MAKING
THE JOURNEY

LEILA CHRISTENBURY

MAKING THE JOURNEY

THIRD EDITION

Being and Becoming a Teacher of English Language Arts

Heinemann
Portsmouth, NH

Heinemann
A division of Reed Elsevier Inc.
361 Hanover Street
Portsmouth, NH 03801–3912
www.heinemann.com

Offices and agents throughout the world

The author and publisher wish to thank those who have generously given permission to reprint borrowed material:

Excerpt from "East Coker" in *Four Quartets* by T. S. Eliot. Copyright © 1940 by T. S. Eliot and renewed © 1968 by Esme Valerie Eliot. Reprinted by permission of Harcourt, Inc.

"Shapes, Vanishings" from *The Flying Change* by Henry Taylor. Copyright © 1985. Reprinted by permission of Louisiana State University Press.

Excerpt from *The House on Mango Street* by Sandra Cisneros. Copyright © 1984 by Sandra Cisneros. Published by Vintage Books, a division of Random House, Inc., and in hardcover by Alfred A. Knopf in 1994. Reprinted by permission of Susan Bergholz Literary Services, New York. All rights reserved.

"Central School" by Jay S. Paul. From *Artemis XVI*. Copyright © 1993. Published by Artemis Artist/Writers, Roanoke, VA. Reprinted by permission of the author.

Acknowledgments for borrowed material continue on p. xii.

Library of Congress Cataloging-in-Publication Data
Christenbury, Leila.
    Making the journey : being and becoming a teacher of English language arts /
Leila Christenbury.—3rd ed.
        p. cm.
    Includes bibliographical references and index.
    ISBN 0-325-00817-5 (alk. paper)
    1. Language arts (Secondary)—United States.   2. Teaching.   3. English philology—Study and teaching—United States—Vocational guidance.   4. English language—Study and teaching—United States.   5. Classroom management—United States.   6. English teachers—Training of. I. Title.

LB1631.C4486 2006
428.0071'2—dc22   2006010222

Editor: James Strickland
Production: Vicki Kasabian
Illustrations: Ann Glover
Cover design: Catherine Hawkes, Cat & Mouse Design
Typesetter: Publishers' Design and Production Services, Inc.
Manufacturing: Steve Bernier

Printed in the United States of America on acid-free paper
10   09   08   07   RRD   2   3   4   5

to Paul and Leila,
my first teachers

If it is dark
when this is given to you,
have care for its content
when the moon shines.
—Robert Creeley
"A Form of Women" (*For Love*)

CONTENTS

ACKNOWLEDGMENTS

In this book I tell stories from my own years of high school and middle school teaching. In some cases it has been appropriate not to use my students' actual names; therefore, when a student's first name only is cited, it is a pseudonym. Many of the stories, however, do not call for anonymity, and when first *and* last names are mentioned they are real names of students who, at one time, were in my classroom. For whatever errors of memory or detail in these stories, I take full responsibility.

Throughout this book I also quote from the papers, journals, and notes of my students at Virginia Commonwealth University, all of whom I have taught in English Education and most of whom are now teaching in their first years in an English language arts classroom. For their permission to use their words and insights, I am very grateful: I think their voices are the strength of this book. I thank Jan Butterworth, Melissa Campbell, Carol Smith Catron, Melissa Chai, Connie Chantelau, Lauren Dean, Werner Doerwaldt, Jane Dowrick, Patty Duffy, Brian Durrett, Kara Elder, Paul Fanney, Susanna Field, Ronnie Fleming, Jenni Gallo, Beverly Garner, Brenda Gates, Sheryl Gibson, Larry Goldman, Sandra Greer, Beth Hagy, Ralph B. Holmes Jr., Jane Hunter, Donna Johnson, Jeffrey Landon, Julie Lepard, Debbie Martin, Laurie Messer, Elizabeth Milne, Johnathan Morris, Julie Morrison, Holly O'Donnell, M. Kevin O'farrell, Barbara Pope, Valerie Schwartz, Lori Shacreaw, David Small, Patti Smith, Katherine Sullivan, Heather Talley, Anne Trippeer, Jake Tucker, Clary Washington, and Jill Williamson.

In Chapter 4, I cite the work of my friend and teaching colleague Nancy Rosenbaum of Patrick Henry High School, Roanoke (Virginia) City Schools; I am grateful, as I have been for many years, for her practical and useful ideas.

Chapter 5 details a research study; to the gifted teachers who allowed my tape recorder into their classrooms—Ellen Seay Young, then of Midlothian High School, Chesterfield County (Virginia) Schools, and Mil Norman-Risch, of The Collegiate Schools, Richmond, Virginia—I say thank you; and I thank their students as well.

The artist whose illustrations are in these pages is my longtime friend Ann Glover. Her work hangs in almost every room of my house, and I am grateful for her talent and craft.

The making of a book, even a third edition, is a complicated process. I thank Jim Strickland of Heinemann, whose enthusiasm is unflagging, and I thank production editor Vicki Kasabian.

Friends mean the world in this writing business. I thank Tucker for his constancy and faith, for believing I could do this, and for being there, as always, on the journey.

All through this book are stories about my students and what they taught and continue to teach me. They are the heart and soul of this book, and it would be hard to overstate my indebtedness to the thousands of people with whom I have shared the classroom through the years. Again, I thank my students, each and every one of them, and gratefully acknowledge their powerful and ongoing influence on my life.

USING THIS BOOK

In many ways, *Making the Journey* is a very personal book, and your reactions and comments are important as you read. The journal suggestions throughout the chapters may help you codify your own response to the activities and ideas presented here; I urge you to buy a journal and to use it with this book. The habit of journal writing is a valuable one, and what you write may surprise you. In addition, a journal is a good place for you to consider issues about you, your ideas, and why and how you are making this journey of being and becoming a teacher.

The Third Edition

Much has happened to me as a teacher since the second edition of *Making the Journey*, and I have tried to reflect my thinking and my reading in this third edition. In the past few years, I completed a term as president of the National Council of Teachers of English, I returned to a high school where for a semester I taught English 11, and, through a grant project, for the first time I became seriously involved with issues of teaching English language learners. Just recently, concerns about timed writing tests led me, with two colleagues, to write books for teachers and students regarding writing on demand. All of these experiences have given me new insights that I share in this third edition of *Making the Journey*.

I am especially grateful, as always, to my students at Virginia Commonwealth University, and I thank them for their advice regarding what this edition needed to offer. In particular, I am grateful to my students and now new teachers: Misty Burton, Beverly Garner, Shannon Garofalo, Bethany Harrar, Heidi Hoffer Garcia, Julie Isman, Zonita James, Allison Kelley, Katherine Leake, Kim McDonnell, Lorraine Rand, Jacob Rheaume, Afaf Salem, and Mark Spewak, all of whom helped me determine what needed to stay in this third edition, what needed to be added, and what needed to change.

I also continue to hear from readers of *Journey* with whom I have corresponded both by letter and e-mail. The positive reaction of these readers, teachers beginning on their journey, has continued to be a moving and wholly unexpected dividend to writing and revising this book. It has also, practically, guided me in this third edition as I have tried to attend to readers' questions, suggestions, and comments.

Working on this revision has, once again, given me a renewed appreciation of the tremendous courage it takes to begin the journey of teaching. It has never been easy to make a life in the classroom, and today it is as challenging as ever to be an effective teacher. To those of you just entering the classroom, I send you my best as you embark upon this daunting but crucially important venture. May you find both strength and grace on the journey.

1

The Teacher, the Student, the School

We Americans have a sublime faith in education. Faced with any difficult problem
of life we set our minds at rest sooner or later by the appeal to the school. We are
convinced that education is the one unfailing remedy for every ill to which man is
subject, whether it be vice, crime, war, poverty, riches, injustice, racketeering, race
hatred, class conflict, or just plain original sin. We even speak glibly and often
about the general reconstruction of society through the school . . . [but] our schools,
instead of directing the course of change, are themselves driven by the very forces
that are transforming the rest of the social order.

—George S. Counts, *Dare the School Build a New Social Order?*

Beginnings

My Story: How I became a teacher

I never planned to be a middle school or high school English teacher. It was very much a
second choice. What I really wanted to be, a college professor specializing in medieval literature, got lost in the now almost legendary English teacher glut of the 1970s and a complete
lack of funds. There were few jobs, and I, who had been on scholarship, faced the inescapable
fact that time *is* money. I had completed my undergraduate degree in three and a half years
and my master's in a record nine months; at the end of this dubious achievement I couldn't
afford any more education—financially or psychologically.

So I filled out about two dozen applications, interviewed at every commutable school
system, and, after this grueling job search, gratefully accepted my first job as an English
teacher, grades eight through twelve, in a tiny high school.

But because teaching high school had not been in my plans, I was not prepared. I had
had no student teaching and had taken no courses that gave me the slightest indication of
what I was getting ready to do. I came to the high school classroom with a Phi Beta Kappa
key, a bachelor's and a master's in English, an appreciation for fourteenth-century alliterative
poetry and the origins of English biography—and not a clue as to how to connect what I
knew to the 120 teenagers I would be teaching. Fortunately, as any teacher will tell you, my

students taught me. During my first semester they endured my unscoreable exams, my lame directions, my changes of curriculum, my indecipherable comments on their essays, my wavering concept of discipline. Directly and indirectly, sometimes tactfully, sometimes sharply, they gave me advice about what I could do to improve over those first few months; when they found me fairly receptive, our relationship stabilized.

And, for my part, I was too overwhelmed at first to feel awfully upset about teaching "just" high school. In fact, it quickly became my guilty secret: I found my students interesting—no, that's not accurate—I found them consuming. I found myself talking a great deal about them and what they said and what I said, often to the exasperation of friends and family. My classroom blunders became fuel for thought, and I began to plot and plan each day, each period, with a new sense of adventure. I began to watch my students' reactions and body language and expressions, convinced that actually the key to what to do was right there in the class, right in front of me—if only I could clear my eyes and just *see* it. I was experiencing something very intense, and I was struggling to make sense of it.

And then, as in a scene from a bad movie, I had my epiphany. One wintry morning somebody in the back row—somebody whose name I no longer remember and, tellingly, from whom I *do* remember I hadn't expected that much—made an observation about the short story we were reading. I heard his comment. And then I really *heard* it. The comment was so original, so insightful, so fraught with possibilities, that I was stunned. It was the proverbial standing still of time; if it *had* been a movie, the heavens would have opened, a shaft of sunlight would have flooded the classroom, and music would have swelled. But real life is usually nothing at all like the movies. My recollection is that I halted and, for a moment at least, just froze. The comment was one that with all my knowledge and education and insight—and class preparation—I had not anticipated. Further, the observation blew the top off our—the class' and my—assumptions about that particular short story.

My next reaction was one of almost overwhelming excitement, an excitement that was infectious as the class began to discuss this wonderful possibility about this story. Well, what about that? Is it true? Why do you think so? If that's right, what else can we assume? I was excited, exhilarated, and the students were too. I know now that I saw that day what could happen in a class and how, if I was lucky, I could spend my life. It was a central and almost searing experience: I turned, really saw that student, that classroom, really heard that comment, and, essentially, in that class, on that day, fell in love with teaching. It was, for me, the experience that Rainer Maria Rilke describes in "Archaic Torso of Apollo" when, after viewing a powerful piece of sculpture, he is overwhelmed and realizes, simply, awfully, "You must change your life" (181). After that experience I had, actually, to change my life. And I did.

My vision of being a medievalist yielded, replaced by the reality and guts and fascination of the classroom and my students. I had found my home, almost by accident, and my blood seemed to run quicker than it ever had in the library looking up the etymology of words in the *Oxford English Dictionary* or while studying alliterative devices in the fourteenth-century poem "Pearl."

I would never recommend that anyone come into teaching as I did; it was unnecessarily hard on me and, more to the point, it was demonstrably not fair to my students for me to learn at their expense. Certainly, after my first fairly isolated semester, I began to seek—and find—other sources of help; I talked with other teachers, took courses, and began reading professional journals and books. Fellow and sister teachers gave advice and shared techniques; organizations such as the National Council of Teachers of English (NCTE) and my own state English-teaching organization published journals and held conferences. I tried to catch up as quickly as I could and become a teaching professional. It was, however, an uneven learning process, some of which had to do with the inevitable difficulty of learning to teach and a great deal of which had to do with my complete lack of professional preparation.

Hit-and-miss is a difficult and dangerous way to enter this business, and I was often highly self-conscious about my shortcomings. Even in the midst of progress, I almost aborted my teaching career after one crisis too many; and, truth be told, I have always suspected that if some of my instructional stumbling and lurching had been regularly observed by those in charge, I might have, charitably, been invited to leave.

But, as is the case in many school settings, I was largely left alone, and because I was self-conscious about my teaching, I was glad to be left alone. I hung in, made what I felt were some breathtaking mistakes, and learned some vivid and painful lessons. During my biggest crisis, when I had left the security of a small school for a larger and more challenging one and was finding the transition overwhelming, I felt I was taking my personality apart and putting it back together so that I could succeed in the classroom. It was a daunting task, and I do not encourage anyone to follow my example.

My interest in helping others become teachers is therefore part of my own experience as a far less prepared beginner than most. There is knowledge and theoretical basis in our field, and you can come into the classroom with a far more comprehensive view than I had.

I also trust you will find what I found: that teaching can be a marriage of soul and mind, that the classroom can be a place of discovery, passion, and very real joy. While not every class is wonderful every day—for there is occasional bitterness and pain and disappointment in this business—teaching is, for me, a consuming and deeply satisfying profession. Once I emerged on the other side and realized that I was a teacher, had *become* a teacher, I realized that I had also found, in essence, my calling, my life's work.

Your story: Becoming a teacher

You are, right now, writing your own story of becoming a teacher, and one emphasis of this book, besides imparting technical and professional information, is to encourage you to look at yourself and your experiences. While it is dangerous to generalize from yourself to each and every one of your students, it is also terribly shortsighted not to use your own insights and discoveries when you think about teaching and being and becoming a teacher. Being self-conscious and self-aware can be a powerful tool as you begin this great adventure. My belief in that power is the major reason I start this book with my own unflattering story of how I became a teacher.

Throughout this book I tell more of my stories and let some of my students—who, like you, are embarking on their first years as English language arts teachers—tell theirs. Their words, coming as they do from the journal entries and papers of "experts" at this being and becoming, may help you puzzle out some of the great issues facing middle and secondary language arts teachers.

Finally, this book outlines existing research and knowledge about classrooms and students and teachers, patterns and techniques and concepts.

The limitation of any one person's point of view

I am, as are many in this business of teaching, conscious of the limitations of one person's perspective. I can tell you that I have been a teacher for almost thirty years, that I have two degrees in English and one in education, that I have publications and editorships and have been elected to professional offices. I can tell you I have taught in private and public schools;

have taught remedial classes and classes for the gifted; have taught experimental courses, summer enrichment programs, and even classes for adults in a city jail. I can tell you that just recently I went back to high school teaching for a semester and learned a lot about schools and young people today. Yet I also need to remind you that I come from a background, a culture, and that I bring with me a specific perspective and a point of view. While to a certain extent I have earned the right to talk to you in this book, to function as an expert, my experiences are not universal, and everything I feel about teaching and learning may not echo the feelings of others, may not, in fact, echo yours.

The books and articles I cite are ones I like and have read. The activities and games and procedures I propose are ones I used as a high school teacher and suggest my students use in their own English classes. I do not want to imply that I have read everything in the field or that I have experienced every conceivable teaching approach. I offer what I know with the acknowledgment that it is—as is all knowledge—undeniably partial.

Finally, I am terribly aware of the many people—pioneers in this business of English teaching, great thinkers, gifted theorists—who have written and practiced at levels I can only dream of. I do not assume that I am one of them. I take heart, however, from a section of *The Four Quartets* and add my slice of teaching experience, largely because, as T. S. Eliot reminds us:

> There is only the fight to recover what has been lost
> And found and lost again and again: and now, under conditions
> That seem unpropitious. But perhaps neither gain nor loss.
> For us, there is only the trying. The rest is not our business.
> ("East Coker," 128)

Making the journey

So what about this *trying* that Eliot talks about? Actually, it goes to the heart of teaching and is the reason for the title of this book. Regardless of how prepared or (like me) unprepared for English teaching you may be, you are from day one a teacher making a journey. But the paradox is that from day one you will continue to become, evolve, and change as a teacher. It is, oddly enough, happily enough, a simultaneous process of both *being* a teacher and *becoming* a teacher. The two events are not separable and, actually, are not mutually exclusive.

Right now you are probably a lot more interested in arriving at your destination than in making the journey. You are more concerned about *being* a teacher: looking like the real thing, acting like a person who can take charge of a class, negotiating a school day gracefully. But as you will see or have perhaps already glimpsed, *becoming*, the ongoing process of changing and shifting and redefining, is also part of this business of teaching.

And that is what makes teaching so exciting: it is never the same. Not only, of course, are the students different each year, each class, but, necessarily, so are you. Unless you lose your curiosity and passion and interest, teaching will continue to evolve and change, *become* more and more, as you continue in the profession.

Teaching today

These are tough times in which to be a teacher. Issues of curricular mandate, of high-stakes testing and reporting, of school violence, of student learning, of community involvement and control swirl everywhere and threaten to overwhelm even the most dedicated. For English language arts teachers the constant battles over what subject areas are of most value, how much writing we can squeeze into a crowded schedule, and how we balance the teaching of skills with the excitement of reading and talking about literature complicate the picture. Despite these issues, you have decided to make the journey, to *be* (and to continue to *become*) an English language arts teacher. For that decision, you have my respect, and all of us in the classroom welcome you into the profession. It is exhausting and exhilarating and important work, work that is as enduring as it is difficult.

Teaching is the central defining truth of my life, the core and heart of my identity. For you, too, teaching may become that important and that sustaining. Not for the complacent nor for the fainthearted, making the journey toward being and becoming a teacher is an adventure of the first order.

················· **FOR YOUR JOURNAL** ·················

Journals are a good way to keep track of your thoughts and ideas. Many times, after reading a section of this book, you will be invited to write a response to the issues and ideas raised. If you wonder how those responses should "look," you might pay close attention to the passages I quote from my students who, like you, are entering teaching and who, in my classes, use a journal to record ideas and questions and responses.

Journals are usually handwritten, and an entry should be two or three pages long; they are informal and should be concerned more with ideas and content than with correctness or spelling or even neatness. The point is to address a subject or issue and to write your way into ideas and answers.

So, in this first journal entry, think of how people get started in a profession and how that may or may not relate to your choosing to be a teacher. One way to start might be to do some quick field research on how people choose professions: interview two or three people about how they entered their job field; informally poll relatives, friends, or coworkers.

Use the following questions as idea starters; you don't have to answer all of them, but they may help you focus this journal entry about people and choosing professions.

Questions to consider for your interviews: How did you choose your profession? What attracted you to that type of work? How long did you stay/have you stayed in the field? Why did you/didn't you leave? What do you consider to be the greatest rewards of your profession? the greatest drawbacks?

Now, think about you. Very briefly, in a paragraph or two, write about what has attracted you to English teaching. Was it an actual experience with a teacher? a film or a book about teaching? some other "trigger" (such as reading—and being moved by—a literary work)? Are your feelings about teaching similar to or different from the feelings of those you interviewed about their careers? How?

Teacher, Student, School: The Dance of the Three

The quotation at the beginning of this chapter, written by George S. Counts in 1932, is true today. And what he thundered about the schools and a new social order is electrifying stuff. The irony is, however, that most of us beginning language arts teaching give scant attention to context—that is, to the schools as part of the social vision Counts describes or as part of any wider vision. Instead, many of us center our thoughts on something closer to home when we begin teaching. We think of ourselves, the instructor, and what *we* are going to instruct—that novel or play we loved so much, that poem that changed our lives, that writing experience that was powerful, that insight about language that seems to stay in our mind. While we know there will be students—some bright, some quiet, some not so bright, some motivated, some unhappy to be there—students are students, right? We are going into the classroom to bring to the students and to share with them what we have learned and learned to love. While we're not exactly missionaries, it's somewhere in the territory.

And, of course, as a beginning teacher, we know that we will be teaching in a setting, a physical classroom, a school with a mailing address and a janitor and other teachers and a principal. And we know that there will be bells and schedules and corridors. But school is a place in which we teach, right? It is, essentially, despite a few pressures to teach to standards and test them, a neutral setting that will allow us to exercise our craft. For some of us, school is a place that will operate as a "safe harbor" where we can continue our delight in our content, the written word.

Right?

No, very wrong.

Most experienced teachers know very well that the vision of teaching just described is not that way at all. In fact these descriptions of students and school are well-meaning—but seriously naive—concepts that are not only shared by the majority of beginning teachers but that also can engender misunderstanding, difficulty, and failure in beginning teachers.

Three truths about teaching

What is the truth about this business of teaching English language arts? Among others, there are three:

1. Teaching is far more than sharing what we learned to love as students in our own English classes.
2. Students and who they are shape what and how we instruct.
3. School as an institution is as real a factor in teaching as any other. Far from being a neutral setting, it limits and influences what we can and cannot do in our classrooms.

Whether we come prepared for it or not, we as teachers are only one part of a triad that also features a bewildering array of students, all of whom have fierce needs and aspirations and brilliance and weaknesses and problems and cultural expectations, and a setting, an institutional context, which we soon find can more often than not keep us from teaching and keep our students from learning.

It's a difficult dance, with the three partners moving and shifting and leading and taking turns. Although we might want to, we don't (can't) teach in the relative isolation or even protection of ourselves and our ideas about William Shakespeare's *Macbeth* or Virginia Woolf's *The Waves* or Richard Wright's *Native Son* or William Wordsworth's "Tintern Abbey." Because we are teachers, we must move among all those loud and messy and frequently challenging and restless people, our students, and we must move through a linoleum-tiled, bell-ringing, rule-driven place: school.

And, if this is true, does it change how we think about ourselves as English language arts teachers and what we can do in a classroom?

Yes.

And no.

So just how much can one teacher do?

Most teachers are not pessimists. During (and because of) their years of teaching they are necessary optimists, workers with lights in their eyes. But what has informed and even protected those teachers is the knowledge of what they are up against. It also took them a while to learn it. So while I as a teacher can't give you 101 nifty activities that work with any group of students in any school setting—I can't because I know they won't work with all students all the time—I want you to know about students, generally and specifically, and to recognize your formidable and sometimes difficult partner in this business—the school. Knowledge of these two elements will help you as you begin to teach. And then you can look more critically at activities and resources and techniques that you can adapt to your own teaching life.

It is worth it? Absolutely. Teaching is some of the most important work in the world; it transcends the concept of job or even career or profession into the sphere of *vocation*—as that word is used in a sense of being called, being chosen for a life role. In fact, if you would like to pursue this idea a bit farther, read Sonia Nieto's *What Keeps Teachers Going?* where Nieto explores the beliefs and practices of dozens of passionate, committed teachers. Personal fulfillment is a large part of teaching and, of course, there are other rewards. Shamelessly put, teaching is also a chance at a bit of immortality. The science teacher Christa McAuliffe, who with others died tragically in the 1986 *Challenger* disaster, has been widely quoted in a statement that now borders on cliché. Although it could seem sappy, McAuliffe's "I touch the future. I teach" is actually to the heart of the matter for many of us who remain in the classroom. This is serious stuff, and while no one will insist that it be true for you or for all teachers, it's true for many teachers; it's why we stay in this business, and it's why we want you to be aware of what we know. Knowledge is not only empowering, it will keep you in the classroom and tell you what is going on in that incredibly demanding—but terribly exciting—place: school.

But now let's turn to you, the becoming teacher.

················· **FOR YOUR JOURNAL** ·················

Let's assume you accept that teaching is a combination of teacher, student, and school, all in one big pie chart as it were. It's your task to divide up the pie. *Questions to consider:* At this point in your career, how would you assign a proportion to each segment? In other words, who or what is more important? less important? What, realistically, is the percentage of each of the three factors? What, ideally, *should* be the percentage of each of the factors? Why? If you take the quick compromise, one-third equally to each, can you see how one segment could feel shortchanged? Why? Why not?

The Teacher/Learner

Why do you want to be an English teacher?

While most people at the elementary level go into teaching because they like children and can see themselves working with the very young for a living, most of us who become middle or secondary school language arts teachers do so because we love our subject, especially literature.

It is rare to want to teach language arts because of the lure of writing or linguistics; most of us were drawn to it by a piece of literature. Every one of us has a story to tell: the first novel that seemed to be written just about us and our lives; that night we stayed up reading until dawn; the poem—some of whose lines we can still recite—that changed our lives. These students would agree:

> When I was twelve I literally vanished from the real world into the world of literature. My older brother handed me *The Hobbit*, and suddenly everything else in my world was thrown aside.
>
> —Werner Doerwaldt

> In a single, pristine moment of understanding, *The Catcher in the Rye* made me realize that books weren't just escapism. They weren't just entertainments—thrills. It made me see that books could have a real effect on people's lives as it had done on mine.
>
> The book put me in a stupor for days. Holden Caulfield *was* me. His words were mine. Every attitude, every action we shared—or so it seemed. After reading *The Catcher in the Rye*, somehow I didn't feel so retarded—not quite so ugly. Holden had come down from the mountain carrying their sacred tablets and had shattered them at my feet. I was free to unashamedly be myself. I didn't have to go along—I could be different—an individual.
>
> —M. Kevin O'farrell

> My teachers . . . used literature as a means of communicating "deeper lessons" about ourselves. I pondered the American Dream through Jay Gatsby, uncovered the harsh realities of murder and guilt through Lady Macbeth, and found strength of human spirit in Hester Prynne. Nearly every piece of literature held an important message about [my] life.
>
> —Jane Hunter

Another student, Holly O'Donnell, wrote just before her student teaching that "literature is personal, not just art for art's sake" and she wanted to use that power in the English classroom. Holly is right; literature is the power that propelled most of us into teaching in the first place.

Teachers we loved

And while literature propelled most of us into this field, a person may have also had a strong effect. Perhaps it was a teacher whose praise or encouragement led us to believe we could understand literature or even write it ourselves. One such student, Paul Fanney, remembers a teacher who was so powerful that in her class "sometimes I even forgot to feel so self-conscious about being a teenager, which is hard to do in high school." English class allowed Paul to come "to a closer awareness of the powerful rush in articulating what it's like to be a part of the human experience."

Here, also, are a few recollections from students about to begin their student teaching:

> I remember being excited about eighth grade English and the writing assignments given to me. To help the class understand the concept of interpreting poetry, our teacher had us write about

the songs of [a popular rock group]. We listened to [an album], discussed several songs and then wrote our personal responses and interpretations of each. We then moved on to the poetry of William Carlos Williams and e. e. cummings. The teacher was successful in tapping into the enthusiasm and imagination of the students by tying what they valued into what he was trying to teach. Because the lyrics of the rock album and the poetry of Williams and cummings were given equal validity, the students were better able to accept and understand the skills and techniques of critical interpretation.

—Barbara Pope

Senior year was a very interesting year in English for me. . . . The first day of class [the teacher] brought in a Kitaro (New Age music) tape, and he told us to free write. I wrote several short stories, including one about a sheik and a British Lady having a romance in America. He loved my writing, found ways to help me improve individually, and boosted my confidence in general. He also had us do a multimedia project connecting words, music, pictures, and ideas to create a philosophical statement of some belief we held (it could be deep, humorous, or fluff as long as it was well done). . . . [He] allowed us to be ourselves, ask questions, discuss things with other students, and do a lot of work independently—which motivated most of us to do our best. He also took the time and energy to help us by doing some individualized instruction, and he's one of the main reasons I chose to teach high school English.

—Elizabeth Milne

Coach, the Minister of Doom, the Grand Enunciator, these all were the names of my eleventh grade English instructor. He was a slender man with a wit for words, always energetic and articulate. As we walked into his class at the blurry hour of 7:45 a.m. his words could be heard filling the class, "My little lemmings, prepare yourselves to enter into a vast panorama of pleasure as we immerse ourselves into the world of Stephen Crane." Words became musical notes and stories became songs, and *Red Badge of Courage* wanted me to keep reading on.

—David Small

The activities [in English class] were probably my favorite—we did group bulletin boards, miniplays, and "Jeopardy" type game shows. The beauty of these activities was that we had fun while we were learning about Romeo and Juliet's plight, the many characters in *The Canterbury Tales*, and the symbolism rampant in "The Waste Land." The bulletin boards allowed us to show off our creativity, "Jeopardy" helped us remember character and plot, and miniplays saturated us in the language of Shakespeare.

—Anne Trippeer

[My English teacher] looked like a koala bear, hence his nickname, Mr. K. Mr. K. was a short, stocky man who was gentle natured and smiled all of the time. He seemed to love all of the students including the trouble makers. I believe that is why all the students loved him. He had a way of never actually answering a question. Instead, he would turn things around and make you answer your own question. It was an art that he had refined so well that the technique rubbed off on his students. We would stop asking questions and evaluate the situation or problem in our own mind and come up with a solution. Independent thinking was Mr. K.'s motto. No thought was ever wrong, it was always correct as long as there was some basis for the thought.

[My other English teacher] was a throw back from the 60s. He wore raggedy pants and his hair was always messed up. He looked like he just rolled out of bed. But he had a great mind and he treated all the students with the respect that he wanted. He . . . had a way to open discussions up and to make everyone feel special. We wrote all the time and some of the stories that the "bad" kids wrote were incredible. These are the same kids that [the other teachers] had thrown out of class for bad behavior.

—Melissa Campbell

One of my best memories of [my English teacher's] class was when we were doing some seat work, reading in groups or something, and she hung up a large white sheet of paper in front of the class. Casually, she told us if we liked we could come up and write or draw our ideas about "Life" on this sheet with the colorful markers she provided. Throughout the class period, students meandered to the front, wrote poems, drew rainbows or angry faces, made a statement. I wrote "Whoops." Near the end of class, she scanned the filled sheet smiling at a few things, nodding her head.

Then she stopped, turned around and said, "Who wrote 'Whoops'?"

I raised my hand.

"What did you mean?" she asked.

"You know, like slipping on a banana peel," I said.

She laughed and nodded at me. . . . That smile and nod she gave me meant more to me than any grade I ever received. It was her way of saying that what I thought was important, even clever, that I had something to contribute. She is what high school English should be.

—Larry Goldman

Whatever the specific impetus, for most of us it was not so much a love of *who* we would be teaching but *what* we would teach (the literature) or *how* we would teach and emulate our model of a great teacher.

For me, it was finding *me* in an unlikely place—in a 1900s North Carolina town in Thomas Wolfe's *Look Homeward, Angel*. It was seventh grade in Linkhorn Park Elementary School, and I *could not* put the book down: I was so taken with it I brought it to and from school for three days. I read at home; I read in class. Wolfe spoke of passion and loss and the difficulty of knowing the world—and one another. He sang of longing and sadness and all the things I could not articulate (but so keenly felt) at thirteen. I concealed the novel on my lap and read it, virtually straight through, during work time in Mrs. Pendleton's room. I am certain Mrs. Pendleton saw me reading during class and—to her credit—left me alone. While the novel has no more charms for me—looking at it now, I find it dated and long-winded, not to mention sexist and self-indulgent—it was my introduction to the power of literature. And I have loved Mrs. Pendleton ever since.

The teacher who inspired me was Larry Duncan, who in eleventh-grade English at Norfolk Catholic High School was both exotic and demanding. He put Ezra Pound's "In a Station of the Metro" on the board and asked us what we thought. He showed how close analysis of the opening lines of Shakespeare's *Richard III* could reveal level upon level of meaning, and then he asked us to try. He told us about the Harlem Renaissance and asked us to consider what *explode* really meant, then in 1967, in Langston Hughes' "Harlem." He chose pieces for the spring play like Eugene O'Neill's *The Hairy Ape* and actually expected us not only to learn but to understand the lines. In general, Mr. Duncan treated his students like intellectual peers. He asked us real questions as if he was interested in our giving him real answers. We didn't always respond, and often our class "discussions" consisted of a lot of puzzled silence on our part and a lot of frustration on his.

We thought he was weird (and I still think that assessment was not only accurate but complimentary), but Mr. Duncan set an example and a tone you had to hear if not accept.

You have a story, too, and a reason for wanting to do this business of English teaching. That reason, that passion, will be part of your strength as a teacher and, further, conveying that story to your students may be appropriate at some time. It's valid; it's part of why you're here, and its power will carry you through the very dailyness and the occasional discouragement of teaching English.

But your love of your subject or a very good experience in English class is only part of the story.

Not everyone loved literature, their English teachers, or even school

Not all of our students like English, love English, will willingly take English classes if they further their education, or will continue to read literature or write poetry or essays after they leave—or escape—us. Many of our students have had very bad experiences with English (the subject and those who teach it) and feel that they and their language are not good enough, are not correct, are not acceptable. Many of our students are terrified of writing, feel they don't have anything to say, or, if they did, probably couldn't say it right anyway. Many of our students don't read frequently or fluently or with a whole lot of understanding. Many of them have encountered few books that seem to have any connection to their lives. For many students, English language arts is the primo arena of the majority—white, Anglo, Western, and male—and they do not see themselves reflected there. Many of our students in English language arts classes are asked questions that seem hardly worth answering about people and life choices and issues that seem to exist solely in books and solely for English teachers' tests. Listen to a few of these stories, written by people who are planning on entering the classroom:

> I know I had an English teacher in every grade from eighth to twelfth. I know that each year someone attempted to teach me high school English because that is what English teachers were instructed to do by the school board. The school board asked teachers to teach literature, reading, and grammar. However, the school board failed to make it a rule that English teachers make high school English interesting, enlightening, and entertaining enough that students be able to recall classroom experiences and teachers' names.
>
> —Jan Butterworth

> Freshman English was conducted by [my teacher], a kindly aging spinster. I say *conducted*, but in actuality she was both the conductor and the chorus. The classroom was her stage, and any interruption by a student was a wrong note. We were there for her audience as she read to us some of the great works of literature. She read *The Merchant of Venice* from beginning to end, and a very effective Shylock she was, I might add!
>
> —Katherine Sullivan

> [My eleventh grade teacher] sat in her desk at the front of the evenly aligned rows of gleaming metal, orange desks. She rested the textbook on her chest which rested on top of the desk and drilled us. She was very predictable. She asked the questions from the back of the book. Her eyes saw everything. There was no talking, laughing, or writing. Of course she didn't react to you sleeping in class as long as it was quiet. Most of the time we had to do busy work, worksheets, crossword puzzles. . . . She would give us any assignment as long as it kept us quiet, so that she had time to read the book on top of her heaving chest and to rub hand lotion on her hands.
>
> —Melissa Campbell

> I once had a friend tell me, "English class ruined every good book I ever read."
>
> —Ralph B. Holmes, Jr.

But since this, by and large, is not the experience of every person who takes English, why dwell on it? We dwell on it, we linger over it, because if we are to improve education, if we are to make the classroom an alive, languaging kind of place, events such as these described must become even rarer in our classrooms.

If you have talked to anyone recently about being or planning to be an English teacher, have you noticed his or her reaction? More than likely you hear them tell you "Uh oh, I'd better watch my grammar" or "I never did well in English." Many times people will tell you that you seem to be too bright or too talented to "waste" your life in the classroom. In particular, many women are counseled against teaching because it is considered too safe, too traditional; many men are reminded of the financial sacrifices that teachers make. Rarely do you meet someone whose eyes will light up at the prospect of talking with you, an English teacher—for many people English teachers represent something negative and almost fearful, and for many people becoming an English teacher seems a futile way to spend a life.

Why is this? I wonder at times if it is because a number of individuals have had bad experiences with English teachers and in English classes and bad memories of school. Those bad experiences, I hope, will stop with you. And while I can write with energy and pride about Mrs. Pendleton and Mr. Duncan, there is also my nameless eighth-grade English teacher at Blair Junior High School. Red pen in hand, she took the poem I had written about mountains (a poem that meant so much to me I not only showed it privately to her after class but had also painstakingly recopied it in peacock ink on my best paper), read it, and first circled the spelling errors and then marked the punctuation with "UNNECESSARY" in large letters. I was fourteen and about as morbidly sensitive as they come. I nearly stopped writing poetry, and I never showed that teacher anything that meant anything to me ever again.

For some students, there will be little chance that they will show a teacher their poetry. Some of our students are fearful about their abilities, their vocabulary, their accent. They feel they have no place, no voice, in our classrooms, and come by compulsion, with no illusions about learning or even having a relatively pleasant experience. For these students, unsatisfactory incidents in English class will be far more serious than one marked-up poem.

What you are planning to do would not be such a challenge if the students with whom you worked saw immediately the reasons for the literature on the agenda Wednesday afternoon and if they fell with zest and comprehension to whatever tasks you assign. The bulk of our job, however, is not to ratify understanding and gracefully preside over the honing and polishing of skills. It is to do what our title dictates—teach. And sometimes that is terribly difficult to do.

We, as an education association bumper sticker proclaims, teach the children. We teach the Anglo, Latino, American Indian, Asian American, African American; the learning disabled, the emotionally disturbed; straight and gay, male and female. Our preparation for the classroom may not give us a deep background with all these learners, but make no mistake about it: they are, once they walk into our classrooms, ours. Ours to teach.

Teacher ego: Having it/losing it

And thus we come to the subject of ego.

You've got to have a special confidence even to think of being a teacher, of being in charge of and accountable for a class, of organizing what 150 or so people will be doing five hours a day five days a week in school. You have to be able to see yourself helping large groups negotiate subjects and facts and concepts. Somewhere along the line you have decided you can be the equal or superior of the teachers—good and not so good—you had in your own background. In short, you have a healthy ego if you can seriously contemplate being a teacher.

But one of the things you may not realize is that very early on, especially if you want to be successful in this teaching business—in other words, if you want your students to learn—you will need to lose a lot of that ego. You will, rapid-fire, need to:

1. Put into perspective what appears to be the occasional indifference or insensitivity of your students.
2. Care more about your students' learning than about your dominance.
3. Talk less and listen more.
4. Answer less and question more.

You will, actually, have to become the quintessential, archetypal adult, one who sublimates personal needs for others, who steps aside so that others can step in, who is silent so that others can learn to speak. If you are used to being the smartest kid in the class, now, as a teacher, you will have to modify if not totally relinquish that role. Can you do it? Maybe not immediately, maybe not even in the first couple of years, but sooner or later the ego will have to soften. And in the space that is left, your students will flourish.

Some of my students who are preparing to teach English already understand this, understand it long before I ever did. Jane Dowrick writes that she realizes the importance of making "oneself empty in order to be ready to receive—that in our efforts to be smart, and ready, and on top of things, we cannot hear what we need to hear" in the classroom. For Jane, the whole process of getting ready to teach is a round of "filling myself up with information, advice, and now I need to make some room" for the emptiness and silence that can be necessary for an effective teacher.

As Sheryl Gibson, a teacher in the early stage of her career, notes:

> I now realize that it is not impossible to be a teacher who does not indoctrinate. Kids need to think on their own and develop their own interpretations. . . . Once I realized that teaching is not being the knowledge factory but the knowledge filter, my desire to teach was rekindled.

Sandra Greer sums it up well. And if all teachers were more like Sandra, the future would be in good hands:

> I know that when it is *me* standing in front of those high school students I want to put on a smiling face because I feel that way, and let those kids "express" to their hearts' content and write till doomsday if that's what they want to do. I don't want to change the world, I just want to encourage them to do what they're capable of and hopefully open up their minds to the exciting and wonderful (I won't get out the thesaurus for any more synonyms!) world of Literature. Yeah! I know . . . it sounds kind of sickening doesn't it. I guess it does sound like I want to change the world. Maybe I do. Maybe I do like to think that because of my effort I'll really help out some kid. But, you see, I want to. I really want to. Even if it's only one student, that's better than none at all. I want to be a good teacher. People ask me all the time, "What do you want to be a teacher for? You won't make much money." You know what I say? Who gives a *?!! about money, these kids need an education because that's about the only thing going for them these days. They are our future. And I'd hate to see our future go to waste.

·············· **FOR YOUR JOURNAL** ··············

Choose one or two of the following. Make a list of three things you
would like to do as a teacher. Write about a memorable teacher who
was great. Write about a memorable teacher who was awful. Write
about one of the first "English" successes you had: in class; tutor-
ing you did with another student; something you read that made a
real difference in your life.

The Student/Learner

What is this thing called adolescence?

It's amazing how once we pass our own adolescence, we tend to forget what it was really
like. With the best of intentions, but certainly inaccurately, we often romanticize those
years—they were great, and we were so carefree—and we cloak adolescence with veils of
what it should have been, not what it was. It is tough being young. It was tough years ago, and
it hasn't changed. Adults, even fairly young adults, tend to become nostalgic or just amne-
siac; as teachers, we really can't indulge ourselves so. In order to be successful, we need to
look at the wily, fascinating, exhausting, exhilarating adolescent and who he or she is. We
also need to make some distinctions about age groups.

Intellectual changes   At this point in your career you have some developmental psychology background, and you are aware of learning stages and cycles. You know about the
work of Swiss psychologist Jean Piaget and his division of cognitive development into four
stages: sensorimotor thought, preoperational thought, concrete operational thought, and
formal operational thought. These last two stages particularly concern us. To briefly review:
Piaget defined the stage of **concrete operations** as taking place from about ages seven to
eleven. This is followed by a **transitional formal operations** stage from about eleven to
fourteen and a **permanent formal operations** stage from about age fourteen on. Broadly
speaking, concrete operations involve real, observable situations; formal operations deal
with abstract, speculative thought.

The work of Piaget is a landmark in education, but you also need to know that it has
not gone unchallenged. For many educators Piaget's belief that the concrete and formal operations stages are truly definable by age is misleading; further, many young people do not
enter a permanent formal operations stage until much later than fourteen years of age.
Researcher Margaret Donaldson, for instance, maintains that Piaget's developmental stages
are not truly accurate when describing development of thought processes in young people
(183ff). At any rate, the movement of your students from one stage to another is a very real
phenomenon but is often not readily perceivable to you, the teacher. While it is helpful for
you to know that some of your students will be struggling with a change in thinking abilities

and patterns (and there is some recent brain research that demonstrates that brain activity in young people is markedly different from that of adults), this knowledge will not, unfortunately, give you a precise guide for dealing with the questions you may have about your students and their response to language arts tasks. While you can accept with some surety that some of your students will be moving through the stages, it is a fallacy to believe that the stages will be exact or readily demonstrable.

Psychological changes   The mythic "crisis" of adolescence may also be just a myth. It is not common to every culture that all adolescents go through the Sturm und Drang of alienation and rebellion. You may not have experienced such huge upheavals nor may many of your friends. Certainly when I went back to teach high school I found that the majority of my students had very positive and close relations with their parents. On the other hand, you may know of others in your own life and see young people in your class for whom growing up is painful and difficult. For sure, three factors are relatively unique challenges of adolescence (Furhmann, 173): rapid, uneven physical growth; a new self-consciousness; and a tremendous cognitive awareness.

Adolescence: Early and beyond   The middle school concept was born out of a concern for what is termed the early adolescent, aged roughly ten to fourteen. About thirty years ago there was a renewed and widespread interest not so much to segregate those students as to try to make their educational experience more appropriate for their development. The idea of a middle school is to offer a more distinctive education than the literal "junior" high school, which had been in place since the 1920s as the educational setting after elementary school and a training ground of sorts for secondary school (Muth and Alvermann, 2–4). While the middle school concept has a very wide variance in this country (and is currently being reassessed as perhaps not the best way to provide for transition) the middle school as an entity is based on the fact that early adolescence is a special time and requires a different sort of educational setting.

What are some of the factors of early adolescence, of the middle schooler?

First, the years before puberty are characterized by more profound physical change than any other time of life—with the exception, of course, of infancy. Second, early adolescence is when cognitive development changes, in Piagetian terms, from concrete operations to formal operations. As previously sketched, the latter is when students begin to think in the abstract, not in the purely observable, and that expanded capability in thinking has serious implications for what we do in our classrooms. Indeed, a "wide range of cognitive ability" is probably most demonstrable at the early adolescent stage (Muth and Alvermann, 31). Third, in the area of reading, early adolescents can encounter serious difficulties moving to a higher level of comprehension and, indeed, the sheer amount of reading often falls off alarmingly at this age (Flood et al., 374–79). Fourth, in the area of writing, early adolescents may have serious difficulty moving to higher-order issues in the way they write and how they think about what they want to write.

What about middle and later adolescents?

In middle and later adolescence, students will show more social awareness, more orientation toward peer and away from parent, and will begin to master skills or fall more seriously behind in writing and reading tasks. They will also (some more gracefully than others) continue to master the tasks of maturation.

So what do adolescents want?

More than anything, young people want a part of the action, a piece of the control. As one of my students laments about her English classes in high school:

> Being a prospective educator myself I know exactly what was lacking in my own high school education. I should have been given the chance to question anything that I was learning; I should have been able to feel comfortable saying I didn't understand something. I should have been challenged to come up with my own ideas instead of my mind remaining dormant. I should have been in an environment where the student's word was equally important as the teacher's. I should have been given not only the opportunity but the instruction . . . to express myself in written work.
>
> —Sandra Greer

A number of educational researchers have looked at what they call "locus of control" and have found that passive students who exhibit "learned helplessness" just don't learn efficiently (Furhmann, 167). Such passive students are also, as you can readily observe, relatively unhappy in their classrooms. Unfortunately, however, it is often in the school's interest to keep students largely passive.

And another story

Listen to this student's description of herself as a teenager in English class; she is representative of the large number of young people who aren't challenged in our classrooms. This young person, who, by the way, is now in her first years of English teaching, was neither gifted nor remedial; she is, however, a voice for the majority of students, and we may learn something from her story:

> I majored in English in college because in high school I thought that I was naturally and amazingly gifted in the subject. For instance, in [my] ninth-grade English class, we had a test, and one of the questions was "Why did Sherlock Holmes beat the sidewalk with his walking stick before entering the building?" I had no clue. As usual, I hadn't even bothered to read the story, let alone study for the test. But I must have been pretty clever, because I took a wild guess and replied, "To see whether or not the ground was hollow—whether or not there was a room beneath." I was right! I got an A! I couldn't tell you what the name of the story was now; I've never even read a story by Sir Arthur Conan Doyle. I just know how to get through high school English without cheating or studying.
>
> I think [my English teacher] used to get frustrated with me and some of my friends, because she was usually pretty crabby when we were around. As hard as she tried, she couldn't nail us for our disrespect. She would stand at the front of the class talking about gerunds or Sherlock Holmes while we carried on our own conversations. Eventually, she would glare in our direction and ask one of us to read aloud. We either had no idea what page she was on or we couldn't control our laughing well enough to oblige her. To add insult to her injury, no matter how disrespectful we were in class, we always did well on her tests. I don't really know exactly how the others got around her, but my secret was that I knew grammar rules intuitively, and I paid just enough attention in class to know what was in the reading that I was supposed to do but rarely did. She was serious about teaching English, but she just didn't challenge me enough for me to show her any respect.
>
> Getting away with murder became a sick little game to make fourth period go by more quickly. [In other English classes with other teachers] I repeated her gerund exercises. . . . Bewilderingly enough to me, the mathematically inclined kids struggled with gerunds. . . . I, on the

other hand, completed the exercises in a matter of minutes, which was nice because that left me with plenty of time to talk and pass notes. Thus I added another year of unearned As in English to my high school transcript.

High school English; what a pathetic experience! I get a little angry now when I think of how much I could have learned but didn't. Maybe it was my fault. I could have read the assignments and behaved better in class. But, why bother? I was doing well as I was. I was secretly quite interested in learning—especially reading and writing—but it wasn't cool to admit it then, and I had no reason to embarrass myself.

I always secretly felt a little sorry for [my English teacher] because, deep-down inside, I always got the feeling that she was trying to teach me something—that she wanted to challenge me more than harass me. I'm not sure why she failed. Why did she make her tests so easy? Perhaps she was too confined by the curriculum. Maybe her teaching abilities were stifled . . . I often wonder what she would think if she knew that I want to be an English teacher. Would she curse me? "Some day, I hope you have students who are just like you were." Or would she secretly feel sorry for me?

—Patty Duffy

Patty Duffy expresses well the sort of mind-numbing contact some students and teachers can engage in in our schools. No one is a particularly bad actor here, no great dramatic events occur, but learning is not the outcome. Further, for both teacher and student, contact is a trial. Patty, as an adult, now understands what her English teacher was doing, but at the time the two did not connect. Why is that?

Some of it is because teachers fail to take into account the adolescent and why he or she really comes to school and sits in our class. Some of it is because our students, in their development cycle, are often difficult to entice into the intellectual life—particularly as it is represented by school. Much of it, of course, is no one's direct fault at all, but we must make the best effort possible with the classes we have and with all the students in them.

A few observations about your students and their behavior

Students don't, by and large, want to be in school for the reasons teachers want them to be there. The action, the heart, is often outside the class in the halls and in the faces and lives of their classmates, not in their teachers. Many of them have already internalized what the society judges them to be and are trying to mirror that expectation. Many feel that the game is biased from the start, and they see you, the teacher, as another of the game masters.

The point is that our students are different from us as adults. Holly O'Donnell, a student teacher, trying to make sense of adolescents and her own perceptions, wrote in her journal:

I'm not surprised by the kids—well, I was at first. But I wasn't surprised about what they talk about—it's *how* they talk about stuff. Maybe I've just got good ears, but I hear more swearing! And I was initially surprised at how "belligerent" they were. I'm not really so sure as it's belligerence, now, as it is adolescence. They are so vocal, so verbal—at first it's scary because adults aren't like this. Adults get up every morning w/o asking why (or w/o asking it very loudly) and do what the capitalistic, bipartisan democracy expects; kids get up and they want to know why—and they're not scared to ask, why? and, who died and left you boss? I mean, they *look* like us, but then they open their mouths and "everything's changed!"

The following observations regarding young people, teens, and preteens may give more specific insight:

- Adolescents can feel misunderstood and often misjudged. They suspect adults don't listen to them. Many times they are quite correct. When teachers only expect students to accept and agree, we are contributing to their sense that no one listens.

- Emotions run high in these years; an hour can be an eternity, and a trivial incident can be a major disaster. Just because an adult's perspective "proves" this to be untrue, the young person's feelings to the contrary are not trivial or discountable.

- The culture of the young person and the culture of the adult are often at odds. It's often the adults, however, who try to impose their culture on the teens, not vice versa.

- Teens look at adults in a highly critical way. At no other time in life is the detection of what teenage Holden Caulfield (in J. D. Salinger's *The Catcher in the Rye*) called the "bullshit factor" more acute. Unfortunately, however, as most adults are well aware, that detection of bullshit is usually other-centered.

- It's all new for adolescents, which is not always that exciting or reassuring. Uncharted territory is scary—as the ancient map of the "edge" of the world indicated, "beyond this place here lie monsters."

- A great many males, especially Caucasian males, begin to find strength in these years; a male-defined culture is ready to receive them. A great many females begin to suspect—and become depressed by—the outline of their future lives and their place in the world. We spend a lot of time on the behavior of our males; young women rarely receive similar guidance. Young women suspect that their lives are changing profoundly: being smart and outspoken in tenth grade carries different implications than it did in fifth grade.

- Students who are a racial or ethnic minority in school feel even more keenly the alienation of adolescence. Being different, not having a sure command of a second language, being one of the few in a group, can be uncomfortable and limiting, and often teachers and other students do not reach out.

- Adolescents don't come to school to see you or to go to class; they come to experience the real action: one another. In some ways you and your class are merely the backdrop of the play.

- In English class, students want to read something that speaks to them and their experience; they want to write about what they know; they want to talk about issues of importance. This does not mean that they can't or won't read about different cultures and different ages, but it must, somehow, relate to now. If you can't give this to them or don't think this is important, you may have problems in your classroom.

- Our young students are not children, and don't want to be termed as such. They usually know more and have experienced more than we give them credit for. Patronize them, let them know that they're just kids, and they'll dislike you for it. First, it's demeaning, and second, it's just not true. One student remembers that "I had always believed that adults didn't expect adolescents to have any worthwhile ideas." That's not what we want to be known for.

- Most of your students are participating to some extent in sexual activities, and many are using or experimenting with drugs, both hard and soft, and alcohol. Some of this is growing up and learning; some of it is highly dangerous. But, despite the earnest work of groups such as Promise Keepers, scare tactics or a shallow approach to moralizing doesn't help here. Some of this behavior is what you and your friends did, too, and just saying no doesn't make the problem—or even the complexity of the issues—go away.

- Many of your students will have jobs outside of school, which, frankly, mean more to them than your class because, unlike your class, those jobs pay them money. Given a chance, some students will tell you this, too.

- Despite how untouched they may appear, your students want you to care about them and to be concerned about them. They do not, however, want you to invade their personal lives or their privacy. It's a fine line they ask you—that they expect you—to walk.

- Despite how indifferent they may appear, your students want to respect you as a teacher and as a person. In fact, despite all disclaimers to the contrary, they look to you for some sort of clue as to how they should live their lives and what choices they should make.

- Despite how broad-minded or sophisticated they may appear, adolescents do not want you to do drugs with them, drink with them, or use risqué language or obscenities around them.

- Despite how infatuated they may become with you—or you with them—adolescents do not want you as a boyfriend or a girlfriend or as a sexual partner. You are an adult, a teacher, in a trusted role, and intimate contact is a flat violation of that trust. Fall in love with someone your own age; put your students' feelings of affection or just experiments with flirtation in perspective. In this area, you have limited rights; you are a teacher first and foremost. To violate that trust is a profound betrayal.

- Remember always that youth is a territory all its own: adults may visit but are guests only on temporary visa.

- Remember also that youth is necessarily, inescapably, self-centered: young people really don't think your life or your problems are anywhere near as important as theirs and, anyway, it's your job to be there because you're the teacher. Furthermore, you get paid for this stuff.

- Remember, finally, that adolescents are the toughest audience in the world—and one of the most rewarding. They may never tell you thanks or write or phone or come back to school to let you know how they are doing, but don't worry; if you did your job, they'll remember, and they just might be better people for it. And you, necessarily, are much the better for having known them. Many of your students will, in fact, stay in your mind and your heart for the rest of your life. And that's a job benefit few professions can offer you.

······· **FOR YOUR JOURNAL** ·······

Try to remember who you were during adolescence. *Questions to consider:* What is one thing you loved? hated? Who were your best friends? What was the major challenge you had during this time? What do you recall about your relationship with your parents? with your teachers? If you worked during the year or during the summer, what did you do? What did you read?

If none of these questions seem appealing, find a young person between the age of thirteen and eighteen and informally interview him or her. *Possible questions for the interview:* What does the person think are the biggest hurdles to being that age? The deepest satisfactions? If there was one thing he or she would like teachers to understand, what would it be? What about for parents? for adults in general? What does the person think being an adult will be like?

Finally, if you hate these questions and the interview, think about another avenue. One of the characters in young adult writer Richard Peck's *Unfinished Portrait of Jessica* remarks, "There were only three ages: *now, high school,* and *grown up.* All adults were the same age" (63–64). If this is true, if this is what most young people really assume, what is your responsibility, obligation, problem as a teacher? What, essentially, are the implications of such a statement?

The School

A little bit of selected history

Arthur N. Applebee wrote the book, literally, on the history of our profession. *Tradition and Reform in the Teaching of English* is the most comprehensive text to date, and if you are interested in the various movements and trends, it's worth your time. And, in a very self-serving way, it is to your advantage to know your educational history, if for no other reason than to appreciate that the latest outcry and call for change has probably been made, with just as much energy and intelligence, sometime in the past. Many of the issues in language arts teaching are perennial, and much of what American education debated at the beginning of the twentieth century is with us now in the twenty-first.

There are, nevertheless, a few historical landmarks and a few issues worth reviewing, a number of which follow.

Education for life versus education for college   So just what is a school for? Should it be geared to prepare a student for the world—that is, work—or for college?

Does this question sound familiar? It was a raging debate in 1892 when the National Education Association sponsored what came to be known as the Report of the Committee of Ten. The group was concerned that high school courses were taught differently depending on whether the students were going to college or not. The Committee of Ten also found that English language arts courses were not being geared to two basic needs: developing communication skills and cultivating a taste for reading. A few years later, in 1918, the significantly more influential *Cardinal Principles* report said much the same as the Committee of Ten, but it also added that English should include "studies of direct value" and that theory and student experience should be related.

The student's interest as the basis for all learning   The *Cardinal Principles* was influential, and the interest in preparing students for life became a major tenet of an encompassing concept called the Progressive Movement. The movement's most influential proponent was the legendary writer and educational theorist John Dewey, and the movement started formally in 1919 with the founding of the Progressive Education Association and didn't really fade until the 1950s.

For the Progressive Movement, the real needs of students were of great import, and in language arts, the 1935 publication of *An Experience Curriculum in English* tried to meet student interests in a realistic course of studies. The curriculum seemed successful, and research involving 240 schools and 3,600 students, called the Eight-Year Study, confirmed the fact. According to the Eight-Year Study's results, students prepared around problems and issues that concerned them did as well in college as their more traditionally educated counterparts. The compelling nature of the Progressive Movement's ideas is enduring, even today, and you will find echoes of its tenets in many contemporary books about American education.

The academic model and the romantic revolt   Carried to its extreme, the Progressive Movement, especially through an early 1950s manifestation called "life adjustment education," lost the faith of the American public. Meeting the real needs of students was carried to the extreme, actually went over the edge, and when units in English class on housing the family, choosing a mate, and even how to answer the telephone were brought to public attention—and ridicule—the bloom was off the Progressive rose. Especially with the fears of international competition, embodied by the former Soviet Union's bold launching in 1957 of the first orbiting space capsule, Sputnik, the English language arts curriculum drew back into what Arthur Applebee terms the "academic model."

It was the early 1960s, and rigor and the concept of English as a discipline held sway. Drawing on the influential writing of Jerome Bruner in the seminal *The Process of Education* and rejecting the "soft" idea of student interest as being the basis of education, the English curriculum in particular became serious, structured, and rigorously tested. While some gains may have been made, the result was an alienation of certain students and teachers although, admittedly, many thrived in the classroom. English language arts in the early 1960s was not about adjusting to society. Instead, there was the academic formalism of studying structural linguistics and the close analysis of the New Criticism.

Nothing, of course, stays in place, and the academic orientation of the previous years was transformed in the mid sixties. Education was not untouched by the upheavals of the age: the civil rights movement, the women's movement, and a general call for societal change. In the schools, a number of educators demanded that the English classroom open up and be more for all students of all persuasions; its intellectual rigor was seen as an impediment to learning, not an enhancement, especially for racial minorities and those not admitted into the prestigious, exclusive, and CEEB-sponsored Advanced Placement classes.

In the mid and late 1960s, it was a time of educational experiment. Students were invited to choose their courses in elective programs, schedule their classes in variable time slots, take courses pass/fail, and take classes with people younger and older than themselves and in spaces without walls or without rows or sometimes without desks. As Neil Postman and Charles Weingartner happily wrote in 1969, teaching could be viewed as a "subversive" activity. According to many 1960s reformers, the classroom could, appropriately, undermine and challenge the omnipresent and scorned "establishment."

Accountability: Let's go back to the basics   Well of course it didn't last. By the mid 1970s the public temperature indicated that it was time to worry that standards were slipping, that teachers slaphappy with freedom and students talking much too expressively were taking over the English classes and not doing or learning a darned thing. A fear emerged that was somewhat akin to that of the late 1950s: where were the testable skills? Where was the practice development? So the wind shifted to going "back" to the basics of English and testing, testing, testing, under the umbrella term *accountability*. Competency tests were in vogue, and the idea of making materials or texts "teacher-proof" resurged.

The "sea of mediocrity" and the standards and testing movements   In 1983 the United States Department of Education issued *A Nation at Risk*, a scathing and influential report that concluded that education was currently drowning in "a sea of mediocrity." It was alarming language, it was widely believed as true, and it set off a national conversation where many concluded that the schools were not doing enough to foster excellence. What seemed to be the solution? Because policy makers, not necessarily the public, suspected that little worthwhile was going on in classrooms, it seemed appropriate to institute more state control over school curriculum.

Additionally, as undisputed evidence of achievement, it also seemed important to test students far more extensively and to report the results of those tests to a broad constituency. Thus more control of the curriculum, more testing, and more reporting and analysis of those tests combined as a three-punch whammy. The need for this change was reinforced by widely publicized—and often misinterpreted—comparisons of American students' test scores in math and science to those of young people from other countries. While many felt that the unfavorable conclusions about American schools and comparisons to students from other countries were unfairly reported, the avalanche had started to snowball. For the first time there was statewide consensus that something unified should be enacted. That something was the crafting of curricular benchmarks and skills standards for every state, accompanied by the testing of those standards. (For a discussion of the standards crafted by our professional organization, the National Council of Teachers of English and for all teachers and students in English language arts, see the last chapter.)

With few exceptions, most states fell into line, and today students and teachers face more testing than possibly ever in the history of American education. Further, the results of those tests are regularly publicized and, through the enactment of the federal No Child Left Behind (NCLB) legislation, where students in grades three through eight are tested every year and in one year of high school, there are sanctions for schools and school districts that do not meet requirements of Adequate Yearly Progress (AYP). This kind of oversight of student achievement, almost completely determined by standardized test scores, is without precedent in American education. It has also not been without controversy: scores of educators and educational associations have raised questions about these tests and about the punitive provisions of NCLB, and parents, teachers, and students have regularly protested and, in some cases, taken their concerns to court.

In a related development, tax-funded alternatives to public education—charter schools—are now developing side by side with traditional public schools although the debate about student achievement in those schools remains fierce on both sides. In addition, the more widespread use of Advanced Placement courses (and the attendant Advanced Placement test) and the International Baccalaureate curriculum are attempts to put more rigor into high school courses. Further, many schools in this country now offer "dual" enrollment, where high school seniors can take college-level courses in their home school setting for which they receive college credit.

Today, we continue to deal with these issues, and we can add to them a few others. There is, in general, a continual concern about the teaching of the "classics" in English, and one change has been that many works in the canon, once taught in senior high schools, are now taught in middle schools, driving literature from middle schools down to the elementary level. Whether most students are capable of reading these works at the time they are taught is not clear, but, for instance, plays by Shakespeare and nineteenth-century novels, once reserved for the last years of school, are now introduced to students far earlier. And the debate goes on.

School as repository of hopes and dreams—and traditions

There is ongoing discussion—as always—of the institution of school and how it is not serving education or young people. More specifically, we continue to hear today that American business is not receiving qualified workers and that the national economy is falling and our country is in second—or third—place because of the failure of school, especially as it is now structured. And despite the consistent comments of reform-minded individuals, it is clear that even today of all the American institutions with which we are familiar, school is the one—virtually the only one other than some organized religions—where a person deep-frozen in the early twentieth century could return to our age and be comfortable and feel a sense of familiarity. In high schools particularly, the same curriculum patterns, much of the same subject matter (including the very same pieces of literature taught in English classes), the same general organization of the school day, have survived from early twentieth-century American public education. And, ironically, the calls we hear now for school reform are many of the same calls that have been issued for almost 100 years, and some of the "new" proposals for flexible/modular scheduling days, for year-round school, and for school on ten-month patterns that do not automatically include a summer (maybe a winter?) vacation are ideas we have heard for the last forty years. The perennial concern about school being preparation for college or preparation for life is a debate from the turn of the century.

America changed its eating habits from home to restaurant to fast-food establishment in less than a decade, shifted from cars to sport utility vehicles in the same time, adjusted to the word processor and the computer in about twenty years, embraced the cell phone, e-mail, and Internet surfing in fewer years than that, and absorbed massive social change regarding women and minorities in a decade and a half. So why the foot-dragging with school?

As a teaching friend of mine notes, "school keeps." We may face tremendous changes around us, but school, with its familiar structure and content, is a reassuring touchstone of sorts for many Americans. It's also, maddeningly enough, a repository for many of our hopes and dreams about our future and what our youth, our young people, represent to us. It may seem to be just a graduation speech cliché, but for many Americans youth is indeed the future, and school is where many of us hope that youth will be formed and shaped.

School is where we try to transmit, carry on, and it's a sensitive issue for the majority of taxpaying, child-rearing adults. When it looks like what we experienced, many of us feel comforted. School is the "universal environment" for adolescents, a "vast, standardized, relatively homogeneous experience" that all students in this country share (Furhmann, 144). When we hear of practices we did not experience—such as the "new" math—there is often dislocation and confusion.

And, as George Counts wrote almost eighty years ago, school is more driven by social change than it is the driver of it. That makes it often a controversial and touchy place to teach and to learn, especially when a society feels that its sense of order and values is threatened by any combination of social shifting. For example, debates over the place of grammar in the curriculum, which piece of literature to study, or how to teach English to those for whom it is a second language are often a product of politics in the very broad sense of the term and not just questions that well-meaning English departments can rationally solve in some sort of vacuum or isolation. Today, schools are also indicators of what educational critic Jonathan Kozol calls "apartheid schooling" where the student population is as segregated as the neighborhoods from which students come. School can be a political minefield, and it is certainly an accurate reflection of the anxieties of the culture.

It is important for you to know about school, the institution, how it is organized, and how that affects you and your classes. There may, in the coming few years, be real changes in the shape of schools—some reforms often talked about may really come to pass—but in the meantime you will experience, at least for the first part of your teaching life, a high school or middle school structured not very differently from the way it was organized when your grandparents walked the halls.

And while that continuity may be comforting on one level, it also is not serving young people efficiently. As one educator grimly notes:

> The comprehensive high school, designed to meet the needs of everyone, is criticized for having become an assembly-line system that denies adolescents access to adults, breeds frustration, creates failure, and is concerned only with conformity and order rather than intellectual curiosity and love of learning. (Furhmann, 148–49)

Further, and this is a reality of the business, the structure of school often gets in the way of teaching and learning. You will find yourself in your classroom wondering if there isn't a better way to set up this contract among learners, and your speculation will be appropriate. Unfortunately, however—and this has been true of educational history in this country for over a century—you, as the teacher, will probably be one of the last people seriously consulted about institutional change. It will be up to you at times to make the best of what can be a difficult situation, at times to make changes as you can in your own school community, and possibly at times to really get a piece of the teacher empowerment that is often touted. But that's another story. Let's look at what the issues are.

Five aspects of school that may not serve you or your students

The compulsory nature of school and your English class   First, you need to remember that your wonderful students, your clientele as it were, even in private or independent school, are there by compulsion. School is required, it is not optional, and by the time you get ready to meet your English classes, your students have been doing this compulsory stuff for many years. They may, by fourteen or seventeen, even be a little jaded. They often come, as Richard Hawley remarks in his article "Teaching as Failing," like an audience with little anticipation of being pleased. You may, indeed, pleasantly surprise them, but do not expect huzzahs as you enter the classroom. While you may know you are different, to many of your students you look a lot like every other teacher they have ever had. And that, by the way, is not necessarily a compliment. As a result, you may be rather surprised at the absentee rate in your school and the practical effects of that rate on your classroom. Student teacher Debbie Martin wrote in her journal:

> These kids never come to school or, when they do, they come late or leave early. I had one student out of 120 who didn't miss a day last semester. By the same token there were 19 students who missed a total of 750 days out of the teaching days of the semester, and 212 students who were tardy over a total of *1,100* times in the same period of time. Trying to keep track of late work is an administrative nightmare.

Second, you need to recall that English is also not optional. School itself is compulsory, as is the one other subject that everyone has to take (with very few exceptions) every year: English. Get the picture? You are not the instructional purveyor of the exotic, like Latin III or theatre arts; what you offer in the classroom is not associated with excessive brilliance or arcane knowledge, like physics or calculus; you will not preside over classes where folks can learn about sex or can sweat and yell and play a game, like health and physical education. You don't help people make things they can eat or put in their bedrooms or hang on their walls like home ec or wood working or art. It's the most common, most broadly required, most repeated game in town: it's English language arts, and you're the teacher.

Grouping students into grade levels   It seems ridiculous to think that the one-room schoolhouse was actually a great educational idea. But, as we'll see, we could do worse than to go back to some of its principles. But that's getting ahead of the story—a little history first.

In the nineteenth century in this country, the one-room schoolhouse was rather grudgingly supported by the community through taxes and levies. It was predominately rural, undersupplied, and badly heated, ventilated, and lit. It was in session in direct relation to the local crops and economy and to the weather. There was often no continuity of instruction—the turnover in teachers and students was startlingly high. The one-room schoolhouse was presided over by one very young, unmarried, and undereducated teacher (most in the late nineteenth and early twentieth century had not the equivalent of a high school diploma), usually female, for whom the job meant low pay, severe community scrutiny, and a great deal of work. That teacher taught and supervised as many young people as the single room could hold, and students often ranged in age from six years old to fourteen or fifteen.

Just for a minute imagine the distance intellectually between a six-year-old and, say, a thirteen-year-old, between first graders and seventh graders. What they can read and comprehend is wildly different, and when you go back in your mind and imagine our turn-of-the-twentieth-century schoolteacher trying, day after day, to structure learning experiences for such a widely disparate group, you can understand why educators thought it would be a great advance to group students by age, to put all of the six-year-olds together and all of the fourteen-year-olds together somewhere else. It was seen as an advance and a sensible way to deal with the differences between young people at varying stages of development. As researcher Larry Cuban observes, "teaching [an] entire class together is an efficient and convenient use of the teacher's time—a valuable and scarce resource—to cover the mandated content and maintain control" (253).

What happened over the years, however, is that many of us in education lost sight of how nebulous and changeable some of those age differentials are. In fact, there will be more variation intellectually *among* your students in your third-period, ninth-grade English class than *between all of the ninth graders and all of the tenth graders* in your entire school. The segregation by age also seems to imply a few things that we need to examine carefully. Let's imagine we're talking about those tenth graders. If we accept grade levels by age, it tells us:

1. There is something all tenth graders should either be ready to learn or should already know, based on their chronological age.
2. All tenth graders should be taught pretty much alike because they are at the same stage of development.
3. Tenth graders will not benefit from intellectual contact with students either older or younger than themselves.

None of these three propositions is true. While we know something about how and when people learn, we don't know enough to be able to say with any certainty what a single year of school should offer intellectually. Further, the kind of crossover that occurred in the one-room schoolhouse—despite its many other manifest drawbacks—is something we could do well to return to. *Each one teach one, collaborative learning,* and *cooperative learning* are all current phrases for the same idea: we benefit when we can teach someone else, and we not only help that person, but, by helping them, we solidify our own skills.

So, when our overworked schoolteacher had to give a geography lesson to the older students, she would, possibly, ask one of the older students to listen to and help two or three of the very young students with their reading. It was a cross-age endeavor. Further, this older student was probably more adept in reading than were those older kids getting the geography lesson; that student would not be kept in a group level but would be allowed to proceed at his or her own pace.

When you begin to teach, or when you teach this week, you may be puzzled at the disparity *among* your eleventh graders. Curricula plans that feature nongrouping—in other words, putting tenth and eleventh and twelfth graders together in a given class—militate against this sort of "Now you're fifteen; that means _____" kind of mentality.

Tracking   Again, it seems a good idea at first glance; put the adept kids together, let them go on, and put the less adept kids together so they can receive extra attention and help. It sounds sensible, but it is based on a few things that we're not sure actually operate in the schools. For tracking to be *successful*, it must be based on the following principles:

1. **Neither teachers nor students should indulge in a "self-fulfilling prophecy" type of behavior;** that is, the kids tracked in the higher brackets cannot always be assumed to be smarter, and the kids tracked in the lower brackets cannot always be assumed to be slower. Lower-tracked students will often assume they aren't smart and therefore won't try. Higher-tracked students may just fail to exert the effort. Also, teachers often internalize these attitudes and deal differently with students in different tracks. And, by the way, disguising tracking designations is virtually impossible. Students and teachers *know*.
2. **Students must be mobile between the tracks;** once in a lower track, they must be allowed to achieve their way to a higher track and vice versa.
3. **The placement of students into tracks must be based on real evidence,** not on:

- Ability gauged by single-measure tests or even standardized tests.
- Race or economic background.
- Personal characteristics such as appearance, ability to interact positively with school authorities, ability to adhere to school rules.

The sad fact is that these three conditions are rarely met in schools; kids are placed into tracks for reasons other than out-and-out ability and intelligence (Oakes, 9–14); kids, once placed, are rarely moved between tracks; and "smart" kids know they are in that track and can act accordingly, as do those designated less able. There is no strong research evidence that tracking is doing what we want it to do, especially for those students who are not at the top of the academic spectrum. (For a thorough look at the subject, see Jeannie Oakes' *Keeping Track*.) And, to compound the problem, we know that students in higher tracks, simply put, receive a better education (Furhmann, 158). Helen Featherstone discusses a study of 108 eighth- and ninth-grade classrooms, where researchers found that

> teachers in high-track classes ask more "authentic" questions, ones that have no predetermined answers, "but instead call for student opinions or for information the student must uncover independently of the teacher." They all follow up on student responses more often. . . . All this makes it sound as though schools conspire against low-track students, but that isn't true. . . . Almost all high school teachers would agree with researchers that students in low-track classes are less engaged than those in high-track classes, but things get more complex when we begin to speculate about the reasons for that disengagement. . . . Placed together in one classroom, without the leaven of more enthusiastic and academically successful classmates, disengaged adolescents create a culture unfriendly to effort. Teachers respond with teaching that asks less of students, perhaps reinforcing the students' disengagement. Before long neither teacher nor students have much heart for academic work. (7)

In addition, there is some evidence that lower-level students benefit strongly from the influence of other, more adept students. The cognitive psychologist Lev Vygotsky found that what students "can do with the assistance of others might be in some sense even more indicative of their mental development than what they can do alone" (85). Vygotsky called this a "zone of proximal development," and clearly students stronger in language arts skills can benefit those less strong.

Jane Hunter notes:

> For many years, I thought that all of the various "tracks" were taught the same things, in the same manner, and that they just varied in pace from one another. I couldn't have been farther from the truth! During my first semester of my senior year, I ran face-to-face into this prejudice after signing up for an advanced poetry class. The first sign that I was out of my territory came from a fellow student on the first day of class. "Andrew," one of the school's most promising students, walked over to my desk that morning and snarled, "Jane, what are you doing in this class?" I responded with a few choice words and wrote him off as being a stuck-up geek. As time went on, however, I began to realize where these kids' attitudes were coming from— the instructors! Students in these advanced English sections were handed a multitude of privileges by the instructors and the administration. These AP classes were run totally different from the "average" tracks—they all sat in a circle and held open discussions/debates amongst each other and with the instructor. They were also permitted to publish a class journal each month that was then distributed schoolwide. And worst of all, they were given first dibs in the computer room!

Finally, as Paul Fanney, a former student of mine, writes, it can be a depressing experience to be placed in the "wrong" track:

> In tenth grade I discovered firsthand the horror of being placed [not in an honors class but] in a "regular" level class. Tenth-grade English had to be one of the most boring, irritating, and desultory experiences I have ever had. The teacher I remember did her best to keep it boring, too. The reason I got into trouble so much with her was because of how she taught and what she taught; like math classes I constantly asked myself "What's the point?" or "So what?" I got the impression that somehow we weren't to be trusted with books, *novels* I mean, based on the "probability" that we wouldn't know what to do with them once we got them. I actually remember feeling as if I was being intellectually insulted, if you know what I mean. I never forgave my advisor for putting me in that class, or the teacher for making me so restless. Instead of an interesting learning environment, we got worksheets; instead of stimulating talks on relevant and meaningful issues good English classes raise, we were given homework in monotone.

What does this mean to you? It means that you will encounter students who, at fifteen, know that it is too late; the school has judged them "slower" or "less able" or, as Paul writes, not to be trusted with books. That's a heavy burden for an adult—it's insupportable when you're a kid.

You will also have classes where the "smart" kids are on the fast track and no longer feel the need to work. They have, by the system's designation, succeeded, so why break a sweat? They have a perennial case of "senioritis" as sophomores or juniors. Finally, you will see a ghettoization of the student body with young people permanently marked and sorted into designations of being smart, not so smart, and so on. It just doesn't do a thing for real teaching and real learning.

A final reason tracking doesn't enhance teaching or learning is that despite your effort to be open-minded, once you enter a classroom you know has been designated as a certain track, your expectations will be subtly and not so subtly affected. You will have assumptions about the low-level class that are hard to shake. Paul's teacher, for example, did not see him as a misplaced bright person. You will also become accustomed to hearing other teachers discuss students and classes solely in relation to their tracking designation. In this game of tracking, then, the students have roles and designations that they are not allowed to change. And you, as their teacher, will also be affected.

Instructional time   When T. S. Eliot's character J. Alfred Prufrock complained about measuring his life out in coffee spoons ("The Love Song of J. Alfred Prufrock"), he might have been discussing the life of a middle school or high school teacher who must deal with short periods of instructional time. Again, with best intentions, with the idea of organizing the school day intelligently, educators first divided the seven or so hours into short periods, in some schools from forty-five- to fifty-five-minute periods. In English language arts particularly, that's a tight block of time to manage every day, every week, every month. Discussions can last longer, reading a piece of literature and then reacting to it often fails to fit into such a slice of the clock, and beginning a piece of writing can proceed in fits and starts much broader than the time allotted. Yet, as beginning teacher Clary Washington laments, "It often seems that the schedule is more important than the learning. This makes me crazy." For high school and middle school students, the class period can be difficult to negotiate, and, for their teachers, it can inspire a mild form of insanity.

In recognition of this fact, many school districts have moved to block scheduling where students and teachers meet on alternate days for longer periods (or "blocks") of time, such as ninety minutes every other day. Certainly in block scheduling there is more free-dom to explore longer projects without the interruption of the bell. Expanded class peri-ods provide time for extensive activities in literature, writing, and technology.

On the other hand, block scheduling itself is not always the magic solution to timing of classroom instruction: for some students, ninety minutes of instruction in the same room with the same teacher can yield less than optimum results and, further, the alternate day scheduling can be confusing. For a teacher intimidated by such long period of instructional time, a block class can be, at least initially, unwieldy to organize.

In general, however, block scheduling militates against the hectic nature of daily fifty-minute periods of instruction. Certainly most teachers find that they and their students accomplish more extended projects in class. And, with judicious use of stretch breaks (*no one* can work unbroken for ninety minutes without some sort of break) and shifts in activ-ities, block classes are highly productive.

In the meantime, understand that both you and your students are responsible to the clock. You must adjust to working within a specific, timed instructional unit. No matter how dull or how exhilarating the class, it comes to an end in a certain amount of minutes, every day, every week, every month of the teaching year. It limits what you can do, and it is a recipe, of and by itself, for routine. You will need to fight that routine so that it becomes not the boredom of utter predictability but the comfort or outline of order. And, unlike the other "constraints" mentioned so far in this section, there are a few things you can do to improve the situation.

How do you do that? You mix it up and shake it up; you keep track of how many days in a row the students had a discussion, worked in small groups, did silent work at their desk, made presentations, or served on panels. You make sure that each week features a variety of large-group, small-group, and individual work, and that class time is alternated appro-priately with films, silent reading, and talk. Again, if you are teaching on a block schedule, you give your students a stretch break somewhere within the ninety minutes. While you do not want to have a class where students really don't know what to expect every day—that can get scary after a while—we flourish, all of us, on variety. One way to beat the boredom trap is to build change into your class. And, as an additional complication, a block schedule requires that you pace your instruction so that students are provided a sense of continuity: seeing them every other day can mean that you, the teacher, need to spend time reviewing on Wednesday what you did on Monday, questioning students so that they can recall on Thursday what they concluded on Tuesday.

Finally, remember that school business may give you much less than the allotted instructional time you expect. Even in block scheduling configurations, announcements, school pictures, field trips, and tardy slips will cut into that period of time. In addition, you may have school-scheduled events suspend your class during the week. After all, how do you think the whole school gets to see the play during the day or hear the special speech imported for their edification? It may be, and with little notice to you, that your Tuesday, fourth-period class doesn't meet, nor does your Wednesday, first-period class. You are responsible for adjusting and planning appropriately. And sometimes, I repeat, it's on short notice. So you remain flexible as you try to teach in this place called school.

Grades and standardized testing   We are a nation of competitors, who's in, who's out, the ten best, the twenty worst, a list and ranking society. We want to know the average, the top, the worst, the mean, the median, and most of us measure ourselves pitilessly against the standard, however we define it. Our students, and our schools, are no different. While we are concentrating on leading an exploration of the power of Martin Luther King's prose, the students—not unexpectedly—want to know whether it will be on the test. We are so pleased with the beginnings of a revision of a student's essay; she wants to know what her grade will be if she keeps on revising. We feel our sixth bell class has made much progress during their year with us, but all the school district wants to know is whether the sixth bell students can score a specified percentage on the state standardized test.

It's the serpent in the garden, but we can't duck it. We are in the business of teaching, for credit and grade, which in turn lead to an official recognition of achievement—a diploma. What we do is required by law, and we are paid for it. Not only are we expected to keep good records, we are also expected to know, for almost every assignment we give, what we are expecting students to learn (objectives), how we will tell if they learned it (evaluation), and how we will rank students' learning (grading).

While issues of grading and evaluation have always been part of teaching, as noted in this chapter, the current intense emphasis on testing is due to public perception that schools are not performing up to standards and that testing will ensure more accountability. On the other hand, educational critics such as Gerald W. Bracey contend that schools *are* doing a good job and certainly better than many members of the public believe: perhaps the doom and gloom of *A Nation at Risk*, published in the 1980s, no longer accurately describes today's schools. Bracey (author of *Setting the Record Straight: Responses to Misconceptions About Public Education in the U.S.*) and others of like mind are, to date, however, in the minority: at least for now, the present educational mantra is one of test, test, test.

Further, if you are skeptical about the relationship between learning and testing, you are probably correct. With drilling and repetition, with daily practice on test items and test time management and test tricks and shortcuts, with total concentration on the test and testing, young people can learn to pass the test and even to improve test scores. Most teachers know this, but they also worry: what do their students really know about the material? Could, in fact, students do as well on a different kind of assessment, a different kind of test? Will they pass that particular test but not know much else?

Many educators don't share uncritical faith in standardized tests. In a perfect world, passing or scoring well on a test would absolutely indicate mastery of the material: isn't that the point? But when one kind of test and test score become the focus of all, and result in intensive practice drilling for that particular test—as is done now in school districts all over the country—then mastering the material can become truly secondary. It's not about learning; it's about learning to take the test.

Surely one reaction to the nationwide emphasis on testing is the proliferation of commercial companies who promise improved test scores. Testing critic Bracey notes that in Virginia, thirty-four companies provide "supplemental educational services"; in California 250 such companies have been approved by the state for such materials. According to a recent report in *Time*, many schools across the nation are turning to commercial companies and their test preparation courses and workbooks to teach students how to eliminate choices in multiple-choice exams, skim reading passages, and fill in bubble sheets. Yet, despite this burgeoning $50 million business, *Time*'s report concludes "there is no solid evidence so far that this kind of preparation makes kids dependable test takers, let alone good learners." Most teachers know this.

Despite this fact, as a beginning teacher you will work in an environment of large-scale, state-administered standardized testing in which students are expected to perform at a specified level. In some states this yearly, largely multiple-choice testing is tied to state curriculum standards, and the results of the testing can determine school accreditation as well as student progress through the grade levels. This is, as a frequently used phrase accurately describes it, "high-stakes" testing, and, in some regions, it has seriously affected classroom instruction and classroom climate.

How high stakes are these tests? Consider some observations from Bracey's "The Seven Deadly Absurdities of No Child Left Behind":

- The state of California projects that by 2014, NCLB will label 99 percent of its schools as failing, and Minnesota projects that 80 percent of its schools will be deemed as such.

- Under the current No Child Left Behind (NCLB) legislation, any school that fails to demonstrate adequate yearly progress (AYP) for two consecutive years must provide their students the option to transfer to another, more successful school.

- In most states, there are not sufficient schools to allow such transfers. In 2004–05 Chicago had 200,000 students eligible for such transfer, but could only find 500 spaces for them. In 2003–04, New York had 350,000 eligible but was so overwhelmed by the numbers that it permitted only 1,000 transfers.

In almost all instances individual teachers have little control over the content or the handling of these tests, but the teachers are, make no mistake about it, responsible for student performance. In most cases this means that teachers must prepare students—who may be used to untimed writing or to short answer responses—to deal successfully with strictly timed multiple-choice questions and their answers. Also, teachers may find themselves spending much classroom time reviewing students in specific content areas so that they are geared for the state test when it is administered. Carol Jago, a longtime California teacher, describes it:

> For some teachers in California, teaching in a time of testing feels like love in a time of cholera. Like Gabriel García Márquez characters, San Diego City schools teachers are being forced to steal moments for authentic teaching from a proscribed curriculum. Literacy must be taught in uninterrupted three-hour blocks from scripted reading programs. Administrators monitor classrooms and "write up" teachers who deviate from the script. One feature of magical realist literature is that it portrays everyday life where extraordinary things happen in a matter-of-fact tone. Too bad this isn't fiction. In his Nobel Prize speech, Márquez explains that Latin American writers turned to magical realism not from excess of imagination, but rather as a way to render the outsized reality of their lives believable. San Diego teachers struggle with the same dilemma. (27)

The expectation to test and measure at all levels—school, school district, and state— is not very good news for us as English teachers, especially when so much of what we do is, frankly, difficult to quantify or difficult to fit into an hour-long fifty-item multiple choice test. How, for example, in the instance of a specific classroom period, do you assign a letter grade to each of the twenty-seven students who for two solid days discussed the meaning of Nathaniel Hawthorne's "Young Goodman Brown"? What constitutes an A or a C in that situation—or do you just give up and give everyone who participated a reasonably good grade? Do you ignore letter grades entirely and move to pass/fail or to check, check-plus, check-minus? If you decline to evaluate individually each student on an activity such as two days of class discussion, aren't you avoiding accountability?

Well, the point is you *can* justify such discussion; you can give students credit—and response—for that discussion, but you can't, unlike other areas of academic endeavor, truly grade everything you do in English language arts. Nor should you.

Much of what we do is cumulative and builds on long periods of time. We are rarely given to know if a student's facility with language or a highly complex idea makes a grade-level change in our classroom. Thus we are kidding ourselves if we believe that progress during any given academic year will always show in the results of a state-administered standardized test.

So what do we do?

We can justify such activities if we can't precisely grade them; we can spend time on classroom exercises even if we know with some certainty that it will not appear on the state-mandated test. We evaluate what we can, and we simply leave the rest to a few instruments: tests, writing assignments, notations of participation and completion. We also do not hijack our own curriculum in total service of the standardized test. To do so abrogates not only our role but our obligation as a teacher.

Patti Smith, writing about preparing our students for the future, presents two aspects of literature, only one of which can be easily graded:

> Everyone agrees that education is supposed to prepare one for the future. The best way to do this is to prepare [students] intellectually, not with the ability to supply the names of the main characters of *Hamlet*, but with the ability to make the connection between *Hamlet* and modern problems. Critical thinking, that's what kids should learn in English class.

And while, certainly, one can grade aspects of a student's critical thinking about *Hamlet* (there has to be some external evidence that a student has connected the play with modern problems), it is a lot easier to grade his or her knowledge of the play's main characters and plot.

Our job, ladies and gentlemen, is not an easy one.

We also want to avoid the following scene (even though we may admire the teacher's temporary solution and even though in this case the students responded positively):

> There was one incident that occurred in [my English teacher's] class that stands out in my mind and describes him and his philosophy of teaching perfectly. Since I was in an Advanced Placement class, the class was small (15 students). Most of my classmates were ambitious, competitive, goal-oriented kids. This is good . . . to a point. All they cared about were grades. They wanted to know at all times what was needed for a grade, and essays and subjective tests drove them crazy. The teacher hated this attitude. He wanted to have discussions and to make these kids think for themselves, not memorize for a grade.
>
> One day the grade-oriented students were really anxious. They kept asking how they were going to be graded on some assignments. They were wasting a great deal of time and we could not get back to the topic being discussed. Something triggered him; he went off! One of the students told him that he had to know how he was going to be graded because of college entrance requirements. Then the student went on to say he wanted to be taught what he needed to know for college and what he needed to know to score high on the SATs. [The teacher] looked at us and said that he wasn't training us for a few crummy classes in college. . . . The next day he came in and tore up the grade book and said that from here on out it would be pass or fail. The only requirements for an A would be real discussions and participation. . . . After that day, class was great. The pressure was gone, and we could really discuss topics.

—Melissa Campbell

Yet, as a student in the middle of her student teaching writes, the pressure to give and get grades is powerful:

> [Teaching] is frustrating because I want so much for all of my kids to do well. I have had to veer away from taking their success (or failure) as my success (or failure). To a certain extent, I must look at the whole class and evaluate if my teaching is soaking in. This can be gathered from looking at them, listening to them, and checking performance. But I realize now that not everyone is going to get an A. It took me a long time to accept this.

> —Julie Lepard

And it may take you some time to sort out your feelings about grades and their pressures and realities. Regardless, they are a feature of school and the teaching life, and until things change markedly in public education, you will need to make your own compromise with grades and quantification, a subject that will run through almost all the chapters of this book. Certainly in the case of your own state's standardized testing of students—a testing that is now almost universal across the country—you will need to balance—as much as any single teacher can—what you see as your students' needs and what is a responsible approach to the yearly, state-mandated test.

Teacher, student, school. The three intertwine perhaps more intimately than you had first imagined. Our job is to find a balanced configuration that truly serves learning and teaching and that does not kill the mind and extinguish the spirit. It is an ongoing issue, an ongoing struggle of school, and no teacher, veteran or novice, has a quick or even permanent answer as to the exact dimensions of the balance. It is, actually, a daily endeavor, depending upon context and myriad other factors, and it is one of the most important jobs facing a teacher.

·············· FOR YOUR JOURNAL ···············

Look back at the five "constraints" you will face in the public school setting. Choose any two of them and make *your* list of options/ alternatives/practices that *you* think could lessen the impact of these potentially negative forces.

Think about your own schooling or what you have observed in school visits; what constraints do you remember experiencing or seeing? Imagine an ideal school: How would it avoid the problems discussed? What would the teachers be like? What attitudes/expectations would students have? How would an ideal community support an ideal school?

References

Aikin, Wilford M. *The Story of the Eight-Year Study*. New York: Harper & Brothers, 1942.

Applebee, Arthur N. *Tradition and Reform in the Teaching of English*. Urbana, IL: NCTE, 1974.

Bracey, Gerald W. *Setting the Record Straight: Responses to Misconceptions About Public Education in the U.S.* 2d ed. Portsmouth, NH: Heinemann, 2004.

———. "The Seven Deadly Absurdities of No Child Left Behind." Unpublished Internet article accessed 9/19/05.

———. *The Truth About America's Schools: The Bracey Reports, 1991–97*. Bloomington, IN: Phi Delta Kappa, 1997.

Bruner, Jerome S. *The Process of Education*. New York: Random House, 1963.

Commission on the Reorganization of Secondary Education of the NEA. *Cardinal Principles of Secondary Education*. Washington, DC: GPO, 1918.

Counts, George S. *Dare the School Build a New Social Order?* New York: Arno Press, 1969.

Creely, Robert. "A Form of Women." In *Contemporary American Poetry*. Edited by A. Poulin, Jr., 57. Boston: Houghton Mifflin, 1971.

Cuban, Larry. *How Teachers Taught: Constancy and Change in American Classrooms 1880–1990*. 2d ed. New York: Teachers College Press, 1993.

Dewey, John. *Democracy and Education*. New York: Macmillan, [1916] 1961.

Donaldson, Margaret. *A Study of Children's Thinking*. London: Tavistock, 1963.

Eliot, T. S. *The Complete Poems and Plays 1909–1950*. New York: Harcourt Brace & World, 1952.

An Experience Curriculum in English. A Report of the Curriculum Committee of the National Council of Teachers of English (Wilbur W. Hatfield, Chairman). New York: D. Appleton-Century Company, 1935.

Featherstone, Helen. "Making Diversity Educational: Alternatives to Ability Grouping." *Changing Minds*. Michigan Educational Extension Service, Bulletin 4 (Fall). East Lansing, MI: 1991.

Flood, James, Julie M. Jensen, Dianne Lapp, and James R. Squire, eds. *Handbook of Research on Teaching the English Language Arts*. 2d ed. Mahwah, NJ: Lawrence Erlbaum, 2003.

Fuhrman, Susan, ed. *From the Capitol to the Classroom: Standards Based Reform in the States, 100th Yearbook of the National Society for the Scientific Study of Education*. Chicago: University of Chicago Press, 2001.

Furhmann, Barbara Schneider. *Adolescence, Adolescents*. 2d ed. Glenview, IL: Scott Foresman/Little Brown, 1990.

Hawley, Richard A. "Teaching as Failing." *Phi Delta Kappan* 60 (April 1979): 597–600.

Hawthorne, Nathaniel. "Young Goodman Brown." In *Hawthorne: Selected Tales and Sketches*. 3d ed. San Francisco: Rinehart Press, 1970.

Hughes, Langston. "Harlem." In *Selected Poems of Langston Hughes*, 268. New York: Vintage, 1959.

Jago, Carol. "Standards in California: A Magical Realist View." *Voices from the Middle* 10 (September 2002): 27–30.

Kozol, Jonathan. *The Shame of the Nation: The Restoration of Apartheid Schooling in America*. New York: Crown, 2005.

Muth, K. Denise, and Donna E. Alvermann. *Teaching and Learning in the Middle Grades*. 2d ed. Boston: Allyn & Bacon, 1999.

Nieto, Sonia. *What Keeps Teachers Going?* New York: Teachers College Press, 2003.

Oakes, Jeannie. *Keeping Track: How Schools Structure Inequality*. 2d ed. New Haven, CT: Yale University Press, 2005.

O'Neill, Eugene. *Selections: The Emperor Jones. Anna Christie. The Hairy Ape*. New York: Vintage, 1972.

Oxford English Dictionary. New York: Oxford University Press, 1971.

Pearl. Edited by E. V. Gordon. New York: Oxford University Press, 1966.

Peck, Richard. *Unfinished Portrait of Jessica*. New York: Delacorte, 1991.

Piaget, Jean. *The Language and Thought of the Child*. 3d ed. London: Routledge & Kegan Paul, 1959.

Postman, Neil, and Charles Weingartner. *Teaching as a Subversive Activity*. New York: Delacorte, 1969.

Pound, Ezra. "In a Station of the Metro." In *Lustra of Ezra Pound*, 45. New York: Haskell House, 1973.

Rilke, Rainer Maria. "Archaic Torso of Apollo." In *Translations from the Poetry of Rainer Maria Rilke*, 181. Translated by M. D. Herter Norton. New York: Norton, 1962.

Salinger, J. D. *The Catcher in the Rye*. Boston: Little, Brown, 1991.

Shakespeare, William. *Complete Plays and Poems of William Shakespeare*. Edited by William Allan Neilson and Charles Jarvis Hill. Boston: Houghton Mifflin, 1942.

"Test Drive." *Time* (February 2, 2002): 53–54.

United States Department of Education. *A Nation at Risk*. Washington, DC: GPO, 1983.

Vygotsky, Lev. *Mind in Society: The Development of Higher Mental Processes*. Cambridge, MA: Harvard University Press, 1978.

Wolfe, Thomas. *Look Homeward, Angel*. New York: Scribner, 1952.

Woolf, Virginia. *The Waves*. New York: Harcourt Brace, 1931.

Wordsworth, William. *The Prelude/Selected Poems and Sonnets*. New York: Holt, Rinehart & Winston, 1948.

Wright, Richard. *Native Son*. New York: Grosset & Dunlop, 1940.

What It Takes
to Be a Teacher

In order to arrive at what you are not
You must go through the way in which you are not.
And what you do not know is the only thing you know
And what you own is what you do not own
And where you are is where you are not.

—**T. S. Eliot, "East Coker"** (*The Four Quartets*)

From Expert Learner to Novice Teacher

Being and becoming a teacher

It was a late afternoon in the fall of my first year of teaching. The students had all gone home, the buses had lumbered off, most of the other teachers had packed up for the day, but I was still mopping up details from the day and working in my classroom. I took a break and stepped for a minute into the long corridor of the first floor. I looked down the hall and saw the row of closed classrooms and a few locker doors left ajar. Some stray student books littered the corridor; a few papers had fallen out of notebooks and had not been swept up. I smelled the rubber stuff the janitor sprinkled on the floors to help with the cleaning and polishing and heard the distant voices of the few teachers and students left in the building.

This was school at the end of the day, and I was a new teacher. But standing alone in the quiet corridor, something made me recall, for a strong pulse, a view of school I had repressed for many years. Right then, I felt and remembered how school had for a brief but important period in my life often scared me, terrified me. School had been a place not of success but of failure and disapproval. I felt my stomach tighten as I remembered three specific, chaotic years.

It was when my family was in crisis: my parents were divorced, and my mother was gone. I came to my elementary school, more often than not, with clothes askew, hair uncombed, and, more to the point, homework incomplete and tests not studied for. My teachers made their disapproval clear, my grades fell, and no one at home was available to help. I managed as best I could, but for most of those three years, I feared and hated school.

I looked around me, down the hall, in the building where I was now teaching—it was, yes, that same place, that familiar, alien, scary place: school. What in the world, I wondered in a sick rush, was I doing *as a teacher in a school*? Was I going to be one of those people who had succeeded in so frightening me for those three years? Was I going to spend five hours a day, five days a week doing to others what had been done to me?

It was a jarring, dislocating moment in my early teaching career. Because I could not deal directly with it or make sense of it in my new context as a teacher, I chose to set that bitter, but accurate, memory aside and literally move on. I went back into the classroom and got to work on a stack of papers. For years I could not think the incident through as I could not really understand it, and I did not want to consider what its implications might be. It was only much later I recognized what was happening: I was shifting, and it wasn't easy or pleasant, from student to teacher. I knew in that moment that school, which had not always been a wonderful place for me, was now my place of employment and teachers, who at one point in my life had terrified me, were now my professional colleagues. I had to make a new vision, which I did, that school was my home and I was a teacher. I also realized later that I could call upon my memories of being a frightened child to help me understand my students for whom school was also hostile and disapproving. The dislocation became actually a positive force, and I accepted my memory—school-as-scary-place—as an asset in understanding.

You may have no such mixed memories in your history, but regardless, there is no way to soft-pedal the fact: the shift from student learner to teacher learner is a tough one. It is no small exaggeration that the world looks very different on the other side of the desk, and for some novices it is almost a loss of innocence to confront the classroom with the chalkboard *behind* you. Making that transition is a difficult one under the best of circumstances; you have had some success in school or you would not envision becoming a teacher, but the shift from a member of the class to the principal organizer of the class is not automatic or, as in my case, a graceful event.

Teaching is also, as you suspect, a tough profession. While some teachers stay in the classroom for many years, others dream of new professions and many, if asked, will tell you they would not enter the profession again.

So why do teachers stay in the classroom?

Although it's now a bit dated, one of the widest studies of the profession, *Schoolteacher* by Dan C. Lortie, involving almost 6,000 teachers, gives somewhat of an answer. Lortie found that teachers' overwhelmingly greatest satisfaction is the interaction with students; other "rewards" such as salary, community status, security, summer vacation time, and freedom from competition are much lower on the scale (105). Lortie calls what teachers cited as the interaction with students a "psychic" reward (103 ff.), and it is true for many veteran teachers and is why they continue to meet first period every morning.

But *becoming* a teacher is a different matter, and often the psychic rewards are not as apparent early in the game. Becoming a teacher sometimes involves unlearning what you know or think you know—and possibly involves recognizing that what you may assume about teaching is, as T. S. Eliot writes, precisely what you do not know.

Lee Shulman, a professor at Stanford and a respected figure in the study of how people become teachers, writes:

> [One of the reasons] it is so difficult to learn to teach is that, unlike many other professions, people who learn to teach learn it after having completed, in Dan Lortie's phrase, a seventeen year "apprenticeship of observation." They have spent seventeen years, more or less, and nearly

20,000 hours as observers of teaching and they've learned an enormous amount about it. . . .
Another reason learning to teach is difficult, is that much of learning to teach depends on learning from experience. . . . The whole idea of learning from experience is: I do something, it
doesn't work, so I try something else until I finally find something that does work. It's a kind
of thoughtful trial and error, but it's predicated on two assumptions: one, we have reasonably
accurate access to what we do, and two, we are reasonably accurate in identifying the consequences of what we do. But it is very difficult to establish those two assumptions.

Thus we come into the classroom with our own history as students—and a relatively
successful history at that—and we assume that what we see in our own classes is not only
what is happening there but that we can figure out the effects of what is happening. Sometimes we are very wrong.

Characteristics of good teachers

There are a number of studies about personality traits that teachers need to be successful,
and some education or certification programs even administer personality tests to their students to ensure that students are psychologically equipped for the profession. Most teachers
know, however, that successful teachers have a formidable range of personalities and that the
classroom atmospheres those teachers foster can be remarkably varied. Beyond that range,
however, there are a few generalizations we can make. Successful teachers:

- **Like people (young people in particular):** Some folks even rather humorously
  advocate being "arrested in development" in order to be a successful teacher, but
  it is true that you must almost have an appetite for the age group you teach. Those
  who thrive in middle school, for example, express a certain affinity for persons that
  age and the characteristics of their developmental level.
- **Are flexible:** You may have the whole day planned only to find that an assembly
  has been scheduled—with little advance warning—for all of your second-period
  and part of your third-period classes. You may find that your lesson plan that
  worked well for the morning section of a course is a bomb with the afternoon section. The two students whose reports were going to take up half the period need
  all the period; one of your students is upset by something and is quietly crying.
  Successful teachers adjust and adjust quickly.
- **Draw appropriate conclusions from classroom observation:** Students are
  bored or disaffected; the small-group arrangements in third period were especially successful; over half the class did not understand the homework reading
  assignment. A number of factors may explain these observations, and the successful teacher makes a judgment regarding subsequent planning.
- **Listen actively and attentively to students:** Students often tell teachers nearly
  all they need to know if indeed the teachers have, as the biblical aphorism tells
  us, the ears to hear and the eyes to see. Students also will share more in class if
  they have the impression their comments are being really listened to. It is important to recognize the overt *text* of what our students say and the covert *subtext* of
  what they are saying. Successful teachers make appropriate eye contact, don't interrupt, listen, and through body language get students to feel their remarks are
  worth attending to.

- **Have a sense of humor:** Laughter, in its best manifestation, is emotional warmth, and both students and teachers can make significant personal contact through lighthearted exchanges.

  You do not need to have the skill of a stand-up comic, but you do need to have a sense of play and liveliness. This, of course, does not embrace the extremes of humor, which are often best left to one's peers. The use of mocking remarks, sarcasm, or jokes at students' expense is unpleasant and often scarring, but the happiness of a more gentle humor can permeate a successful teacher's classroom.

- **Have a sense of intellectual curiosity—both their own and their students':** Truly exciting things happen in the classroom, especially when the parties involved are somewhat prepared to be surprised and pleased and intrigued. "Why is that so? If it is true, what else could be true? Does anyone know about, has anyone heard of _____?" are all questions that can open doors of exploration. Good teachers ask these questions frequently.

·················· **FOR YOUR JOURNAL** ··················

Think about your personality and who you are. How would you describe yourself to others? Don't be modest; list six or so of your best traits. Then look at those traits and pick two or three that you think will *help* you be a good teacher. Why do you think those traits are important? How do you think they will function in your interaction in the classroom?

What a Teacher Needs to Do

Despite your enthusiasm and preparation, you may experience what my student Brian Durrett described in his student teaching journal. Brian raises important questions:

I think the thing that bugs me . . . is . . . the whole teacher student battle for the classroom. I have heard many a lecture about how it is important to have students experience the curriculum in a way that applies to their lives. Is it possible to do that with a student whose mind is closed? The students who are rude are the ones that are not into the material and have nothing better to do. I know that it is my job to teach every student and it is my responsibility to make my lessons interesting enough that they engage the students. I know that if there is a student that is not learning and he or she is being rude, I need to do what is necessary to make sure that the student learns. Period. But the important piece of that puzzle is that there is only so much I can do. I had been the idealist and thought that I would do everything in my power to touch every student. I thought that might be possible. Now that I have spent time [student teaching], I am not sure if that is possible. . . . There are a number of students [in my classes] who genuinely do not want to be at school, have failed for the year by the end of the first semester, and could care less. There are other students who are bright and at most times do what is necessary to get by, but do not apply themselves. And there are very bright students who for whatever reason just play and don't do their work . . . So how far do you go?

How far do you go? For me, there are some answers in one of my favorite books about teaching, *After the Lesson Plan: Realities of High School Teaching*. Amy Puett Emmers is a veteran teacher, and her book is both hard-nosed and compassionate. Emmers believes a teacher has four major tasks. They are:

1. **A teacher must gain students' attention.**
2. **A teacher must insist that students perform at the level of their ability.**
3. **A teacher must provide consequences for learning.**
4. **A teacher must recognize and insist.** (xiv, xv, 60)

Gaining students' attention

We all remember classes where the students were having a great time carrying on their own conversations while the teacher futilely tried to either quiet them or just talk above them. During her student teaching, Debbie Martin recalls one class:

> Third period—GAWD!!!! . . . When I asked them to pleeease quiet down for the video [we were seeing], it was as if I wasn't in the room—there was a total disregard for anything & every-one except what they were interested in. I repeated my request several times by standing in the middle of the room saying, "Excuse me, excuse me, please. Let's get quiet. Let's not be rude to those who wish to watch the video." One student shouted, "Hey! show some respect." I thanked her and started the video.

On a longer-term basis, we also can remember semesters where we just endured a course (and a teacher), resigned that we were not going to learn or do much of anything interesting. Sometimes we wondered if the teacher noticed what we certainly knew. Some-times we made the best of the class by daydreaming, passing notes, or surreptitiously talk-ing with friends.

Actually this activity has been studied and researched. In an article you may find interesting, Robert Brooke discusses and categorizes the "underlife" of a classroom, a sociological term that "refers to those behaviors which undercut roles expected of par-ticipants in a situation . . . [for example] students disobey, write letters instead of taking notes, and whisper with their peers to show they are more than just students and can think independently of classroom expectations" (141). While much of this is normal classroom behavior, when carried to an extreme it can be highly disruptive and certainly can be demoralizing to class order. And when it happens in your classroom, it can be a real problem.

Emmers suggests a number of principles to help us gain—and keep—our students' attention:

- **Interest students in the subject matter and relate it to their lives.**
- **Build on what the students know.**
- **Discuss, don't lecture.**
- **Answer student questions.**
- **Provide an element of excitement through reasonable competition.** (23–47)

As you will see later in this chapter, the discovery model of teaching may be closest to what Emmers suggests. Certainly, when we care about our students' learning, it is rather automatic that we will adopt many of Emmers' suggestions in our teaching.

Insisting students perform at the level of their ability

This may seem so obvious that it is simpleminded, but the difficulty is that we are often clueless about where our students truly are in their level of ability. Test scores and grades are not the reliable indications you may have been led to believe. People also, we know from cognitive psychology, can "plateau" in their development—stay at the same level for long periods—and then make remarkable gains in relatively rapid periods of time. How do we know where they are? While students with disabilities need special help and those who are unwilling need prodding, Emmers is most concerned about our setting limits on the other students. She counsels:

> We still know very little about what actually occurs in the brain when people learn. Moreover, teachers cannot possibly be aware of all of the many factors that contribute to their students' motivation to learn. Is it really the function of teachers ever to discourage a student from attempting something he wants to do? If he can't do it, he'll discover that soon enough for himself. He certainly won't thank anybody for advance information about his shortcomings.
>
> When asked whether he knows how to do any specific task, whatever it is, a friend of mine usually replies, "Maybe I do; I haven't tried." Most people smile at his whimsy, which they do not regard as a very realistic appraisal of ability. Perhaps, though, students would benefit if teachers could be just this optimistic. Teachers would not be requiring anyone to do what he can't. They would not be forcing anyone to do what he really doesn't wish. Rather they would be trying to extend a student's possibilities. After all, maybe he can! (87)

And perhaps the tragedy of many classrooms is not that we ask too much of our students— but that we ask too little. Certainly when we assume that a "less able" or "slower" group cannot handle classroom tasks above the level of filling in worksheets, we are not trying to get our students to perform at the level of their ability. Nor are we giving them the chance to move to a higher level.

Providing consequences for learning

There are many ways to reward learning: with praise, class privileges, posting of work on bulletin boards or publishing it in anthologies, congratulatory notes sent home, grades, awards. Once students are motivated and capable of the work level, they will perform. What about students, however, who are not motivated or not capable? While teachers need to make their best effort and attempt, rather unceasingly, to capture students' attention and motivation, there is a limit. Emmers writes:

> For teachers to blame themselves unnecessarily when students are inattentive or unmotivated is a waste of time and emotion, for it is, after all, an individual student who must change these conditions. Teachers can't do it for him. All they can do is try to conduct the kind of class in which uninterested students will at least be tempted to reverse their feelings about the subject. (57–58)

Beginning teachers especially feel the sting of students who refuse to engage in class. While we have an ethical obligation to do our best in a class, we also must acknowledge that teachers cannot learn *for* the student, cannot study for them, and cannot be motivated for them. We can create the classroom atmosphere that emphasizes all students should—and can—do their best, but we cannot ensure that everyone is engaged all the time. For students who, despite our best efforts, resist working in our classes, often we have no choice but to give them the grades they have earned. And just showing up is not enough; if we make that a sufficient standard, we certainly cannot expect that students will do anything resembling work once they cross the classroom threshold.

Recognizing and insisting

Besides the three tasks just listed, Emmers also articulates a teaching principle that is worth lingering over: *recognizing and insisting*. She explains:

> At the opposite extreme from those students who for whatever reason can't do the work are those who are capable but won't do it. While there are various causes for students' not working, or at least not working as much as they should, most . . . think they can get by without doing the assignments. They are also convinced that what they neglect won't make much difference in their lives. (68)

Again, our students come largely by compulsion—which can make the relationship in the class a difficult one. On the other hand, a student's very presence in a class can imply that she or he is there to learn; as teachers we recognize that. We can also insist that we be allowed to teach the reluctant students as well as the others. Class is for learning; participation, in some form, is a way toward that learning. What we have to recognize and, at the end, resist, is what Lauren Dean describes in one of her classes during student teaching:

> Today I called my first parent. Three weeks ago I had to make a seating chart for my fifth period class. . . . Many of the students are extroverted, sarcastic, and hyper (just after lunch). Six of these students are on the basketball team, and they are all friends. Needless to say, they like to push my buttons, so I developed a seating chart in an effort to increase student focus and decrease the chatty distractions. Since that day, one student refuses to sit in his appropriate seat. Each day he comes in and sits in the wrong seat until I notice, and then have to tell him to move. Each day this disrupts the first few moments of class, unless of course I catch him before the bell rings. At first it was kind of funny. Now it is just disrespectful and frustrating.
>
> So today when I noticed this student was again in the wrong seat, I asked him to step out in the hall. First I asked him why he thought the new seating chart rule did not apply to him and it did for the other students. He shrugged. I then told him his behavior was disrespectful and disruptive. He shrugged. I asked him if he understood why this was disrespectful and disruptive. He shrugged. I asked him if his mother would be upset to hear about his behavior. He shrugged. I asked him if I should call his mother. He shrugged. So I did. That very afternoon I called her.

Perhaps one of the worst things we can do with our students is ignore them, minimize them. We need to let students know we know them and that they are in our classes; while they are there, we need to insist upon their participation. Indifference is, ultimately, killing. We have an obligation to see and recognize our charges and to demand from them as much as we can—we must insist on their learning. To do less is to turn our backs on them and, ultimately, on ourselves.

·················· **FOR YOUR JOURNAL** ··················

The four tasks that Emmers believes teachers should address are similar to many such lists. If we use what she counsels as a springboard for discussion, how would you rank or prioritize those four tasks? Which is the most important? Why? Which seems the least important? Why? Remember to think more from a teacher's point of view than a student's.

Beginning Your Life in the Classroom

On your journey of being and becoming a teacher, you will live a significant portion of your waking hours among young people and in a classroom setting. If you have worked in any kind of a business office or corporate complex, either for the summer or full time, you may find some of the aspects of living and working in school challenging as there are real obstacles. While there is no single book that can anticipate all of your questions and issues during your first few years of teaching, this section is an attempt to outline some things that might get lost otherwise. There is, actually, much to your life in the classroom that is serious—such as dealing with the politics of school and discipline—and a lot that is pretty mundane—such as where to scrounge supplies for your room or what to do about eating lunch. Both the serious and the mundane, however, are important to your early success in the classroom.

The journey begins.

The Politics of School

Every school is different, a city with its own laws and rules and culture and climate and, yes, its politics. While it would be wonderful to think that you will truly understand the climate and politics of your first school before you sign that contract, the character of a school community is often not clear until you are actually on staff and teaching. You would be well advised, in your first few months in your new school, to observe closely as to what you can tell about what is important in this school and, essentially, what are the mores and values. For instance, some schools and staff are very warm and personal; others are more formal and expect the same from you. In some schools teachers talk freely among themselves about their lives, their personal convictions, their family. In other schools such conversation is more limited to close friends. As other issues, there is wide variance in schools regarding forms of address within the staff (do you call everyone by their first name?), chain of command (when do you go to your department chair, when to an assistant principal?), and regulations regarding dealing with parents (how often are you to call parents and on what issues?). You will undoubtedly make mistakes and have misinterpretations, but if you approach your teaching setting as if it were neutral, you are being naive. There is a distinct climate of sorts in every school, and the sooner you scope it out and learn how to manage it—if not adjust to it, because after a year or so you may want to transfer schools—the less stressful your beginning career will be. Things to consider for your early successful career:

- What kinds of topics are discussed in the teachers' lounge? What seems to be off limits? To what extent should you add your comments?
- How much of your personal life do you—should you—share with members of the staff, especially in the beginning?
- How do you deal with teachers who may be negative about their careers and their students? To what extent do you spend time with these teachers and listen to their advice—or complaints?
- Who are the teachers who have a reputation for success in the classroom? How can you get to know them and learn from them?
- How do you feel about having lunch with certain groups or even socializing with them after school? To what extent are you expected to attend weekend and night school events (such as football or basketball games, plays, music concerts)?
- What are the requirements for dealing with parents, a group that can be a potent ally and also a potent enemy? What kinds of communication strategies and regulations are in place? How much notification to parents is expected regarding your classes and regulations?
- What are the staff rules or deadlines that are nonnegotiable? What should you be sure that you do on time and very well? What appears to be less crucial?
- What is the role of your team leader or department chair? What are the functions of the assistant principal or the principal? Who is approachable and who is not? To what extent do—can you—talk with these individuals and ask them for help?

While the answers to these questions may not be clear to you, especially in the beginning, it is important to know that your school community has distinct characteristics and ways of doing things. The sooner you assess these, the better you can make choices and negotiate successfully the politics of school.

Discipline

Most people getting ready to enter a classroom for the first time, especially after having completed courses on teaching and having read books on students and classroom management, expect that they will be able to quickly establish an orderly atmosphere and run a classroom fairly smoothly. This expectation, however, is rarely fulfilled, and some novices are bitterly disappointed that they were not "taught" what to do or how to react in real classroom situations.

The fact of the matter is that no class or book can teach a beginner or novice what to do and how to do it in every specific instructional incident. Even a very successful student teaching experience is no guarantee that the first year in the classroom will go smoothly in the discipline arena.

Discipline seems a simple concept, but it is actually very complex and is the sum of a number of variables, not the least of which is the beginning teacher's rather nascent perception of what is acceptable behavior and what is not. School context is important here, as are school rules. In certain schools there is a surprising level of informality that is expected and acceptable; in other schools, the opposite may be true. What you assume to be polite or respectful behavior between teachers and students and students and students may not, indeed, be what your students assume. The only way to determine this is to watch and learn, ask and adjust your own expectations—and, yes, you have the right to have those expectations—to the reality of your school context. And, of course, if for whatever reason you find the school context antithetical to your beliefs, you need to change schools or school systems.

In addition, in the beginning of anyone's teaching, the fit between what a teacher thinks is happening in a classroom and what is actually occurring is often not exact. Thus a beginning teacher may honestly feel that the entire class is out of control when actually two or three students are being disruptive. A novice may think that her tone of voice was sufficiently commanding when, in actuality, it barely could be heard. The teacher may be frustrated that students, although instructed to raise their hands to be called upon, simply call out answers, and unaware that he routinely accepts answers from students who do not raise their hands and thus reinforces the behavior.

Having someone observe your classes, watching other teachers' classes, and trying to become more self-perceptive are three ways to establish a clearer view of what you are doing in your own classroom. Videotaping yourself is also helpful. Further, although they are as general as anything you will read in any similar book, the following principles may help you establish and maintain good discipline. They are not magic, and implementing all of them will not automatically ensure a well-managed class, but they are sensible and common sense.

Be firm; be fair Once you decide on a procedure or a consequence for behavior, stick to it. Of course, be sure the procedure or consequence does not favor or punish in an inequitable manner. Thus if something goes for one student, it must go for the other, and, unless it is an unusual circumstance (a judgment call in and of itself), you should not be talked out of or into anything different for different students.

Be consistent If it's a rule on Monday, it should be a rule on Wednesday. Constant change confuses students and confuses you. While there are often real and compelling reasons for altering classroom procedures or consequences, don't do it willy nilly.

Use "I" messages As much as you would like to tell a student that he or she is the problem, phrasing statements such as "*I* can't accept this behavior in class" or "*I* would appreciate/ prefer that you sit down" helps students see the issue as an issue, not as a direct attack on them personally.

Single out students but don't humiliate them Often, talking with or disciplining individual students—not the entire class—is sufficient to change a disorderly atmosphere into an orderly one. Be aware, however, that such attention to individual students needs to be done thoughtfully. If you wish to talk to one student, take him or her out in the hall or meet them before or after school; don't discuss their behavior in the presence and hearing of their peers and their class.

Use praise and rewards Students need praise for working well or for working better than before. Students are people, too, and they often appreciate positive attention from you. Students also respond to rewards, rewards that can range from something class-related (you can have a choice on this procedure; you can have ten minutes of free time in this class) to something more tangible (pencils or pens; a copy of a paperback book). Offering praise and rewards to students if they achieve or continue to achieve can be helpful. While certainly we would all like to think that students come to our class and study and work without the need for reward, that is often not true. Judiciously used, praise and rewards can help students stay on track and stay out of trouble.

Do not ignore bullying   One of the sad lessons to emerge from the past decade's melancholy list of school shootings is that students who are consistently bullied become enormously frustrated with teachers, school, and the other students who harass them. This frustration, as we have seen from the tragic events at Columbine High School and other places, can erupt into deadly violence. Whether the bullying is subtle or obvious, physical—involving hitting or shoving or touching or groping—or verbal—such as name-calling—your class should never be a place where such harassment is tolerated. You may want to ignore it and hope it goes away, but when students see that you will allow bullying in your presence, it is likely to escalate either in your classroom or outside it. You have an obligation to intervene and squelch the behavior.

Make your students too busy to misbehave   A class that starts on time and in which much happens is a class where a student will have to work to get in trouble. While you do not want to assume that students might have misbehaved just because the class was not sufficiently organized or rigorous—some incidents will occur regardless—you can head off a lot of trouble by establishing a productive, busy atmosphere. E. B. White in *Stuart Little* may have said it best, "Make the work interesting, and the discipline will take care of itself."

Involve parents   In a recent article about parents in *Time* magazine, Harvard education professor Sara Lawrence-Lightfoot acknowledges that most teachers feel anxious when dealing with parents. Indeed, a recent survey of new teachers indicated that only a small percentage enjoyed working with parents. In fact, almost three quarters of new teachers surveyed felt that "parents treat schools and teachers as adversaries" (Gibbs, 45). This may well be true, but as noted in the Politics of School section in this chapter, parents can be potent allies, too. Use whatever communication channels your school suggests (e-mails, phone calls, written notes) and inform parents when you need their help—or even when things are going well. While harmony between teacher and parent is not always assured, you might be pleasantly surprised to find that you and your students' parents agree more often than you think.

·············· **FOR YOUR JOURNAL** ··············

Discipline is a large issue for most beginning teachers. Which of the principles just described seem to you to be the easiest to enforce or adopt? Which seems to be the hardest? Why? What do you assume will have to happen in your classes before you have what you feel is an acceptable and orderly environment?

Classroom Environment, Room Arrangement, Creature Comforts, Food

I had not been teaching very long before I realized that the schedule of school was my schedule, too. Somehow I had assumed that while students were responsible for being in a specific place at a specific time on a daily basis, teachers' schedules just had to be somewhat different. Not so. I soon realized that, just like my students, I too was in a classroom for hours every day, and I too could not leave. Students had to be strictly on time for the beginning of every class; so did I. Students had five minutes to change class; I had five minutes to set up for the next class. Students had twenty minutes for lunch; I had the same. Students could not leave the school when they wished or make phone calls when they wanted; neither could I. Students turned in assignments—which meant that very soon after I had to grade those assignments. Students met deadlines which, in turn, meant I met deadlines, too. In fact, I soon learned there is a profound reciprocity to this business of living and working in school that is more exacting than I at first realized.

You may already be aware of this, but it was news to me. Bluntly put, teachers have the same schedule restriction as students—in fact, in some ways it is more demanding because, unlike our students, we can't routinely go to our locker or be excused to go to the bathroom during class. What this means for you is that the freedom to pursue your own daily schedule and rhythms during class is forever changed. For some of you, this will not be much of an issue. For others, however, adjusting to living life in a classroom may take some time.

Classroom environment

Practically speaking, you need to know that you will be logging many hours inside a classroom and that if that environment is not a friendly or pleasant place for you, it probably will not be for your students, either. While no one is suggesting that you spend a great deal of money or consult an interior decorator for your room—if indeed at the beginning of your teaching career you have your "own" room and teach there for all day or even part of the day—there are some things you need to think about.

Most school buildings, despite the best intentions of the architects and the district administration and the local school board, are relatively bare, antiseptic institutions, and the heart of those schools, the classrooms, are rarely better. You want to think of bringing color and light and, yes, beauty, into what may at first appear a sterile space. Without spending a huge amount of money, you can purchase or scrounge (yard sales are great sources) some of the following for your classroom:

- **Posters:** There are many inexpensive, colorful, and thought-provoking posters, which range from inspirational (with art, photography, and famous quotations) to the informational (offering facts about authors, literary works, components of language, historical events). I am particularly fond of posters from ALA, the American Library Association (write ALA at 50 E. Huron Street, Chicago, IL 60611, or go to their website at www.ala.org). ALA sells all kinds of posters, many in a series, advocating reading and supporting intellectual freedom. Other educational organizations and commercial teacher outlets also sell posters; check their catalogs.

Your local bookstore, either of the small or of the mega variety, often will give away dated posters touting new authors or books. Your local music store will often do the same with posters of rock bands for promoting new CDs. Very contemporary music posters are often especially appreciated by students, and, as a small side benefit, may earn you the reputation of being pretty cool.

Practical tip: If you get some posters for your room, do change them every marking period or so: even the most attractive of posters gets stale after months and months.

- **Bulletin boards:** A great place to put those posters is on your bulletin board (most school classrooms have at least one, sometimes more, attached to the classroom wall), but you can also use this space to display student work and to put reminder announcements. At times I reserved part of the bulletin board and made it a student comment/graffiti area where students were encouraged to write. Students could leave quotations that they have found, ask thought-provoking questions, or just write something that they want expressed publicly (you may have to provide a few etiquette guidelines here, but it shouldn't be that difficult). Watching students wander over to that section of your bulletin board to check for what's new is, by the way, gratifying.

   Covering the board with bright paper as a background is helpful and, again, you want to think of changing the paper and the look of the bulletin board about every marking period. Do not, by the way, be intimidated by a bulletin board! Even those of us who are artistically challenged can staple paper on the board, slap up a poster, and leave space for other items of interest to the class—the effort is worth it.

- **Books and bookcases:** You will need a modest classroom library for that day when the schedule is shot and students need something to read or for when those three students finish the test early and turn it in, telling you, in all earnestness, they now have nothing to do or read. (In a later chapter we will also talk about free reading and, if you provide time for that in your teaching, you will definitely need a classroom library.)

   For your class library, get old magazines from your friends and relatives, scrounge old paperbacks (remember those yard sales again), throw in some crossword puzzle books; use anything that is readable and appropriate for the age level of your students. If you can find an old bookcase (some classrooms come equipped with these already, some do not), put the magazines and books there.

   For me, the classroom library, the books and bookcase, were indispensable additions to my room, and before class and even when the room was empty at lunch, I would find students going to the bookcase to check for what might be new or interesting. Without explicit instructions from me, students were getting into the habit of browsing through what I had brought in.

   Practical tip: Post nearby a sign-up sheet for when students want to borrow something from the library. On the sheet students can write their names and the dates they removed materials. This record will help you keep some track of what goes in and out of the bookcase—you don't want the bookcase bare by the first month of school. You can, of course, decide that nothing goes out of the classroom on loan; that is up to you, but if you do let students take things home, keep a record. Certainly, though, you need to think of your collection as "disposable": even with teacher vigilance, a sign-up sheet, and conscientious students, some of your materials will naturally leave your room and never return. Thus, the library will change content significantly from semester to semester.

- **Rugs:** This is really optional, but old rag rugs can provide a great place for students to sit and read. They also "warm up" a room and, if there is no objection from the administration (some principals freak when they think of kids sitting in or on anything but an official desk), get an inexpensive rug and put it near the bookcase.

    Practical tip: Washable rugs are best.

- **Plants:** Again, this is optional, but plants are great living things to have in a room. There are, thank you, Mother Nature, many varieties that require little care and will flourish under florescent lights and drinking water from the hall fountain. Most everyone responds to the look of plants, and I had one or two in every classroom in which I taught.

Room arrangement

For generations students learned in a classroom where the teacher's desk stood centered in front of the blackboard. The remainder of the room was filled with students' desks, set in long rows, all facing the front. So what is wrong with this picture?

Well, for one thing the teacher's desk impedes the students' view of the blackboard (or whiteboard or smart board or whatever your school provides). For another, if the students are all facing front, during discussions they will be unable to see much of anyone else but the teacher. Finally, how do students work in small groups or pairs if they are permanently located in long rows of desks?

While there is no perfect—nor should there be—room arrangement, you need to consider placing your desk somewhere other than centered in front of the blackboard: the side of the blackboard, either side of the room, and the back of the room are three options, all of which give you a different perspective on the students as they sit at their desks.

Another thing you need to consider is how the students' desks are arranged. While there is nothing wrong with students sitting facing the front in long rows when they are taking tests or listening to a short lecture or presentation, there is something wrong with that arrangement at other times. Large group discussions are not natural when people talk to the back of other people's heads: accordingly, think of putting your students' desks into a horseshoe or in four long rows, two rows facing two rows (Figure 2–1). If you use the latter, remember to leave space between the left two and the right two of the rows so that you can walk between them comfortably. If you have table-type desks, you can put students in pairs or in a trio or a quartet; this is, obviously, ideal for small group work.

And, of course, any desk arrangement can be changed so that three or four students can all work on a project in one general area together (Figure 2–2).

My feeling is that you should not become attached to a single room arrangement; you should shift the desks in accordance with what the students are doing, not in accordance with some inflexible ideal of order. This may mean, at times, that the desk arrangement changes from class to class; that's okay, too.

Practical tips: If the desks need to be moved at any given time, don't do it by yourself. Ask your students to help: it's far quicker for twenty-five people to do such a task than for

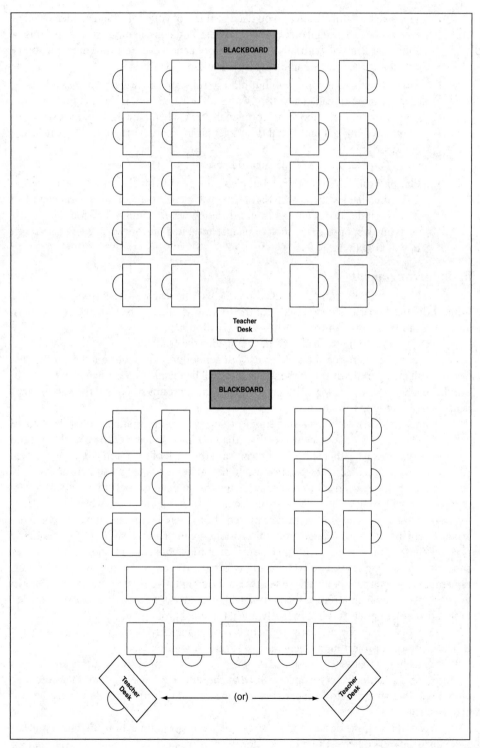

Figure 2–1

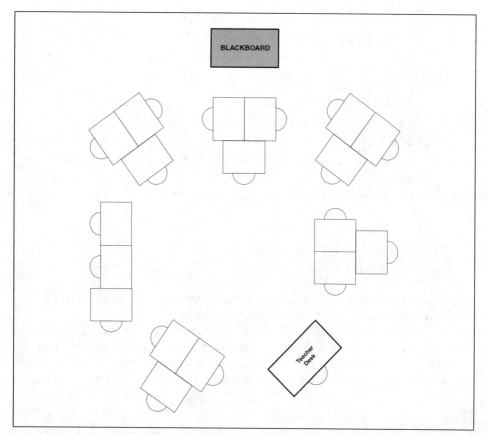

BLACKBOARD

Teacher Desk

Figure 2–2

a single individual. Also, if you alter a room arrangement and will not be in that room for the succeeding bell, be considerate and have the students change the desks back as you found them. The teacher who comes in next will appreciate it. Finally, there are some classrooms, such as portables or trailers, where space is very tight, and it is extremely difficult to move desks. If that is your teaching setting, think of moving chairs and using circles of students whose materials are either on their laps or, for that instructional time, not needed.

Creature comforts

Beyond the classroom itself, there is the issue of *you* and what you need to be comfortable as well as productive. While much of this may not be true for the school in which you teach, you can never assume that what you need will automatically be accessible in the building—and in most schools, teachers are expected to stay in the building the entire contract day. You can't hop in your car and go buy something for that headache; you can't run home for just a minute to pick something up. Thus try to think of school as a civilized version of camping out: you may be far from home and not able to get what you need at any given moment for your comfort. Depending on your individual needs (use your imagination for all of the varying crises), those items may include:

- some form of aspirin
- some form of antacid tablets or liquid
- eye drops, nose drops, lip balm
- Band-Aids and disinfectant
- bottled water
- if you wear contacts, cleaning solution and, if you wear them, an extra pair of glasses
- emergency sewing kit (needle, black thread, white thread, a few buttons, safety pins)
- extra sweater or jacket
- tissues and/or paper towels
- hand sanitizers

Keep a permanent supply of these items in your room or desk. You may find, one day, that it makes the difference between comfort and mild misery.

Practical tip: Teachers are not allowed, in almost any school district in the country, to give students medication, such as aspirin. It may seem really dumb not to share with a student who has an unexpected cramp or headache, but you are placing yourself in some jeopardy by giving out to students, even upon their request, any form of medication.

Food

You will also need to think about eating. For many schools lunch occurs much earlier than the traditional 12 P.M., and that may affect what and if you eat for breakfast. Be aware early on of your lunch schedule and consider your stomach and your nutritional needs. Further, will you pack your lunch or eat in the cafeteria? While many people hate making their own lunches, if the cafeteria is really crowded one day, you may find yourself going hungry so you can make your next class on time. If you have blood sugar issues, you will need to bring your juice or snack or whatever you require to keep your blood level constant—and, remember, most schools will not allow you to run down the hall during class to do this!

In addition, many people need to drink a significant amount of water during the day. If you are one of those, you need to consider and plan for your trips to the bathroom: and if you cannot get to the bathroom and back to class in time, you'll need to adjust how much water you consume during the teaching day.

Some schools have serious restrictions about eating or drinking in the classroom. If you need, for the health reasons, to do either in class, you will need to notify the administration and, more important, mention to your students why you get to drink or eat, and they can't. It seems like a little thing—in business offices this is a nonissue—but students can be resentful if they see you eating and drinking, and they can't.

One day, when I was feeling a cold coming on, I brought a cup of hot coffee into my classroom, never thinking to mention to my students, even informally, why I was sipping away when they were similarly forbidden. About halfway through the period I left the coffee cup, only partially drunk, on my desk, and the class moved into small group work. At one point while I was circulating around the room one of my kinder students whispered to me that I should not finish the coffee sitting on my desk as someone—nameless, but someone—had scooped chalk dust into the cup. I had few discipline problems with that class, and I realized that my coffee had become an instant source of some resentment, and someone wanted to let me know. I quietly thanked the student for her warning, and I never said a thing to the class. As far as I was concerned, lesson learned.

············· **FOR YOUR JOURNAL** ·············

This is a list and a chart journal assignment.

Think about your classroom: what would you like to see there? You will have a desk and chair provided, desks for the students, and possibly file cabinets or bookcases. Beyond that, however, most schools leave the furnishings and arrangement up to the individual teacher.

With that in mind, make a list of items you would like in your classroom and then, to the best of your knowledge, attach both a source (yard sale, friends, attic, store) and, if you can, a price for each one. How many items are on your list? Where will you get them? How much will they cost? Finally, draw a simple classroom chart: what is located where? How are the student desks, at least initially, arranged? Where is your desk?

A Few Other Things: Getting Started, Openings, Voice, Body, Touch, Dress

Getting started

It's not just students who have fluttery tummies at the beginning of a school year: teachers do, too. And for you, your first few years of teaching, getting started can be a bit daunting. Some of the routine and pattern of getting started, even if you have completed a successful student teaching internship, will be new to you, and certainly you are not going to have thought out every eventuality in your classroom. While you can't decide on the answers for all of the following questions, there are some things you need to consider as you get ready for your first teaching year. I have ideas of my own regarding some of these questions—which are explored in the following—but here's a list of things you might want to look at and ponder. Where do *you* stand on these topics?

Introductory activities   How much time should I spend on introductory (or get-to-know) activities? What activities could I do? What does each accomplish? What do I need to know about these students and about this class?

Rules   What class rules do I make? To what extent should students help make the class rules? Should these rules be different for different classes? Can my rules change? What is my policy on students and their materials (books, paper, pencils, notebooks, etc.)? What is my policy on absences? tardiness? being excused for the bathroom? Where do I go or whom do I call if I need immediate help with a classroom discipline incident? Are my rules consistent with those of the school?

Names and information   What do I tell students about me? How do I learn students' names? How do I address my students? How should students address me?

Starting and running a class   Where should I be before the bell rings? What information should be on the board at the beginning of class? How do I begin a class? How will I take up papers and assignments? When and how do I call roll? How do I handle interruptions? How do I handle announcements over the PA? How do I end class and when? How do I assign homework?

Personal   How do I dress? How do I speak? To what extent do I use colloquial language in the class or in the hall? How much do I share about myself with other teachers? Do I encourage or allow students to call me at home? To what extent do I talk with students about their—or my—individual problems? If a students tells me something personal that is very serious, what do I do? To whom do I consult in the school building and when?

Again, you may not have answers for many of these questions and, in point of fact, the answers you have in September may be very different from the ones you might give in March. But thinking about the myriad issues of getting started may help you define what kind of classroom procedures and management you want to establish.

Openings

Beyond these general questions, the answers to which will often extend throughout the entire teaching year, one of the most important days of teaching is the first day of class. How you set a tone and deal with students that first day can make the rest of the year or the semester a smoother one. Being organized, relatively calm, and prepared your very first day gives students the expectations that this is how you will be the rest of the year. Getting ready, therefore, for the first day may actually take some time: leaving tasks until the last minute—when presemester school meetings and paperwork may interfere—is not a good idea.

But what, besides the handing-out-of-books administrivia, should happen the first day? There are a few things:

1. You need to think of what is important to you and the classroom and **establish and communicate rules or general principles.** If you want students to evince certain behaviors or attitudes, the first day is the day to mention them. Use positive language; giving students a list of *don'ts* is a surefire route to a negative start.

2. As mentioned earlier in this chapter, you need **to arrange the room** in a way that reinforces what will be going on in your classroom. This includes bulletin boards and artwork, study areas or reading areas, and a quiet corner for a class library. Again, desks should be positioned so students can see each other for large-group activities or, when needed, work individually or in small groups.

3. You need to **provide an introductory activity** that will let students get to know each other as well as you. Activities can include:

   • **Interviewing each other and then introducing the other person to the class.**

- Having members of the class get out of their desks and stand in a large circle. **Students place themselves in alphabetical order using the first letter of their middle name.** Students go around the circle, taking turns first telling their middle name and then describing how that name was chosen for them.

- **Drawing a coat of arms that represents interests and then sharing it.** Students draw a symbol or series of symbols that represent the importance they give the following (number 5 is the most metaphorical):

  > 1—Outside Interests or Hobbies
  > 2—Family
  > 3—School
  > 4—Reading
  > 5—My Essence

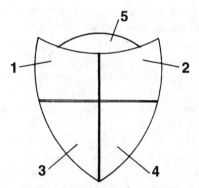

- **Giving students a "scavenger hunt" list** where they have ten minutes to go around the room and find the names of other students in the class who, for example: live within one mile of school; have traveled in the past year outside the United States; speak a language beside English; have been in a natural disaster such as an earthquake or a tornado; have more than two brothers (or sisters); are a twin; play two musical instruments; have memorized a poem in the last year, and so on.

- **Writing a letter of introduction to students and having them do the same to you and their peers.**

- **Asking students to complete the following statement: I am the only one who _____.** As students share, put each phrase on the board so everyone in the class can view the differing comments.

- **Filling out a brief interest inventory and then sharing it.**
  Providing fill-in-the-blank statements can help, such as:
  When I go online I like to_____
  My favorite possession is_____
  What I like best/hate most about English class is_____
  My friends value me because_____
  School would be better if_____

These activities are ways of letting students establish who they are and who the others are. While every classroom minute counts, the time spent on these activities will give you useful information about your students and will highlight their crucial importance in the success of the classroom. Your sharing something about yourself will also help students connect with you as a person, not just a teacher. If students do a coat of arms, for instance, you do one, too. If students share the origin of their middle name, you do, too.

4. You need to begin to **learn and use all your students' names,** being very careful to pronounce them correctly or, within reason, to use their preferred names. What is on the roll books may not be what your students want to be called, and your sensitivity to their names will establish a positive and immediate bond.

5. You need to **tell students about the class** and how you envision what you will be doing together. Don't forget to use humor and positive terms and enthusiasm. If students think the class will be interesting or fun, they are more likely to work with you and with each other. If you also stress that students will have a say in the class' organization and procedural rules, students will feel that the class is not just yours, the teacher's.

6. Finally, while it may seem hard to do both at once, you need to establish that **you are in charge of the classroom** and that **you are a friendly, pleasant person.** Smiling and looking at your students as if you are happy to be with them will, frankly, reassure many of them. On the other hand, being pleasant does not mean that you are a pushover; classrooms need order to proceed, and you are in charge of that order. I am sure you have heard the old saw about not smiling until Thanksgiving; while many teachers actually take that as serious advice, I think it's silly. You are a human being working with other human beings. Not showing a pleasant demeanor is, to me, self-defeating. Your class is not boot camp, it's school, and you and your students should have a good and productive time together.

Voice

Most of us in this culture associate a commanding presence with a relatively deep voice. While many men have an edge over many women in this department, it is somewhat of an exaggeration. It helps, however, to use an authoritative or relatively professional tone when trying to get students' attention, particularly, say, at the beginning of a class. Know also that if you speak over students or shout at them—and you'll be tempted—you are establishing an atmosphere that is hard to break or retract. If you use a quiet voice, they will, too.

And trust the power of silence; constant talk from you is not helpful; pauses and silence can get students' attention effectively.

Using your body

Do not believe people who tell you that to be successful in keeping a class in order, you must be big or tall. The key here is *presence,* and people who are short of stature—both male and female—can have tons of it, and tall folks can have none of it. Remember your body is a tool and one that you can use effectively. Moving around a class, standing near a student, standing erect, using your eyes to scan a room or to catch a student's attention, using your hands to gesture appropriately can all send messages to students that indicate care, attention, or discipline.

When I taught some years ago in a high school where discipline was an ongoing issue, I made it a practice to stand at my class door and greet or smile at each student as he or she came in the room. It established my presence, it made immediate, individual contact with each person, and, further, students had to pass by me—acknowledge me—in order to enter the class. Thus the signal of standing at the door was both a personal touch and an order measure.

Similarly, walking around the class can help students—although not to the extent where, in one of my classes, a student told me *just sit down*. My pacing (and in this class, that's just what it was) was making her nervous, and she decided to give me some advice and to attempt to save her relatively shattered nerves. While I wasn't particularly thrilled to be criticized, I listened, and I learned from that encounter to be more aware of my own movement and to move a bit less frenetically.

The personal touch

Touching is contextually and culturally determined. While much of what we do in class is pretty personal—write about how that makes you feel; discuss in your group if anything like that has ever happened to you—it does not give us a license to invade our students' private space, that is, their bodies. My personality characteristics are that I am affectionate in speech and gesture, but I try to curb that enthusiasm. It is smart to know students and classes before one ever touches—even in the relatively neutral locations such as forearm and upper arm.

For sure, if you are having a conflict or disagreement with a student, *do not touch them* while you are discussing the issue; it may be seen, rightly or wrongly, as an act of hostility or aggression, and you may get—and deserve—a disproportionate reaction.

In addition, *inappropriate touching* can also be a control issue with students and teachers. As Clary Washington found in one of her classes during her internship teaching, touching signaled a discipline issue:

> Yesterday's class made it quite clear to me that I can't be their pal, and that I've inadvertently let them know that I am. One student, Mike, kept grabbing my hands each time I walked past his desk, saying, "I want you Ms. Washington." My reaction (I was totally shocked and forced myself free each time) didn't make it clear enough that this was inappropriate behavior. I could squash this kid like a grape, but that is not even the point. My hesitation to draw boundaries sent him and the rest of the class the wrong message: it's okay to manhandle Ms. Washington. It's not okay.

Male teachers also need, especially in this era of heightened sensitivity, to be extremely cautious about touching female *and* male students; while culturally the reverse is generally not quite so true for women, it is still good advice. While we are human, and some of us have been raised in families where touching is customary, know, however, that our affection and care are not always reciprocated. It is not always understood in the way in which we intend it, and it is an imposition on our part to force a student to accept our gesture, however well meaning. Know before you reach out to touch.

Dress for context

Dress is another context issue. Certainly two hot topic areas are tattoos and piercings; while some schools are tolerant, in other school settings administrators do not want to see teachers showing visible tattoos and piercings. So what do you do? Look around you and see what the other teachers come to school wearing and if they show tattoos or pierced rings.

Do not model yourself after the one person on the faculty who everyone thinks is weird or who most assume is repressed or stuck-up and who, others assume, illustrates that by his or her clothing. You can be weird and stuck-up or whatever—later in your career. In the beginning, without wholly sacrificing your own individuality, it is best to take the middle of the road in attire. Frankly, you have enough to concern yourself with without adding your sartorial choices to the mix.

First, with all of this in mind, try to dress in a way that seems comfortable to you. If, as a woman, certain kinds of shoes—such as high heels—make you feel silly, wear flats. If you feel stupid in flats, by all means, wear those heels. For women, the restrictions regarding pants and dresses are often real ones: if no one in your school wears pants (or dresses), understand that you will be noticed if you come to school in such. If, as a man, ties just mean awful stuff, wear a jacket and shirt and no tie. If dress shirts seem stultifying, try more informal ones. If no one on the teaching staff wears jeans, don't be the first to trot out your pair. Again, if you feel like you can't teach or talk with any authority without a tie, put one on.

Real teachers wear clothes that make them feel attractive, comfortable, and professional. Look at your closet, check out the other teachers, and make your choices. By all means, however, remember that you are a teacher and not one of the students. That may take some wardrobe adjustment for some of you, but you'll get over it.

I taught in Iowa for a year and came to my first classes dressed as I would to teach in my home state, Virginia. I found my students were truly intimidated by what I assumed to be standard attire; they asked about my clothes before class, and I would often see them checking me out.

Accordingly, I put the suits and skirts and pumps in the back of the closet and came to class in flats, trousers, and sweaters and jackets. My students noticed the change immediately and made approving comments about my "looking nice." They seemed happier; there were fewer comments about my being from "the East"; I felt their ease and was happier in the classroom.

Back in Virginia, when I wore the dashiki friends had brought me from a Caribbean trip, my African American students took time to remark on my appearance. They liked my wearing an interpretation of African fashion, and it made me, to them, seem more personal. These kinds of things may also happen to you; students react to our appearance and can also give us invaluable advice about something so personal as how we dress.

Teaching as Failing

This section may be one you'd like to skip; the idea of failing in the classroom may come a bit close to home. As a beginner, you may rightly fear that a great deal of your teaching will be failing. Actually, while that is true, it is also true of veteran teachers, as one of my favorite articles outlines. Richard Hawley opens his essay with almost uncomfortably harsh truth:

> Whenever a teacher enters a classroom to engage students in the process of increasing their understanding of some subject, some process, some created thing, some event—that is, whenever a teacher enters a classroom to teach—he or she risks great failure and, regardless of his or her gifts, *experiences* that failure to a significant extent. (597)

It is daunting and distressing to think that each class will reveal your failure as a teacher, but Hawley is on target. The poet T. S. Eliot wrote in *The Four Quartets* that "The only wisdom we can hope to acquire / Is the wisdom of humility: humility is endless" ("East Coker," 126). Hawley tells us:

> Human beings generally dread the prospect of speaking authoritatively before a group. The dread is greatest when the group being addressed is not particularly receptive or welcoming, when they do not anticipate being pleased. Teachers play to tougher houses than actors do. They also play to them in more intimate settings, and the scheduled run is generally longer, regardless of the reviews. An actor, often with reason, may blame a flat performance on his material. Teachers are less able to do this; it is rarely Euclid's or Melville's fault that a class has fallen flat. Teachers move among their audiences, address them, converse with them. Any inattention, boredom, hostility is clearly visible before them. Because there are normally no co-stars or supporting players, the experience of teaching imperfectly is essentially a private matter. And again, because failure is by nature humiliating, we tend to keep it to ourselves. (597)

For this reason more than any other, it is necessary that we become reflective teachers and also that we find a teacher friend, teacher buddy to bounce ideas off. Joining in a professional organization can literally be a lifesaver, as with friends it is possible to share what we have done and not done well.

But beyond the concept of failing, there are two other factors intertwined with teaching and failing. Both deal with defenses against classes that "did not go well." The first is blaming the students, the second is blaming the method. The latter is addressed in Chapter 3. And do remember, although the bumper sticker "Of all possible worlds / we only have one" is true of our earth, it is just not true of teaching. Of all possible methods, we may indeed only choose one at one time, but there are a universe of ways to approach a given instructional question. But let's look at the other approach—blaming the students.

Blaming the students

Blaming the students is counterproductive and probably has a lot to do with teacher frustration. While you will have in your career many "difficult" students—which often means they are insufficiently prepared for your class, culturally different from you, learning disabled, emotionally disturbed—it is a trap of the first order to blame classes that do not go well on the students. As a beginner, you will, by a grim custom of the schools, often be given the youngest and least tractable students and classes. Tempting though it may be, you cannot afford to blame failure on them. You must be able to move beyond the rather bitter comment of one of my student teachers who recently remarked after her very first experience teaching a class: "Teaching never follows a perfect plan. The students just seem to get in the way." I am hoping my student soon changes her mind because as teachers I don't think we can afford this kind of attitude. We must continue to teach, enthrall, seduce, illumine students *where they are* and *how we find them*. Decrying their lack of attention, preparation, or ability does no good—it is cursing the darkness. Be a lighter of candles, not a curser of the dark; it will save energy, and, further, you and your students just might surmount the problems and learn.

This is not a perfection business: it is an approximation only, and in a rather mystical sense, we teachers are rarely given to know exactly what the outcome of our classes are—what students remember, retain, what comes back to them years later, is really outside our control. It is also really not reflected by the grades they earn, the tests they take, the essays they write, or even our memories of who they were and what the classes in which they enrolled were like.

Some stories

Like many teachers, I remember incidents with students that make me squirm: times I misunderstood, mistrusted, did not pay attention to an individual.

I lost all patience with Florean Witcher who, even after being repeatedly advised, just would not look up the term she needed in a book's index. She had the book in hand and knew how to spell the term. I was losing patience. Florean had a legendary temper, and after her third request for help and my third identical reply (*look it up in the index*), she pulled furiously away from me.

I saw the anger—and the frustration—and in a well-meaning but misplaced gesture, I tried to stop Florean from storming to the other side of the class. It was winter, and, as was her custom, she had on her coat even though we were inside. In one of those fateful split-second decisions, I reached for her coat's belt to keep her from moving away. But Florean did not stop, and the belt ripped from its tie. Florean, I, and the class froze; Florean's right hand went into a very convincing fist and, indeed, she was fully capable of flattening me for, in essence, tearing her clothing. She didn't, the moment passed, and I both apologized for damaging her coat and offered to repair it. The apology was accepted, the offer to repair was declined, and the atmosphere cooled.

I then renewed the index discussion and found out that Florean would not look up her term in the index because she had never even heard the word *index*; I was asking her to look something up in an igloo for all she knew. We both became calm and businesslike, Florean learned what an index was, and I thought, first, about trying to anticipate students' background and knowledge and, second, about making split-second decisions involving touching and restraining angry students.

And I slowly learned other things. How could I have insisted that Linda Kern's self-confessed nervousness about giving a report in front of the class was overestimated and all that she needed was to just get up and *do it*? She tried, she started, and succeeded, as she had warned me, in becoming so overwhelmed by the experience that there, in front of all of us, she turned and, in her terror, vomited her lunch on the classroom floor. On my knees, as Linda and I cleaned up the remains, I thought about listening to my students.

I could not ever stop the social bullying and name-calling of the physically slight, but very smart, Tho Dang—the first of the Vietnamese refugees to come to my high school and the first student I had ever taught for whom English was a second language. I also just did not rattle the school's resources sufficiently to get the help he needed to negotiate my "remedial" English class. Tho struggled on his own—and successfully—without me. He passed all his usage tests with triumph, but it was not due to me, his English teacher, but to his own very hard work and a tutor in the Vietnamese community. When I complimented him on his high scores, he was polite but noncommittal. He knew, I knew, I had not taught him.

In fact, my feeling of failure with Gino Forrest was so strong that, when I saw him in a restaurant years after graduation—he was working as a waiter there—I struck up a conversation with him so that, essentially, I could try to set things right. I told Gino that night how I regretted the day some years past when I upbraided him after class about his consistently comic behavior. The fact was that Gino was a naturally funny guy, had even, after high school, traveled to Los Angeles to try to establish a career as a professional comedian—but I, his English teacher, did not find him at that point very humorous or very helpful with overall class discipline. Looking back on the encounter with Gino after class—I can remember it vividly—I know that I came down on him as hard as I had ever done with a student and was unfair, even harsh. Now I understand my overreaction more clearly: justified or not, I was afraid that Gino was taking away from me the control of that particular class. Regardless, it is still not an incident of which I am proud—surely I could have handled it less forcefully—

and I was glad to see Gino so I could tell him so. But this is another interesting aspect of the teaching life—Gino listened to my regretful comments and told me, in all honesty, he didn't remember the event at all.

There is a roll call I have—as all teachers do—of students I have failed in the sense that I did not live up to my obligations as teacher.

Like many teachers, I also have had students, years later, tell me brilliant insights or words of advice or encouragement I gave them—good, serendipitous deeds that were wholly individual and that were so context-dependent that I do not often remember, at least not in the same way as the student. But, nevertheless, a number of students have cited crucial incidents in which I, evidently, played an important role.

The failures are dramatic, the good stories are heartening, but some of teaching is a bit more mixed. I also must recount the memorable—and utterly typical—incident when a former high school student of mine, who was then in college and functioning as a summer hostess in a local restaurant, stopped me in the restaurant foyer with exclamations of pleasure and recognition. I was with a group of friends and, actually, rather pleased to have an audience for my student's greeting and such obvious delight. When she wanted to tell me what she remembered most about our class in English those years ago, I glowed with pleasure, somewhat confident that my friends would now hear some stellar incident from the class. I braced myself to accept what she would recount; my friends smiled at each other and at me in pleasant anticipation.

"Oh yes," she recalled, her eyes lighting up with pleasure, "I just never forgot when you told us about your wedding cake and how you decided on it and had it specially ordered."

My dismay, if not my disbelief, was immediate and total; was that, I asked her, what she had remembered?

"Oh yes," she gushed enthusiastically, "it was made entirely of *cream puffs*, and you had ordered it from that new French restaurant."

Well she had me. My wedding cake *had* been made of cream puffs and ordered specially from a new, local French restaurant. But, good grief, had I ever spent class time telling students about my *wedding cake*? About *cream puffs*? What in the world was I thinking to talk about a wedding cake? Even as an aside? Where was my brain that day? Where was my lesson plan?

I squeaked a thank-you and quickly moved with my amused friends through the foyer and out of the door. My wedding cake—on which I had evidently actually spent class time—was what my former student remembered. Humility is endless.

Hawley sums it up well:

> Failure—real failure—is palpable everywhere in the teaching process. We need to name it and to face it, so that we may continue. If we insulate ourselves sufficiently with defenses, we may go unhurt, but we will teach nothing, while providing students models of flight and disengagement. Acknowledging failure and acknowledging defenses, we may come to know as much about our business as the medieval scholastics knew about God: what he is not and that he is necessary. Now off to class. (600)

And perhaps that is one encouraging aspect of this business of teaching; there is always another class and more students and, thanks to the fates, another chance to teach. As a teaching friend of mine says, "Teaching is the *only* profession where we can clear away all the failures at the end of the school year and start afresh in the fall."

A final word from a poet (and student and teacher)

Henry Taylor, a Pulitzer prize winner, wrote a poem I like to share with my students. It's about failure and domination and a terrible incident in a long-ago but not long-forgotten math class. It presents a bright but not truly confident student and an insecure, overbearing teacher. But the last part of the poem is even more powerful for us, because Taylor, now a teacher himself, writes of what all of us teachers know; we all fail each other and, to a certain extent, we must forgive each other in the classroom:

Shapes, Vanishings

1

Down a street in the town where I went
to high school twenty-odd years ago, by doorways
and shadows that change with the times, I walked
past a woman at whose glance I almost stopped cold,
almost to speak, to remind her of who I had been—
but walked on, not being certain it was she,
not knowing what I might find to say.
It wasn't quite the face I remembered, the years
being what they are, and I could have been wrong.

2

But that feeling of being stopped cold, stopped dead,
will not leave me, and I hark back
to the thing I remember her for, though God knows
how I could remind her of it now.
Well, one afternoon when I was fifteen
I sat in her class. She leaned on her desk,
facing us, the blackboard behind her arrayed
with geometrical figures—triangle, square,
pentagon, hexagon, et cetera. She pointed
and named them. "The five-sided figure," she said,
"is a polygon." So far so good, but then when she said,
"The six-sided one is a hexagon," I wanted things clear.
Three or more sides is *poly*, I knew, but five only
is *penta*, and said so; she denied it,
and I pressed the issue, I, with no grades
to speak of, a miserable average to stand on
with an Archimedean pole—no world to move,
either, just a fact to get straight, but she
would have none of it, saying, at last, "Are you
contradicting me?"

3

A small thing to remember a teacher for. Since then,
I have thought about justice often enough
to have earned my uncertainty about what it is,
but one hard fact from that day has stayed with me:

If you're going to be a smartass, you have to be right,
and not just some of the time. "Are you
contradicting me?" she had said, and I stopped
breathing a moment, the burden of her words
pressing down through me hard and quick, the huge
weight of knowing I was right, and beaten. She
had me. "No, ma'am," I managed to say, wishing
I had the whole thing down on tape to play back
to the principal, wishing I were ten feet tall
and never mistaken, ever, about anything in this world,
wishing I were older, and long gone from there.

　　　　4
Now I am older, and long gone from there.
What sense in a grudge over something so small?
What use to forgive her for something
she wouldn't remember? Now students
face me as I stand at my desk, and the shoe
may yet find its way to the other foot,
if it hasn't already. I couldn't charge
thirty-five cents for all that I know
of geometry; what little I learned is gone now,
like a face looming up for a second out of years
that dissolve in the mind like a single summer.
Therefore,
if ever she almost stops me again,
I will walk on as I have done once already,
remembering how we failed each other,
knowing better than to blame anyone.

　　　　　　　　　　　　—Henry Taylor
　　　　　　　　　　　　The Flying Change

And so, off to class.

·········· FOR YOUR JOURNAL ··········

As you think about your teaching career, what is the one area more
than any other in which you would hope you would not fail your
students? Is it intellectual? emotional? social? Would it have to do
with something inside the classroom? outside? If you could ask
your teaching Fairy Godmother to keep you from one area of failure, what would it be? MAKE A WISH—

References

Brooke, Robert. "Underlife and Writing Instruction." *College Composition and Communication* 38 (May 1987): 141–53.

Eliot, T. S. *The Complete Poems and Plays 1909–1950*. New York: Harcourt Brace & World, 1952.

Emmers, Amy Puett. *After the Lesson Plan: Realities of High School Teaching*. New York: Teachers College Press, 1981.

Gibbs, Nancy. "Parents Behaving Badly." *Time* 165 (February 21, 2005): 40–49.

Hawley, Richard A. "Teaching as Failing." *Phi Delta Kappan* 60 (April 1979): 597–600.

Lortie, Dan C. *Schoolteacher: A Sociological Study*. Chicago: University of Chicago Press, 1975.

Shulman, Lee. S. "Learning to Teach." *AHHE Bulletin* (November 1987).

Taylor, Henry. "Shapes, Vanishings." In *The Flying Change*, 14–15. Baton Rouge, LA: LSU Press, 1985.

3

Planning for Your Teaching

Order and simplification are the first steps toward the mastery of a subject—the actual enemy is the unknown.

—Thomas Mann, *The Magic Mountain*

Planning for your teaching can at first seem overwhelming, but it is actually something you will need to learn to do consistently and well. There are so many unpredictable aspects of teaching that can be accommodated when you have a solid teaching plan, and your confidence in your own ability will strengthen as you actually carry out well-conceived plans. Thus planning well is a crucial part of successful teaching, and it is something you don't, especially at first, want to minimize. While most veteran teachers are sketchy planners, you will need, in your first few years in the classroom, to map things out fairly explicitly, even if you end up changing those plans as you teach. Planning is part of the learning process, and short-circuiting it is often not in your—and your students'—best interest. Further, some school systems like to see teachers' lesson plans on a regular basis and may ask you to submit plans to your department chair or even to your principal. At any rate, as well as the confidence that planning will give you in your teaching, as a beginning teacher there are numerous folks who will take an active interest in the extent—and the presence—of your plans.

In this chapter we take a look at some theoretical aspects of planning and some practical strategies. You will need both on your teaching journey. Let's start with models of teaching.

Five Models of Teaching

Adopting a teaching model

My own teaching model was shaped, first, by what I had experienced as a student and, second, by the experience of my own students as I myself became a teacher. What I remembered—and treasured—from my favorite teachers was their ability to set a stage for discovery and talk. The best of my teachers seemed interested in what we had to say and let us grope through many wrong turns to find out what indeed was not only important to us but what was true. From these teachers I felt I had had an opportunity to learn, to find on my own. And I remembered the learning, which was *my* learning, not someone else's.

It was learning to love the questions, for, as seers have often pointed out, we are often not ready for the answers. I still am not ready for some answers—that, by the way, is part of the wonderful discovery of teaching; it is a self-renewing enterprise when it is at its best, and, with our students, we explore.

My students helped me develop a model of teaching. Most of them, even the more traditionally polite, had a highly limited patience with listening to *me*. At the extreme, I found students who not only were impatient about listening but who would just not do it. They needed to be involved and active and to find answers and ideas on their own. It was, essentially, an instructional issue for them as much as it was a discipline question.

I found that asking, not telling, was almost always more powerful. Students had to make their own meaning of events or text or writing; it became *our* class, not just mine, and when it was ours, many discipline problems seemed to evaporate. The nonclass-related chatter diminished, and talk revolved around the subject.

When teachers are not interested in their students, when their own telling is the most important, we have a classroom as described by a student, Susanna Field:

> [My English teacher] could have improved her class by coming closer to the students. She could have been more interested in what we had to say. (Because she was not interested, we cared to say nothing.) . . . Also, she could have arranged the desks in a circle, so then we could all discuss with each other, rather than facing the front of the room and merely listening to the teacher.

Thus I set for you a model of teaching that is almost wholly based on asking and constructing events and opportunities for students to find the meaning. It is a skill that takes some practice; it takes patience, yet it, I think, yields probably the only learning that is worth our energy. If we want students to know facts, they need to consult information sources. If, however, we want students to think and explore and weigh and argue, they need an environment and an arena to come up with their own learning. A popular aphorism states, "Give a person a fish, he eats for a day; teach a person to fish, he eats for a lifetime." We must teach our students to fish, not keep handing them the dead ones *we* have gotten from the stream.

There are, in essence, a number of models of teaching—ways of teaching—that are not so much correct and incorrect, right or wrong, but that reflect different philosophies of instruction and approaches to students and appeal to different personality strengths of teachers. Some of this is individual and essentially neutral in character; some of this is part of good practice. There is, however, an essential approach to teaching that is beyond the kind of individual aspects unique to each of us, teaching as discovery, and that model will be presented here as a goal toward which you should strive.

One book on the subject, Bruce Joyce and Marsha Weil's *Models of Teaching*, presents multiple groups of dozens of separate models of teaching. The following is a stripped-down version of five models you may need to consider in your own teaching. Please note that some of this is developmental; you will naturally be attracted to certain models early in your career. Some of this also is hierarchical; I see the later models as superior to the others. Teaching as telling is the earliest model and the one we want you to move away from. It is also a very necessary step for a beginner: the other models will come, I believe, for you, as they did for me and for many other teachers, with time.

In his study *Twenty Teachers*, Ken Macrorie sees teachers, regardless of grade level or subject matter, as those doing "good works" in the classroom. In the award-winning *The Making of a Teacher*, Pamela Grossman describes a number of beginning teachers and discusses especially how many of them try to replicate their English major experiences in college with their high school students. Robert V. Bullough Jr.'s *First Year Teacher* explores the experiences of a beginner and her attempts first to survive the classroom and then to truly become a good teacher. *Educating Esme* and *Brief Intervals of Horrible Sanity* describe some of the tough times for teachers who are in the classroom for their first years. Social studies teacher Stuart B. Palonsky writes of the strain of teaching in a book appropriately entitled *900 Shows a Year*. There are dozens of good books about teaching and teachers and, as you get deeper into this business, you may not only want to read them, you may want to add your voice to the collection. Almost all of these accounts, however, include some of the following models of teaching.

Teaching as telling

When you first thought of being a teacher, one of the early images in your mind was probably that of you standing in front of a class and telling students about a novel or poem, explaining to them a concept or idea, and writing on a chalkboard while students listened to you or watched what you wrote. The sun is shining through the classroom windows, the room is attractively furnished, the students are quiet, and there you are, at the podium, teaching. You are teaching eloquently, and the students are rapt with attention, taking notes and asking, only occasionally, a salient question on the issue. It is an orderly scene, and you are at the head, faced by interested, attentive students.

For many people getting ready to enter the classroom or even for some veteran teachers, teaching is telling, the teacher talking and the students listening. Certainly for most of us early in our career, teaching was a great deal of telling, although as many later found, the longer we taught the farther we moved from this model of teaching.

If this is your image of what middle school or high school English teaching is, I want you to think about it for a minute. Consider: Who is doing the talking? Who is making the connections? Who is giving the examples? Who is in charge? Who is the active one? Shifting the scene: Who is doing the listening? Who is receiving the connections, the examples? Whose mind may be wandering everywhere? Who is the passive one?

How does the teacher know, especially if he or she speaks for a long period—an entire class period—if the students understand, have questions, already know all of the material, part of the material, can extend the material beyond what the teacher is discussing? Is asking "are there any questions?" or checking to see that students are silent or taking notes sufficient to answer this concern?

Clearly I see severe limitations in the model of teaching as telling; I think it is inefficient, overused, and encourages a great deal of student passivity and intellectual laziness. And, from a teacher's point of view, it is exhausting: the teacher is the center and the one upon whom all are dependent. To take that responsibility, undiluted, five periods a day, five days a week, is a recipe for burnout as well as a waste of teacher resource.

Being a talking head is not my idea of teaching, and I have lost faith in the idea of students being a tabula rasa, a blank slate upon which the teacher writes. Similarly, I am concerned about the idea of what Brazilian educator Paulo Freire criticizes as the "banking concept" of education where the teacher makes knowledge deposits into students' heads. These ideas of teaching are often attributed to the factory model of the western Industrial

Revolution where education was considered analogous to manufacturing; the students were the raw materials, the factory was the school, and the teachers were the workers who shaped the students into some sort of product, or educated person. All these ideas, teacher as knowledge knower, student as knowledge receiver, sound fairly logical and, indeed, some of them are deeply rooted in our culture. The models, however, are largely based on a few assumptions that we need to examine seriously:

- **Teachers' functions are largely to funnel specific pieces of knowledge to students.**
- **Students' functions are largely to absorb that knowledge, much as they would read a book or view a film.**
- **The reception of such knowledge is active and efficient and also incorporates critical assessment of that knowledge.**
- **The giving of such knowledge is tailored to students' experience, prior knowledge, and difficulties with the subject.**

Many teachers just don't agree. The major problem with teaching as telling is that it is overwhelmingly a one-way street: the person doing the work, including making many of the learning connections, is the teacher, not the student. Listening is rarely that active of an experience, and listening for long periods of time is downright wasteful, if not impossible to sustain, for most students. A teacher who talks most of the class cannot tailor the knowledge or the insight to all of his or her students; students, moreover, do not have the experience of questioning, arguing, and putting into context what they are hearing if the overwhelming activity is simply receiving another's talk.

This is not to say that there are not times when a teacher needs to give students instructions, history, major points. Some of those times, judiciously chosen, are when students need background before they can begin to approach a subject. There is a place for the brief lecture on the use of imagery in modern poetry, for the uses of the semicolon, for the difference between alliteration and assonance. But, very soon after that lecture, it is time for students to take the information and use it, question it, incorporate it, illustrate it, *something* it so that the knowledge does not become someone else's point but their own. As one young man in student teaching, using his first student groups as an effort to help him break the teaching-as-telling mode, wrote:

Tuesday, April 3

English Literature Class: 3rd Period was motivatingly scary. The students worked in groups (another way for me to cut down on talking). I feel I am actually getting the message of why it's ineffective to talk too much to students. They received their instructions, played some, and talked some, and laughed, and joked, and worked some. And when the groups were presenting their answers, they did it as if they had actually learned what I had intended.

—Ronnie Fleming

Teaching as inspiration

I have taught a number of students who were rather successful in their own school careers and, understandably, took that skill with them into their new lives as teachers. For many of these students, however, they also took their ability to "wing it" and used that ability in the classroom. While there is surely a place for inspiration—changing the direction or focus of an activity in response to what happened in a previous class, or, indeed, what is happening in that very class at that very time—I urge you to reconsider the model of teaching as inspiration. Teaching as inspiration must grow from the planning that has already been done. Planning, as discussed in this chapter, is really the foundation to good teaching, and while no one can realistically map out everything that will happen in every class—nor should they—relying on inspiration and waiting until the last minute to pull a class together won't do you or your students much good.

Teaching as inspiration is based on the following assumptions:

- **Getting students excited is more important than leading them to some sort of intellectual conclusion.**
- **Things always have a tendency to "work out" in a classroom setting.**
- **The freshness of inspiration is always superior to the certainty (read *dullness*) of planning.**

Certainly, as I said before, there are times when it will strike you that an activity could change or be added to right here and right now, and that will help you with your classes, but relying solely on teaching as inspiration will not substitute for mapping out instructional activities before class. Teaching a short story you have not read, asking students to do exercises you have not reviewed, showing a film you have never seen, or making up a classroom activity on the spot is part of poor planning and can—not always, but can—result in some tense classroom moments and some instructional gaffes. Further, it is likely that some smart student will know just how unprepared you are.

Part of your job as a professional is to come to class prepared; relying on inspiration is a sloppy way to run your teaching life.

Teaching as maintaining a creation

In the opening of Nancie Atwell's *In the Middle*, she describes herself early in her career as an organizer and planner who carefully, minutely created a class and its organization and then, essentially, maintained that creation throughout the year. With the best of intentions, she set a complicated system "in motion" and simply made it endure throughout the school year. Atwell writes:

> I confess. I started out as a creationist. The first days of every school year I created; for the next thirty-six weeks I maintained my creation. My curriculum. From behind my big desk I set it in motion, managed and maintained it all year long. I wanted to be a great teacher—systematic, purposeful, in control. . . . I didn't learn in my classroom. I tended and taught my creation. (3)

A teacher, such as Atwell describes herself, is indeed in control and manages a classroom much as one would manage any system. As she writes in another article, "Sitting there at my big desk, developing new assignments and evaluating the results, I remained oblivious to . . . my students' ideas, experiences, and expertise. I remained in charge" ("Everyone Sits," 35).

Teaching as maintaining a creation is based on the following assumptions:

- **Teaching has more to do with systems and patterns and rules than with the shifting demands of learning.**
- **Once a classroom organizational pattern is established, it can successfully guide an entire semester or year of the class.**

- **A teacher can successfully anticipate student needs to the point that any organizational pattern that he or she establishes will be durable for a fixed pattern of time.**

The problem is, of course, what Atwell describes: *I didn't learn in my classroom.* It is not just spineless sentimentality or softheartednesss that leads us to believe that, yes, our students can teach us. Indeed they do—different ways of approaching and different aspects of knowledge. As Atwell describes, we can, and should, shift to another model:

> These days, I learn in my classroom. What happens there has changed; it continually changes. I've become an evolutionist, and the curriculum unfolds now as my kids and I learn together. My aims stay constant . . . but my practices evolve. . . . What I learn with these students . . . makes me a better teacher. (*In the Middle*, 3)

While setting a class' agenda is part of teaching, we have to strike a balance between being the organizer and being the dictator. The latter is not only inefficient—all responsibility falls on the teacher—but it also often means that the students' interest is not captured and capitalized upon. Being in charge, absolutely, always, can stifle our students and box us into an unshakable role as sole authority. Planning and organizing can become a trap: we fall so in love with our own system for our classes that we neglect to revise, adjust, change, to accommodate our students.

Teaching as discovery

We now come to the model I believe will be the most enduring for you as a teacher. A teacher who uses discovery:

- **Doesn't necessarily avoid questions to which there is no answer or mind saying, "I don't know."**
- **Lets students talk.**
- **Allows pauses in the talk—just like in a real conversation. This means there are periods of silence in the classroom.**
- **Asks, asks, asks and falls out of love with telling.**
- **Starts teaching with where the students are, not where the book is or where the teacher is.**

It is not as efficient, as many suppose, to be told the point and then find the examples to support it. It's like being told the punch line and then trying to recreate the joke to fit the end, like being told the answer to the algebraic equation and being asked to reconstruct the problem. Using the discovery method, we learn and internalize that learning by finding the point ourselves, by making it our own, by saying it, by stumbling toward it. We avoid overt didacticism, as our knowledge is not our students' knowledge, our revelation about a poem or play or language principle is not our students'.

If we adopt this teaching model, we must stop asking our students to admire the fine conclusions we have reached or to be in awe at our knowledge of any given subject. Instead, we allow them to lurch through to their own. This is one of the most powerful aspects of the act of teaching. I often wonder if, actually, it is the only one.

Teaching as a reflective practitioner

It is important that you add into your teaching life the concept of reflecting on what you do in your classes and what your students do and what seem to be the outcomes. The aphorism "Those who do not know history are doomed to repeat it" may have some bearing on this discussion: if you are unaware or do not consider not only why a class was unsuccessful but why it was *successful*, it would seem virtually impossible for you to progress in your teaching life. In fact, the whole idea of a teacher being a researcher within the context of his or her own classes is a large part of being a reflective practitioner.

The field of reflection can be summarized, perhaps, by four very salient questions. Researcher Bud Wellington cites them:

1. **What do I do?** ("observational description of practice")
2. **What does this mean?** ("principles of theories-in-use . . . which underlie and drive the described practice")
3. **How did I come to be this way?** ("forces our awareness beyond the classroom . . . correctly reveals educational practice as essentially political")
4. **How might I do things differently?** ("gives us the call to action") (5)

Wellington notes that these questions "are not intended as rhetorical . . . for casual consideration over tea. Rather, they are intended to raise consciousness, to challenge complacency, and to engender a higher order of professional practice" (5). When we ask these questions about our classes and our teaching—before we embark on a class or after it, as evaluation and follow-up—we are being reflective about our models of teaching. When we alter our teaching in response to the answers to the questions, we are being responsible and responsive.

Teaching *Their Eyes Were Watching God* and the Five Models

So, let's take a piece of literature and look at it from the point of view of each of the five models. Writer and anthropologist Zora Neale Hurston's *Their Eyes Were Watching God* has become popular in many high school English classes. While its use of dialect, mature themes, and frank language makes it unacceptable in most middle school settings (and, indeed, those factors can also prevent it from being used in secondary schools), it is nevertheless on a number of reading lists across the country. The novel, set in Florida and originally published in 1937, is a strong one that deals with important questions; it has feminist underpinnings, uses beautiful imagery, and carries a clear message regarding love and endurance. *Their Eyes Were Watching God* is also characterized by a powerful and gripping plot, and its protagonist, Janie, is memorable. Further, important issues of race, class, and poverty are all part of the novel.

If the teaching model were **teaching as telling**, a teacher using *Their Eyes Were Watching God* could more than likely engage in the following activities:

- **Give students a brief lecture on the definition and characteristics of the regional novel and ask them to find examples in *Their Eyes Were Watching God* to illustrate those characteristics.**

- Cite the major themes of the novel and ask students to find illustrative incidents.
- List the major characters of the novel and ask students to define their roles.
- Give students worksheets with important quotations and have students explain why those quotations are significant.
- Review the parts of a plot for students and have them identify rising action, falling action, and one climax.

If a teacher was relying upon **inspiration,** he or she might make a few notes on the novel and start the class hoping that someone would bring up important issues. The teacher would follow the students' lead and pursue whatever came up. The length of the "study" might be one day, might be a week; it might lead to other literature or not.

A **maintaining-a-creation** model would involve *Their Eyes Were Watching God* as part of a thematic unit or genre study, orchestrated and integrated with other pieces and following the same pattern of discussion and investigation as pieces of literature in the previous part of the unit. The topics to be discussed would be strictly established as would the time spent on each topic or activity. It would not be unusual for the test on the novel to be written before the actual teaching of the novel.

A **discovery** model would look different. Instead of the teaching as telling questions just listed, instead of meticulous mapping out of the topics and time and even testing, the teacher would change the focus and emphasis to exploration and discussion. What topics would be lingered on and for how long and what the final evaluation would be would not be immediately established; it would depend on the students. With that as a conceptual frame, the teacher might:

- Ask students about the dialect in the novel: Was it difficult? Was it essential? What would happen if the novel did not use any dialect at all? Can you rewrite one section of dialogue using standard English and then compare and contrast the dramatic effect? What is gained? What is lost?
- Ask students about the theme(s) of this novel: How do you know which are the themes or theme? Which seem the most/least important to you? Why?
- Ask students about the characters: Is this novel about more than one character? (Janie? Tea Cake? Jody?) How do you know? How can you tell? To what extent is it important to decide? Why?
- Ask students to select three quotations that seem important: Why are these quotations important?
- Tell students that some critics have suggested *Their Eyes Were Watching God*, written decades ago and brought back into print and popularity in contemporary times, just doesn't deserve the attention and praise that it is given. What do you think of that argument? To what extent do you think this novel deserves/does not deserve the attention it is currently receiving? If you were giving a literary prize, what would you select as criteria?
- Ask students about the feminist and political aspects of the novel: What appears to the message regarding love between men and women? Marriage? Commitment?

- **Ask students to determine if there is a climax to this novel: Is there more than one climax? How do you know? Why do you think that? What, by the way, is a *climax*?**

A **reflective practitioner** would consider what to do and why in teaching *Their Eyes Were Watching God* and would be sensitive to options (how might I do things differently?). If a reflective practitioner used discovery activities, he or she would be attentive and make adjustments; the literary merit question, for instance, which assumes that students have an interest in literary prizes, may be tedious to answer and puzzling. It also raises the specter of racial discrimination and might be difficult for some classes, especially if the teacher is of a racial majority making the inquiry of a class largely of minority students. Adjustments would need to be made. These could be reflected in the class immediately and in future plans to teach the novel.

·················· **FOR YOUR JOURNAL** ··················

Pick a piece of literature or a skill and consider it from the point of view of the teaching models. If you were to teach it by *telling*, what would you do? If you were to rely on *inspiration*, what might be the shape of the lesson? If you taught the concept in the frame of *maintaining a creation*, what might you ask students to do? Finally, if you had students *discover* the concept, how would you structure the class? Then, as a *reflective practitioner*, what questions would you ask yourself about any or all of these teaching models and their effectiveness?

It Didn't Work

Teaching as considering instructional options

Another aspect of teaching, especially beginning teaching, is the seductive—but false—idea of teaching as correct and incorrect. Beginning teachers, like beginning anything, tend to think in terms of *right* and *wrong* when it comes to classroom practice. Having sat in on the classes of dozens of student teachers for some twenty years, I have yet to find a novice who is not concerned about what he or she did that was in terms of *correct* and *incorrect*. It's maddening news for the beginner, but it's true: there is very little right and wrong in this business. It is, actually, almost wholly a matter of options, the choice of any one of which yields different outcomes.

Teaching is not right or wrong, things don't just "work" or "not work." It is, both happily and unnervingly, much more complicated than that. As Stanford University professor David F. Labaree notes:

Teaching remains an uncertain enterprise [because of its] irreducible complexity. What we know about teaching is always contingent on a vast array of intervening variables that mediate between a teacher's action and a student's response. As a result, there is always a *ceteris paribus* clause hovering over any instructional prescription: This works better than that, if everything else is equal. In other words, it all depends. (53)

What in the world does Labaree mean? Let me explain: if we could hypothetically assume a lesson plan that would be identically presented to two different classes of students in the same grade in the same school, the outcomes and student learning of those classes would be, despite all efforts of the teacher, very different. The variables are crucial: not only are the students different but their "mix" is different; the sheer number of students is different; the time of day of the class period is different; different things happened the day before in class; and so on. Some of those factors are choices made by the teacher of subject matter and methodology, but some are simply indigenous to school and the varying classes a teacher deals with every day.

And also, as experienced teachers know—sometimes intuitively, sometimes through bitter trial and error—the same lesson plan, technique, or instructional approach cannot be used successfully with all students semester after semester or even from period to period. This may come as an unhappy surprise if you were hoping that after the first year or two your lesson or unit plans would become sort of unchangeable blueprints on which you could rely for many years. Certainly experience will be helpful to you as a teacher, but you will not be able to replicate from year to year or semester to semester entire class plans. Change and adjustment to the many factors that go to make up a class and a group of students is part of successful teaching, and there are many factors to consider.

The variables involved

What can make a successful class? What can contribute to a less than successful one? There are a variety of components, all of which you should know and recognize. As a beginning, however, it is useful to know that there is rarely a single reason for a successful or unsuccessful class. While you may be tempted to point to one thing, it's not just you, the teacher; it's not just your students. It's not only what anyone is studying or how they are studying it or even how long they have spent on it. It's rarely just the school or even the weather. It is a little bit of all of these; every one of these factors can and does interact and affect learning outcomes and learning environment. Let's look at the variables one at a time.

One variable that can affect a classroom is **subject matter**, its **nature**, **amount**, and its **purpose**. The **nature** of subject matter can be a factor because that which is familiar and that which is not can affect not only learning but student attitude and classroom environment. For example, sometimes literature that is difficult can be more intriguing to students than that which is readily accessible; on the other hand, starting with familiar material and then moving to the more difficult can give students a sense of security that they might not have if the difficult material was immediately begun.

The **amount** of subject matter is also a crucial variable in classroom success. For example, let's consider the extensiveness of material: a number of nonfiction essays might provide a successful and enjoyable study with a specific group of students for two weeks but be a disaster if stretched into a month. Likewise, a day of poetry can be wonderful; five straight days might be tedious and boring, taking all of the surprise and newness out of the genre. On the other hand, two days working on an essay may leave students puzzled and confused; three days might give them more time to revise and rework.

Looking at **purpose**, material students know has to be learned for a standardized test or because it is a curricular requirement may be viewed very differently from material they have chosen or in which they are taking a newly discovered interest. Even if that material is essentially the same in difficulty, why someone is learning something can affect attitude and actual learning itself.

Often, too, **methodology** is just not successfully interchangeable with all classes. Students, for example, who are used to working in small groups will, with direction, continue to function efficiently and productively in those groups. On the other hand, abruptly putting students who have been fed an exclusive diet of worksheets into small groups can be a disaster. In another area, verbal and assured students will often respond well to a large-group discussion; for some students, however, large groups are intimidating or alienating, and the opportunity to talk as a whole class will not be successful.

Setting or school context can also affect classes. As outlined in other chapters, knowing who your students are and what their lives are like outside school can give you crucial clues about what links to establish in making material relevant and what material to select or emphasize. To give a fairly low-level example, students in rural midwestern settings may need background information if they read a short story set in New York City; Western urban students may need the same sort of information regarding poetry about Southern fields and farms.

Veteran teachers also know that at a certain portion of the day (a split period broken by lunch, for example) or at a certain time of the year (late spring, for instance) certain activities and courses of study will be more successful than others. To illustrate, creative dramatics, which require movement and noise and expressiveness, might best be avoided when students are really excited or keyed up. The first school day after a holiday or the last period of a Friday are times when creative dramatics might not be such a good choice for a classroom activity. I think, from my experience, of the senior research paper. I have found that scheduling the completion of that project in late spring is not very smart. Most seniors by that time of year and at that late date of their high school life really don't have their minds set on research or the format of a bibliography. It is better, I have found, to schedule the completion of such a long project in the late fall or winter.

Time is another variable. While many teachers love certain topics or pieces or literature and want students to know every aspect and understand almost everything before they consider the issue "covered," numerous days or class periods spent on a single topic can engender boredom and restlessness. Less in this case is often more—it is usually advisable not to spend huge chunks of instructional time on single topics. Despite its great appeal to you, a month of study on *Romeo and Juliet* will make most students crazy; two weeks on the persuasive essay may be overkill.

In addition, another variable is you, the **teacher**. Your degree of experience, your enthusiasm for and knowledge of any given subject, even your mood on a particular day can truly affect your classes. Imagine that you are, for example, still unsure of the difference between restrictive and nonrestrictive clauses and yet you are going to give fifth bell a ten-minute minilesson on the subject. All other things being equal, just how relaxed do you anticipate that ten minutes will be? How receptive do you think you might be to a possible barrage of questions from puzzled students? How many inventive examples do you think you will be putting on the overhead? Chances are, with the best of intentions, what you present will be tight, to the point, and not very expansive. And, as you can imagine, that type of presentation might have an effect on your students and the class atmosphere. Contrast this in your mind with a class period talking about one of your favorite plays. Can you imagine how your attitude might affect the class itself? Finally, you may have had personal issues or problems that are worrying you; leaving your own problems, however legitimate they may be, at the classroom door is a habit you may just be learning.

Of course, the **students**, their experience, background, and maturity are a powerful variable in the success of any classroom. Knowing and adjusting to your students is vital in making instruction "work."

The teaching act, as experienced teachers know and beginning ones quickly learn, is a complex event and is influenced by a myriad of variables: when novice teachers report "it didn't work," they are actually talking about numerous factors.

To recap, the problem begins with the nebulous "it." Is "it" the interest or appropriateness of the subject matter? The success of the students' activities? The teacher's instructional methodology? The students' learning outcomes? The students' responses and general satisfaction?

We also need to look at the even more vague "work." What didn't "work"? Did the majority of students fail a test? Did the students seem confused about a concept? Did class discipline disintegrate? Was the teacher simply dissatisfied with the lesson or unit?

There are a number of variables involved, and while "it didn't work" is not an unimportant or easily resolved worry, it can be more readily handled with a conceptual framework that can help break teaching and learning into component parts.

A paradigm for analyzing the teaching act

Let us imagine a paradigm for learning that is, essentially, A producing B or B resulting from A:

A Paradigm for Analyzing the Teaching Act

Subject matter of this nature
                  in this amount
                  for this purpose
with *methodology* of this type,
in this *situation* or *setting*,
and for this *time* of instruction,
with a *teacher* of this disposition
                  this background and
                  these qualities,   A

PRODUCES

these *patterns of affective and cognitive learning*,
in *students* at this level of development and maturity
                  with this level of experience and   B
                  with this kind of background.
(Christenbury, 233–39)

Without belaboring what may appear as a perfectly self-explanatory model, let's look at some obvious (if not simpleminded) questions to highlight the components.

Subject matter of this nature   To what extent is the complexity of British seventeenth-century metaphysical poetry accessible to all students? What kind of ethnic studies can be/should be taught in a community? What kind of student response will there be to an intensive consideration of spelling rules? Do all students need and find useful the formal argumentative essay?

Subject matter in this amount   Should a teacher present major punctuation rules in an intensive unit or intersperse them with other material? Should novels be read and taught extensively or intensively? Do students learn more producing a final draft of a piece every week or every other week?

Subject matter for this purpose   Is there a difference between teaching something as a review or because students requested it? How do students respond if a teacher spontaneously adds material to a class? If a subject is taught as part of a curricular requirement, to what degree can student interest be affected?

Methodology   Do some classes enjoy large-group discussion? Do some classes respond well to small-group work? Do some students seem to like silent reading and working alone? Is work at a computer successful with the majority of students? How can pair work be used?

Situation or setting   Is the last period or bell of the day appropriate for certain types of instructional activities? In what ways are the bells that are usually usurped for assemblies and pep rallies affected by the disruption? Should the approach for a split lunch period be different from that for first period?

Time   Considering the students in a particular class, are two days enough to review imagery? Is one month too long for the reading of a novel? Are three weeks sufficient for the reading of a play? How many days do students need to work on a rough draft?

Teacher   Does a teacher's experience, academic qualifications, and personality characteristics affect a class? To what extent can his or her level of confidence and ease with students be a factor in teaching success? Can all teachers readily adapt to all types of methodology?

Patterns of affective and cognitive learning   Are all groups of students equally able to understand all levels of material? Do some students understand material but remain disengaged? Can some students thoroughly enjoy some material but not completely comprehend it? Should a teacher demand emotional (or affective) responses of any kind? A mix of cognitive and affective? Cognitive only? When? Why?

Students   Do some students, regardless of chronological age, seem more mature than others? What forms does this maturity take in the classroom? Do "above average" students react differently and learn differently from "disadvantaged" students? Are urban and suburban students alike in their instructional needs? What about students for whom English is a second language?

Now that you are completely depressed and overwhelmed by these questions, know that they are the issues that veteran teachers perhaps never fully answer but do learn to consider, especially when we wonder why something didn't "work" in the classroom. Knowing the questions in this case may be more important than knowing the answers, and it may help you when you know that a class didn't go well or, yes, just didn't work.

Playing a game with teaching variables

So let's play a game with the teaching variables. Let's imagine you know everything *but* the type of learning that may occur. Thus, you will have six variables and will need to speculate or predict *one*. You will need to work in a group of three.

First, the group will need to prepare index cards representing the six categories of variables discussed previously. To begin, let's simplify the game and imagine that the subject matter is a short story and that the discussion will center on the other five variables and that short story. Using a different card for each variable under each heading, write out the variables and place them in six piles of three.

(I) Subject Matter (nature, amount, and purpose)   Cards one, two, and three: a seven-page modern American short story in the anthology, part of the school curriculum.

(II) Methodology   Card one: reading the story out loud and following it with a large-group discussion. Card two: reading the story for homework and doing a short journal entry/writing response as a prelude to small-group discussion. Card three: reading the story silently the previous day and then discussing it in small groups.

(III) Setting (period/day of week/time of year)   Card one: first period, Monday, early fall. Card two: fifth period, Friday, late spring. Card three: third period, Wednesday, winter, assembly day.

(IV) Time   Card one: all of the period/bell. Card two: two consecutive periods/bells. Card three: two nonconsecutive periods/bells (e.g., Monday and Thursday).

(V) Teacher   Card one, two, and three: you. (When you are further along in your career you might want to consider including two of your colleagues; you will then know teaching "styles" a bit more intimately.)

(VI) Students   Card one: class of 18, considered average. Card two: class of 31, considered high ability. Card three: class of 22, collaborative class with some reluctant learners.

Once the cards have been written out, have a group member shuffle the cards in each category and, in turn, select one card from each of the six categories. When you are through, each member of the group should have six cards, one card representing subject matter, one representing methodology, and so on.

Now, silently study what the fates have given you and imagine that this mix is your class. Spend about five minutes and make a few notes to yourself. Then in the group, go around in a circle and have each person briefly present what his or her variables are and what, regarding the success of teaching this short story, the person guesses would be the possible results.

Factors each member of the group should consider include: What, given the best guesses you can make, do you predict about learning outcomes with specific students? What problem areas (if any) do you think you would need to be aware of? What adjustments do you speculate you might need to make in the classroom?

Even if your assumptions and predictions are off-center, it will give you a chance to consider, given the components of a teaching act, what kind of effect this combination of variables might have on the learning of these hypothetical students.

As a variation, make up your own game and, in your group of three, brainstorm for a minute the possible specifics that could be placed under each of the six categories. To get you started, look at the following as *Subject Matter* suggestions:

Card one: a 250-page nineteenth-century British novel, required by the school district curriculum

Card two: ten modern American poems in the anthology

Card three: a three-page persuasive essay written to the school principal on a subject the class has selected

Card four: the 500-year history of the English language presented by the teacher who studied—and loved—history of the language in college

As before, write each variable in each category on a separate index card; provide at least three or four variables in each of the five remaining categories: **methodology**, **setting**, **time**, **teacher**, and **students**. Repeat the procedure of choosing six cards, spending time to consider what has been "dealt" you and writing on what you have and what you speculate about learning or classroom outcomes.

While certainly this game is about as hypothetical as it gets—you are making a number of assumptions about students and schools that are largely speculative and, in some cases, based on not much experience or knowledge—it does give you a chance to think about variables and issues of options and change within the classroom.

Deciding that an instructional pattern just "doesn't work" is rarely the case. You must try to get an eye for the variables; while the class may not have "worked," there may be more reasons or different reasons than you might automatically assume.

····················· **FOR YOUR JOURNAL** ·····················

Write a response to the teaching game. What did you learn from it? What were your assumptions and predictions?

Creating Activities

There are excellent books available on planning and a number of books on writing objectives. There are also, especially from the National Council of Teachers of English (NCTE), hundreds of journals, books, and newsletters with teaching activities (the series Notes Plus may be of especial interest). While these resources and the good ideas of your fellow and sister teachers will often help you with your planning (and, indeed, your school and school district may ask you to follow a certain outline for all your plans), you need to know how to do it yourself. In general, then, you need to plan a class with the following headings in mind:

- **Objectives:** What are you trying to achieve in this class? What do you hope students will learn? What seems important to highlight about this strategy or skill or piece of literature? What relevant standards are you addressing?
- **Method:** How are you going to meet these objectives? What activities will you use? Will the students write? discuss? work in small groups? read and then respond? act something out?
- **Materials:** What will you need? cards? books? films? overhead? VCR? computers? art materials? props?

- **Outline:** What will be the general procedure for the class? what comes first? second? What is the timing for each section?
- **Evaluation:** How will you judge if students have learned? understood? appreciated? If you give a test, what will be on it? If students write, what will be the content and focus? How long will it be? What kind of rubric will you use to grade it? If students discuss or work in small groups, how can their contributions be evaluated? by frequency? importance? originality?

You also need to remember three principles of creating activities: simplicity, relevance, and specificity.

Simplicity   A simple teaching idea is not a simpleminded one but one that has a major thrust and focus. Teaching ideas that rely on multiple, complex components—most of which, necessarily, would be interconnected—can fall apart due to their own elaborate nature. Both teachers and students can get hopelessly confused if a teaching activity has too many parts, too many concepts, too many grading rubrics, too many components. Keeping an idea and its attendant activities simple—and thus central—makes the idea more successful in almost any setting. Using *Their Eyes Were Watching God* as an example, you would want your students to do something that is fairly small scale. Asking students to research statistics on African American families in the novel's era, for example, or bringing in a local social worker to discuss spousal abuse is probably more complicated than necessary and, further, deflects attention away from the novel. When designing activities you need to keep the focus direct and simple.

Relevance   Relevance is a highly complex topic and, in this context, does not relate to the contemporary or applicable nature of an activity. Relevance is a characteristic that means that the activity itself is directly tied to the text or the concept itself. While this caution may seem self-evident, it is often lost when we try to make an otherwise interesting activity fit a piece of literature or when we fixate on a subordinate aspect of the literature and use it as a major springboard for discussion or research. For example, it may seem outrageous, but some beginning teachers might think that any assignment would be adaptable to *Their Eyes Were Watching God*. Having students research the economy or geography or even weather patterns and prevalence of hurricanes in Florida in the early twentieth century versus today would not, for instance, be that significant to the study of the novel. Nor, in addition, would an exploration of how this remarkable book was "rediscovered" and brought back into print. Activities need to be directly related to the novel and its study.

Specificity   If you want students to write, tell them the general direction and the length. Similarly, if they are to do an art project based on the novel, list the components needed. While too many specific directions can be stultifying, giving students no directions ("write about what the novel meant to you"; "draw a picture based on *Their Eyes Were Watching God*") is unfair. Such vagueness will also, as you can imagine, lead you into difficulty when you have to evaluate and grade such assignments. Further, specificity in assignments will help you clarify what you want from students and also make you consider how long students need to complete the activities successfully. Remember that when we ask students to attempt new or unfamiliar activities, they can often appear reluctant, possibly even uncooperative. What many of us forget is the fear that almost all students have of trying something new—and failing. While part of our job as teachers is to extend student skill, to nudge them into new territory, we must be willing to give students clear explanations and, when appropriate, specific models of what we want.

.... **FOR YOUR JOURNAL** ....

Imagine you are teaching the controversial short story "The Lottery" by Shirley Jackson. Sketch out an outline plan for teaching to your students in a single fifty-minute class period. Use the headings (Objectives, Method, Materials, Outline, and Evaluation) and the concepts of simplicity, relevance, and specificity. Share your ideas with a friend. What is similar? different? What do you think you could add or delete?

"Central School": From Poem to Plan to Class

A few years ago, I read a poem in a regional literary magazine. I really liked its power and I think it speaks to something that is very familiar to almost everyone. I've been using it in the classroom ever since.

Central School

From the bus garage beside the river, where motors
idle like the middle of stories, the road
labors uphill to street signs, the faces growing.

You stand in headlights, climb into the certainty
of acceleration, stagger between the lines of jokes.
You want a small place at the end of a seat,
hoping not to be noticed, not to weep when your shoe
flies from shout to shout and against a window.

Leaving the houses to speed along fence, the road
brakes into daily screams at the steep bank, the turn
above the invisible pasture. You name
each day by the wrong they do, reciting
days all day till counting loses count. One year

the shoe they hand is small. They hand it to you.
　　　　　　　　　　　　　　　　　　—Jay S. Paul

For me, there are a number of positive aspects to "Central School" that make it both teachable and worthwhile. The poem deals with a relatively universal situation (most students will quickly get the scene; many have lived it); it is plain in much of its poetic language (if not its imagery—we'll come back to that). Its conclusion is absolutely open-ended (providing a perfect invitation for discussion and writing), and, finally, the poem carries an unexpected punch, a punch that is squarely located in its consideration of what can truly be described as an ethical dilemma.

Despite these positive points, there are also problem areas in "Central School" that affect the approach to teaching it. For instance, many students will be puzzled by some of the language of the poem (How can a road "labor uphill"? Why are the faces "growing"? What is "leaving the houses to speed along fence"? How can a road "brake into daily screams"? What's this "invisible pasture"?). The mystery behind many of these phrases, however, will be resolved when students realize that in order to establish the scene in stanza two, a person has to wait for the bus, see and hear it approaching, board the bus, and then, on the bus, travel to the title destination, Central School.

As a teacher, though, for me the occasionally puzzling phrases are minor problems. What I really want to get at is the last half of the last line (now what? why?) and the resonance of the title (beyond the name of the destination, what layers of meaning can reside in *central school*?).

If this represents my teacher thinking on "Central School," the following is my lesson plan for what I might do with older middle school or any age senior high school students (I think the poem works well with both age groups). I would want to teach this poem during a block class of 90 minutes, using discussion and writing. And, because of this poem's surprise ending, I would want to pace students through the reading so that there is less chance to "rush" the poem and to come to closure too quickly.

Though at this stage in my life my actual plan might not be as specifically written out as what follows (like many teachers with some experience I tend to plan using shorthand descriptions), this is what, for an outside reader, I would present as my plan:

Objectives
- The students will appreciate "Central School" by predicting its content and outcome.
- The students will explore the imagery in the poem.
- The students will consider the relation of the incident of the poem to their own lives and to other pieces of literature they have read.
- The students will deepen their understanding of "Central School" by crafting a creative extension to the ending of the poem and defending their choices.
- The students will extend their comprehension by exploring the levels of meaning of the poem's title.

Method
- Large-group discussion
- Individual writing
- Sharing of writing in pairs
- Sharing of writing in small groups

Materials
- Blackboard and chalk/whiteboard and pens
- Student journal and pen

- Overhead projector
- Acetate copy of "Central School" for projection
- Duplicated paper copies of "Central School" for each student

Outline   I tell students that we will be looking at a single poem today, talking and writing. They first need to get out their journals and a pen. They will receive their own copy of the poem later but, for the time being, they will see the poem only on the overhead projector.

I place an acetate copy of "Central School" on the overhead, blocking out with a piece of paper all of the poem except for the title, "Central School." I ask students to consider this title and to speculate silently for a moment as to what they suppose this poem will contain. We wait about ten seconds.

I then ask students to share what they think the poem "Central School" will be about. Students, in response, offer phrase or single word suggestions; I, without comment or evaluation, write all student ideas on the board.

Time: 5–7 minutes

After thanking students for their suggestions, I then move the paper down the acetate to reveal the poem's first stanza. I read the title and the stanza. I pause about five seconds (silence, even ever so brief, is important here; if there is too much teacher talk, students don't have time to absorb what they have just heard). I then ask students to write in their journals silently for three minutes as to what in the world they think is going on. I ask them to speculate on answers even if they are not particularly clear at this stage. If they wish, students can also write for three minutes on how this stanza does or does not appear to relate to the poem's title. Students and I write.

Time: 5–7 minutes

I call time. Without preface or apology (and this should be true of all oral sharing by all readers), I read my entry aloud. I then ask students to turn to someone near them, a pair partner, and share their response aloud, without comment. Then they let the other person read their response aloud. Students take turns reading to each other.

Time: 5 minutes

I now move the paper down the acetate to reveal the second stanza and then read the entire poem again, from title through the end of the second stanza (there is method to this madness; the repetition helps students focus on the poem as otherwise there is a tendency to fragmentation). At the end of the reading, I give directions, as before, to write silently for three minutes, this time on what they think is happening in the poem so far.

Time: 5–7 minutes

I call time. Again, I read my entry and ask students to take turns reading theirs aloud to their pair partner. Students take turns reading to each other.

Time: 5 minutes

I now move the paper down the acetate to reveal all but the last sentence of the last stanza (this can be tricky, but it is essential). I tell students that what they are seeing is all but one remaining five-word sentence of "Central School." Again, I read the entire poem from title through the end of the last stanza. I ask students to write for three minutes not on what is happening (at this point, it should be generally clear) but on what they think the last sentence will reveal. How will this poem end? Students and I write.

Time: 5–7 minutes

There is, at this juncture, no sharing by myself or between students. I remove the paper from the acetate copy of the poem so that all is now visible, and I read all of "Central School" aloud (again, the repetition is powerful). I pause—many students find the end of "Central School" somewhat of a surprise. I tell students we will talk in a minute—sometimes students want to talk immediately—and ask them to consider the whole poem and what *they* would do in the situation.

I hand out the paper copies of "Central School," one for each student, and ask them to look over the poem and, either on the sheet they have or on a separate sheet of paper, to write a four-line stanza that would pick up from the end of the original poem and finish it.

Time: 7–10 minutes

Now it is time for students to share in the large group. I invite students who wish to share their stanza by putting them up on the board (you may need to limit numbers here; if you have a class of 20 or more, it is unlikely that all students will be able to share). When students have placed these in view, each student, in turn, reads his or her creation aloud: thus we hear and have a visual record of some of the new endings. We read and listen without comment.

Time: 10 minutes

As a large group, using the student poetry on the board as a reminder, we then discuss why people chose what they chose as an ending. There will be, in any given class, a real range of endings, and we compare and contrast what people decided to do and why. As appropriate, we discuss the topic of bullies and their victims—is any of this familiar to any of you from your school experience?—and we mention, as appropriate, similar pieces of literature that feature such (e.g., Robert Cormier's *The Chocolate War*, Jerry Spinelli's *Wringer*, William Golding's *Lord of the Flies*, and the short story "Priscilla and the Wimps" by Richard Peck are all possible examples).

We return to the list on the board of our assumptions about the poem and discuss how we first had them and how close—or not close—those assumptions were. We consider how the two timed writings after "Central School" 's first and second stanzas were, again, close or not close to the original, revealed poem. We write for three minutes and then share in the large group.

Time: 10 minutes

Now is the time to make sure students understand most of the imagery; asking students if everything that happened in the poem, in particular in the first and third stanzas, is clear, may elicit student comments and questions. It is my belief, however, that few students will find their understanding impaired by difficulties with image and language in the two stanzas.

Time: 10 minutes

Extension possibilities for this poem are numerous: students could write another poem based on "Central School" (possibly from the perspective not of the bullied child but of the bus driver or one of the tormentors); they could do a prose description of a similar incident that they or friends have experienced.

Evaluation   Students receive credit for class participation; students receive a daily grade for the journal entries, including the four-line addition that bears relationship to the poem.

This lesson plan is not particularly original or startling; what it does do, however, is pace students though the poem so that they can take time with it. This kind of time is necessary for this poem, I think, as otherwise its power, its surprise get lost. Also, this kind of lesson plan allows students to speculate and make their own assumptions. Finally, it invites them to consider what indeed will happen beyond the last line of "Central School," and that kind of resolution will be very individual for each student in the class.

The House on Mango Street:
From Chapter to Plan to Class

Sandra Cisneros' *The House on Mango Street* is an accessible novel that is widely used in many schools across the country. It is a first-person memoir of a young girl, Esperanza Cordero, who tells of her neighborhood, parents, friends, school, and, most importantly, her wishes and dreams. The format of *Mango Street* lends itself to classroom use as most of the almost three dozen chapters—which could also be accurately termed *vignettes*— are exceptionally short and also feature helpful and, at times, evocative titles. Written in a deceptively simple style, *Mango Street* combines prose craft and emotion. Here, in its entirety, is the three-paragraph chapter entitled "Those Who Don't":

Those Who Don't

Those who don't know any better come into our neighborhood scared. They think we're dangerous. They think we will attack them with shiny knives. They are stupid people who are lost and got here by mistake.

But we aren't afraid. We know the guy with the crooked eye is Davey the Baby's brother, and the tall one next to him in the straw brim, that's Rosa's Eddie V., and the big one that looks like a dumb grown man, he's Fat Boy, though he's not fat anymore nor a boy.

All brown all around, we are safe. But watch us drive into a neighborhood of another color and our knees go shakity-shake and our car windows get rolled up tight and our eyes look straight. Yeah. This is how it goes and goes.

There are many useful things that we could do with our students using this chapter. Certainly its subject matter, prejudice and the disparity between appearance and reality, is immediately obvious. Consideration of this topic could spark a number of discussions and responses as students not only look at what Cisneros has written (and her character, Esperanza, has articulated) but also make links to their own perceptions and experiences with such prejudice and assumptions. Students may also be able to share other pieces of literature they have read that address similar concerns.

Additionally, there is also the craft of the prose in "Those Who Don't." Having students look at the language that, even in this very short piece is both simple and highly effective, could be interesting. Students could note the memorable rhyme (*all brown all around*), the distinctive adverb *shakity-shake*, the two sentences that start with the conjunction *but*, and the one-word sentence *Yeah* and how it functions.

But I would also make a case that "Those Who Don't" could be used effectively to teach logic and organizational structure. What I would like students to do is consider how the speaker sets out her thesis, gives relevant examples, and then switches the concentration from the others, "those who don't," to herself and what she and her neighbors and friends do. This kind of structural analysis, though it is taking place in the context of a fiction piece, is also relevant to nonfiction, in particular persuasive essays. I would want to spend about 30 to 40 minutes of a class doing this, 30 minutes that include reading, discussion, filling in a template, and beginning a similar persuasive essay. How would I try to achieve this? Here's what I would plan.

Objectives

- The students will appreciate "Those Who Don't" by discussing its theme.
- The students will consider the relation of what the chapter describes to their own lives and to other pieces of literature they have read.
- The students will explore the prose craft in the chapter, deepening their understanding of the organizational and argumentative structure of "Those Who Don't" by first sketching the sequence of the major points and using that sketch to write a similar piece, a short persuasive essay.

Method

- Large-group discussion
- Pair work
- Individual writing
- Large-group sharing

Materials

- Blackboard and chalk/whiteboard and pens
- Copies of *The House on Mango Street*
- Copies of template sheet for students

Outline   First, I would tell students that we're going to read a chapter from *Mango Street*, and I would write the chapter title, "Those Who Don't," on the board. I would ask students what they predict this chapter might be about, and I would record three or four answers on the board. We would then take out our copies of *Mango Street*, turn to "Those Who Don't," and I would ask for a student volunteer to read the chapter aloud.

   Time: 5 minutes

   After hearing the chapter read aloud and following it in our books, I would ask the class what they now thought this chapter was about, what were its themes. I am seriously doubting many students would miss the point of "Those Who Don't," and as we discuss the fears of those who are in an unfamiliar neighborhood and of what they might be afraid, we would move to one of the speaker's major points, that there is little indeed to fear. How do we know this? Students would likely point to the second paragraph of "Those Who Don't" and cite the human beings the speaker describes behind the possibly scary exteriors.

   Time: 5–7 minutes

   At this point, many students would be through with "Those Who Don't" (*been there, done that, got it*). It is important, though, to continue on. Cisneros, in fact, complicates the entire issue in her third paragraph, when Esperanza turns the tables. What does Esperanza tell us in paragraph three? How is this important? How does it relate to her previous contention that while "stupid people" who wander into *her* neighborhood have unreasonable fears, when she and her friends go into *other* neighborhoods, their fears are real? So who is right and who is wrong? Are Esperanza and her friends also "stupid"?

Time: 5 minutes

At this juncture, students may not have any real answer to the questions posed about whose perceptions are correct, and for this lesson it is not essentially important. What is important is to move students into how Cisneros makes her persuasive argument, an argument that is three points in three linked paragraphs, using the signal word *but* to indicate shifts in concept.

To make this clear, I would hand out this template and ask students, in pairs, to fill in the blanks. In all cases, they are to use the language of "Those Who Don't," not a paraphrase of what Cisneros writes.

Looking at the Logic and Organization of "Those Who Don't"

Paragraph #1

Point #1_____

Examples illustrating Point #1   _____

_____

_____

Paragraph #2

Point #2_____

Examples illustrating Point #2   _____

_____

_____

What word is used to signal new point? _____

Paragraph #3

Point #3_____

Examples illustrating Point #3   _____

_____

_____

What word is used to signal new point? _____

Conclusion_____

Time: 10 minutes

I would now ask students to write their own "Those Who Don't" using the previous structure, a short persuasive essay of three paragraphs with three different points, examples illustrating each of the three points, and some sort of signal word between paragraphs two and three and to indicate a shift (or extension) in logic. Students would write alone, and can start using Cisneros' words: Those who don't know any better _____.

After working alone, students can then share their drafts in the large group.

Time: 10–15 minutes

Evaluation   Students would receive credit for turning in their completed template (with both names on the sheet) and for their final three-paragraph "Those Who Don't." Using a 100-point scale for this activity, students could receive 40 points for the completed template and 60 points (20 points a paragraph, modeled after the template) for the short persuasive essay.

A Brief Word on Creating Tests and Test Items

While in your first few years of teaching you may rely heavily on tests and test items that are provided in the teacher's edition, suggested by the textbook publishing company, found on a website, or even given to you by other teachers, you will, as you become more sure of yourself, start to alter those tests and test items and, eventually, make up your own tests. Creating your own tests can be very positive because when you craft your own tests, the items will more accurately reflect what was actually taught or discussed in a given class. Whether, however, you are revising tests and test items or creating your own from scratch, you want to remember a few points, some of which may seem so obvious they are simpleminded, but some of which are often overlooked by beginning teachers. If you follow these points, you will find that grading your tests will be simplified and that student concerns—or even objections—will be minimized.

When you are **creating a test or test items,** remember to:

- test what you have taught
- test more than recall and memorization
- make sure all test items total your target figure (100 is standard but not mandatory)
- indicate on the test for each section the number of points the question or questions are worth
- consider providing extra credit items (but be sure not to let extra credit become a large percentage of the final test grade)
- write clear, unambiguous directions for all test questions and test sections
- leave sufficient space on the test for essay and short answer items if the students are to write on the test itself
- put a blank line on the first page of the test for the student's name
- make sure the blanks for multiple choice, matching, and so on are lined up so that you can easily grade multiple tests at one time
- proofread your test carefully!

Before the test:

- review with students the material that will be tested
- give students fair warning about when the test will be given

During the test itself:

- allow sufficient class time for the test to be completed
- make sure students know your procedures regarding taking tests (including talking to other students, asking you questions during the test, having materials on their desk, turning the test in, what to do if they finish the test early, etc.)
- advise students during the test as to when time will be up

When you **grade** the test:

- discount a test item if a significant number of students fail to answer it correctly
- check your arithmetic so that your final grade is accurate

When you **return** the test to your students:

- take class time to go over the questions with your students so that they understand what items they missed or what they did correctly
- be willing to meet with and talk to students one-on-one if there are questions regarding your grading

Finally, if most of your students do not do well on your test:

- retest if necessary
- learn from your own tests and continue to refine them

And, if you are creating your own test items, remember:

- **true/false** items are not truly discriminatory unless students are asked to explain their choices
- **multiple choice** and **matching items** need to have sufficient options to be challenging (multiple choice needs to have more than three options; matching should not feature equal numbers of concepts)
- **fill in the blank** items must be phrased very carefully OR you must be prepared to accept multiple answers OR the fill in the blank must mimic a matching item format
- **short answer** items need to be specifically phrased so that students know what you are asking
- **essay questions** must be precisely phrased, and, as noted, sufficient time must be given to answer them.

The Place of Standards in Your Planning

At some point in your early career, you should make yourself familiar with your state and or/school district standards for English language arts. Most states use skills-based standards, organized by grade level, and while nothing is ever perfect, most states' English language arts standards are usually not hard to accommodate in a lesson plan or activity. In your school, you may well be asked to indicate specifically which standards you are addressing in your lesson plans and in your classes and, as across the nation, your state's standards will also surface eventually on the state test. This kind of linked consistency may well help you and your students, and for most of us, regardless of locality, English language arts standards are generally reasonable.

But where to start? You might think of taking some time to assess your state or local standards from the perspective of a single grade level. If so, think about the following:

I. Choose **one grade level** in secondary English Language Arts (grades 6 through 12) and download or photocopy your state or school district standards for that **one grade level**. These standards are, essentially, your instructional map for the year.

II. Consider each of the standards (there are usually a manageable number for most grade levels) and answer, **for each, four questions:**

1. To the best of your understanding, to what extent is this skill **appropriate or inappropriate** for this grade level?

2. To the best of your understanding, to what extent is this skill **important or unimportant** in the broad context of mastery of English language arts?

3. If you had to **teach** this standard to your students, **what activity and/or content** would be appropriate to help students master this standard?

4. If you had to **test** mastery of this standard with your students, what kind of **test item or mastery demonstration** would you use with your students?

While two of these questions are theoretical (numbers 1 and 2), two are very practical. How to teach a specific skill using an activity or reading and how to test that skill is to the heart of the matter. Taking a bit of time to review your district and/or state standards and to assess them may save you some panic as you enter the whirlwind of the school year and plan your teaching.

Let's see how this might play out with two state standards (from my state Virginia) from two different grade levels. For instance, one of the oral communication standards for tenth grade directs that:

Oral Communication Standard 10.2 (Virginia)

The student will critique oral reports of small group learning activities.

Evaluate role in the group

Evaluate the effectiveness of group processes

What can we say about this standard 10.2?

First, this standard is indeed **appropriate** for this grade level as it reinforces the importance of group and pair work, a staple in the English classroom and an activity familiar to most students—if not always effective. The standard is also **important**; students will work in groups for most of their academic careers, and being able to assess individual roles and critique group processes are crucial to the success and smooth functioning of the group strategy. **Teaching** this standard would involve an actual group **activity**—which could be used with any language arts **content**—and the teacher would need to review with students group roles and processes and develop and use an assessment inventory or check sheet regarding roles and ultimate effectiveness. Having students take specific roles—such as recorder, reporter, questioner, such as used in literature circles—might more clearly delineate the issue of what a student can or should do in a group, and having all students complete a check sheet or inventory will help them focus on the issue of group processes and their effectiveness. **Testing** in this case is probably not appropriate, but a **demonstration of mastery**—teacher and/or class assessment of students' ability to critique oral reports of small-group learning activities—can be done with simple evaluation instruments.

Let's move up a grade level to juniors. Standard 11.5 in Virginia addresses literature:

Literature Standard 11.5 (Virginia)

The student will read and critique a variety of poetry.

> Analyze poetic elements of classic poems
>
> Identify poetic elements and techniques that are most appealing and make poetry enjoyable
>
> Compare and contrast the works of contemporary and past American poets

Poetry study is **appropriate** for all students in English language arts, and American poetry is taught frequently throughout the curriculum. Obviously, it is extremely **important** to have older students not just read but critique poems. On the other hand, poetry, even in the upper grades, should be viewed not just in terms of analysis but also in terms of enjoyment. Finally, it is **important** for mature students to compare and contrast poems and to consider the difference between classic and contemporary literature; this skill will be important for them in future English study.

Teaching this standard would not be difficult. Using the **content** of virtually any American poem or pair of poems, teachers can have students engaged in a number of **activities**. Students could identify metaphor within the poems, discuss to what extent its use is effective, and if the poem is paired with a classic poem, compare and contrast the differences in metaphor use (this is always fun as contemporary poetry is far more stripped down than most of its early twentieth- and nineteenth-century cousins). **Testing** this standard could include **identification** or **matching** or even **definition** of metaphor. Students, presented with two poems, could compare and contrast the metaphor in both. A **demonstration of mastery** could be shown through successful individual work, group work, an all-class discussion, a brief paper, or even a journal entry on the topic.

Standards will be part of your planning as you begin your life in the classroom and they will be far more helpful to you and easier to negotiate than you first might have imagined.

·············· FOR YOUR JOURNAL ··············

Select a grade level and look at the English language arts standards for your state. Consider the four questions discussed, especially the one on activity/content and test items or mastery demonstration. How difficult was it to come up with ideas? To what extent were you able to imagine multiple activities and mastery assessments for a single standard? Share your ideas with a friend. What is similar? different?

A Final Caution About Planning

Despite all the exhortations about the importance of planning and how it will help you in your teaching, remember that plans can—and should —be changed depending on context. Loving the plan, following the script regardless of what is actually happening in your classroom will not ensure learning. Make your plans, but also don't forget that you will need to be flexible. Brian Durrett found this out in student teaching, and, after a conversation with his cooperating teacher, he realized at the end of one week:

> It hit me like a ton of bricks while I was driving home Friday afternoon. My cooperating teacher had been telling me over and over that I should try straying from my lesson plan or improvising a little when I felt that things were not going well. I listened to what she said but I was not hearing her. It finally sunk in when I was reflecting on what had happened that day. When things began falling part in my classes, I would tend to barge on and get through what I had planned. I did this even though I had become completed frustrated with the students for not paying attention and following my instructions. I never really asked myself how I could make this any better. I would keep driving my point home because I had the plan written down, people told me that my plans were well thought out so I assumed that they would work. For some reason, I never considered all of the elements that could thwart a lesson plan. I just knew what I had planned and that was what I was going to do in the classroom . . . the best laid plans will not always work. The students are dynamic. Some days they are very receptive and are eager to tackle what I throw out to them. Other days, even the coolest lesson goes over like a lead balloon because it is warm and sunny outside or there is a tension that causes the students with the shorter fuses to explode at the smallest thing. Being able to read the students and doing what they can handle makes me happier because I am not doing battle throughout the class. It makes the students happy because I'm not trying their patience and pushing them beyond their limit.

Planning for your teaching may at first seem hard to do, and knowing when to deviate from the plan may, at first, be even harder. Certainly your early life in the classroom will have a different rhythm and a different reality than what you may remember experiencing as a student. The classroom will, though, also reveal itself to you as a very intense and wonderful place where plans are made but also unpredictable and exciting things occur, new insights, significant conversations, real learning, real connections. It may be a little moment, but it happens to all teachers. Beginning teacher Beverly Garner describes it well:

> There have been days when I've had second thoughts, and days when I've felt exhilarated. Right now, I'm feeling horrible with a virus and an accompanying secondary infection, so I'm a bit down. What bolsters me, though, are those FACES, when they're LISTENING, and something is CLICKING between them and me—those times when they're laughing, or arguing even, let me know there's something going on, and it's a great feeling.

Some afternoon soon you too will find yourself standing at the end of a full and good teaching day—while you may be doubtful at this point, you will indeed have a number of these. You will look around your room and think of what you planned and what you and your students then said and did in class. You will not think of the difficult times when you felt you were facing the unknown. Some afternoon it will strike you, at least on that day, that teaching is actually a rather wonderful way to spend your life.

References

Atwell, Nancie. "Everyone Sits at a Big Desk: Discovering Topics for Writing." *English Journal* 74 (September 1985): 35–39.

———. *In the Middle: New Understandings About Writing, Reading, and Learning.* 2d ed. Portsmouth, NH: Boynton/Cook, 1998.

Bullough, Robert V. Jr. *First Year Teacher: A Case Study.* New York: Teachers College Press, 1989.

Christenbury, Leila. "A Paradigm for Analyzing Components of the Teaching Act." *English Education* 11 (May 1980): 233–39.

Cisneros, Sandra. *The House on Mango Street.* New York: Vintage, 1984.

Codell, Esmé Raji. *Educating Esmé: A Diary of a Teacher's First Year.* Chapel Hill, NC: Algonquin Books, 1999.

Cormier, Robert. *The Chocolate War.* New York: Dell, 1974.

Freire, Paulo. *Pedagogy of the Oppressed.* New York: Continuum, 1981.

Gold, Elizabeth. *Brief Intervals of Horrible Sanity: One Season in a Progressive School.* New York: Penguin, 2003.

Golding, William. *Lord of the Flies.* New York: Coward-McCann, 1962.

Grossman, Pamela L. *The Making of a Teacher: Teacher Knowledge and Teacher Education.* New York: Teachers College Press, 1990.

Hurston, Zora Neale. *Their Eyes Were Watching God.* New York: Harper and Row, [1937] 1990.

Jackson, Shirley. *The Lottery: And Other Stories.* New York: Farrar, Straus & Giroux, [1949] 1982.

Joyce, Bruce, and Marsha Weil. *Models of Teaching.* 5th ed. Boston: Allyn & Bacon, 1996.

Labaree, David F. *The Trouble with Ed Schools.* New Haven, CT: Yale University Press, 2004.

Macrorie, Ken. *Twenty Teachers.* New York: Oxford University Press, 1984.

Mann, Thomas. *The Magic Mountain.* New York: Knopf, 1927.

NCTE. *Notes Plus.* Urbana, IL: NCTE, 1990 and years following.

Palonsky, Stuart B. *900 Shows a Year.* New York: Random House, 1986.

Paul, Jay S. "Central School." *Artemis XVI.* Roanoke, VA: Artemis Artists/Writers, 1993.

Peck, Richard. "Priscilla and the Wimps." In *Sixteen: Short Stories by Outstanding Writers for Young Adults.* Edited by Donald R. Gallo. New York: Dell, 1984.

Spinelli, Jerry. *Wringer.* New York: HarperCollins, 1997.

Wellington, Bud. "The Promise of Reflective Practice." *Educational Leadership* 48 (March 1991): 4–5.

White, E. B. *Stuart Little.* New York: Harper Trophy, 1974.

4

Those Whom We Teach

We need to hear adolescents, and not when we are shouting at them or when they are shouting at us. They need to be heard when sitting face to face with someone who is interested in them as individuals. . . . The point is not simply that good kids can be bad, or that the school system needs fixing, but rather that labels so easily planted on teens obscure their more interesting reality. In fact, one of the most powerful themes exposed through the simple act of taking the time really to know . . . kids is that they hold enormous potential.

—**Patricia Hersch,** ***A Tribe Apart: A Journey into the Heart of American Adolescence***

Patricia Hersch is not a teacher. She is a journalist who spent three years observing eight young people in school and out and talking with them about their lives, their beliefs, and their dreams. One of her major conclusions in *A Tribe Apart: A Journey into the Heart of American Adolescence* is that young people need more—not fewer—adults in their lives and that, as you might have suspected, for us to have any effect on them, young people need to have a positive relationship with us, adults and teachers:

> It is a popular notion that adolescents career out of control, are hypnotized by peer pressure or manipulated by demons for six years or so, and then if they don't get messed up or hurt or killed, they become sensible adults. That's ridiculous. The youngsters I have spoken to are trying the best they can in the present world to do what is right for them. . . . An eighth grader explains: "We're kind of like adults. We've learned how to run our own lives, think for ourselves, make decisions for ourselves." . . . The turbulence of adolescence today comes not so much from rebellion as from the loss of communication between adults and kids, and from the lack of realistic, honest understanding of what the kids' world really looks like. The bottom line: we can lecture kids to our heart's content but if they don't care what we think, or there is no relationship between us that matters to them, or they think we are ignorant of the reality of their lives, they will not listen. (365)

And if they will not listen, they also will not learn. For sure, students are our profound partners in the classroom, and our willingness to understand them and our sense of connection with them constitutes a large part of teaching success. I knew this early in my teaching, but I got a chance recently to relearn it.

I returned to teach high school after many years at a university teaching other people how to teach, and I found, not surprisingly, that my students in English 11 were very different from those students who I taught years ago. I knew that an ability to adjust and change is important: getting into an instructional rhythm with these students, trying to take their perspective about assignments and grades, understanding their motivations to work—or not to work—were crucial to my teaching success. And, when I had difficulty connecting with some of those students in my high school class, I understood clearly how serious that problem might be. Ignoring or minimizing students, teaching around them or in spite of them, are just not options for us. If we are to be conscientious and successful teachers, engaged students are at the heart of our work.

So who are these young people you will teach and with whom you need to connect? Generalities are misleading—and young people as a group despise being labeled and classified—but some observations are in order. And do remember that even though you may right now be close in age to those you teach, their experience at this moment in school is not yours, and your past experience will soon not be up-to-date. Like most adults, you will rapidly—inescapably—have to be re-educated by your students regarding the here and now, what is going on in their lives, and what is important to them.

Some factual information may help capture a snapshot of students today. A recent large-scale survey of young people in the Washington, DC, area—a very urban/suburban and multicultural, multiracial, and multilanguage area—describes teenagers in late 2005:

> They're a generation in a hurry, hurling headlong to adulthood but not yet shed of youthful innocence or naiveté. They're mixed up—and the girls in particular are stressed out. They view the future through cracked rose-colored glasses, anxious about the direction of the country and the world. Most predict another terrorist attack as big or bigger than September 11 sometime in their lives. One in four expects a nuclear war . . . at the same time [they] are brimming with youthful optimism and self-confidence about the world they will inherit. . . . Sometimes their confidence borders on delusional: The vast majority say it's likely they will be rich. Sometimes it is poignant: Most are convinced they will be married to the same person till death do them part. But more often their expectations are sensibly realistic: Most expect that just about everything, from a new house to a college education, will cost more when they are their parents' age. (Morin et al., 14)

What do teenagers in this survey cite as fears? The survey lists: pollution, AIDS, drug abuse, immorality, divorce, war, the economy. What do teenagers in this survey value? By percentage and topic, the researchers found:

75%   being successful in a career
65%   having a family of your own
65%   having lots of close friends
64%   making a difference in the world
62%   having enough free time to do things you want

And there are, understandably, gaps by race and gender. In general, African American teens feel "the country's best years are in the past" while only a fraction of white teens agree. Boys view the future positively; a majority of girls are not as optimistic and also think about a recurring terrorist attack. Girls in this survey feel far more stress than boys, especially regarding school issues; a majority of black teens believe they will be famous someday, while whites are not as confident. Most of the teens surveyed would consider interracial marriage, and a significant number had dated or were dating someone of another race. Finally, the importance of religion in everyday life was a positive factor for over one-third of all teens surveyed.

How exposed are these teens to the harsh realities of life? It may be indicative of the metropolitan nature of Washington, DC, and not all teens across the country may respond in the same manner, but in this survey, almost half the teens surveyed know someone who is in a gang, and a fifth have had a friend who was killed or injured by gun violence and personally have been a victim of crime or violence. Interestingly, the results of a separate national survey were not very different: "one of the biggest surprises of the [two] surveys was how closely the attitudes of [Washington, DC] area teens mirror the view of high school-age teenagers across the country" (17).

················ **FOR YOUR JOURNAL** ················

Who teenagers are at any given moment and in any given community is a moveable target. To what extent do you agree with the statistics and observations just cited? How different are your beliefs, fears, and concerns? Are they different from the teenagers in your community? Finally, are these observations just generally helpful, or are there any statistics and facts to which teachers in particular need to pay particular attention?

No One Ever Said It Was Going to Be Easy

Interacting with students is the heart of the teaching process: when that interaction is lively and relatively smooth, the joys of teaching come easily to mind. When, however, the interaction is strained, awkward, or even unpleasant, then teachers often wonder why they got into this in the first place. Teaching is, as you suspect, a terribly *intimate* business, and when we and our students are not in sync, the level of discomfort can be frighteningly high. While the days and weeks of teaching can go by in a very routine manner, there will be days when things go wrong between teachers and students and when the entire enterprise becomes remarkably difficult. It is, first, that students are in groups and identify in ways different from adults; it is also that some students don't identify very much at all.

If you have been a visitor in a teachers' lounge recently and no one particularly worried about your presence there, the remarks you overheard might have surprised you. In many teachers' lounges across this country, in countless school workrooms and offices, relatively sharp and unflattering remarks are made about students by teachers. Much of that talk is the release of tension by people who interact intensely and over sustained periods of time with large groups of young people. Thus, much of that talk means little. Some of it, though, can be cynical and cruel. The latter is not worth your sustained consideration and often comes from adults who are overwhelmed and very tired and disappointed by the entire enterprise of teaching. But where in the world does the former come from?

The cynical comments come from the difficulty of teaching as we define it in this country in the public school system: teaching people in same-age groups, teaching people in groups, and the political act itself of teaching people. The fact that these patterns can make teaching difficult is probably not very surprising to you, especially when you recall your own life as a student. It is naive to expect that your teaching career will not have some hard moments. Teaching students can be a tough business; it can have ugly times. Some of my former students—males and females—are in jail; some are dead. Some are hard to remember fondly.

The Tough Times of Teaching: Apathy and Violence

For all of the wonderful experiences I have had in the classroom and the countless satisfying and even exhilarating encounters with students, like many teachers, I have also had my share of rough moments.

Fighting student apathy is part of my history as a teacher: I have been unable to motivate every student in my classroom. Some, for a variety of reasons, have refused to engage, be involved, or attempt to do assignments. Some slipped in and out of my classroom more like ghosts than real people, only temporarily there, perched, just waiting to move on. Some were so quiet, so removed, I almost forgot they were on my roll book and, after some months of trying to get them involved, I turned my energies and efforts elsewhere.

Despite my attempts, my energy, and my enthusiasm, I have seen students turn away from an activity, a learning contract, a book. I have had students who have, without exaggeration, done virtually nothing in class for days at a stretch. I have asked students to sit up in class and not sleep, to open books that have remained resolutely shut, to bring a pen or pencil or paper to class, to get up and actually *sit* with their group. I have had students who made themselves so unobtrusive in class that very soon after our time together I could not begin to recall their names. This happened in my early teaching career, and when I recently returned to teach high school, it happened then, too.

I, like many teachers who have taught for some time, have also had more dramatic difficulties with students. I have been threatened physically, cursed, and had my car damaged. I have had my locked classroom broken into and test materials stolen. I have had bulletin boards I assembled and for which I bought or made the artwork defaced or vandalized. Some of this was directed at me personally; some of this was directed more generally.

I was hit "accidentally" in the act of shielding a slightly built student from the class bully; sadly for me, the larger student's fist went into my stomach but, thankfully, not into the other kid's face. While standing in the hall during a class change I was slammed into a door by a student I did not recognize and who was trying to get away from a pursuing assistant principal. On hall duty I was knocked out of the way while walking a confused and drug-dazed student to the school infirmary; his friends, observing the scene, feared any intervention and did not want a teacher involved. The student was taken away from me forcibly and spirited somewhere across the school campus.

When I was taking over a hospitalized colleague's study hall, I was warned that the group had been a problem in the past. Sure enough, the second day of my assignment I was backed up against the classroom door by a student who wanted to leave the room before the bell rang.

Cheerfully, I stood at the door, but the encounter changed character quickly; the game became one of seeing whether the student could frighten me by producing a lighter and threatening to set my long hair on fire. With his face inches from mine and his arm blocking my movement, the student, with a fascinated and repelled audience behind him, watched to see whether I would back down. I did not, would not; there seemed to be too much at stake. But I was scared. In this case, the fates were merciful: the lighter stubbornly refused to operate (did the student know this? was this part of the game?), the bell finally rang, and study hall ended.

The reasons for these events vary: some involve individual students and their responses not only to teachers but to situations; some reasons involve reactions to school as an institution and teachers as representatives of that institution. Many arise from students' response to situations not related to schools or teaching; students can "act out" against family or community problems and can do that acting out in school. And, today, it is not just students who can bring this anger to school: often parents, when dealing with administrators and teachers, are similarly hostile. While you may have many serene years in the classroom without anything such as the ones I've recounted, student apathy, physical and verbal assaults on teachers, and the occasional flare-up of anger or hostility are actually fairly commonplace in schools across the country. Vandalism is an issue for school systems, as is maintaining an atmosphere not only of relative civility but of some form of mutual intellectual engagement.

But why does this occur? Why in the world would such an atmosphere exist in school?

We need to look at how school is an alien place for many of our students and why the we/them dyad can be one of the most damaging of relationships. You, the beginning teacher, are *them*. Many students see themselves absolutely as *us*. For some students that will mean withdrawal, apathy; for others it will involve a more active and combative role. For both types of students, school is foreign territory and they come with their defenses up, committed to getting over, getting by, and ultimately, mercifully, getting out.

Two Researchers on Students:
William Glasser and Linda McNeil

There are two classic books you might want to know about, Linda McNeil's *Contradictions of Control* and William Glasser's *Control Theory in the Classroom*. Both researchers have studied schools and students and conclude that, in Glasser's words, the whole game needs to change. Glasser, a psychiatrist, sees school as a place where students do not feel part of the process:

> The problem is that at least half of all students are making little or no effort to learn, because they don't believe that school satisfies their needs. To make school harder—to increase the length of the school year or the school day, to assign more homework, to require more courses . . . is not going to reach those students. . . . We can't do anything *to* people, or really even *for* people, to get them to produce more. We have to change the school itself, so that students look at it and say, "In this school and with these teachers I can satisfy my needs, if I work hard." (656)

For McNeil, the enterprise has become seriously poisoned at the source—at what teachers actually present to students in the form of content. McNeil writes that teachers, in an effort to maintain a semblance of power or control in school, actually diminish what they teach— their content—and create "brief, 'right' answers, easily transmitted, easily answered, easily graded [in order to accommodate] to a school where their only power came from the class-room" (157). Glasser advises cooperative learning to counter this lack of control. For McNeil, however, Glasser's control theory has some insidious implications:

> Adults who visit high-school classrooms are often struck by the dullness of the lessons. Those who visit systematically note the overwhelming prevalence of boring content, dull presenta-tions and bored but patient students. . . . The dull presentations are not caused merely by poor teacher preparation or teacher burnout, but by deliberate, often articulated, decisions teachers have made to control the students by controlling the content. . . . Defensive, controlling teach-ing does more than make content boring; it transforms the subject content from "real world" knowledge into "school knowledge," an artificial set of facts and generalizations whose credi-bility lies no longer in its authenticity as a cultural selection but in its instrumental value in meeting the obligations teachers and students have within the institution of schooling. . . .
>
> As the course content is transformed into "school knowledge," there is little incentive for the student to become involved in that content. It is there to be mastered, traded for a grade and, as some students have said, deliberately forgotten afterward. (191)

At times I wonder if there aren't ways in school that we can literally set up situations where kids become—or are encouraged to become—stupid. When we insist that all students know—and repeat back to us—minute details, when we place emphasis on senseless tasks or minor aspects of assignments, when we ask questions that are not worth answering we set students up for compliant passivity. When the whole point of a school year is to pass a sin-gle high-stakes test, we narrow the curriculum and the student's sense of intellectual engage-ment. When we demand strict obedience to all behavioral regulations, when we, in essence, try to micromanage all student interaction, we can create classrooms where students become cowed, passive, and also profoundly resistant. Once we make it clear that students are to fit themselves into narrow boxes we can rarely expect that they will exercise much of the intel-lectual life: questioning, challenging, exploring. If, on the other hand, we decide and con-vey to our students that they do have minds and lives (desires, ideals) of their own, that in a way they are not so different from us, their teachers, then we can create vibrant classroom situations.

For McNeil, "the very relations within classroom[s] and within schools will have to be transformed" (215) for real knowledge and school knowledge to become one. And this leads us to one of our great concerns, the alienated student.

·············· **FOR YOUR JOURNAL** ··············

At this point in your career you have observed some high school or middle school English classes. Reread McNeil's comments about visiting high school classrooms and consider it in light of what you have recently seen. Do you agree with McNeil's characterization of many classes as models of "defensive, controlling teaching"? If so, what, in specific, did you see? If, on the other hand, this is not your experience and observation, what kind of positive, intellectually challenging teaching did you observe? What did the teacher do? How did the students respond?

The Alienated Student: Not Always Who You Think

Susan Beth Pfeffer, a writer of adolescent novels, has lightheartedly defined what she calls the "basic rules of teenage life." Some of them include: *My Family Is Awful*, *Anyplace Would Be Better Than Here*, and *It Is Inconceivable That I'm Going to Survive This Awful Moment*. Her most important rule, however, is: *I Am the One True Outsider*. Pfeffer notes: "No matter how popular teenagers might be, they always know that they and they alone are the one true outsider" (6).

Even though Pfeffer is being humorous, the issue is a serious one. Certainly it is a hallmark of many young people to feel like the outsider, the only one, the stranger. Adults have a tendency to smile at this feeling, knowing that, in some measure, it is rarely a perennial condition that persists into mature years. On the other hand, the power of feelings of alienation cannot be minimized by us as teachers in the classroom.

Years ago in a series of issues of *English Journal*, a number of teachers wrote about their experience in the classroom with what they termed "alienated" students. Daniel A. Lindley Jr. wrote "we know who they are, and we know what they do to us, the alienated ones, those students so far removed from our values, our beliefs, our whole way of life" (26). Lindley asked teachers to distinguish between the "possible" and the "impossible," and certainly we know that a teacher can control or influence only certain aspects of school and life that might contribute to a student feeling alienated. Certainly we cannot bring students home with us, give them money, trade places with their parents, get them off drugs, make them motivated, or even learn for them. But we can, within our classrooms, make contact with them as human beings and provide opportunities for them to succeed and participate.

What are the factors that make it likely students will not do well in school, and as a last resort, drop out? Most studies cite a familiar list of markers (these are taken from a National Center for Educational Statistics study of eighth and tenth graders from over fifteen years ago):

- living in a single parent family
- having a yearly family income less than $15,000
- being home alone more than three hours a day
- having parents with no high school diploma
- having a sibling who has dropped out
- having a limited English proficiency

In fact, in 2004, the National Center for Educational Statistics virtually replicated these findings and cited the following factors as indicators of achievement difficulty, especially in reading, if the student's family was characterized by:

- a household income below the poverty level
- a language other than English as the primary home language
- a mother with less than a high school diploma or with a GED degree
- a single parent household

Additionally, some of these findings are confirmed by the 2003 National Assessment of Educational Progress, NAEP, which found that the presence of books in the home and parents with an eighth-grade education were associated positively with higher reading scores on the NAEP assessment.

How are these findings important to us? Notice that family income is only one of the risk factors; notice also that most of the factors are not under the control of the school. On the other hand, students whose families exhibit these characteristics may well be in our classes in great number, and it is our responsibility to teach them and teach them well.

Characteristics of the alienated student

What kind of students will you be teaching who might have reason to feel alienated in school? You will be teaching people who are parents, who have their own babies at home. You will be teaching people who have parents who are in the midst of divorces or bankruptcies or emotional breakdowns. You will be teaching people who feel they live, despite material comfort, in emotional poverty. You will be teaching people who are finding identity in gangs, who are trying to see if sexual intimacy can lead to psychological intimacy, who are escaping with drugs or alcohol or even compulsive shopping. You will be teaching people who are repeatedly told that they have everything—and who feel that they have nothing. You will be teaching people who, at their age, profoundly suspect that life doesn't hold a whole lot for them—and, for sure, that school is not going to help them make it any better. You will be teaching people who wonder if they will see another set of twin towers fall in the smoke and fire of a new terrorist attack, who wonder if the world will even exist when they become adults. You will be teaching people who are told that getting into college is the most important goal of their lives and who know they will not be admitted—and people who are sure they will get into college and question whether that will mean very much at all. You will be teaching people who are told that this is the best time of their lives—and who wonder, if that is true, what in the world do the succeeding years hold?

You will be teaching people in the great and dramatic process of growing up, a growing up that often is marked as much by fear and danger and unhappiness as by joy and discovery. For some of our students the latter feelings are intermittent and transitory, lasting a few days or weeks; yet for others, the feelings are relatively permanent.

For many students, school and our classes are arenas where they do not feel safe or a part; they do not want to be there. While there are always exceptions to the following generalizations, these are the students who only put in their time in school, who want to be left alone, and who will occasionally "act out" if pushed or challenged. Alienated students, both the truly apathetic and the more combative, do not talk a lot in large-group discussions, do not do much homework, do not see themselves as any part of the life of the school—either during the day or after the last bell. Consider this description Johnathan gives of himself in high school:

> I was what I think one would call a "problem child." . . . In my junior English class . . . I sat in that back corner of the room as always. I could never stand the feeling of people looking at the back of my head. This class was a little strange for me because there was not one person in the room that I was friends with. And, of course, I never participated in class discussions. This meant that I never spoke in class, I never said a word.
>
> This has been, over the years, a very typical situation for me. And once the silence starts it becomes increasingly difficult to say anything. The silence builds such a momentum that in order to utter one word I would be facing a mountain of shame, and at once losing my anonymity, drawing attention to my paralysis.

One day in this English class we had a test. I had forgotten to bring a pencil. Class had already started, the door was closed, I was trapped. I thought about asking the people near me for something to write with; I thought about asking the teacher. Instead, I just made writing motions with my finger the entire period and turned in a blank test, face down, quickly as I left the room.

The next year English class was better. One of my best friends was in the class, and he sat next to me in the back corner of the room. I still never said anything in class. The other students were just faceless heads, masters of all social situations. The teacher was someone whose gaze I averted for fear he might think I was interested and call on me. I didn't have to worry.

—Johnathan Morris

Alienated students are often like Johnathan, the ones who, at least in class, are likely sitting by themselves, who are apt to try to sleep or otherwise withdraw from the life of the class, who are absent from school more than the average, who consistently forget or lose their instructional materials. With some exceptions, these are the students who just don't turn in major assignments and who don't complete even minimal parts of tests. These alienated students are those who are termed "at risk" and who are often extreme underachievers.

Jeffrey Landon describes a young woman he encountered in his student teaching who fits the at-risk description and whose behaviors outside school as well as in it are cause for concern:

Jewel is a sophomore, six feet tall, and she walks hunched over to disguise both her height and her chest. Her skin is the color of an acorn, and her cheeks are acne-scarred. I have never seen her talk either in class or out; in class, she is almost invisible.

I have read two short essays by Jewel. In the first she talked about Christmas, and how it depressed her. Her parents live in another city, but she hasn't seen them in 2 years. She writes, "they are too busy." She thought she would see them on Christmas, but it didn't work out. Instead they sent her a yellow dress 2 sizes too small for her body.

On New Year's Eve, Jewel injured herself, falling down some stairs while holding onto a butcher knife. It was called an accident by her grandmother (who she lives with). Jewel required many stitches. Apparently, she had accidentally (and repeatedly) punctured her stomach and sliced open at least two veins in her arms. . . . In another essay comparing herself to a figure in literature, Jewel wrote, "I always wanted to have a happier life, but that won't happen I guess. I don't want to hurt myself, because I care about myself. But sometimes I can't stop what they do."

For Clary Washington, a student teacher in a suburban high school, Derek put a human face on the alienated student. Upper middle class, ostensibly bright and promising, surrounded, in fact, by concerned adults, Derek was nonetheless on his way to trouble. After numerous discipline incidents in Clary's class, Derek failed a research paper. Outraged by his grade, he threatened to write a complaint letter about his "horrible," "awful" student teacher, Ms. Washington. Clary writes in her journal:

While he put absolutely no effort in [his] paper, last week Derek asked me how he did, apparently believing that I was not bright enough to figure out that he didn't write what he took credit for. What was really sad was that what [he] essentially copied was full of misspelled words and punctuation errors due to sloppy transcription. . . . What is almost amusing (if it weren't so sad) is that [Derek] could write a letter complaining about me as a teacher, and few would take it seriously because he cannot write. . . . His mother wants him to be considered learning disabled, and there has been discussion of possible brain damage due to Derek's car accident late last year. (After the accident Derek was tested positive for alcohol and cocaine.) . . . I'm obviously not a medical expert, but Derek's attitude is what I see standing in his way—not an impaired brain. If he's given special treatment, he'll just assume that he'll be taken care of for the rest of his life, something that was confirmed when I asked him what he planned to do after high school, and he said work for his father. He's got everything figured out at 17. Almost 18 he keeps reminding me. Old enough to go to jail, I think . . . [Later] Derek told me in class, "You're going down, Ms. Washington, you're going down. You'll never work in [this county]. I'll see to that. I can." . . . When Derek first came in the class, I didn't want to stereotype him as the "bad boy," but he really fulfilled his reputation. I don't like him, and it has perhaps taken me a while to really become comfortable with this notion. He really made part of my [student teaching] experience miserable. His problems are really too numerous for me to tackle alone.

You may, in your teaching, have students such as Derek.

Alienation, gender, and race

There is also research evidence that both gender and race can be alienating factors. Researchers Carol Gilligan, Nona Lyons, and Trudy Hanmer, as well as psychologist Mary Pipher, have found that female students seem to lose a sense of confidence and assurance as they move through the middle school years. Many girls become silent in our classes and doubtful of their intellectual strength as they become high school students. Female students begin to perceive and become troubled by the contradictory roles they will face and are currently facing as women. Many are puzzled by these changes and, as the book title *"We Want to Be Known": Learning from Adolescent Girls* notes, girls often feel relatively invisible and that they and their needs are not necessarily "known" (Hubbard, Barbieri, and Power, 198). Often girls will not participate vigorously in class and will not challenge either male students or the teacher. In fact, in one survey of 2,400 girls and 600 boys in fourth through tenth grades, "adolescent girls experience genuine, substantial drops in self-esteem that far outpace those reported by boys [and have] less confidence in their academic abilities and fewer aspirations to professional careers" (Bower, 184).

Some of this may be what child psychologist Mary Pipher sees as the issue of girls and adolescence: "With puberty girls crash into junk culture . . . [a culture that] is just too hard for most girls to understand and master at this point in their development. They become overwhelmed and symptomatic" (13). And often we see this in our classes.

For boys, there is similar pressure, and a spate of recent books (*"Reading Don't Fix No Chevys"*; *Teaching Reading to Black Adolescent Males*; *To Be a Boy, to Be a Reader*; *Boys and Literacy*; *Misreading Masculinity*) explores how school—and the English classroom—mirrors more perfectly female values and interest than those of males. For former eighth-grade teacher Alfred Tatum, writing in *Teaching Reading to Black Adolescent Males*, "schools are hostile and unpredictable environments for many black males, who come to view themselves as nonachievers and nonparticipants in society because of what happens to them there" (33). Tatum outlines how young men adopt a "cool pose" which is "a ritualized form of masculinity, uses certain behavior, scripts, physical posturing, and carefully crafted performance to convey a strong impression of pride, strength, and control" (29). Tatum observes, though, that the ritualized forms of masculinity, the "cool pose as a coping mechanism," can carry negative aspects as it encourages a refusal to get involved in experiences; a disinclination against self-disclosure that makes it difficult for teachers to know how to help; an avoidance of institutions and activities—such as school, museum, and churches—which, though they could help with personal turmoil, are seen as terminally uncool (29).

And, in addition, those who feel they are the representatives of their race can also feel tremendous pressure. In *A Tribe Apart*, Patricia Hersch describes Charles whose parents, black professionals who have high expectations, have inculcated in Charles a special burden: "He never feels at ease in his classes because he is never free of the burden of proving he is Mr. Perfect Black" (87), the flawless representative of his race. For Charles, and for many other racial minorities who choose to embrace school and all it represents, who wish to achieve on the terms of the mainstream, there can be real alienation:

> Charles' dilemma represents the word of the striving black middle-class adolescents. It is a life lived on the defensive, a constant tightrope to be navigated between two cultures: a white culture that never fully embraces them, and a black peer group that disdains black achievers. If hip-hop extols the black underclass, then where does a kid like Charles belong? (88)

Other sources of alienation: Teachers/administration/school size

Another, perhaps hidden, source of alienation is not only the shapes of our students' personal lives and the composition of the student body itself but you, the teacher, and your school's administration.

It is likely that you, the reader of this book and the beginning teacher, are Caucasian and middle class. It is also likely that you are a female. Further, it is also probable that most of your colleagues in your school will share these characteristics. In other words, you the teacher and your school administration are largely homogeneous in class and race. While this is not to imply that Anglo teachers cannot deal effectively with nonwhite students or that female teachers are limited in their connection to male students or that middle-class values are always at odds with those of other classes, the issue is that the power structure of schools—of which you are or will soon be a part—is usually overwhelmingly represented by the white, middle class, and female. When your students are different, there can be conflict and misunderstanding, issues that while not your sole responsibility are nevertheless your predominant responsibility to attempt to bridge. Carol Smith Catron remembers the magic of a teacher who seemed to bridge that gap:

> Junior year I had [a teacher] who I loved. My favorite thing about her class was that there were no favorites. We had everyone in that class from a guy named Wendyl with a pierced nose and chains on his boots to a girl named Julie who was head of the cheerleaders and won every beauty contest to come her way. And then there were all the people in between, like me. I felt like I was this teacher's favorite person in the world. So did my friend Vanessa, and my fiancé, John. And, no doubt, Wendyl and Julie felt the same way. There were no "shadow" people, or people who dominated every discussion. Everyone was called upon in class and everyone's answers were given respect and consideration.

Within her class, the teacher Carol Smith Catron recalls made all of her students individuals. On the other hand, you must remember that the way middle and secondary schools are organized, you will be seeing upwards of 120 students a day in a school of anywhere from 1,200 students to 2,000. While many schools attempt to ameliorate the drawbacks of such "largeness," kids can, as a well-respected NCTE statement notes, feel "lost in the crowd." It is quite possible to hide in such large configurations and, quite possibly, to feel even more apart and disengaged.

A final note on alienation

While not all of the factors discussed here mean that a student will feel alienated, it is helpful to remember, once again, the great range of pressures that confront young people. Being a minority racially—Caucasian students in predominately African American student bodies, Latino students surrounded by Anglos, Asian Americans in a sea of Caucasians—and the reverse of each—can engender a certain sense of aloneness. Students for whom English is a second language can also feel much apart from school culture. Muslim and Jewish students are often the exception in a student body of Christians; Roman Catholic students can be a small proportion of a largely Protestant group. Gay and lesbian students can also feel alienated. It is too easy for us to look at those youthful, clear faces, those expressive clothes and hairdos, those tattoos and piercings, and assume that what is in our students' lives is equally cheerful and well balanced. The appearance can often belie the reality.

Let us turn to some students whose stories are based on real people and, in one case, on a composite of two people; I taught them, and they are all, in their own ways, alienated students.

Three Students: Marianna, Antoine, and Marc

Once I had a student who had very pale skin and pale, wispy blonde hair. She had a pretty, sweet face with watchful eyes that would widen enormously. She was shy, had no friends I could discern, and ate alone in the cafeteria and walked alone between classes. She was, at sixteen, undergoing a difficult period in her own life and with her alcoholic mother. When she took an overdose of pills between classes, the rescue squad came and carried her from the girls' bathroom floor to the hospital. A month later, she returned to school and was placed in one of my classes. I knew her recent history but was cautious about treating her differently from the others. But equal treatment was hard for two reasons: Marianna was virtually incapable of speaking above a soft whisper. Almost no one in the class, even those sitting right around her, could hear her comments, and no one, including me, her teacher, could induce her to raise her voice. But it got even more complicated because when she turned in her first writing assignment, I realized I was in the presence of one of the brightest students I had ever seen in my teaching career. Whispering and writing, the troubled and brilliant Marianna was in my class.

Once I had another student whose almost angelic features, mocha skin, and dark eyes belied a volatile temper. It was never clear to most of his teachers and even many of his friends what would "set off" Antoine, or why he would decide at a given juncture in class to raise his voice in question, protest, or complaint—or stalk out of the classroom, slamming the door behind him. When he did his work, Antoine was a wonderful student, and he could be a strong addition to any class discussion. He was aware, smart, and explosively under pressure.

One day he came into class ten minutes late, a fairly usual behavior. But in the missed ten minutes, Antoine had not heard the class introduction of why the day's reading, the South American short story, was paired with the Biblical story of the Good Samaritan. Standing up to announce, "This is no religion class," Antoine once again stalked out and slammed the door behind him. Not very much later, no one was happy—but no one was terribly surprised—when, one Saturday night, Antoine returned to an after-hours club to retaliate for a perceived slight. Antoine's father, who had taken him to the club, had been insulted, the story went, and Antoine went back to the club ostensibly to retrieve his coat—but actually to shoot the owner dead. On bond and awaiting trial for murder, and later after he was convicted, awaiting the beginning of his jail sentence, the volatile and very bright Antoine was, like Marianna, in my class.

And once I also had a student who didn't exactly look like James Dean—he was too stocky and his cheekbones weren't as prominent—but wanted to act like him. When he bothered to come to school (he attended only about two-thirds of any given week) Marc either would not bring his books to class or, when he did bring them, would not open them. He would not answer questions, turn in homework, take tests, or do much of anything but slouch in his desk and watch the class. Whenever he decided he had "had enough," he would get up and walk out. He was moody, abrupt, and in the middle of his fifth year of a well-known and tempestuous love relationship with a classmate. His sole interests were Angie and motorcycles; the rest was irrelevant. When Angie, pregnant, withdrew from school, Marc stayed to get more Ds and Fs. Putting his face down on his desk with his jacket pulled over his head, bereft of his girlfriend, Marc was also in my class.

Teacher reaction to the alienated student

In a newspaper years ago, I read a study of nurses and their critically ill patients that I think has some bearing on teacher reaction to alienated students. Researchers found that registered nurses would spend a considerably shorter period of time interacting with and caring for patients who were critically, often terminally, ill. The researchers concluded that because such patients were less rewarding to deal with, the nurses, more than likely unconsciously, spent less time with them. So it is, too, with us as teachers. In fact, the subtitle of the Lindley article on alienated students, "For Teachers of the Alienated," is "Three Defenses Against Despair," which, while a rather melodramatic phrase, captures the intensity of the issue. Most of us will tend to avoid the truly alienated student because he or she is often not rewarding to be with. We can make a number of efforts, but it is not axiomatic that they will be successful. And, in fact, some teachers, fearful of burnout, make it a point to be less than fully engaged with such students. Others have experiences that confirm that the school, as it is currently organized, cannot be effective with such students.

For example, it is with no little shame that I recount my encounter with the alternately vacant-eyed and occasionally giggling student I had and whose behavior was a complete puzzle to me. Her hair was unkempt, her skin blotched, and her clothes were held together by a dozen or so safety pins. Even in my less than affluent school she stood out as poorly, inappropriately dressed. She insisted, though, that she had big plans for the immediate future: she would be on a bus to Hollywood the next week. The movies were her goal, she asserted, and she was only in my class as something to pass the time before she set out for California. And her instructions to me were equally direct: she told me to leave her alone, put her desk away from the others, and not speak to her. She would not cause me problems, she assured me, if I would just cease and desist.

As I recall, that's just what I did. She dropped out of school in a month or so, for the system's resources and my energy were no match for her problems.

For a colleague of mine facing a different situation, there was also little recourse but, in this case, she made a better effort than I had with the student just described:

Nothing prepared me for the day two of my students who had killed a cat wore the bones to school around their necks. One gleefully described how he had killed the animal while his classmates alternated between disgust and laughter. I asked him why he had killed the cat. He told me that his god was calling out for a sacrifice. A week later he wore the cat's skull to school on a string, complete with a red cross painted on top.

I exhausted all of the channels possible—guidance counselors, department chairman, administration. The facts seemed to be that unless the two had killed the animal on school property, there wasn't anything that could be done.

Tell that to the cat.

Tell that to the parents in the school district.

Tell that to the next teacher who hasn't a notion how to handle this. . . . If we can't deal with students in crisis we are potentially turning them away from possibly the only place where they may be influenced positively. If we sit in class and fervently hope that [such students] will drop out, we are being woefully shortsighted.

On the other hand, caring is just not enough; for these students there needs to be attention to different sorts of strategies to bring them into the life of the classroom. And, as in the case of my Hollywood-bound student, we are not doing our job if we just, as I did some years ago, give up and turn away.

Guidelines for dealing with the alienated student

Perhaps it is more a sense of degree than kind when we think of guidelines for dealing with alienated students and an effort to individualize our approach with them. Certainly there is no magic set of activities that will turn apathetic students into involved ones or calm the disaffected student. Certainly many of those students do succeed with minimal—even no—intervention. For many of them, however, extra help is necessary, and we need to do more than just leave students alone. Here are a few guiding principles:

- **Refuse to ignore your alienated students:** let them know that you know they are there in the class and that you are aware of them and their performance and want to see it improved. **Things to do:** speak to these students every day, make eye contact with them, ask them how they are doing. Do not avoid them, since it only reinforces their behavior.

- **Maintain expectations for the alienated student's academic performance:** regardless of the origin of the "problem," the student must be held accountable for his or her own achievement. **Things to do:** remind these students where they are in terms of assignments and deadlines; look for opportunities to tell them when you genuinely expect they will do well or be interested; praise them when they have earned it, without letting them know you really feel "it's about time."

- **Use performance contracts to shape behavior:** written contracts can define behavior and goals for students. **Things to do:** you and the student agree that answering so many times in class will equal such and such a reward, that so many assignments completed with such and such requirements will equal such and such grade; you establish a written contract or form, and both you and the student sign and date it.

- **Make deals:** on large issues (such as the performance contracts) and small, giving students a sense that they can exert some control over their fate. **Things to**

do: tell the students that if they turn in homework two days in a row they can go to the library for half the period; if they answer questions on Monday you will not call on them on Tuesday; and so on.

- **Remember that variety in curriculum and flexibility in instructional style is probably more important to your alienated students than to others:** the lack of choice can be numbing to the alienated student. **Things to do:** tell the student, you can read either this or that; you can do one of these four projects.

- Finally, without creating a wholly artificial situation, **try to structure activities where the student can be engaged and can legitimately succeed.**

With Marianna, whose whispered, virtually inaudible speech was a problem in class, the first step seemed to lie in her great strength in writing. I encouraged her to write out her comments rather than speak, and after some discussion, on an occasional basis I asked her to read her writing aloud. I also put Marianna in group and pair work where speaking in front of many others would not be such an issue. When these two strategies seemed to be consistently successful, I initiated a step-by-step attempt to get Marianna to speak audibly in large-group discussion. Along the way I realized that I had, inadvertently, reinforced Marianna's behavior pattern not only by physically moving closer to her to hear what she had said but by asking her to reiterate her comments and then praising her rather effusively when she did repeat them. I stopped those behaviors and started calling on Marianna as I would any other student. If her speech was only partially audible, I accepted it as she presented it, although other students would occasionally insist that she speak up. The combination of techniques seemed to work, and Marianna became more a part of the class, not the whispering student she had been before. This procedure took about two semesters; it was my impression Marianna gathered some confidence and seemed to shed her "speaking aloud" block. By the time of graduation she was headed to college some states away and seemed more confident.

I was not able to do anything about Antoine's outbursts of temper. While he was awaiting jail, however, his behavior became understandably subdued. We worked out a reading list/project contract that directly addressed the years he would be spending in prison, and Antoine made excursions into sociological studies on crime in America and the penal system. Antoine did the best work he had ever done in class, and his written reports were careful and detailed. As tragic and sad as his situation was, his work allowed him to pass his English class. If nothing else, he went to prison with very recent academic success, not to mention some factual knowledge of what awaited him.

Marc and I consistently struck deals. Although it was against departmental policy for juniors in British Literature to write a research paper on anything but British literature, I threw out the rules. Marc's research paper, a major part of his year's grade, detailed the history and production schedules of the Harley Davidson Company, complete with specifications and descriptions of all the current models. I used the successful research project to build on other behavior; Marc now had a chance to pass my class despite his previous academic deficiencies, and we worked out an arrangement for minimal participation. Marc agreed to answer at least twice a week in class if left alone otherwise; he was not allowed to put his head down in class, but he did not have to bring his book and could share with someone else. He was absent a great deal and would not take unit tests. He also initially refused to take the final exam, but I got Angie to intervene, and Marc did, just barely, pass for the year.

The place of the guidance counselor, the parents, the administration

It is likely that when a student shows up in your class and appears to be apathetic or disaffected—or alienated—someone else in the school is aware of that student and his or her difficulties. It is not a given, however, and when you perceive, as a teacher, that the student is displaying signs of relatively desperate behavior, you must inform your guidance staff, make an effort to call the student's parents, or otherwise alert your administration. To this day, I still worry about my Hollywood starlet; I let her slip away. I decided not to expend the energy, and it's hard to know if the intervention of a counselor would have helped her cope more successfully with reality.

In the case of Marianna, other students were well aware that she was teetering on an emotional edge and were the ones to get a teacher involved as soon as she overdosed and slumped on the girls' bathroom floor. In her case, her parents, who had problems with their marriage and their drinking, had not been heretofore helpful and, because Marianna was a student who had never been any "trouble," she had escaped most of our notice. When she returned to school, however, it was under a certain amount of supervision and care. She was also placed in a foster home through the efforts of the guidance staff.

In the case of Antoine, the school was not directly responsible: he got a gun and shot the nightclub owner on the weekend and off school property. There had previously, however, been little organized effort to intervene in what escalated into a major problem and left one person dead and one life shattered. Antoine's outbursts were not recognized for what they eventually became; instead, his behavior in school and difficulty with teachers were perceived, possibly cynically, as fairly typical for a teenage African American male.

With Marc, parents, guidance counselors, and administration were aware of his difficulties in school, and, as a strategy, all three had resorted to reward structures, threats, and a variety of punishments. All three seemed ineffective: it was only when the rules were bent, deals struck, and his girlfriend Angie enlisted into the struggle that Marc showed improvement.

And just recently, it was teamwork with a parent that seemed to make the difference for my student Susan.

Parent and teacher: An intervention with Susan

When I returned to teach high school, Susan was one of the students in my class I worried about the most. She was a pleasant young woman but extremely quiet and self-effacing, one who would not share anything in large-group discussion and who, in small-group work, always paired with folks who seemed to be more energetic than she and could accomplish the work. At one point she appeared to give up in class, put her head on her desk, and just refused to be engaged.

She completely stopped writing in her journal, even though all of us, myself and the students, wrote for ten minutes at the opening of every class. What was the problem? Previously Susan had written a strong journal entry on her father, a man who had ceased to be in her life some time ago and who, even on Christmas and her birthday, failed to acknowledge her presence. His new family and younger children seemed to be his focus, and it hurt Susan immensely. I talked with her during and after class—I too had had a difficult time with my own father—but got almost nothing from her but averted eyes and mumbles. Her behavior was beginning to alarm me; I checked with other teachers, and there were rumors about her health, her love life, both of which could have explained her lack of affect in school. There was an older boyfriend for whom Susan had, alarmingly, made two court appearances, but, despite all that and her indifference to work, she believed firmly that in a year or so she would escape high school and be a student at a university (her heart was set on Louisiana State University, LSU). Using any "in" I had, I talked to Susan about LSU and asked her about the connection she might see between her grades in school and her admission to college-level work. But Susan was not buying my teacher version of reality: she was going to LSU and somehow whatever she did or did not do in our class was beside the point.

As the semester continued, Susan's work was so marginal and skimpy that when the second midterm grades were given, I called her mother yet another time. Susan's mother was one of the parents with whom I connected positively and strongly, and she appreciated my efforts to keep in touch. This crisis, however, was getting serious, and over the phone we discussed what we could do. All other approaches had failed—and at home Susan went into her bedroom, closed the door, and would not talk to her mom. So Susan's mother and I plotted and planned and arranged for what we both hoped would be a small but effective shock. Without warning Susan, her mother arranged to come early to school so that we could call Susan out of class and sit down jointly with her. Perhaps the surprise of the two of us—making an impromptu, tag-team intervention—would cause some change.

Certainly Susan registered surprise when she was called to the office during first period, only to see both myself and her mother waiting for her, but the effect was not as I had hoped. We three sat in the empty cafeteria, and it was cold in all senses of the word. The earnest (and rehearsed) presentation made by the two of us to Susan was greeted with silence. Susan listened but would not respond, had no answers, offered no reasons, and made no promises to do anything different in class. I was saddened; the whole effort seemed a waste of time.

So on we went, and I concluded I had done what I could do for Susan.

Life, however, can be surprising. Just a few weeks later as part of a class project, Susan chose a young adult novel, and a breakthrough appeared to come. She actually read the novel she selected and, for the first time in the entire semester, elected to work alone. She chose one of the creative projects I had offered and made an ABC book based on the novel. Using different markers and type styles, she put her phrases on carefully trimmed construction paper, tying the pages together with yarn. Susan had raided her mother's sewing kit to put on each page pearls, sequins, sparkles, beads, and all sorts of glitter. The content was not remarkable, the presentation was messy in places, but the entire effect was wonderful, full and consistent with the spirit of the book itself. It was, in many ways, a triumph. More to the point, it was the first completed work Susan had done in months, she had done it on her own, and it was pretty good. I couldn't praise her enough.

To what extent the intervention/discussion with myself and Susan's mother had been the catalyst or not, after that there seemed some shift in Susan, and, thanks in part to her good grade on the ABC book project, she did just barely pass the semester. I can't prove it, but I do believe that somehow the mother/teacher teamwork and our dogged refusal to ignore her finally made an impression on Susan and helped her to succeed on one small project. She never did go to LSU—I followed up on her a year or so after I left the high school—but, for me, getting Susan's attention and getting her to engage at least once was a small victory.

One Teacher's Strategy for Dealing with Alienated Students: "Big Bucks"

The students described and the strategies devised to help them are representative of attempts to deal with alienation in school. In the following account, however, an individual teacher had an entire class that was relatively unmotivated and certainly apathetic. What can a teacher do about a *group* that might be termed *alienated*? This teacher decided to use a behaviorally oriented plan that depended on extrinsic reward; for her the solution was successful, and while it may not represent any sort of plan you would like to implement in your classroom, it is worth detailing. "Big Bucks" offers a tangible, real-life reward for school activities, and in this school context, it worked.

One of the saving graces of the second half of my teaching career in high school was the friendship and guidance of a buddy down the hall. Nancy Rosenbaum, more than most anybody I knew, could come up with systems that worked and that were directly related to a student or instructional problem. I always admired Nancy for the crafty way she could adapt a principle or a concept to her students.

We have stayed friends through the years, and we share personal and school-related news. At one point in her teaching, Nancy had a crisis of sorts. She had moved to a new school and just did not like what was going on in one of her classes. Here was her situation: she was teaching Project College, an intensive reading course to prepare athletes and others who were not particularly motivated or geared to go on with their education. Built within the class were a number of field trips and guest speakers to give students an idea of what was "out there" in the world. It seemed a relatively ideal structure.

But the students in Nancy's Project College class turned out to be a highly unmotivated group of juniors and seniors. As a group, they consistently came to class late and without materials. A disproportionate number wanted to go to the bathroom immediately when class began; some of them insisted on using class time to study for what they perceived were more important tests in other subjects. They were not convinced about going to college or jobs; for a few, an athletic scholarship might be an entry ticket, but even that was a bit remote. They were not angry or hostile: they were just indifferent, disaffected, and tuned out. They did not want to do a whole lot of work; for many, even participation in field trips was declined because it would mean make-up work in other, missed classes. For a number of students in this group, very little that was going on in school related to what they perceived as the reality of the world. And, as Nancy knew, they might just have been right.

What to do?

It was during a routine weekend trip to the local office supplies store that Nancy had a vision. Browsing in the aisles, she spied oversized note pads with a reproduction of a $500 bill on one side and space to write a grocery list or a memo or whatever on the other. It was a gimmick to jazz up ordinary note pads, but to Nancy it seemed to open a door. Big bucks, she thought. Hmmm . . . Big Bucks. She bought a lot of them. She made some notes, did some planning, and was ready to institute a barter-and-reward system in her class, a strategy she called "Big Bucks."

The next week in class she put the stack of $500 memo pads on her desk. Gesturing toward them, she began. What, she asked her students, do you have to do to earn Big Bucks? What, after these final years in school, can you do to get those greatly desired Big Bucks?

The class perked up; here was a subject they were interested in. Students brainstormed, they brought up illegal activities, they snickered, they got serious.

Okay, the students concluded, to earn Big Bucks you have to do something fairly extraordinary—or maybe something pretty well for a sustained period of time. The students knew from their class that college graduates make about $100,000 more over a lifetime than high school graduates do. They even cited some of the guest speakers they had had in their class who could command higher fees in law, interior design, accounting for just those types of achievement. And, of course, with those Big Bucks you can have at least some of what most people call "the good life"—the conversation moved a bit to cars, houses, jewelry, vacations, and the like.

Nancy then gestured toward the note pads and outlined how students could earn the $500 "bills," one at a time, for certain behaviors or achievements:

- Being on time to class four times in a row: $500.
- Showing a 10 percent improvement in score from pretest to posttest on certain subjects: $500.
- Sharing great ideas with the class, including study techniques that really worked or memory tricks for any subject: $500.
- Quizzes with scores of over 98 percent: $500 each.
- Being exceptionally polite and pleasant: $500.
- Keeping a semester calendar for assignments and deadlines: $1,000, payable the last day of class.
- Going on field trips that required make-up work in other classes: $500.
- Meeting deadlines, getting money and/or permission slips in before the due date: $500.

Nancy then outlined what her students could do with the Big Bucks they earned, a list that was directly related to the issues of this particular class:

- Going to the bathroom during class cost $500.
- A trip to the library to study for something else was $3,000 for half the class period, $5,000, for the whole period ("not cheap," Nancy noted, "but a bargain if you need it").
- School rules dictated that four tardies to class equaled one after-school detention; a student could be tardy to class, without further penalty, for $500.
- The big-ticket item: buy all or parts of the final exam. For Big Bucks, students could purchase their year-end Project College English exam ahead of time and study accordingly. The entire exam sold for $9,500; individual sections cost varying amounts.

As Nancy set up "Big Bucks," students could lend money to others or give their money away. They could not, however, borrow from the teacher, forge the Big Bucks (Nancy initialed and dated each bill), or get their money replaced if they lost it. And a student who had purchased all or part of the final exam could show it to others who hadn't been able to. That decision was left entirely up to the individual.

The point of this one teacher's strategy for dealing with the alienated is that it was based on an established order all of us, students and teachers, intimately understand—money. It may have been symbolic—note pads with enlarged $500 bills—it may have relied a great deal on extrinsic reward, but it took on a power and a reality of its own. And in this one class, Big Bucks reinforced good behavior, study habits, esprit de corps, and a very good final exam. Nancy also observed, "Most of these students had jobs, and occasionally I'd hear one remark that this was just like life; as soon as they had a payday, they'd have a bunch of bills that used it all."

What would Nancy change? She wrote:

The use of Big Bucks cut the tardies and bathroom trips even more effectively then I first thought it could. It gave me a chance to reinforce behaviors I think will help students—sharing study ideas, practicing on quizzes with each other to get the 98 percent, keeping a calendar so that deadlines do not totally sneak up on them, consciously thinking of the extra politeness or helpfulness that may help them in their relationships with others. It also did not make every reward a grade.

Students suggested things to earn and spend Big Bucks that I could never have thought of, and some of them were great ideas. . . . Students also can save!! During second semester, everyone's priority was accumulating the $9,500 first—everything else could wait. When they had their nest eggs, spending could begin.

At the end of the semester (and sometimes before) students could be incredibly generous with each other. One girl was the surprised recipient of $1,000 from a student who gave or "loaned" Aimee the money because Aimee needed it right then.

I never had any big quarrels or fights about money. Students did like to keep up with how much they had and how much other people had—a couple of people counted their "cash" at the end of the period every day. But the emphasis was never all money—money was a bonus.

While the administration had to be notified, Nancy wrote that members of "the administration, including the department chair, came to observe when I was first beginning with Big Bucks and were very interested and supportive" and the program then went along on its own. It is one teacher's solution to a problem in one disaffected class, a solution that relates to the class—and also uses what we so frequently refer to as the outside and "real" world.

·············· FOR YOUR JOURNAL ················

Projects such as Nancy's "Big Bucks" are not universally embraced by all teachers, some of whom would characterize such programs as overly behavioral and controlling. Although certainly "Big Bucks" worked for Nancy's students, it is not a solution for every similar situation. What kind of practices would *you* institute if you had a class such as Nancy's—disaffected, indifferent, tuned out? What kinds of rewards or structures do you think might work with these students? Brainstorm and describe at least *two* practices you would like to try.

The Average Student: Lost in the Middle

At one point in American history a large group of citizens was characterized as the "silent majority." That phrase still has some power and can be applicable to what is often termed the *average* student: the ones in the middle who are neither characterized as gifted nor alienated and who do not otherwise call attention to themselves. These students are the majority of those we teach in middle school and high school and are tracked and labeled as average. When they are flanked either in a single class or in our teaching day by others at the extremes, it is easy to gloss over them and to forget that they, too, are a vital part of our teaching life. While most of the activities in this book are directed to them, the average student, it is helpful to consider them as a group with as much definition as our alienated students.

Kids who don't cause any trouble, who largely do their assignments and cooperate, can be given short shrift by us as teachers. We need to remember that these students also require attention, praise, reinforcement, and, indeed, an acknowledgment that what the system may call an average student can be highly misleading. Within your average group can be startlingly original thinkers and, conversely, kids who are in over their heads academically. Being seen as average is not necessarily a pleasant experience, and for some students, it can also be a conscious strategy to keep notice from being called to oneself, a way to hide. We as teachers need, as best we can, to remember to examine the labels we so often glibly place on or readily accept for our students and not lose our responsibility to our average students.

An eloquent comment on this subject came to me in a letter. A young woman preparing to be a teacher had read the first edition of *Making the Journey* and wanted to talk further about average students. Ashley Ruff observed:

> I have often been lumped into that category [of being average] myself, and it tends to be glossed over more frequently than any other category. I have found that within my own high school "the average student" is often treated very different in relation to the other preexisting tracks. We already knew that we would have to read a lot more literature than the basic track. We also knew that we wouldn't be going on as many field trips as the gifted class. I remember feeling in high school that I simply didn't fit into a category anywhere. I felt as if I wasn't smart enough to be gifted, and I wasn't slow enough to be basic. I simply was just another "average student."

Being a face in a large crowd, being considered unremarkable is not always an enviable position. Teachers need to consistently challenge students who are tracked as average in academic ability and to provide them with the same kinds of stimulation they provide so-called gifted students. Getting by, unremarked and unnoticed, is the goal of a number of average students, and it is not something with which we as teachers should glibly cooperate.

The Gifted Student: Burdens and Responsibilities

The pinnacle of success for many teachers is to be given a class of "gifted" students, those who have risen, at least at a given point in their school lives, to the top academically. Some enjoy this teaching immensely and find it very satisfying to deal with motivated, competitive, college-bound students, either in classes or in programs such as Advanced Placement (AP) or International Baccalaureate (IB). Such students, however, have their own special challenges, and not all of them are academic.

There is for these students often an incredible pressure to produce, succeed, and, in some cases, to be relatively "perfect" in a variety of other areas, notably social and athletic. While some of this pressure comes from parents and teachers, a great deal of it also comes from the students themselves.

It was during my teaching of Advanced Placement English that I had my most extensive contact with students who could be termed gifted. While not every one of those I taught was truly gifted, the majority were academically talented. These students needed intellectual stimulation but also needed less an atmosphere of competition and aggression than one of mutuality and cooperation.

In almost all cases, the students needed to consider their own paths to success and, in the case of the AP class, the limitations—perceived or not—of their segregation from the rest of the student body.

Accordingly, I tried to use more cooperative learning with these students and, to an extent, to deemphasize what was for many of them the major motivating force of their lives, the grade. It was possible with these students to make a convincing case for postponing a tangible reward or to use participation and completion as benchmarks.

Keeping in touch with my gifted students' parents was also as important as keeping in touch with those of my less successful students and helped, in some cases, to soften the pressure from home.

And we need to remember that gifted students are as varied as all our other students. Jill Williamson recalls her AP English class and paints a portrait of the varied gifted student:

> Shawna and Amy were best friends, but their personalities were entirely different. Amy spent most of her time popping gum and cracking silly jokes and took her poetry quite seriously. Shawna worshipped her GPA yet did the very least amount of work she could to get by. And Shawna had the most beautiful head of long, wavy, red hair. I was so jealous. Jason, Jim, and Jeff always became the teachers' pets. Jason was my modern-day Adonis. Jim slept most of the time but was quite charming nonetheless. And Jeff missed class frequently to celebrate Jewish holidays, and he always seasoned his speech with multisyllabic words. T. J. was sensitive and had a quiet laugh. York had the quickest wit of all of us and had seven brothers and sisters. Greg was our token burly, slow-witted jock, and Sean was our token surfer dude. Jennifer came from a broken home and her expression was blank most of the time, yet she wrote the most eloquent and creative short stories. John was my favorite classmate. On the outside he was a Virginia gentlemen, but secretly he spent quite a bit of time drawing phallic symbols and telling dirty jokes. He was also a terrible speller. Nikki was my manic-depressive friend who spent way too much time reading Ayn Rand and stopped coming to school about halfway through our senior year. I was the class spelling champion.

Students as varied as Jill's friends in her AP class will be in your class, too.

The Delicate Contract with Students

Dealing with and getting along with your students is a central priority of teaching; depending on your personality, while you may not enter into any sort of lovefest with your students, there needs to be a sense of mutual respect and care and feeling on both sides that this endeavor is worth embarking on. While indeed school is compulsory and your language arts class is required, there is also a necessary mutuality to this business.

Regardless of the "level" of the class, the degree of alienation, giftedness, or averageness, students can refuse to cooperate. What if, we might wonder, we held class and nobody came? What if the teacher asked a question and nobody, but nobody—ever so sullenly or ever so politely—answered? What if a test was distributed, and nobody picked up a pencil and took it? It is a delicate contract because, indeed, there is little we can do if students, at the extreme, absolutely refuse to cooperate or, at the not as extreme, change the class expectations until they are virtually meaningless. This lack of faith can occur with any level of students, and in some ways it is a teacher's worst nightmare. So how do we make sure that the students in our classes do not say no, do not decide not to participate? It is, indeed, a delicate contract. We need, I think, to remember four things:

1. **We need to be reasonable, to offer students activities that are meaningful, doable, and have real connection to skills and knowledge.**

2. **We need to articulate why what we are studying or writing or reading or discussing is important.**

3. **We need to listen to students and to accord them the same courtesy we would accord our friends.**

4. **We need, finally, to remember that school, enduring as a concept, is perennial largely because the majority of students have come to our classes over the decades with a certain hopeful belief that they will learn from us and that the learning will make their lives better.**

···············: FOR YOUR JOURNAL ················

One of the ways we can work more successfully with students is to think not of rules and regulations, but of options for that delicate contract. Look at the following classroom situations. How many options can you suggest to deal with such typical classroom/student events? What do you predict would be the result of each of the options?

1. A student repeatedly comes in late and disturbs the class in progress.

2. A student consistently uses materials from your desk without asking but, when confronted, always apologizes and promises to replace the materials.

3. Two students, best friends, consistently whisper loudly whenever you are giving directions.

4. A student gets in an argument with another student and, when you intervene, calls you an obscene name.

5. As you are explaining the details of a new project, a student complains that you are giving the class too much work and that the project is "stupid" anyway. Other students nod and appear to agree.

6. At least half a dozen students constantly interrupt others in the course of large-group discussions, disrupting the flow of conversation and also dominating the discussion.

7. A student refuses to cooperate in group work and wants to work alone.

8. A student consistently comes to class without materials or books or with the wrong materials and books.

9. A student has a habit of not turning in homework assignments, citing a lack of clarity from you regarding directions and/or deadlines.

10. Almost once a week this student comes to class, puts his head on the desk, and resists participation in class.

11. Right before the bell rings and class starts, a student often needs to talk to you about why she does not have her assignments or about difficulty she had completing the assignment. You try to give her attention, but the bell often rings, and the class waits for both of you to finish your conversation.

Two Students: Tanya and Barry

Despite my stories of difficult students and failed expectations, I have to end this chapter on a positive note. An exceptional benefit to teaching—a benefit that perhaps I have not emphasized enough—is that working with students is often close to magical. Not every month, not every semester, not even every year, but often, often enough to keep you going, you will meet and work with students who shape and positively influence your life. You will remember these students and even keep in touch with some of them—as I still do with two I have written about in this chapter, Marianna and Angie. You will receive from these students kindness, consideration, and often genuine affection. They may make you laugh, and they will make you feel, perhaps as only those who work with the young can regularly feel, that the world is indeed a big and exciting and glorious place.

And beyond the parting hugs and handshakes and occasional tears, beyond the letters of appreciation and the little gifts from classes and groups—the necklace from the literary magazine staff, the locket from Advanced Placement, the coffee mugs and blank journals and books and glass apples and pens from the homeroom, the junior class, individual students—beyond all the little tokens and tributes that I, like most teachers, have received over the years, beyond the tangible gifts are those moments when your students often reveal to you their trust and friendship.

I have chosen, of those students, two who affected me in memorable ways.

Tanya and I kept a running argument going for three years; first in sophomore home-room, then in a junior English class, then, her senior year, in my Advanced Placement where she was one of a handful of African American students in the pilot course. She was terribly bright and very sarcastic, and while I knew she was both vulnerable and talented, she could occasionally bring out the worst in me, her teacher. I loved Tanya's spirit, but she also had a way of asking the wrong question at just the wrong time, of challenging at precisely the vulnerable moment when the class was ready to have one bright member take on the teacher. Sometimes I could appreciate Tanya's wit and verve and really admire it: with the roll of an eye or a quip or just a well-timed question, Tanya could turn a class around. Sometimes, however, she tried my patience.

A good student for her sophomore year despite some run-ins with other teachers, Tanya became a *very* good student her junior year and learned to play the politeness game. In Advanced Placement during her senior year, she was aggressive in discussion and bright, and I especially enjoyed her writing. She and I tried to rise above our differences.

And it was Tanya who called me at home late one night with a very adult and truly serious personal crisis. She called, she said, to ask my advice. I would not betray her, she said, and she wanted to know what I would do in her situation. She was brisk and almost busi-nesslike. I was mildly stunned—Tanya and I were more worthy adversaries than friends—but I gave her what insights I had, and we talked frankly on the phone for a half hour or so.

Back in school, Tanya waited some weeks before she told me that the crisis had been resolved. I was relieved for her and, operating in a rather new sense of relationship, under a truce of sorts, Tanya and I went on to finish the semester together. She graduated with hon-ors, and as I shook her hand in congratulation, I felt a renewed sense of affection and con-cern for this complicated and smart young woman who had, surprisingly, possibly all along, trusted me. Her graduation was bittersweet: while I was happy to see Tanya leave high school for a very prestigious university, I seriously doubted her chances for success. And I knew, of course, as with many students, that I would never know the outcome.

It was fully four years later when a graduation invitation from that prestigious uni-versity arrived in the mail. I could scarcely believe the name on the return address, but it was from Tanya. After four years of silence, she had sent me the news. Of course, it was typ-ical Tanya; written on the back of her calling card was her one-line comment, teasing, jaunty, and proud: *Ha! Ha! Bet you're surprised!* Indeed I was and touched that, years later, Tanya knew that I would want to know the news.

Tanya taught me something about students and teachers, about influence that is not always obvious, and about relationships that are forged over the years. Maybe I had failed to see it all along, but my sparring partner, the bright and aggressive Tanya, had turned out to be a student with whom I shared a bond and who seemed to know that I cared. And Tanya continued her triumphs; she is now a medical doctor.

Barry was a new student to my high school who did not get along very well with school rules or policies. Very early in the semester he had been in a difficulty with a num-ber of his teachers. Typically, he and I had had a series of confrontations in my third-period class, which escalated so quickly that I really wondered if we could stand to work together for the rest of the semester. I tried to talk to Barry, but he blew me off pretty convincingly, and I decided to exercise a rare option in our school. I asked, on the basis of personality conflict, that Barry be transferred to another teacher and another class. It was probably a cowardly move on my part, but there was something about the challenge of Barry I did not feel equal to that semester; I felt I had enough to handle with five classes and 140 students.

Regardless of my motives, Barry saw the request as an insult, and, possibly on general principles, was enraged. In a subsequent conference about his schedule—and his behavior in my class and others—he assaulted an assistant principal and was immediately suspended from school.

When I saw him in the halls after he returned to his classes—and his new English class—I stayed clear; Barry was one student who I had crossed and, inadvertently or not, my transfer request was the precipitating event that resulted in his suspension. Barry, I suspected, would be more than willing to retaliate. But the year went on quietly, and I saw little of him.

It was, then, with some serious trepidation that I found myself, with other teachers and students, on a bus with Barry. My school had arranged a modified Outward Bound experience, and I was one of a dozen teacher volunteers to go into the mountains with students who had been, for varying reasons, identified as at risk. The Outward Bound day was an exercise in communication and trust building, centered around physical tests of strength and endurance that were performed in teacher/student teams. Barry, of course, was a prime and logical candidate and was, with some of his friends, on the trip.

When we began the Outward Bound day, I had no control over the activities or grouping. There was some risk in some of the "events," and participants were warned about the danger of falling or slipping—teamwork was essential to preventing injuries. At any rate, teachers and students were randomly placed in teams for varying tests of strength, agility, and trust building. My team's turn came to scale a horizontal crossbar held twelve feet above the ground by two vertical uprights. The whole structure, crossbar and uprights, had no ropes, no handholds, no ladders, and certainly no safety features such as a net. As luck would have it, I was selected to be the first to be launched over the top and handed down to an opposing team working on the other side. I hated the look of this activity, the height and the possible danger, but I just couldn't be the teacher/coward of the team.

Fearfully but doggedly, trusting my team members as I was encouraged to do, I climbed up the back and on to the shoulders of a volunteer. Standing on his shoulders and balancing the best I could, I stood up and reached for the crossbar, twelve feet above the ground and some two feet above my head. I jumped, grabbed for dear life, threw a leg over, hugged the crossbar, and desperately looked to the volunteer on the other side to help me get down.

I must have been more concerned about breaking my neck than I had realized, because I hadn't noticed the members of the other team. I literally couldn't trust my eyes—on the other side of the crossbar and the only thing between me and the void was my former student Barry.

He reached for me. I had a real sense of fatalism, twelve feet above the hard-packed earth, and possibly for that reason I felt I had to say something. Who knows, it might have been my last words before I went to the hospital with my broken leg or arm or both, and anyway, Barry and I had not talked since he had been removed from my class and suspended.

I looked at him. Barry was expressionless. It's a long way down was all I could think. And then I just blurted out what was really on my mind, "If you want to get even, here's your chance." Certainly here was his chance: this was one of the most dangerous of the day's activities, and the accidental slip and fall of a volunteer, though regrettable, would not necessarily be that suspicious. Some of these facts had been outlined before this trip; I knew it, and I supposed Barry did too.

For an eerie moment Barry remained expressionless and silent but then, twelve feet in the air, he smiled, shook his head, and grabbed my arms. Not gently—but not roughly—he delivered me safely to the members of his team—and the ground. I did not look back as I walked away and went on to the next activity, but I remember my legs were shaking.

Later that day during a break I went looking for Barry. I found him, sat down with him, and we talked. I thanked him for not dropping me, and that opened a very intense twenty-minute conversation. Barry was, as I guess I should have known, about as decent a person as I had ever met. He hated school, he didn't get along with his parents, he worried about his life and his girlfriend. I told him I was sorry about what had happened in my class; he told me he was sorry too. We shook hands, went our separate ways to finish the day, and, later, when we saw each other in the halls during the remainder of the semester, we waved and smiled. We were, in a way, friends who had done something together, shared something important. I almost hoped I would have Barry in class the next year, but his parents moved out of the area, and I never saw him again.

I never forgot Barry or that day, though, and I think about how frustrated and angry he probably was, how tempted he could have been to have an "accident" with a hated teacher, and how he, with every temptation to get even and every possibility he could get away with it, refused to. To this day I wonder, if given a similar situation, I would have resisted as he did. I learned something from Barry, something about doing the right thing regardless, and his example stays with me after all these years. In fact, most of our students, like Tanya and Barry and many others, believe that we, their teachers, not only know something but are people of good will and will treat them fairly.

And, in a way, the belief of the young in us, their teachers, and their belief in what we represent, the power of education, is both heartening and heartbreaking. It is the essence of optimism and faith, and, unfortunately, it is often not confirmed by experience. If we take this business seriously, however, we are bound, to the best of our abilities, to never disillusion our students or dishonor what is nothing less than a sacred trust. This can be a hard assignment, this stuff of teaching, but the people before us in our classrooms and the lives they represent are briefly, yet profoundly, entrusted to us. As daunting—terrifying even—as that may be, it is also our little piece of immortality.

·············· FOR YOUR JOURNAL ··············

Think of your middle and high school friends or of some students you may have recently observed. Can you find ones who possibly could be characterized as "alienated"? "average"? "gifted"? What behaviors do or did those students exhibit? What kinds of assignments or teachers appealed to them? did not appeal to them? What variations or refinements would *you* make on the three categories of students presented in this chapter? If you care to, how would you describe yourself, in middle school or in high school, in relation to those categories?

References

Bower, Bruce. "Teenage Turning Point: Does Adolescence Herald the Twilight of Girls' Self-Esteem?" *Science News* 139 (March 23, 1991): 184–86.

Brozo, William G. *To Be a Boy, To Be a Reader: Engaging Teen and Preteen Boys in Active Literacy.* Newark, DE: International Reading Association, 2002.

Gilligan, Carol, Nona P. Lyons, and Trudy J. Hanmer, eds. *Making Connections: The Relational Worlds of Adolescent Girls at Emma Willard School.* Troy, NY: Emma Willard School, 1989.

Glasser, William. *Control Theory in the Classroom.* New York: Harper & Row, 1985.

Gough, Pauline B. "The Key to Improving Schools: An Interview with William Glasser." *Phi Delta Kappan* 68 (May 1987): 656–62.

Hersch, Patricia. *A Tribe Apart: A Journey into the Heart of American Adolescence.* New York: Random House, 1999.

Hubbard, Ruth Shagoury, Maureen Barbieri, and Brenda Miller Power. *"We Want to Be Known": Learning from Adolescent Girls.* York, ME: Stenhouse, 1998.

Lindley, Daniel A. Jr. "For Teachers of the Alienated: Three Defenses Against Despair." *English Journal* 79 (October 1990): 26–31.

Lost in the Crowd: A Statement on Class Size and Teacher Workload. Urbana, IL: NCTE, 1990.

Maynard, Trisha. *Boys and Literacy: Exploring the Issues.* New York: Routledge, 2002.

McNeil, Linda. *Contradictions of Control.* New York: Routledge and Kegan Paul, 1986.

Morin, Richard, Liz Mundy, Kevin Merida, Claudia Deane, Lisa Frazier Page, and Jose Antonio Vargas. "What Teens Really Think: A Poll of Washington Area Kids Gives Us a Piece of Their Minds." *Washington Post Magazine* (October 23, 2005): 14–29, 32–50.

Newkirk, Tom. *Misreading Masculinity: Boys, Literacy, and Popular Culture.* Portsmouth, NH: Heinemann, 2002.

Pfeffer, Susan Beth. "Basic Rules of Teenage Life." *The ALAN Review* 17 (Spring 1990): 5–7.

Pipher, Mary. *Reviving Ophelia: Saving the Selves of Adolescent Girls.* New York: Putnam, 1994.

Rosenbaum, Nancy. Personal correspondence with author. November 2005.

Ruff, Ashley. Personal letter. August 28, 1998.

Smith, Michael, and Jeffrey Wilhelm. *"Reading Don't Fix No Chevys": Literacy in the Lives of Young Men.* Portsmouth, NH: Heinemann, 2002.

Tatum, Alfred. *Teaching Reading to Black Adolescent Males: Closing the Achievement Gap.* Portland, ME: Stenhouse, 2005.

United States Department of Education. *National Education Longitudinal Study of 1988: A Profile of the American Eighth Grader.* Washington, DC: United States Department of Education, 1990.

———. *National Center for Educational Statistics: The Condition of Education 2004.* Washington, DC: U.S. Department of Education, 2004 (NCES 2004-077).

The World of Literature
Teaching and Selecting

And gladly wolde he lerne and gladly teche.

—**Geoffrey Chaucer, Prologue to** *Canterbury Tales*

The Fear of Not Knowing Enough

I am back in my high school, standing in a wide and empty corridor. It is time to go to class; in fact, I am late, and behind the closed doors are other students already seated and working. I need to go to class; I have a test today. Funny thing, though, I have not been to class in months, have done no homework and no studying. I know I am going to fail the test, fail the course, and not graduate from high school. I just hate that class; I don't understand the subject and have avoided it until now. Right this moment, however, I would give anything to have been working all along; the feeling of fear and impending doom is overwhelming.

This, of course, is my dream, my special, recurring anxiety nightmare. Like many people, this dream comes periodically to visit me, and I think it stands for fear of failure or worry about achievement and preparation. While you may not have such recurring dreams, you are probably a bit apprehensive about how much you know as you prepare to enter the classroom.

There is hardly a one of us on the eve of teaching or in the first few years in the classroom who felt that she or he knew *enough*. All of us are haunted by the worry that we are ill prepared, underread, insufficiently educated, ignorant about a number of crucial areas. And the fact is, we probably are. Bluntly put, the amount and depth and breadth of knowledge that we need to be fully conversant with all aspects of language arts is just not possible for most of us to achieve in the preparation years before teaching. It is also not reasonable to expect that level of expertise in the first few years.

The fallacy, however, of the fear of being ill educated is the unspoken assumption that our reading and study should really be completed by the time we become teachers. Most teachers know that the first year in the classroom simply marks the start of a new phase of education and, indeed, that we will never "own" pieces of literature or facts about language or grasp writing principles so firmly as when, year after year, we handle and manipulate and use and create activities based on those elements of language arts. We have to, it is true, be a teacher from the very first day; but as veteran teachers know, we do not have control over all of our subject matter for some years to come. As the title of this book insists, we also continue to *become* teachers, and that includes expanding our knowledge and our skill in the classroom.

We do, as Chaucer reminds us, not only "gladly teche" but also "gladly lerne" (1. 308). And for those who see Chaucer's oft-quoted phrase as more of a definition of a political stance regarding teaching, it is, interestingly enough, also a pure practicality: teachers, in order to teach, really must continue to learn. The two activities are, unless one makes a conscious effort to resist, symbiotically related.

The idea that you don't know enough, that your learning is continuing—possibly, in one sense of the word, just starting—may be a depressing thought for you. If you look at it another way, it also might be relatively heartening. It would be, in the long run, horrifically boring if you could really know everything, master everything almost immediately. There might be more surety than you are feeling now but how emptily the teaching years would stretch before you! There is also the undeniable benefit (especially in literature) of discovering with your students and thus seeing somewhat with fresh eyes. Those thoughts may be most of what sustains you during the first few years in the classroom when, with mounting panic, you realize that you will occasionally be teaching something over which you yourself have only the most marginal control.

Take heart, new teacher, and forge ahead: the excitement of learning will probably outweigh the sheer fear. You will also have the pleasure of watching your own tastes change and expand as you add to your storehouse of learning authors and ideas and techniques. Unless you are very different from almost all teachers, you will, as the years go on, become far more accomplished—and educated—than you can really imagine right now.

And, of course, it almost goes without saying: if your own education has left you deficient in some area, it is your responsibility as a teacher, as a professional, to make up that deficiency. And, at this stage in the game, it really doesn't matter whose "fault" the deficiency may be; you didn't take the course or the teachers were not effective or you just didn't think the information was that important. It is, however, up to you to get yourself up to speed.

If you are confused about assonance and alliteration, look them up and learn them; if you've never gotten point of view straight, start studying now; if you don't know the difference between the Middle Ages and the Enlightenment, you can read about them; if somehow you've missed the major American twentieth-century novels, select a reasonable number and set aside some weekend time to enjoy them. If the distinction between phrase and clause eludes you, if you are not certain what a parallel construction looks like, you can learn it. You will now gladly learn as well as gladly teach. It comes, happily, with the territory.

················· **FOR YOUR JOURNAL** ·················

This is an entry you may want to keep private; it is for you, not anyone else. At the top of your journal page make three columns: *What I Know I Really Know, What I Sort of Know, What I Know I Need to Know.* Right now, at this point in your life, make a brief list regarding your knowledge of literature, language, and writing. Now look over the three columns; which is longest, which shortest? In the What I Know I Need to Know column, which one or two items do you think you will absolutely need in order to deal with your students? absolutely not need for some time to come? Which of the items can you learn this week? this month?

Literature: The Heart of Language Arts

As writing became more valued in school instruction, and computers and word processing took a more prominent place in the classroom, there was a fear that literature would be dethroned as the "queen" of the language arts curriculum. Certainly the days of literature always occupying the lion's share of the curriculum are somewhat on the wane. But literature, the reason most of us are English teachers—and the area with which we are usually the most familiar—remains the backbone of English language arts.

As I talked about in Chapter 1, most of us entered this profession because of our love of literature. Many of us are convinced that reading is, of and by itself, a good thing to do, and we want to encourage our students to engage in it and be captivated by its magic. Many of us also associate with literature an experience that moved us and that was represented in fiction, nonfiction, poetry, or drama. We have favorite authors, lines, scenes that we carry with us much as other people carry recollections with them from their childhood. Literature is, for many of us, a cosmic memory bank of sorts, and the conflicts and characters and metaphors of our favorite books can take on a deep and highly personal resonance.

While not all of our students will appear to react with the same enthusiasm regarding all the literature we read and respond to in the classroom, literature is, for most of our students, the most enjoyable part of language arts. First, it is an opportunity for them to **escape**, to literally lose themselves in reading. It is an old-fashioned phrase, antiquely put, but Emily Dickinson's belief that "there is no frigate like a book" (poem #1263) is indeed apt; a book, like no other vehicle, is stunningly equipped to carry us somewhere else. Second, students also **find themselves** in other characters. Third, through literature students can **live vicariously other lives** and in other eras. Fourth and finally, reading literature can be, for students, an opportunity to experience the sheer art of a well-crafted plot, the delineation of a character, the unfolding of an important theme. This **aesthetic appreciation** is often considered the most important reason for reading literature, but by placing our entire emphasis on aesthetics—how a piece of literature achieves what it is—we can destroy the reading and the pleasure of literature. It goes back to a cynical statement cited in Chapter 1, "English class ruined every good book I ever read." We do our students a great disservice if we confine all of our discussion and attention—and testing—to aesthetic appreciation. Which leads us to literary criticism and another reason you need to spend a great deal of time with your students and their response to all aspects of literature, not only the pure aesthetics.

> ·············· **FOR YOUR JOURNAL** ··············
>
> Considering the four reasons for reading literature—to escape, to find yourself, to learn about others, or to gain aesthetic appreciation—think about when and how you can relate to each reason. Perhaps a specific novel or short story or poem might stand out as being the major example. What do you remember about yourself as a reader and each of the four reasons for reading? Can you link any pieces of literature to specific reasons? Are there books you read that, for you at least, fulfill all four of the reasons for reading?

Schools of Literary Criticism: Why You Should Care

It may seem that in school you were just taught literature; you read a short story or a poem in class or for homework and discussed it or wrote about it or took a test on it and that was that. Actually, whether you were aware of it or not, the way you were taught literature was based on a number of philosophical assumptions and schools of literary criticism. Certainly, as an English major you are quite aware of literary criticism and of its impact as you read and talk about literature. Whether in middle school or college, literary theory can have a powerful effect. Raman Selden in *A Reader's Guide to Contemporary Literary Theory* writes that:

> One can think of the various literary theories as raising different questions about literature. Theories may ask questions from the point of view of the writer, of the work, of the reader, of what we usually call "reality." (3)

What that "reality" is can certainly vary according to the interpretation of the theory. For example, if you look at any literature from the perspective of feminist theory, if you realize that many times gender has shaped literature in powerful—and often not immediately apparent—ways, you see it very differently than you would otherwise. Taming the wilderness, hunting the white whale, going to war, ascending the throne, rescuing the maiden, all take on a distinctly gender-oriented cast, and these activities, which are still certainly "privileged" over the domestic aspects we associate with "female" life (cooking, tending a child), take up the predominant time in literary air space.

The contemporary popularity of Kate Chopin's *The Awakening* is somewhat a case in point. The story of a woman who literally awakens from her traditional role as a wife and mother, the novel languished in obscurity until almost seventy years after its 1899 publication date. While termed "poison" by nineteenth-century reviewers, *The Awakening*'s subject matter is now very acceptable to readers, and the novel is highly rated.

But to turn to the four major schools of literary criticism: if your teachers spent a great deal of time giving you information regarding the era the literature was written, the context in which it occurred, and who else was writing then, those teachers were concentrating on **historical** or **literary** background. For some teachers, that background is of less interest than the life of the author; if you remember being asked to pay attention to a writer's birth and death dates and other such information, your teachers were probably emphasizing **author biography**.

As a third approach, many of us were taught through the approach of what has been called the **New Criticism**. According to New Critical theory, where and when and even by whom a piece of literature is written is ultimately irrelevant. In New Critical theory, literature is considered a piece of art; very little other information is important or even of interest. This was a highly influential way to approach literature and was used almost exclusively in colleges, filtering down to the high schools, for some decades. The focus of New Critical approaches was largely on close reading of the text and aesthetic appreciation, one of the reasons for reading that I outlined previously.

Finally, yet another way to approach literature—to ask students to relate literature to themselves, their lives, and what else they have read—is termed **a reader response approach**, and the emphasis here is on what the reader brings to the piece. Gone is the interest in historical context, the author biography, or the aesthetic twists and turns as major concentrations. Using a reader response approach, what teachers ask of students is how the literature intertwines with what they know, who they are, and what they believe. Clearly, a reader response approach does not involve the factual information of a literary or historical emphasis; it does not address the author's biography and the New Critical aesthetic considerations. Reader response contends that most readers approach pieces differently, can have a shift not only from reader to reader but through a person's reading of the same text at different times in his or her life.

The Four Schools: What to Do?

There are valid reasons for all four approaches and, given a perfect world and more than enough time (to paraphrase Andrew Marvell's "To His Coy Mistress"), we as teachers would skillfully combine all four (and possibly add others, such as feminist theory), shifting our emphasis in response to the demands of the literature and the interests of our students. Such blending and adjusting, however, are not possible in most classrooms. Thus we need to ask ourselves as teachers: what is served by each of these four approaches?

New Critical approaches to literature came about because of serious dissatisfaction with extensive concentration on historical context and author biography. Whether the poem was the first or the last of a writer's career or was written after the artist's midlife nervous breakdown seemed not only irrelevant but also to deflect from the consideration of the work itself. Whether the literature occurred in response to some historical or topical event seemed equally irrelevant. Certainly there are clear exceptions to this: students probably need to know, for example, why Jonathan Swift was so outraged by events in Ireland that he would write the scathing "A Modest Proposal." Students might also need to understand that Nathaniel Hawthorne's *The Scarlet Letter* is not a historically accurate account of the Puritans but is a highly selected, highly filtered, nineteenth-century interpretation of a period of history. Do they need, however, to know Swift's or Hawthorne's biography? On the other hand, the colorful and tragic life of Edgar Allan Poe often seems to inspire students to wade through his dense prose and to attempt to understand it; the incidents surrounding Samuel Taylor Coleridge's "Kubla Khan," whether reported truthfully by Coleridge or not, are intriguing to most readers and lend some further depth to the magical, mysterious poem.

The problem comes when such information usurps—and it can, very quickly—the point of the reading. If students spend the bulk of class time learning about history and biography, where is the time to actually engage with the literature? This leaves us with New Criticism and reader response, and many argue it is the latter to which we should be paying most attention in our middle and high school classrooms.

Transactional Theory/Reader Response

Many English teachers learned in their literature study to love the close reading of poetry and prose. In this kind of analysis, known largely as the New Criticism, literature as seen as a relatively isolated object to be discussed and analyzed, almost as one would turn a multifaceted object such as a cut diamond and consider it from all points of view. The diamond itself would not be altered by the turning and handling; it would retain its entire integrity as an object. Thus the New Criticism, as defined in John Crowe Ransom's 1941 book of the same name, was literature without the influence of the reader, the historical context, or the personal history of the author. Yet for all its obvious advantages over other forms of literary criticism, teachers schooled in this tradition often find that it does not translate well into the middle school and high school English classroom. Analytical reading divorced from personal or historical context, a celebration of the intricate art of literature, can became for students an almost repugnant dissection of an already difficult text, robbing it of joy, making it a task, not a connection to life. An alternative to this approach is that of Louise Rosenblatt, the major voice of transactional or reader response theory. Rosenblatt's seminal book, *Literature as Exploration*, was first published in 1938, and she offers a very different view than that of Ransom. Rosenblatt reminds teachers of their "responsibility to the students as well as to the discipline" (ix) and cautions us:

> We go through empty motions if our primary concern is to enable the student to recognize various literary forms, to identify various verse patterns, to note the earmarks of the style of particular author, to detect recurrent symbols, or to discriminate the kinds of irony or satire. Acquaintance with the formal aspects of literature will not in itself insure esthetic sensitivity . . . Knowledge of literary forms is empty without an accompanying humanity. (52)

I discovered reader response out of my own difficulty enticing my students to celebrate what I perceived to be the great craft of literature. What I think I had forgotten is that that appreciation came to me after, sometimes long after, I had experienced how a novel or a short story could make me feel, could tell me about my life, my problems, my capabilities. Louise Rosenblatt tells us three things:

1. The literature itself must have some connection to the students' lives.
2. The approach must, in order to capitalize upon the students' lives, be inductive.
3. Students must be involved, must be engaged to the point where the discussion leads them, as Rosenblatt writes, "to raise personally meaningful questions . . . [and] to seek in the text the basis for valid answers." (ix–x)

What did it mean for me and my students to move into transactional theory and into reader response? It meant a radical transformation, one that is still challenging to many today. Indeed, the message of Louise Rosenblatt—"analysis of the work . . . acquisition of new insights and information, will have value only as it is linked up with the student's own primary response to the work" (120)—is as fresh and startling today as it was when first articulated 70 some years ago in *Literature as Exploration*. What Rosenblatt means—what transactional theory demands—is that we and our students do far more with what is read in a classroom than look for patterns and devices and even comprehension or answers to multiple-choice test items on the state exam.

Rosenblatt insists that literature is engagement, response, search for insight, and, ultimately, that that study can be both individual and idiosyncratic as it is heavily, necessarily dependent upon what every reader brings to the text. And that profound faith in what the reader brings—what the reader has a right to bring—is continuingly radical, startling, and upends the hierarchy of the traditional classroom. Rosenblatt gives us the very definition of a democratic classroom. Such a classroom can be unsettling, as Rosenblatt well knows: while "teachers and pupils should be relaxed enough to face what indeed happened as they interpreted the printed page," the dominance of the teacher is ceded. Rosenblatt tells us:

> Frank expression of boredom or even vigorous rejections is a more valid starting point for learning than are docile attempts to feel "what the teacher wants." When the young reader considers why he has responded in a certain way, he is learning both to read more adequately and to seek personal meaning in literature. (70)

What a conjunction Rosenblatt offers us—not only to read but to seek meaning. Is she telling us that the two are complementary, even inseparable? Indeed she is.

Characteristics of a reader response classroom

In a study, I taped and analyzed classes of two teachers who use a reader response philosophy in teaching literature. The teachers, in two different schools in different sections of the same urban area, had their students discuss a trio of contemporary poems. A detailed look at what was said within the classes revealed five characteristics of a classroom that uses a reader response orientation:

1. Teachers encourage students to talk extensively.
2. Teachers help students make a community of meaning.
3. Teachers ask, they don't tell.
4. Teachers ask students to make links to personal experience.
5. Teachers affirm student responses.

I also found that the discussions refute two common objections to the implementation of a reader response methodology in the classroom: first, that attention to student response to literature will deflect seriously from any literary analysis of the work itself; and second, that a reader response approach, in and of itself, takes too much instructional time to be efficient—it is quicker to tell students than to ask them to explore their own interpretations or reactions to a text.

Let's take a brief look at the following three poems on young people and their fathers and how two classes discussed them:

Breakings

Long before I first left home, my father
tried to teach me horses, land, and sky,
to show me how this kind of work was done.
I studied how to be my father's son,
but all I learned was, when the wicked die,
they ride combines through barley forever.

Every summer I hated my father
as I drove hot horses through dusty grass;
and so I broke with him, and left the farm
for other work, where unfamiliar weather
broke on my head an unexpected storm
and things I had not studied came to pass.

So nothing changes, nothing stays the same,
and I have returned from a broken home
alone, to ask for a job breaking horses.
I watch a colt on a long line making
tracks in dust, and think of the kinds of breakings
there are, and the kinds of restraining forces.
—Henry Taylor
An Afternoon of Pocket Billiards

Those Winter Sundays

Sundays too my father got up early
and put his clothes on in the blueblack cold
then with cracked hands that ached
from labor in the weekday weather made
banked fires blaze. No one ever thanked him.

I'd wake and hear the cold splintering, breaking.
When the rooms were warm, he'd call,
and slowly I would rise and dress,
fearing the chronic angers of that house,

Speaking indifferently to him,
who had driven out the cold
and polished my good shoes as well.
What did I know, what did I know
of love's austere and lonely offices?
—Robert Hayden
Angle of Ascent

Black Walnuts

The year my father used the car for hulling
was the best. We cobbled the drive
with walnuts gathered in baskets
and cardboard boxes, then rode with him
down that rough lane, forward and backward,
time and again, until the air was bitter to breathe
and the tires spun in the juice.
For years after, every piece of gravel
was dyed brown, and the old Ford
out on the open road would warm up
to a nutty smell, especially in winter
with the windows closed and the heater blowing.

Crouched over hulls mangled green and yellow,
we picked out corrugated shells
even the car's weight couldn't crack
and spread them on the grass to dry.
My father, on his hands and knees, happy
over windfall, talked of how good
the tender meats would taste; and in that moment
I wished with all my heart that he might live forever,
as leaves ticked down around us
and the fresh stain darkened on our hands.

—Neal Bowers
North American Review

Teachers encourage students to talk extensively   If engaging in a transaction with literature (having students make the literature their own) is an instructional goal, then students must be able to join in a conversation. This is to be distinguished from a series of responses to a teacher's question, responses that are ultimately regulated, guided, and abbreviated within the class context. Students must, if they are to thrive in a reader response classroom, really talk, converse, speak at length, pause, argue, question. They should not be confined to one-word, one-phrase answers in response to a teacher's question and in a pattern determined by the teacher. In a reader response classroom, teachers encourage students to talk extensively.

In the two classes studied, the discussion is lively. Students remain on task with the three poems during the entire class period, and the teachers do not have to guide students "back to the subject." In fact, in both the classes student responses are not always one-word or one-phrase answers but extended sentences (largely in clusters of five to seven seconds with a dozen or so twenty-second responses). When students do make brief-phrase answers, they are in the context of a rapid-fire argument/discussion with other students that seem to come in response to the drama and tension of the discussion.

Teachers help students make a community of meaning   Because each student's response will draw on individual, even idiosyncratic, personal background and experience, and because exchange and exploration is the goal, reader response teachers must be patient with factual misunderstanding. Eventually, individual misconceptions are corrected in a community of meaning. In a reader response classroom, nevertheless, paramount attention is not focused on right answers.

Accordingly, both classes studied are characterized by open discussion and exploration of multiple interpretations. For example, about five minutes into the discussion of the first poem, "Breakings," one teacher (Teacher A) initiates a discussion on a passage referring to the breaking of a colt. The colt's experience is metaphorically linked to the poem's speaker's own "breaking" by life/reality, but the teacher waits as the students struggle with the meaning. While they later (as a whole class) understand the poem's major point, it is a journey of interpretation. As in discussions outside of school, meaning is found and lost and found again:

TEACHER A: What does it ["Breakings"] mean, James?
JAMES: He learned how to be a farmer on his dad's farm and then he left first to find a
                     new job, and he got—he couldn't find nothing better—he couldn't find noth-
                     ing good—so he had to go back to working on the farm and hopefully . . .
                     (garbled).
KAY: He left his dad and the dad wanted the son to be just like him—so he got tired
                     of it.
TEACHER A: What do you think he's learned at the end [of the poem]?
BILL: I thought he was at a racetrack.
TEACHER A: What made you think that?
JAMAL: Because it said—the colt—he's kicking up dirt. I thought he was at a racetrack.
TEACHER A: What's he doing with the colt on a long line?
JAMES: He's plowing.
KAY: He's breaking.
JAMES: He's plowing . . . he's training.
KAY: He's training.
ANN: He's trying to get it so that he can break the—
TEACHER A: He's trying to break the colt? . . . Ann, you work with horses, don't you? Have
                     you ever seen them when they put them on a long line—what are they trying
                     to do?
ANN: It's a *lunge* line. They're trying to get them to—have them get used to . . .
TEACHER A: Get used to the thing around their head—what do they call that, a *halter*?
ANN: Yeah. They call it a halter.
TEACHER A: So what else could they be breaking here?
BILL: Breaking him into a plow . . . getting him used to a plow.
TEACHER A: Breaking on the plow. What does a plow do?
BILL: It plows the field.
JAMES: It breaks up the ground.
TEACHER A: Does it break up anything?
BILL: It breaks up the dirt.
TEACHER A: Okay. What does this guy say about his feelings about his father?

As the discussion goes on, much is said about what the speaker feels about his father and while it would appear the students do not immediately understand the metaphorical significance of *breaking*, they eventually come to the following conclusion:

TEACHER A:	What do you think this title, "Breakings," means?
MARY:	Breaking of him.
ANN:	Breaking the horses.
CURT:	Breaking both [of them].

A community of meaning is made.

Teachers ask; they don't tell   Teachers who tell students, who talk most of the class time, do not have reader response classrooms. It must be the students who struggle with the literature, who give the answers, and who make the meaning—their own meaning—of the text.

The major tool in these discussions is the question. While one teacher in this study does give vocabulary synonyms, and the other speaks extensively on a related aspect of one of the poems, the teachers resist almost all direct instruction. When confronted with a student question, both teachers turn to other students rather than become the answer giver.

Teacher A does not provide students with a list of preselected terms but asks twice for words the students do not understand ("Find another word that you don't know the meaning of"), asks for confirmation regarding terms ("Ann, what do they call that, a *halter*?"), and, when she actually looks up one word for a definition, asks students to give her the spelling of the word. She encourages students to struggle to find meaning themselves and, in a typical exchange, tells a student: "Look at *corrugated* in context . . . have you ever seen corrugated cardboard?" When the student responds, "That word doesn't make sense," the teacher does not correct her or argue but acknowledges the fact and tells the student, "We're going to find out why it doesn't make sense." When confronted with a twenty-second silence regarding the meaning of "Breakings," Teacher A gives two prompts but waits for student answers—which do come, from three students. Even when asked for clarification, the teacher turns to her students.

TEACHER A:	What do you think changes in the roles that the dad and the son play? Anything?
ANDRE:	What do you mean by the *roles*?
TEACHER A:	Does anyone know here what I mean by the *roles*?

She receives responses to this question, as she does when she asks for an interpretation of a line in "Those Winter Sundays."

TEACHER A:	He says in here, let's look down at this bottom line, "speaking *indifferently* to him." What do you think that means?
MIKE:	Not any differently than . . .
BOB:	Not in a different language.
CURT:	Same as everyone, everyone else.
TEACHER A:	Why would that be that significant if he's talking to his father the same as everyone else?
ALAN:	All fathers are like . . .
CURT:	It's probably that same weekend routine.
BILL:	Does that mean like *indifferently* to, like than what he usually does—or just to everybody?
TEACHER A:	I don't know . . . what do you think?

BILL: It's everybody—he should be talking to his father differently because his
               father . . .

Similarly, the other teacher, Teacher B, when asking "Which of these three [poems]
seems to be a *father poem*?" receives two student questions: "What do you mean by that?"
and "Which one do you like?" She does not answer, however, letting students argue as to
the definition. And the students do subsequently argue in what is the most heated discussion of their particular class.

Teachers ask students to make links to personal experience   Requesting that students
make links to personal experience is the paramount activity in reader response classrooms.
In capable hands, however, it becomes more than students simply venting their opinions.
While personal experience is shared and cited, the students in both teachers' classrooms
also pay close attention to the text of the three poems, using it to buttress their points.

One teacher asks students on two separate instances to relate to the anger of the
speaker against his father in "Breakings" and receives multiple answers—some students link
their assigned household tasks (such as mowing the lawn) to the speaker; some discuss
their general anger toward their parents. During the latter, three students share responses,
one for twenty-two seconds.

Certainly the fact that the three poems are central to students' lives—they all have
parents, if not on-site fathers—makes such an insistence on linkage of personal experience
possible. All of the students have stories and opinions and a history in this area; the discussions, as cited here, might not be as rich if the topic were about building highways or
going to war. Yet as the discussions reveal, the students do more than simply link the poetry
to their own lives and experiences. Most of the students return to lines, concepts, and ideas
in the literature and, while they relate to the text, they also do a capable job examining and
even analyzing it.

Teachers affirm students' responses   Another characteristic of the methodology of a
reader response classroom discussion is that teachers affirm student response to the literature. They can affirm response by overt praise or agreement, but these two classes show that
the teachers reinforce their students' responses through two major instructional methods: by
referring to student comments in discussion and by asking other students to respond specifically to those comments. Such actions give powerful confirmation to students that their
ideas, their responses, are legitimate.

In one section of the discussion, approximately seven students respond for a total of
three relatively teacher-uninterrupted minutes, taking turns looking at the phrase in question. Another student then moves the discussion to the "speaking indifferently" section and
talks, without interruption, for almost one and one-half minutes.

Teacher B repeatedly moves students to respond to other student observations—at
least a half-dozen times during the class period. In "Breakings," for instance, she notes: "Jim
said you break the spirit of the colt. If we make an analogy here between the father and son,
does that make the son bitter—as Rick said?"

The technique has the effect of inspiring students to continue to respond to each
other. From this very heated, wide-ranging argument there emerges a question of whose
poem is it anyway, a discussion that is about reader response. Theresa starts the discussion,
and her comment is almost lost in the uproar. The teacher does not repeat it for the class,
but signals the other students to listen.

TEACHER B: Check out Theresa's remark, and let's hear if you agree.

THERESA: I think it [the interpretation of the poem as about fathers and sons or fathers and daughters] is determined by the reader and not the poet.

JOHN: Yeah, it's neutered. (Garbled voices; Teacher B calls the class to order.)

TEACHER B: Do you agree that there's a different meaning for the reader, that that's possible?

THERESA: Yeah.

RICK: Yeah. Sometimes the poem—you put these allegorical meanings [in it], then it can. But if you just write a straightforward poem, it can't be disputed then. There's, like, no second meaning.

TEACHER B: What kind of poem is a "straightforward" poem?

RICK: What the poet wants to write.

ROB: Like a descriptive poem.

KAREN: Like when he says *he*.

ROB: Like a haiku.

KAREN: Yeah.

JOHN: I think you can interpret it however you want—but you may well be *wrong* in your interpretation. Because I think the poet had a set audience in mind and what he was remembering and what he was trying to get out. So if you want to think of it as a father/daughter thing, you may be wrong, but you're welcome to your own opinion.

JIM: The poet's a man.

KAREN: But you don't know the poet.

RICK: But if the author like released what this . . . pamphlet, this book . . . is about, is meant to mean, that would take all the fun out of discussing it.

ROB: Well, you see the poet is writing for the poet himself, and that's how he is interpreting it. But other people can read it, and that's how they interpret it.

And how they interpret it, and the very excitement, the very pleasure of discussing it, is surely at the heart of this reader response classroom.

Certainly there is a place for the literary lecture and for an author's biography. Certainly the New Critical examination of that well-wrought urn can also be an illuminating and rewarding activity. But as Rosenblatt, Barthes, and others remind us, when we consider our middle school and high school students and their engagement with literature and the formation of their joy of literature, we must allow them not only the discussion floor itself but also the authority of their own thoughts and instincts.

In my school history, I can recall few teachers who advanced the opinion that a poet's ideas might be akin to mine or any other student's. By contrast, the two teachers represented in this study allow their students joy and time, and they honor their ideas. These teachers know and convey that different readers can have different interpretations, and they suspect that poets and young people have similar feelings. What they do is not mysterious or arcane or even terribly difficult. What they do, however, is mandatory if we care about literature and about developing our students into lifelong readers.

Reader response: Uses and abuses

Especially after reading these exciting give-and-take conversations of the students, it may be hard to think of reader response being abused in a classroom, but a few cautions are in order.

Many well-meaning teachers cite Louise Rosenblatt and reader response theory but are not sure what Rosenblatt has written and what reader response activities mean in a classroom. Certainly reader response does not imply that any student response under any circumstances carries complete authority. Reader response asks the student to bring his or her experience to the literature, and it honors that connection. It maintains that an individual reader can shape a piece of literature through his or her own interpretation, although the limits of that shaping are relatively crucial to delineate. Using a reader response approach in a classroom is not an invitation to students or teachers to:

- Ignore completely what is in the text.
- Read into the text facts or inferences that are clearly not present or not defensible.
- Insist that "well, that's my opinion" constitutes the last—and unassailable—word on the discussion.
- Reveal sensitive aspects of their personal lives in order to discuss the literature or defend their points.

A reader's response must be intelligent, thoughtful, and have some tie to the text, however tenuous that might first appear. To consider a discussion where students do not have to pay any attention to what they have read is not reader response—it's irresponsible.

On the other hand, we cannot insist that students reveal responses to literature that may violate their sense of privacy. Much literature that is worth reading and discussing deals with mature issues. Students can have legitimate responses to that literature—and experience with those issues—but prefer to keep the specifics to themselves. Asking students to make general connections or to discuss if they know of anyone else who has been in a similar situation or felt a similar way can relieve the pressure to reveal. Teacher as *voyeur* is an ugly sight; we do not want to extract from our students, in the name of reader response or any other approach to literature, personal revelations that they would prefer to keep outside the classroom.

We must attempt to create a classroom climate where students can bring their own lives and beliefs to the text. Balancing and adjusting that climate is part of the craft of the teacher. What we do not want is described by a student on the eve of teaching:

> I had the audacity to contradict (or question) [my English teacher's] view on the analysis of poetry. For several weeks we read and analyzed poems. My poor memory cannot recall specific works, but I do recall my shock and dismay when my teacher informed me that my perception of a poem, my own personal analysis, was wrong. He then proceeded to lecture the class on the correct perception. I was incredulous. Is not poetry like a work of art? Is it not there for each of us to perceive differently? Some poems are as abstract as the most modern of art. Who is to say what the poet really means except the poet himself?
>
> —Donna Johnson

While some could also argue that even the poet may not "know" what the poem means, we do know that each reader needs to be respected. Donna was not crushed by her teacher's rejection of her interpretation; some of our students, however, may not be so fortunate.

In Lisa Schade's classroom in Michigan students become active readers and also critics. In an award-winning article, she outlines how she deliberately introduces to her senior world literature students five literary critical models and then asks them to analyze a variety of pieces using each, in turn, of the five models. In Schade's classroom, she has settled on these critical approaches: Jungian/Archetypal, Formalism, Reader Response, Socio-Historic and Biographical, and Philosophical. It has worked well for her students, and Schade uses lecture, small-group work, large-group discussion, and individual work as organizing structures. She explains how she sets this up:

> After I introduce the essential theory of any school of criticism, I follow some basic steps to test for comprehension and encourage application. It usually takes one class session to introduce the idea of a critical method and practice application to a short poem or story. On the following day, students must take a quiz about the specific aspects of the criticism for literal knowledge of the theory. Then students divide into small groups and work with a poem or short story to practice together approaching it from the perspective introduced the day before. As I move around the room to help, students work through the poem; we share responses at the end of the hour, discussing the difficulties and advantages of the approach. When I'm satisfied that they're comfortable, we move on. . . . They read at home and respond to reading from the critical approach we're currently working with. On the following day, they bring their response back to the small group setting to share and discuss. Each group must reach a consensus in interpretation using the current method of criticism, and then we come together into a full class discussion. (30–31)

For Schade's students, looking at literature from five different perspectives is enriching— "students' curiosity is piqued by different theories of literature and life" (31)—and it helps students find a way into world literature texts that might be otherwise difficult or inaccessible. At the end of her class, Schade gives her students one last piece of literature and asks them to individually decide which of the critical approaches is not only most "logical for the given text" but how that method of criticism would help in interpretation (31). Schade feels that her students "become more adept at utilizing criticism and making their own choices and interpretations" (30), the great goal, in fact, of most good teachers of literature. (For a more extensive look at teaching literary criticism, see the Deborah Appleman book cited in References section at the end of the chapter.)

·············· **FOR YOUR JOURNAL** ··············

Pick a short story or poem or play or novel you have read and might like to teach. Think about it from the perspectives of the four schools of literary criticism: historical or literary background, author biography, New Critical, and reader response. Make a list of questions you might want to ask students that reflect each of the four schools. Now look at the questions you developed, and write a brief entry on which of the four schools interests you the most as a teacher/learner. Why? How do you think your students will respond?

Organizing Literature

You may find, especially in the beginning of your teaching, that you follow a textbook's organization of literature and go from Chapter 1 to June 1. You may, practically speaking, be a bit too overwhelmed to do much more creative shaping. As you become more self-assured, however, as you continue not just to be but to *become* a teacher, you will want to experiment and play with how you organize literature for your classes. Such experimentation will help you respond to what your students may be interested in pursuing. After all, ninth-grade or seventh-grade or any-grade English, even when you and your students have a literature anthology/textbook, can include many different—and wonderful—things not only to read but to discuss and write about.

Let's consider. Most textbooks are organized in standard patterns, and some of the major ways textbooks—and teachers—organize the study of literature are by:

- **Chronology** (the Romantic Period, the Middle Ages, and so on)
- **Author** (James Baldwin, F. Scott Fitzgerald)
- **Theme** ("Discovering Oneself")
- **Genre** (the short story)

There are, as you can imagine, benefits to all four of the patterns. Certainly in survey courses of American and British literature the chronological pattern is the most frequently used; in more general literature courses, theme and genre are popular. Some classes focus on individual writers for brief periods of study. By dipping in and out of chapters, though, by taking some pieces from one section and some from another, the organizational pattern can be adapted. Some textbooks even list in the (often unread) introduction or teacher's manual suggestions on how to use the literature in different configurations. Obviously, you can also mix up the categories and study, for instance, a more complicated version of one pattern by adding to it.

Let us consider poetry (genre) by adding to it:

- Modern (late-twentieth and early-twenty-first century) poetry (**chronology and genre**)
- Modern poetry by American writers (**chronology, genre, and authors**)
- Modern poetry by American writers who focused on the loss of the American Dream (**chronology, genre, authors, and theme**)

What such a series of combinations may do is enrich the consideration and discussion of the literature. Making connections intellectually is what much of our reading is all about; when students are confronted with one of these combinations, they make connections they would not otherwise see.

Theme and genre: Pleasures and pitfalls

Asking students to consider literature under the umbrella of a **theme** can be very helpful as students try to make sense of a poem or a novel or a play. It can connect what could otherwise seem so disparate it is impossible to grasp. Linking, for example, pieces of literature that come from different countries and different eras—but that all have a similar theme—may also help students see connections and stimulate questions that might not be, otherwise, so obvious.

Certainly the three poems discussed in the section on reader response ("Breakings," "Those Winter Sundays," and "Black Walnuts") all share, loosely, the same theme of fathers and children.

On the other hand, we need to be very aware that by asking students to see or find a predetermined theme, we can be circumventing their discovery of the literature. And this caution regarding theme does not necessarily mean students should seek some terribly far out interpretation in the name of rampant individuality. Literature is essentially made new by new readers, and we need to create a classroom atmosphere where, while there is guidance, there is not a preset determination of what a work or poem just might be about. The point is to use a framework such as theme in a rather loose manner. Your students may see themes you have not anticipated and may possibly reject the thematic relation of two pieces of literature—and for good reason. Announcing or insisting that a certain piece or pieces of literature have a set theme is intellectual hostage taking.

In a similar way, the very act of looking at literature as only representative of a specific **genre** can be as limiting as it can be helpful. Literature is traditionally categorized into genres, a term which attempts to capture the marvelous and myriad universe of writing. You recognize the three major terms: prose, poetry, and drama. Prose is further defined/refined into fiction (novels, short stories) and nonfiction (literary nonfiction such as essays and longer pieces; informational nonfiction such as contracts, reports, research studies).

All of this is helpful in a way, but it is also misleading. You will find, as will your students, that genre is tricky at best. One of my favorite activities is to make three columns on the board, each headed by the names of the three genres: prose, poetry, and drama. I then ask students to brainstorm characteristics that they think are appropriate for each genre. Students rarely hesitate as most can recall with little difficulty a few characteristics of a play they have seen or a poem or a novel they have read.

After about twenty minutes of coming up with terms and descriptors and moving from genre category to category, I stop and ask students to look, without comment or elimination, at the lists we have made on the board. Students generally find that each genre shares almost identical characteristics, and they realize that when you think about it, it is truly difficult to *define* a genre or type of literature. In fact, each genre often has the characteristics of the others; and sometimes we may feel as if we are, in this game of definition and codification, reduced to saying, "I can't define it, but I know it when I see it."

While this argument may seem negative to you, think about how the questions of the genres can be manipulated into wonderful discussion departures. Consider these intriguing contradictions:

- **Fiction vs. Nonfiction:** How true is fact? How false is fiction? Where can you draw the line between story and account? What makes fiction fiction? nonfiction nonfiction?
- **Prose vs. Poetry:** How much poetry uses flat, proselike statement? Which prose uses figurative language? How compressed is language in poetry? in prose? What makes prose prose? poetry poetry? What are prose poems?
- **Short Story vs. Novel:** What makes a short story a short story? a novel a novel? Is a short novel (a novella or a novelette) really a long short story? Why or why not?
- **Drama vs. Fiction:** What is the drama of a play? Why isn't the dialogue in a short story or novel—or a piece of nonfiction, for that matter—playlike? What makes drama not fiction? fiction not drama?

Talking about genre in these ways can be interesting to students and can, further, get them to look more critically at what they are reading. And now let's turn to the major genres and how you can select and teach each of them.

Looking at Fiction: Novels and Short Stories

Both contemporary and classic fiction are staples of the English language arts curriculum. Many classic novels used in secondary English classrooms are Western European, specifically, British (such as George Orwell's *1984* or Mary Shelley's *Frankenstein*) and American (such as William Faulkner's *As I Lay Dying* and John Steinbeck's *Of Mice and Men*). While there are a number of other recent novels written outside the Western European tradition and used in secondary English classrooms—one such widely read African novel is Chinua Achebe's *Things Fall Apart*—British and American tend to dominate in secondary curriculum.

Short stories also have their classics, and while some famous ones are in translation— such as those by Guy De Maupassant—British and American short stories are widely anthologized in many textbooks across the grade levels. We think of widely anthologized short stories such as Kate Chopin's "The Story of an Hour," Edgar Allan Poe's "Cask of Amontillado," Shirley Jackson's "The Lottery," and that old chestnut, Richard Connell's "The Most Dangerous Game." In addition, there are numerous contemporary short story collections that you can use with your students. (Teacher Don Gallo has compiled a number of wonderful young adult short story collections, and the titles are cited in the References section at the end of this chapter.) Regardless of the piece of fiction, however, there are three major issues teachers must consider before approaching a novel or a short story: background, length, and focus. (For further discussions of approaches to novels, see Chapter 3 for *Their Eyes Were Watching God* and *The House on Mango Street*).

Background

What will students need to know to appreciate the novel or short story? When I returned to teach high school, the classic we read and studied was F. Scott Fitzgerald's *The Great Gatsby*. While I thought I had prepared my students for the 1920s setting and characters— not to mention telling them that the book was an American classic and filled with shimmering language—it was clear that I had not done so sufficiently. My students had little problem with the vocabulary, but they needed more background than I anticipated. About a third way through the novel, in class discussion the students showed that they were clearly flummoxed by characters who spent all day entertaining themselves and were so wealthy that they never needed to work or clean the house or do the usual mundane chores that most of us perform. How had I missed stressing this essential point about economics? We went back to talk about it, but I feel that my misjudgment regarding the need for extensive background preparation made the reading of this novel not as powerful I had hoped. While many of the students genuinely disliked the movie we saw after our reading, it did give them a visual on which to focus and made the setting of the novel far more explicit. In hindsight, I should have used the movie earlier to capture for students the wealth and opulence of Gatsby's life and the setting of the novel. Sadly, my misperception about background my students needed made the reading of *The Great Gatsby* tedious and puzzling.

It's a bit different with short stories that often give readers everything they need regarding background in the first few paragraphs and are rarely as tricky as novels. Some short stories can, though, require prereading information. Regardless, try to look at the piece as if you were reading it for the first time—what will your students need to know before reading or very quickly into the reading so that they do not become frustrated? To understand the setting of a short story such as "Cask," students will need to know about wine and wine cellars as well as what Poe calls "the supreme madness of the carnival season." "The Story of an Hour" may need some vocabulary glossing for despite its very short and straightforward tale, words such as *aquiver*, *bespoke*, *elixir*, *importunities*, and *gripsack* may interfere with student understanding.

Length

Short stories are rarely longer than a dozen pages, and this brevity is part of their great utility and interest. You and your students can read a short story in one class and respond and discuss it fairly efficiently. Novels, however, are often a different matter, and keeping students motivated and reading can be tough. If the novel is a very long one, such as *Frankenstein* or Theodore Dreiser's *An American Tragedy*, you need to think of pacing for your students. Having some students responsible for some chapters—using a jigsaw arrangement where students in groups read selected chapters and then become experts who teach other students about the chapters—and limiting your time is important. If the novel is short, it may well be possible to read much of it aloud or in class. Study guides for chapters can also be helpful, especially if students create them themselves. In the high school class I recently taught, student groups crafted guides and picked out, on their own, important vocabulary, interesting quotations, striking poetic passages, the latter of which was especially appropriate for *The Great Gatsby*. And, from these study guides, shared in class, we as a group were able to select items for the final novel test, making the test far more student centered than what I could have created on my own. As noted before, the class as a whole did not like *Gatsby*, but the study guides were helpful, and the test grades were high.

Focus

If you worry about being a conscientious English teacher, you think that you need to cover all of the major "parts" of a novel or short story, that is, plot, character, theme, setting. Don't forget, though, that all fiction is not alike; some writers are great on plotting and moving characters through intricate settings; some use a bare plot and concentrate on character. Setting is important in some fiction and purely backdrop in others. So what do you do? Pay attention to the literature you choose and try to resist trotting your students through every literary element. And remember, too, that for some students new to the literature, there will be insights and emphases that you had not anticipated. It is powerful when you can follow students' interest as they may choose to focus on an aspect of the fiction that you had not anticipated.

One final caution about reading classic novels and short stories: with the wide availability of Cliffs Notes, Spark Notes, and other such "study aids," some of your students will surely read commercial summaries rather than the literature itself. If nothing else, this is a real reason to look beyond canonical, classic literature and choose something recently written for which there are no prepackaged materials. In addition, keep this very much in mind if you ask your students to write formal essays or responses on works such as Richard Wright's *Native Son* or Jane Austen's *Pride and Prejudice*; there are countless standard research papers for sale on the Internet, and many students will not be able to resist the temptation.

The Lure of Nonfiction: Literary and Informational

For many of our students, nonfiction is the real deal, literature that transcends their interest in any form of fiction. Most of us as teachers, of course, have progressed through our English majors as readers and lovers of literature—meaning fiction, drama, and poetry—but we should not lose sight of the power of nonfiction to enthrall. In fact, as discussed earlier in this chapter, the very question of what is fact and what is fiction, though actually a fairly sophisticated consideration, can lead students to understanding and debate. At any rate, nonfiction—both literary nonfiction and informational nonfiction—needs more attention in our classes and needs more acceptance by us as teachers. Further, the very nature of nonfiction means that much of it is contemporary, and that can be a real boon when classic fiction is often set decades or even centuries in the past.

For students for whom fiction or drama or poetry is not appealing, nonfiction is a viable and useful alternative. Lists such as those compiled by the American Library Association, booklists published by the National Council of Teachers of English, Joyce Carol Oates and Robert Atwan's *The Best Essays of the Century*, excellent references such as *The Best in Children's Nonfiction* edited by Myra Zarnowksi and colleagues, and articles such as Larry R. Johannessen's "When History Talks Back: Teaching Nonfiction Literature of the Vietnam War" are also helpful. For teachers, nonfiction—whether it be a full book or an article or an essay, letters, diaries, memoir, speeches—can also be a vehicle to give students practice with important skills. While many English language arts teachers are first and foremost lovers of fiction, nonfiction is powerful and highly useful in the classroom.

Literary nonfiction

Mostly due to the recent film and the surprising discovery of some unpublished material, Truman Capote and in particular his groundbreaking *In Cold Blood* has experienced a resurgence of interest. Capote's daring (and, as we know now from newly revealed material, at times fanciful) combination of fact and imagination broke the mold in the nonfiction genre. Students may be interested in reading this account of murder and motivation as well as other classics such as Jacob A. Riis' *How the Other Half Lives*, a portrait of tenement poverty in 1900 New York, and James Agee's *Let Us Now Praise Famous Men*, a look at life in rural American in the Depression. Both books by Riis and Agee combine photography and prose, and Agee's work in particular is what we now term multigenre, using many forms of writing to capture the people and the landscape of the Depression-era South. More recently, there are also current popular books on disastrous hurricanes (Erik Larson's *Isaac's Storm*), whaling accidents (Nathaniel Philbrick's National Book Award-winning *In the Heart of the Sea*), deadly mountain climbing (Jon Krakauer's *Into Thin Air*), working poverty in the United States (Barbara Ehrenreich's *Nickel and Dimed*), the food industry (Eric Schlosser's *Fast Food Nation*), a legendary and unlikely racehorse (Laura Hillenbrand's *Seabiscuit*), long-distance and endurance swimming (Lynne Cox's *Swimming to Antarctica*) as well as recent biographies of figures as disparate as Elvis (by Peter Guralnick) and *John Adams* (by David McCullough).

Memoir is also experiencing a resurgence, and students who might be turned off by classic fiction may well be interested in contemporary accounts of individual lives. For instance, young adult writer Paula Fox's *Borrowed Finery* and Frank McCourt's *Angela's Ashes* may both find eager readers in students. Fox recounts her life with elegant but indifferent parents in urban New York City; McCourt's book takes place in Limerick, Ireland, and details, often with grim humor, poverty, and hardship. Another favorite of mine is poet Kim Barnes' *In the Wilderness*, the story of her childhood in northern Idaho where her logger father raised the family in a remote wooded area and, in an effort to make sense of his hard life, turned to Pentecostalism. In addition, slave narratives from the nineteenth century and many excellent accounts of war—both older conflicts and more contemporary—can be riveting to students despite their often-depressing content.

Informational nonfiction

How things work, how things are built, statistics regarding weather, sales, and achievements are all the province of informational nonfiction, which fascinates students. Sources for these abound—everything from nonfiction magazines, to *The Guinness World Record*, issued and updated every year (one of the most popular books in any school library), to nonfiction books. Books such as the Orbis Pictus winner *Phineas Gage: A Gruesome but True Story About Brain Science* by John Fleischmann tells students much about an emerging scientific area of study, and George Sullivan's *Built to Last: Building America's Amazing Bridges, Dams, Tunnels and Skyscrapers* offers, for younger readers, narrative, photographs, and statistics on important structures in America. The DK (Dorling Kindersley) Eyewitness series, examples of which are often housed in reference sections in the school library, combine in oversized books beautiful photography and interesting information on topics as wide ranging as the ocean, weapons of spies, and animals of all kinds. Again, for students who believe that the world of reading is confined to boring stories about uninteresting people who mostly live in the past, informational nonfiction opens a very different landscape.

Working with nonfiction

What should we do with nonfiction? Actually, we should do similar activities to what we do with fiction: read it, discuss it, and write about it. Certainly one crucial aspect of nonfiction is point of view and how that shapes what is highlighted in research and fact: any nonfiction book or essay or article will have an undeniable slant on the topic, and asking students to discuss and discern an author's point of view or even bias is an important intellectual aspect of reading and assessing nonfiction. While this may seem very obvious with biography and autobiography, it is also crucial in other pieces. What an author selects or fails to emphasize can shape the reader's view of any topic. For instance, in Lillian Schlissel's *Women's Diaries of the Westward Journey,* a collection of American women's writing as they trekked the Overland Trail in the mid-nineteenth century, the editor's emphasis is far different than what most historical accounts include. Schlissel highlights, for instance, the repeated mention of graves on the side of the trail, final resting places for adults and infants who did not survive the journey. This detail, which some of the women diarists consistently choose to include, is rarely mentioned in men's accounts and is part of the different point of view.

Finally, as noted in the opening of this section, nonfiction is also an excellent vehicle for skills instruction; using any kind of nonfiction, students can take notes, locate information, summarize passages, generate questions that the text may not answer, and connect and relate ideas. Many nonfiction books use maps, drawings, charts, reproductions of period photographs and newspapers, all of which can widen students' reading ability.

Teaching and Selecting Poetry

Let's tell the truth: many teachers are scared of poetry. Some feel that every poem has a set meaning and that if they do not teach and convey that meaning in their teaching, any work with the poem is incomplete. In addition, because many teachers are fearful of the "meaning" of poems, they often deflect the issue entirely by spending most of their time teaching literary terms and making sure that every student knows the two metaphors, the one instance of assonance, and the rhyme scheme of the poem. Obviously, I don't agree: poems don't need owner's manuals before they can be read and appreciated. In fact, you can teach poems that are puzzles (think of Emily Dickinson's poems, many examples of which are deliberately ambiguous and tantalizing) and not necessarily explain to students—or even know yourself—every aspect of every line. Further, I think that to enforce the knowledge and identification of all literary terms in a poem seems to me artificial and counterproductive. Reading poetry and talking about it can enrich your class—and if every student and even you are not sure exactly what every line means or cannot pinpoint every image in the piece, you can still fill your classroom with the music and magic of poetry. Poems can touch students in ways that fiction and nonfiction and even drama do not, and when you add poetry to your literature teaching, everyone is enriched.

Textbook anthologies routinely contain poetry classics, and while your favorite piece may be something by Gwendolyn Brooks or Walt Whitman or John Keats, remember that contemporary poetry is a treasure trove and you should think of bringing in poems from other sources. Billy Collins, Mary Oliver, Rita Dove, Nikki Giovanni, Robert Pinsky, and others have numerous fine poems that students can readily read and understand. Regardless, as with any literature, you need to be sure that students have sufficient background if the poem makes important (and obscure) allusions. W. B. Yeats' "The Second Coming" cannot be read without some sort of introduction to the poet's world view as well as some background on Christian theology (think of "slouches toward Bethlehem," for instance), whereas Robert Frost's central image of "two roads diverged in a yellow wood" requires little background. At any rate, if you tackle something as complex as John Donne's "A Valediction Forbidding Mourning," know that you cannot just hope students will get the poem on their own. For truly mature and older poems, your expertise will be needed or students will be frustrated and turned off. And, frankly, that is one good reason to use poetry that is more accessible than the canonical poems of the greats.

How can we use poetry in our classes? Teaching extensive poetry units is not a good idea because reading and studying numerous poems over an extended period of days can exhaust even the most enthusiastic of students (see the Limit Your Time section in Teaching Tips later in this chapter). But poetry can be used in many different ways and dropped into classes or studied and read for a day or two. In addition, poetry can be its own object of study, it can be used as a companion to or extension of other literature, as vehicle for literary appreciation, and, happily, as an inspiration for creative writing. Let's look briefly at each one in turn.

Poetry as an object of study

Some poems are true classics, such as many of the sonnets of Shakespeare, the nature poetry of Williams Wordsworth, and the poetry that emerged from the Harlem Renaissance. If you are teaching one or more of these poems, poetry can indeed then be an object of study. Its historical placement may be of real interest, and the background of the author may also be important to include. Poetry as an object of study can also include genre consideration—yes, how in the world do we define a poem? What kinds of features do we most often find in poems? And, in this case, consideration of the huge range of poetic devices and their effect is appropriate. Poetry can also, however, be beautifully paired with other literature.

Poetry as a companion to other literature

Poems can also be used as parallel pieces to prose and drama, and some poems can be linked to characters or themes. The range of this possibility is huge; your students can search out poems that they think represent themes in something they have read; they can select a poem that they feel the main characters would appreciate and tell why. One obvious pairing is Langston Hughes' "Dream Deferred" and Lorraine Hansberry's play *Raisin in the Sun*. But also think, for instance, of Emily Dickinson's poem which begins, "Hope is the thing with feathers": which of the Loman family in Arthur Miller's *Death of a Salesman* might like that poem especially and think it represents his or her life? Which characters might find it irrelevant?

Poetry as a vehicle for literary appreciation

It may seem a bit odd to suggest that you could read a poem aloud at the beginning or end of a class and just let it be heard, not discussed or tested, or written about, but poetry can serve just that kind of function in the English classroom. Nonsense poems and poems with strong rhyme are often wonderful for this activity, and I also give my students nature poems when the season shifts abruptly (Mary Oliver's "First Snow" was shared this fall when we had an unexpected two inches of the white stuff). In addition, performance of poetry can help students appreciate the sound of poems; acting out in pairs or larger groups, students can experience the drama and music of large numbers of poetry. Poetry slams and performances in settings other than school, such as local bookstores, show students that poetry is not just restricted to a rarified atmosphere.

Poetry as an inspiration or creative writing

While they may not win any prizes, most students enjoy attempting a variety of poetic forms: haiku, acrostics or name poems, sonnets, poems that are in shapes (think of George Herbert's "Easter-Wings"). Found poetry, the making of poems by breaking prose in lines (newspaper articles are good sources as are some sections of novels), can also intrigue students and show them the close relation of prose and poetry. I also occasionally like to make a game with poetry writing. I prepare four grab bags, and students must choose slips of paper from each and then write a poem. One recent selection by one of my students yielded an animal, *elephant*; a color, *scarlet*; a sound, *boom*; and a taste, *salty*. Writing in response to poems and using a genre other than the essay or journal entry—such as a letter, a diary entry, a series of questions—can be similarly intriguing. Poetry is meant to uplift and inspire; using it in this manner can open writing and creative expression in your students.

Finally, students can make their own poetry anthologies, based on themes or personal tastes, and collect and showcase a number of poems. These anthologies need not be just paper books but can be integrated with art projects and also, at the end, displayed in the classroom or even in the school library. Including in these anthologies, by the way, lyrics from songs as accepted poetry can broaden student appeal.

When you begin to work with poems, remember that even though students have a paper copy of the poem in front of them or projected on the overhead, all poems need to be read aloud. The sound and the music of the words is essential to their understanding and appreciation of the poem, and if all your students do is read the poem silently, many of them may not hear the emphasis and may struggle unnecessarily with the craft of the lines and the meaning. And if the poem is not a complex classic that requires preparation and background and you still are puzzled about approaching it, after it is read aloud ask your students to follow these quick and sensible suggestions from *Do I Really Have to Teach Reading?* by Cris Tovani:

- Circle passages you like.
- Write three questions about the poem.
- Make a connection from this poem to a personal experience.
- Look at the title of the poem; how does it seem to relate to the poem itself? (119)

For other examples of approaches to poetry (along with the discussion in this chapter of "Breakings," "Those Winter Sundays," and "Black Walnuts"), see Chapter 3 for "Central School" and Chapter 8 for "Cold Snap."

The Power of Drama

I can't find the article reference, but I recently read that drama is one of the most positive factors in a school curriculum, and that many students find that experience with acting changes their attitude toward school life and toward themselves. Certainly that was true of me: working with all sorts of drama was an activity I treasured, and my junior and senior English teachers encouraged our participation in musicals and plays and even, as a project, had us write and stage an original play. I started acting and singing in junior high school, and then in high school I moved to directing. In my very first teaching situation, I was named the Drama Coach—and while the rehearsals and performances added many hours to my already full schedule and I'm not sure I knew as much as I needed to do the job, I found that working with kids and plays was almost exhilarating. Students who were not responsive in class came alive on stage, and those who would not turn in homework really did learn their lines. Shy students seemed to become bolder when they interacted with characters on stage, and I experienced a level of trust with students that at times was hard to achieve in my own English classroom. (For more information on drama in the classroom and its effect on student learning, see Betty Jane Wagner's *Educational Drama and Language Arts: What Research Shows*; Paula Ressler's *Dramatic Changes* outlines how gender identity issues can also be approached thorough drama.)

Drama does indeed have power, and you do not have to launch a full play or know about blocking and lighting to use it effectively in your teaching. When you select or use a play, though, know that it is not just a short novel with dialogue and those pesky interruptions of stage directions. Drama only comes alive in its natural element, performance. So whether you have students take parts and read lines as they are seated or standing in front of the class or if you have small groups act out selected scenes in your room or even on a stage with props and lighting, plays must be *heard and seen* to be understood. While student reading is important, this is one reason that many teachers also use filmed versions of plays so that students can see how those stage directions actually work and how emphases on lines can be varied. While the language and plot and character of drama is all worthy of examination, the *play* is the thing indeed, and you are not honoring the power of drama unless you actually use it as it was intended—performance.

But what plays can you use? Yes, there will be some in your textbook anthology and probably some play sets in your department office. There are also other sources. A recent *English Journal* issue devoted to drama asked high school teachers what plays other than Shakespeare had been effective with their students. The teachers mentioned a number of American and international classics, such as *Twelve Angry Men* by Reginald Rose, *The Crucible* by Arthur Miller, and *A Doll's House* by Henrik Ibsen ("Teacher to Teacher," September 2005). One article by Nathan Coates in that same issue also explored the enduring charm of *Lost in Yonkers* by Neil Simon. I also would add to that list Miller's *Death of a Salesman* and the plays of the late August Wilson. And if you are looking for other titles, Don Gallo's *Center Stage* and Judith Barlow's *Plays by American Women* both offer a variety of short drama. In addition, *Beyond the Bard: Fifty Plays for Use in the English Classroom* by Joshua Rutsky is focused and gives solid teaching suggestions for half a hundred plays.

Regardless of what play or plays you choose, however, do not fall into the trap of thinking of drama as just another text to be read and discussed. Short or long, classic or contemporary, let the lines and the characters live in your classroom. And don't feel that students need to read all of the play aloud; having them prepare for small portions that they can then present is as powerful. Especially with complex plays, asking the class to attempt the entire work can be overwhelming. For suggestions about warms-up before reading and performance, see the Let Them Act It Out section in Teaching Tips later in this chapter.

And now to the most widely read playwright in the secondary English curriculum, we turn to Mr. Shakespeare.

Using Shakespeare

Like most teachers, I have changed instructional strategies and emphases over my years in the classroom and, like most, I think about those changes. Some alterations, no doubt, have resulted in improvements in my teaching and understanding; some, possibly, are just changes that reflect my own shifting interests and interpretations. You will watch yourself make these changes, too, and find them renewing your teaching.

Regardless of changes, however, I have not abandoned my love of probably the most traditionally revered writer in the language arts curriculum. I firmly advocate teaching and reading and performing Shakespeare and think every student should, in varying intensities, be exposed to the magic of his writing. I rate Shakespeare above anything or anyone else in the so-called canon of classics. I will give up time with some of the best new writers to have students read and respond to the sonnets and the plays; Shakespeare is eminently worth my time and that of my students. You will find that you teach a Shakespearian play or two almost every year; it's a staple of most English language arts curricula, and there are ways, as you will see, to use the Bard.

Giving your students background

Before we move into Shakespeare, however, let me caution you briefly about background when reading and discussing the plays. While your students may benefit from knowing something about the Elizabethan Age—the language, the culture, the politics—I have always felt it misguided that many teachers spend a truly large amount of time on that subject, taking away time from the literature. Further, what English class has not been subjected to countless lectures on *where* Shakespeare's plays were physically performed—the Globe Theatre, its construction and layout—if not asked to construct detailed models of that theatre? While nothing is wrong with some attention to historical context, again, it can usurp the major point of studying Shakespeare at all—and the point is the literature. So give that background briefly: if it takes over a third to a half of the time you have allotted for Shakespeare, you need to reconsider the proportion of your classroom time you spend on it.

And if you haven't done so yet, look at E. M. W. Tillyard's *The Elizabethan World Picture*. It is interesting, packed with information, and brief; it remains, in my mind, one of the best short works on the Elizabethan Age you could use for your own and your students' reference.

Shakespeare's language

One of the major reasons I love teaching Shakespeare is the language. Across the centuries, it stands and endures and calls. Shakespeare has crept into our conversation, our phrases, quips, and titles—from "all the world's a stage" (*As You Like It*) to "green-ey'd jealousy" (*Merchant of Venice*) to "hark, hark, the lark" (*Cymbeline*) to "double, double, toil and trouble" (*Macbeth*) to "how sharper than a serpent's tooth it is / To have a thankless child" (*King Lear*). Our students know to "beware the Ides of March" (*Julius Caesar*); they can complete the line "Romeo, Romeo, wherefore art thou Romeo" (*Romeo and Juliet*); and "the winter of our discontent" (*Richard the Third* and as borrowed by John Steinbeck) may strike a vague chord of recognition. Most of our students, consciously or unconsciously, know some Shakespeare. On a more elevated level, the words of Shakespeare have a freshness and sharpness that is worth our students' attention and study.

Using quotations to teach Shakespeare

Along with strong imagery, gripping plots, and believable characters, Shakespeare gives us, as teachers and students, an utterly ringing collection of phrases, aphorisms, and quips. There are thousands of memorable quotations from Shakespeare's plays, and they illumine not only the plays but life itself. As Pope writes in *An Essay on Criticism*, "True Wit is Nature to advantage dress'd, / What oft was thought, but ne'er so well expressed" (l. 297). Shakespeare is the essence of true wit to advantage dressed. Studying quotations can be a helpful tool to organize discussion of his plays in the English classroom.

Using quotations to teach Shakespeare:

1. Makes students focus on the specifics of the language.
2. Helps students deal with the complexity of the plays by using smaller units to discuss and focus.
3. Provides a structuring device of part for the whole.
4. Encourages students to memorize—or own—the language.

The broad range of the plays can be highly intimidating to our students. Reducing a scene to the consideration of a single quotation can help students "manage" the play and, further, consideration of the smaller idea within the quotation can help them get a handle on the larger theme. While it is, of course, a fallacy to blithely assume that the part can stand always and conveniently for the whole, a more limited observation or a more circumscribed comment can illumine a wider field. Finally, close work with a small number of quotations can encourage students to familiarize themselves with if not actually memorize the language—students can thus "own" the words of Shakespeare, and the effect can be long range and electrifying.

Quotations and scene summaries   When I first started teaching Shakespeare in high school, I used a common and pragmatic technique to help my students understand the bare bones of the action. I had students, after reading a number of scenes, summarize the events/facts by writing a one-sentence précis for each scene. Students had three choices of how they could write their scene summaries: standard English, Elizabethan English, or school slang/street talk. Each choice yielded somewhat different results and added a bit of creativity to the assignment.

The summaries in standard English seemed to be more geared to student understanding or attempted understanding of the facts of the scene. The summaries in Elizabethan English offered this same advantage, but the students' approximations were not only often hilarious, they could be wildly inventive and occasionally almost frighteningly close to the original. The summaries in the latest version of school slang or street talk of hip hop were often witty revelations of the students' factual appreciation of the action; in addition, this unusual language occasionally commented subtly on the play. Obviously, however, such an emphasis on scene summaries—on what happened—tended to make students concentrate on plot, requiring them to digest and understand more of the action than the subtlety of subtext.

My teaching of Shakespeare changed accordingly. I moved away from summary to quotations. Students would pick from each scene the single line or lines they felt were the most significant. Students would then write a brief paragraph of justification, including who said what to whom, in what context, and why this quotation was chosen over others.

The instructional advantage of using quotations, as opposed to the summaries, was that students could then discuss what they picked and why. Putting the two or three most frequent choices on the board or overhead and opening the floor for large-group discussion or having students who chose the same—or very different—quotations work in groups yielded lively discussion and talk. Let's see how this works specifically with a quotation from *Othello*.

A quotation from Act V, Scene ii of *Othello*   After students have read or acted out scenes in class, it is also possible to have the class as a whole agree on a central quotation and discuss why it merits being the majority choice. Why, for example, did my students argue that, in Act V, Scene ii of *Othello*, "I that am cruel am yet merciful; / I would not have thee linger in thy pain" (ll. 86–87) was a more significant line than the famous "Put out the light, and then put out the light" (l. 7) and the even more well known "one that lov'd not wisely but too well" (l. 344)? Just what was cruel, what was merciful, and what Othello perceived as lingering in pain were part of the discussion. The light imagery and all its resonance of putting it out was not, for this class at least, of interest; perhaps the very famous loving wisely but too well comment seemed hackneyed and, furthermore, so patently false it was not worth consideration: how could this murderer be accused of loving, at least on a surface interpretation, "too well"?

In addition, students also passed up from that scene Emilia's poetic and powerful incremental repetition of "My husband!" as she listens incredulously to Othello's accounting of just how he knows of Desdemona's betrayal; students similarly gave barely a glance to the "as ignorant as dirt" (l. 164) quotation (an insult still used widely in my region); they did not select the powerful justification Iago makes for his own perfidy ("I told [Othello] what I thought, and told no more / Than what he found himself was apt and true" (ll. 176–77). For these students, the "cruel yet merciful" quotation was of central importance: we discussed Othello's assessment of his own character and actions and his stubborn refusal, at this point in the scene at least, to see the truth of Desdemona's fidelity.

Acting out quotations   The use of dramatics, performance-based teaching of Shakespeare, is an indispensable part of considering the plays. As discussed previously in this chapter, drama is not meant just to be read but to be heard and seen. Using quotations, students can experiment with inflection and intonation as they perform the quotations they choose, performances that necessarily reflect alternative interpretations. Miriam Gilbert, in her "Teaching Shakespeare Through Performance," recommends "deprivation" exercises: not only miming the lines rather than speaking them but also "telegramming" them or "reducing [the lines] to the smallest number of words that will convey the message" (605) and then performing them. She reminds us that "performance-based teaching needs to work toward discussion" (605) that will reveal the number of interpretations any group of students will find in Shakespeare's lines. (For more ideas on performance approaches to teaching Shakespeare, see the Resources section at the end of this chapter.)

Quotations and tests   As quotations can be used to discuss the plays and their implications, so also can they be used with essay tests. It is possible to present a number of quotations to students, have them pick out a requisite number (for example, ten out of twenty or seven out of fifteen), and ask them to write on each one. In their essays, students should include who said the lines to whom at approximately what juncture in the play. Students should then discuss the significance of the speech and its wider meaning. Context—who is speaking to whom when—can be most interesting, and even if students are mistaken in their memory or judgment, it can invite them to consider just what that line or lines might mean and why they were spoken. The wider significance is helpful in that it asks students to consider the ramifications of the lines both before and after the actual incident.

In selecting such a list of quotations, it would seem that students should have some familiarity with the range of lines before the test; to present students a list of relatively unknown quotations—regardless of the possibility of choice—is self-defeating and anxiety producing. The point is to look at the line or lines and see context and wider dimension. Similarly, students can choose a limited set of quotations—one for each act is a possibility, a central single line is another—and write on why that quotation or quotations is/are important.

············· FOR YOUR JOURNAL ·············

Pick a Shakespearian play you like or have enjoyed before. Pick an act and reread it; what quotations seem important to you? Why? What discussion questions could come from those quotations? Which quotations could be used to act out parts of the play? Is there any quotation students could write about? What should students focus on as they write?

Building Bridges to Adult Reading:
The Place of Young Adult Literature

There has been, even before the advent of the "dime" novel in the nineteenth century in this country, literature that has been written specifically for the younger reader, the young adult, and marketed to that audience. Known first by the term *juvenile* (which has unfortunate contemporary connotations and is slipping out of usage as a term simply synonymous with *young*) and then alternately by the terms *young adult, YA,* or *adolescent,* this literature started in modern form in 1967 with the publication of sixteen-year-old Susie Hinton's novel *The Outsiders,* the gripping story of two embattled groups of teenagers, "the Greasers" and "the Socs." Realistic dialogue, a strong plot, and compelling characters are all part of *The Outsiders,* and the novel, somewhat akin to J. D. Salinger's *The Catcher in the Rye,* struck a chord with young readers. Susie Hinton's first effort signaled an avalanche of writing that continues, unabated, to this day and goes by the name of Young Adult literature.

For many teachers, especially those unfamiliar with quality Young Adult literature, the whole field seems unnecessary or, possibly, only necessary for students who are unable to handle the intricacies of "real" adult literature. That argument ignores the fact that many of our students just stop reading around the middle school years and never take the habit back up. Developing lifelong readers is tricky, and for some young people, the shift from elementary school to middle school and above leaves their reading far behind. Young Adult (YA) literature can provide an important and crucial bridge

To keep our students reading, YA literature provides a useful and quality transition. Certainly the formula fiction of the Sweet Valley High series, popular with middle and high school students, and the Goosebumps and the Baby-Sitters Club series, popular with upper elementary and middle school students, are all well-known YA titles. But they are only a part of the YA genre. More challenging YA work is reviewed in national journals and newspapers, critiqued by professors and librarians and professional writers, and awarded honors and medals such as the Newbery, the Coretta Scott King, the Michael L. Prinz Book Award, the Orbis Pictus, and others. And there is a startling variety in the field: poetry, short stories, plays, nonfiction, and, of course, novels of adventure, romance, horror, science fiction, historical fiction, fantasy, almost any conceivable area of interest. YA literature, though certainly written on a smaller scale than adult literature can be judged using the same literary standards we would apply to any piece of writing.

Definition of YA literature

What makes a YA novel? Essentially, the genre is characterized by a few components, the most important of which is the first, followed by other, more structural characteristics:

- a teenage (or young adult) protagonist
- a stripped-down plot with very few, if any, subplots
- a limited number of characters
- a compressed time span and a restricted setting
- an approximate length of 125 to 250 pages (though current fantasy YA novels, such as the Harry Potter books, may be much longer)

While young adults, your students, will read "classics" with teen protagonists—such as Mark Twain's *Huckleberry Finn* or William Golding's *Lord of the Flies*—such novels are not strictly considered YA literature. Similarly, contemporary novels popular with adults and young people, such as those written by Danielle Steel, Tom Clancy, John Grisham, David Baldacci, and much of the work of Stephen King, are also not in the category of YA literature. Commencing with the publication of *The Outsiders* and written for and marketed to young people, the YA genre is somewhat apart. It is also a definable genre that leads students (many of whom are not ready to make the shift from children's literature to adult literature, from *Charlotte's Web* to *Jane Eyre* and *Great Expectations*) into reading and the enjoyment of literature.

Concerns about YA literature

There is no fudging the fact of the matter, though: YA literature, at least in the schools, is still a stepchild and has not entered the curriculum in any widespread way. Three issues are the more than likely culprits:

1. The question of quality.
2. The concern for the classics.
3. The subject matter and language in YA novels.

The question of quality   As mentioned before, many people, especially those who have not read YA literature, worry that the novels are just not well written. Certainly those novels that earn the Newbery Award are not in this category, nor are those that make the best lists of the numerous journals that review YA literature, among them *The ALAN Review*, *School Library Journal*, *Booklist*, *VOYA*, *Horn Book Magazine*, *Journal of Reading*, and others. Quality YA books are also found in NCTE's publications: *Your Reading* (for middle school), *Books for You* (for senior high school), and *High Interest—Easy Reading* (for the struggling reader). The fear persists, however, especially for those who are unfamiliar with YA literature, that these "junior" novels are nothing other than monuments to mediocrity and not worth students' time. According to these critics, students will stay mired in the worst of this literature and never develop a taste for more mature works.

My experience both as a reader and a teacher does not confirm this belief. It seems to me that our students need to read a whole lot and that not all of what they read should necessarily be immortal prose or poetry. G. Robert Carlsen, a strong voice for YA literature, wrote years ago in *Books and the Teenage Reader* regarding what he called *subliterature* and suggested that students need to read such material and would move beyond it. While very little of YA literature could be termed subliterature, the point is a valid one. Our reading has to go through stages, and when we tell our students that one year it is quality children's books, such as *The Phantom Tollbooth*, and the next it is a classic, such as Nathaniel Hawthorne's *The House of Seven Gables*, we may lose a number of readers and never regain them.

The concern for the classics   Another fear is that if students read YA literature, they will not read the classics. This implies an either/or situation in which students have a highly limited time to read and does not seem to be borne out by the experience of real readers. In fact, it would appear that many readers read both genres simultaneously, just as adults relax with popular magazines and keep at their bedside a more serious novel. Pairing young adult novels with classic novels is also an effective way to use both kinds of literature, and there are books listed in the Resource section of this chapter that offer suggestions and lesson plans for taking more traditional books and putting them with quality YA novels.

At any rate, insisting that students read classics or nothing often results in the latter: students, confronted with literature with which they can make little personal connection, choose, often quietly but often permanently, to stop reading altogether—or to confine reading to only that which is required by English class.

The subject matter and language in YA novels   Along with other issues such as the place of the classics and Young Adult literature, the question of censorship is a very real one when teachers consider using YA literature in class. All of the hot topics—sex, drugs, suicide, parental tensions, race, poverty—are touched on in much YA literature, and often the characters speak in realistic dialogue incorporating slang and an occasional obscenity. In fact, the realism of much of YA literature may be part of its popularity with young people. Again, the issue is polarized: all good literature addresses the hot topics, but for many people, unfortunately some teachers and librarians included, hot topics are acceptable in antique dress but not in today's clothing. There is nothing Robert Cormier's frequently censored *The Chocolate War* discusses that William Shakespeare or Nathaniel Hawthorne or Herman Melville avoid. Put the same themes in modern times, however, and discuss them in contemporary language, and many people become wary and worry that young people will be exposed to something they might otherwise never learn—or will learn sometime in that distant future when they can "handle" it. Truth be told, life is not that way, and young people need truth in today's language as much as in the language of yesteryear.

Keeping students reading is one of the gifts of YA literature; it is a powerful tool we can use both in and outside the classroom and can provide a bridge to more sophisticated, lengthy and complicated reading.

New Kid on the Block: The Graphic Novel

While YA literature occupies a corner in some English classrooms, graphic novels have not been readily accepted into many school district curricula. Their time, however, may indeed come soon; the genre is rapidly developing, and it is expanding into wider spheres. For instance, Scholastic, a well-respected and long established publisher of young adult and other fiction, has launched Graphix, a division devoted solely to graphic novels and has begun the publication of a classic series, Jeff Smith's funny and appealing *Bone*. The American Library Association has established a "Great Graphic Novels for Teens" list among its more traditional booklists and book awards and regularly updates nominations to the list. Scholarly and historical books such as Scott McCloud's *Understanding Comics* and Stephen Weiner's *Faster Than a Speeding Bullet: The Rise of the Graphic Novel* provide background and frame for this unusual genre. *Time*, a national news magazine, is currently including in its weekly issues the work of Chris Ware, the creator of American Book Award-winning *Jimmy Corrigan*.

Some of this may be a surprise to you, and some of it may not. Certainly you may know graphic novels from two examples that have been more widely read in schools, Art Spiegelman's Pulitzer prize–winning *Maus* (followed by *Maus II*). Though the format uses the frames and dialogue of a comic book and the characters are animals, the subject is a deadly serious fable of Nazi Germany where the Jews are portrayed as mice and the Nazi as cats. You may also have familiarity with Manga, Japanese graphic novels that feature superheroes. There is, however, more range to the field than the examples cited here might suggest. While many know the field of graphic novels largely through super heroes (such as Spider

Man, X-Men, Batman, and the Hulk), graphic novels also include horror, realistic fiction, science fiction, fantasy, nonfiction, and literary adaptations and interpretations.

Don Gallo, in a recent *English Journal* column, defines the genre of graphic novels as "elaborately illustrated stories that look like high-class, book-length comics" and "something between an emerging literary form and a cultural phenomenon" (114). Indeed, for many of our students, graphic novels are not just fancy comic books but exciting and interesting reading. Another brief but potent thing to remember about graphic novels is their unique appeal; they are, in a phrase, cutting edge, and that fact alone may make them especially enticing to certain students. Peter Schjeldahl, writing in *The New Yorker*, observes:

> Consuming them [graphic novels]—toggling for hours between the incommensurable functions of reading and looking—is taxing. The difficulty of graphic novels limits their potential audience, in contrast to the blissfully easeful, still all-conquering movies, but that is not a debility; rather, it gives them the opalescent sheen of avant-gardism. (162)

From a teacher's perspective, graphic novels provide an innovative combination of art and prose, and the many unusual topics of graphic novels make them interesting choices for supplementary reading in the classroom and as lures for students who would otherwise be reluctant to pick up and finish a traditional book. In addition, graphic novels' extensive use of dialogue and unusual narrative form can be studied and replicated in the classroom. Interested students can both transform parts of traditional prose works into short graphic novels and can also assess the art and its effect in graphic novels.

What else can a teacher do with a graphic novel? Depending on the novel's subject matter, there are actually a number of things.

Comparing the graphic novel superhero to a classic epic hero   While the stories of Batman or the X-Men may seem like something from childhood, their exploits are detailed seriously in graphic novels. Ask students to compare and contrast Ulysses, Beowulf, or King Arthur to a superhero. To what extent are the trials and challenges the same? different? How do the visuals of the graphic novel give a reader more—or different—detail than the poetry of Homer or Tennyson?

Using graphic novels that are based on classics   For students eager to go to Spark Notes rather than read the original, a graphic novel may be a good companion choice. Puffin Graphics has a series that has adapted *Frankenstein*, as well as other classics, to the graphic format. Ask students to read a graphic novel adaptation in companion with some of the original work. What is changed? preserved? How does the graphic presentation enhance or alter the original prose?

Contrasting the graphic novel to the film   *The Adventures of the League of Extraordinary Gentleman* are recounted in a series of graphic novels as well as in film. Ask students to view both and compare and contrast in particular the visuals. To what extent does the film mimic or alter the graphic novel? Which is more effective and why?

Enticing reluctant readers   There are graphic novels that also feature specifically young adult themes. One recent example is *Queen Bee*, the story of Haley, a middle schooler and former geek who has special powers and will be using them to attempt to win a local American Idol-type contest. Another is the series Runaways, the tale of six teens who find that their parents are secretly super-powerful villains who they must resist. Given the subject matter and the format, both of these graphic novels may be very appealing to reluctant readers.

Using graphic novels as approaches to difficult subjects   Like *Maus*, some graphic novels are very serious, and Joe Sacco's *Safe Area Gorazde* is the story of the war in Eastern Bosnia from 1992 to 1995. Well researched and factual, *Safe Area Gorazde* is journalism presented in the form of a graphic novel and is a mature and complicated read.

For more suggestions regarding graphic novels, see the Resources section at the end of this chapter.

······················ **FOR YOUR JOURNAL** ······················

YA and many (but not all) graphic novels are not lengthy, and you will probably be able to read one in a brief period of time. Go to your local library or bookstore and browse in the young adult section; consult the Resources section at the at the end of this chapter. Read a YA work or graphic novel and write about it briefly: how did you react to it? Who do you think would like to read such a book? How do you assess it in terms of tightness of plot, believability of characters, realism in dialogue, appropriateness of setting, importance of theme, accuracy of information? Regarding the graphic novel, what do you notice as far as art, color, placement? To what extent does the presentation enhance the subject matter? Can you think of any adult or "classic" work you could pair this book with? What similarities/differences do you see?

The Specter of Censorship

Whenever a teacher uses a poem, a novel, a play, or a piece of nonfiction in a classroom, he or she is open to the question of censorship. There is—the evidence is virtually irrefutable—no piece of literature "safe" from challenge and censorship. From all kinds of popular magazines to the most revered of the classics, reading material is regularly questioned and occasionally removed from library and classroom shelves. Sometimes the courts, as high as the Supreme Court, are involved in censorship cases. Most times the challenges are handled at the individual classroom, the school, or the school board level.

While there are few of us who would relish such a battle or the attack on our professionalism, we as teachers need to be prepared to give a rational defense of why we are asking—or, as some people might think, allowing—our students to read certain materials in our classes. The American Library Association (ALA) and the National Council of Teachers of English (NCTE) have many resources available to teachers and schools regarding books that are challenged. A few that may be helpful are the NCTE's publication *The Students' Right to Read* and Burress and Jenkinson's *The Students' Right to Know* (both have overviews of censorship and a helpful form for those who would like a book reconsidered). Similarly invaluable is the ALA's *Hit List: Frequently Challenged Books for Young Adults*, which gives teachers sources outside their own judgment as to what is a good book. In the meantime, however, the following five principles may help you.

1. **Find out if your school has a materials selection policy and a procedure for dealing with books that are challenged.** If it does, get a copy. If it doesn't, raise the issue: without something in writing, schools are unprepared to deal quickly and effectively with a parental or public complaint.

2. **Find out if your department has a file of rationales for books that are taught in classes.** Making up rationales and keeping them on file is powerful ammunition when books are questioned by parents and members of the public. Printed rationales or techniques for writing your own are available from ALA; NCTE has books on the topic and has also, in cooperation with the International Reading Association (IRA), compiled a CD-ROM, *Rationales for Challenged Books Grades 4–12.*

3. **Get a copy of NCTE's publication "Citizen's Request for the Reconsideration of a Work of Literature" (from the NCTE publication cited, *The Students' Right to Read*).** It is a workable and usable form to give parents and others who question a work you might be teaching.

4. **As you teach and select, do keep in mind what merit you feel the material has for your students.** If you really don't know why you are using something, even if it is in the mandated textbook, maybe you don't need to teach it. Conviction is important in this business, and there are so many great things from which to choose and which are highly defensible.

5. **Finally, if a work you have selected or allowed is questioned, it is in your best interest to always assume that the challenger is a person of good will.** Civility, respect, and helpfulness are characteristics you should strive for, even in such an emotionally charged situation. Remember, parents and members of the public do have the right to ask questions and receive answers. Sometimes the underlying reason for their inquiry is simply that they are uninformed or unsure about the merit of literature with which they are unfamiliar.

If your school has a materials selection policy and a procedure for dealing with complaints, and you have a rationale on hand, the issue can usually be resolved amicably. On the other hand, if you find yourself without those resources, there are others who can help you—your local education association, your local language arts association, or, as mentioned, ALA and NCTE. The attempt to censor and restrict is almost as old as writing itself; while you may have never thought of it in this way, it is an ongoing effort to keep library shelves freely stocked and students reading widely. In no case, however, should you stand alone. Censorship challenges can be emotional and scary (the Nat Hentoff YA novel *The Day They Came to Arrest the Book* tells one such story), and teachers need to avail themselves of outside resources.

When we discuss this issue, it is also almost impossible not to cite John Milton's stirring and still very apt *Areopagitica*, his defense of writing against the censor. Milton wrote this pamphlet in 1644 in response to the censorship prevalent in seventeenth-century England. Addressed to the British parliament for the "liberty of unlicensed printing," Milton thundered about protecting the reading public through "a fugitive and cloister'd vertue, unexercis'd and unbreath'd" (691). He argued that even in a restrictive, theocratic society, reading would not sully anyone; he concluded it was better to kill a person than a book—because a book was so akin to a likeness of the divine:

> as good almost kill a Man as kill a good
> Booke; who kills a Man kills a reasonable
> creature, God's Image: but hee who destroyes a
> good Booke, kills reason it selfe, kills the
> Image of God, as it were in the eye. (681)

On a less elevated—but no less compelling—plane is E. B. White, who wrote in 1949 in *The New Yorker* regarding the New York Board of Education's criteria for selecting books. The criteria are strongly reminiscent of today's concerns:

> The Board of Education has twenty-three criteria for selecting textbooks, library books, and magazines for use in the public schools. We learned this by reading a fourteen-page pamphlet published by the Board explaining how it makes its choice. One criterion is: "Is it [the book or magazine] free from subject matter that tends to irreverence for things held sacred?" Another criterion is: "Are both sides of controversial issues presented with fairness?" Another: "Is it free from objectionable slang expressions which will interfere with the building of good language habits?" (140)

White worries in his essay that "these three criteria by themselves are enough to keep a lot of good books from the schools." He goes on to note:

> Irreverence for things held sacred has started many a writer on his way, and will again. An author so little moved by a controversy that he can present both sides fairly is not likely to burn any holes in the paper. We think the way for school children to get both sides of a controversy is to read several books on the subject, not one. In other words we think the Board should strive for a well-balanced library, not a well-balanced book. The greatest books are heavily slanted, by the nature of greatness. (140)

I wish I had written that.

Using Literature: Some Teaching Tips

There are a number of books available, especially from NCTE, that regularly provide teaching tips on specific works. Use your *English Journal* (the NCTE magazine for secondary teachers), state language arts publications, and *Notes Plus* and similar publications for teaching ideas. Publishers also offer teaching guides, many of which are written by teachers in the classroom and by YA authors. In general, however, there are a number of principles to keep in mind when you think of using literature.

Limit your time

Covering every aspect of any piece of literature is deadening, and furthermore, real readers don't approach literature that way. Why is it in the classroom we beat poems and short stories and novels to death, exhausting every avenue of discussion and, in the process, our students, too?

Think about limiting the time you spend on what your students are reading and try to fall in love with the concept that it is better to leave them wanting to discuss more, do more, than to end a unit of study with everyone cranky and worn out and just sick of the piece. It's the extensive versus intensive debate, and I, for one, always opt for the former. I would rather range over a wide variety of works than spend significant portions of time exhausting a single piece. From my experience, extensive, not intensive, reading seems to give students a wider range of ideas and facility.

Practically, what does this mean? As mentioned in the poetry section in this chapter, it means, that with the Godiva chocolate of literature, poetry, less is definitely more. Five straight days of poetry should drive you and your students crazy; think of a maximum of two or three, and never, never do a complete "unit" of poetry. The literature is too condensed for most younger readers—that's middle school and high schoolers—and should be interspersed with other forms of literature. It may seem like heresy, but, as I have noted in this chapter, I also find it helpful to "drop in" a poem every week or so; duplicate one, read it aloud, briefly discuss it, and move on. Sometimes, of course, even brief discussion is unnecessary; poetry, like those delicious Godivas, needs to be sampled and savored.

With longer works, such as multiact plays and novels, two weeks—ten days of instruction—is a reasonable limit. And, yes, this means Shakespeare, too: most students' enthusiasm will flag, as will yours, if you spend class period after class period on the same, single work of literature. Even the most dedicated of classes will wilt if, day after day, you and they mine the piece for every bit of gold it holds.

Short stories, particularly when they relate thematically or chronologically to other pieces of literature, are highly useful for "breaking up" poetry and longer pieces of study. Short stories, like poems, can also provide vehicles for "self-contained" classes in which in one period, one day, students can read and respond to a piece of literature. This not only avoids homework—which in some school settings or at some junctures is difficult, if not impossible, to have all students complete—but it also provides an impact that is hard to replicate when the literature is read outside class.

Give them a context/lead them in

Many beginning teachers forget how puzzling a piece of literature can be, how it can seem, especially on first reading, to come from absolutely nowhere. They often assume that students will "get it" much quicker than is realistic; accordingly, in their classroom discussions or activities involving literature these teachers just start—often seemingly out of thin air— as if the mere act of having heard the poem read aloud or reading the short story as homework was a sufficient introduction.

Always think about how to lead your students into a piece: call it a *hook*, a *warm-up*, an *anticipatory set*, call it what you will, but do it. Give students some sort of context for what they will be dealing with, and try at the onset to help them puzzle out a connection.

For example, in Samuel G. Freedman's *Small Victories*, the story of students in New York City's Seward Park High School, English teacher Jessica Siegel talks about how she uses a number of techniques. To introduce "Walden," the Henry David Thoreau essay on leaving the complications of civilization to live simply in the country, she opens the class discussion by asking "What's a luxury?" and uses student answers to set the stage for what Thoreau would describe as going into the woods to "live deliberately" and, necessarily, without luxury. To open a unit on early American literature that encompasses writing about what the early settlers hoped for in the New World, Siegel asks her students, predominantly the children of relatively recent immigrants, why their parents came to the United States. She then uses their answers to link today with the eighteenth-century first settlers of America. For "Upon the Burning of Our House, July 10th, 1666," which is about the destruction of seventeenth-century American poet Anne Bradstreet's house by fire, students write in their journals a brief description of their favorite possession. Following this, Siegel asks students to imagine their feelings about the destruction of that favorite possession. In all three cases, students are encouraged to think of a concept or an idea that ultimately relates to the literature.

In her first few months student teaching, Debbie Martin did a similar activity:

Today I probably had my best day of teaching yet. I mean *real teaching*. . . . I wrote on the board: Defining death is a very difficult task. If a six-year-old asked you, "What is death?," what would you say to him/her? Students had ten minutes to respond. They were told that we would share answers.

Which we did. I had no trouble getting students to share. They wanted me to read their writing first, but once I did they eagerly volunteered. I let those who wanted to read, read and those who just wanted to tell me their ideas, tell me.

When they did so I made very little comment. I didn't need to. The remainder of the class jumped in. We even had quite a disagreement between two students in one class. As long as it was rational and kind, I let it go on for a few moments. I ended it by saying that a definition of death was often tied to religious beliefs and that in any case [it] was tied to beliefs that were very personal. Further, that if we had the time to really get into it, more than likely not one of us would agree.

We then read John Donne's "Sonnet X" or "Death, Be Not Proud." The relationship between the writing and the sonnet were crystal clear. One of my students who does *nothing* said later, when I mentioned a review, "We don't need to review this one; we've practically memorized it now."

While there is a danger, as with the pitfalls of theme, that such openers, warm-ups, or anticipatory sets will steer students only too precisely into what *we* want them to see in and believe about a piece of literature, the opposite is probably more dangerous, especially for younger and unsure readers. Leaving students to flounder, repeatedly confronting them class after class with literature that seems relatively contextless, is to invite disaffection and unease. The luxury of no context and discovery may be more appropriately left for college and graduate school, where more adept readers are not so confounded by what they are discussing. By and large, our middle school and high school students, many of whom are pretty new to this game of looking at unfamiliar literature, may need to be pointed in a general direction. What Jessica Siegel and Debbie Martin do in their classrooms seems to have far more benefits than disadvantages.

On the other hand, if a focused warm-up is too targeted for you, consider doing one or more of the following:

- Ask your students to speculate on the title: what does it mean? How do they know? Can they provide synonyms? Can they create a parallel title?
- Read them the first line of the poem or the first paragraph of the prose, and ask them to write about what they expect will happen next. Ask them to share their answers and discuss.
- Excerpt a slice of dialogue from the play; have a number of students read the parts, and ask students what is going on. Have another duo or trio read the same lines and ask the question again. Do the readings differ in tone and interpretation? How?

Let them create it—within reason

A way into poetry is encouraging students to write their own; similarly, short skits can also help students appreciate drama and feel its power. Be very wary, however, of asking students to write epic poems or five-act plays; while there are some classes and some students who may be able to do it, insisting that an entire class embark upon a complete, whole work of literature may not invite creativity so much as despair. Asking students, similarly, to write an entire short story is an assignment many teachers rather routinely give, and the results are very rarely satisfactory. Unless you are committed to helping students work through the process of creating a long work, stick to more attainable goals. It is one thing to do a very short, self-contained piece; it is another to piece together prose that features, in the case of the short story, setting, characters, and dialogue, not to mention theme and a coherent plot with conflict and climax.

If you doubt the truth of this, consider what it took you to write your most recent long poem, play, or short story. What?! You've never written such a piece? Well, actually, you are like most people, English majors or not. Few of us have attempted or completed such works. Accordingly, try it before you blithely assign it to your students on a Monday morning. It may give you an appreciation of what you are asking; in addition, it may help you define what you expect from your students.

Consider having your students create short pieces of text that are related to the original. For instance, shifting genre, you can ask students after reading a novel to respond by writing two original thirty-line poems, rhyming or unrhyming (your choice), using at least two stanzas, which reflect the spirit and intent of the novel. The first student-written poem should relate to the first half of the novel, and the second poem should relate to the second half of the novel. The poems should show knowledge of the novel, appreciation of it, and some creativity.

Similarly, with a chapter from a novel or with a short story, students can look at plot, setting, and character. For example:

- Have students **pick a favorite or pivotal scene.** Then let them add a character, delete a character, or alter a piece of dialogue by changing a crucial word or key phrase. Ask your students to rewrite that one scene and share it by reading it aloud and discussing how it changes the plot.

- Have students **write a new ending or a sequel** by extending the ending by one hour, one day, one week, one month, one year. For some pieces of literature, what happens immediately after the final period is of great interest; for other pieces, what the characters are doing after a year is more realistic. Have students share their new endings and discuss how they arrived at them. As an alternative, have students create a letter five years after the end of the novel, written by the main character to someone significant who may or may not know what happened in the novel. The letter should show understanding not only of the novel itself but of the implications of the events of the novel five years later.

- Have students **do a new beginning to the literature**—in media speak, a *prequel*—that begins an hour, a day, a week, a month, a year before the literature actually starts. Again, have students share.

- Let students **change the title** and **rewrite the opening paragraph** and/or the closing paragraph to reflect that new title. How did they come up with the new title?

- Have students **rewrite the setting** of a section. Setting can be a snooze to students, but what if a section of the literature is set in a different era? in the country rather than on the street corner? in spring instead of winter? Have students discuss the changes they make.

- Let students **rename characters, change the sex of characters, change a major personality trait or physical characteristic** of a character, and then have them rewrite a section. Character is pivotal in most literature. What happens when one of these characteristics is changed? Why?

Certainly we as teachers need to be careful with students, whose egos are, necessarily, intimately, tied up with their creative attempts. I offer as an example the following poem, given to me some years ago by one of my high school students. It is a piece whose major merit lies in its effort to express an idea important to the writer and, actually, an idea important to this discussion as well. Gabriella writes:

> **Trying won't hurt**
> I have never fallen down so hard
> for it to hurt so bad,
> But the biggest hurt of all
> is when I don't success.
> For if I don't success and try my best
> It won't hurt as much,
> But, if I don't success and
> don't keep trying, then it hurts.

We have to give our Gabriellas opportunities to try. As they articulate and explore in our class, there will be time to talk about verbs and nouns, about the difference between *success* and *succeed*, and we can help them make their poetry and their prose writing not only expressive but more correct. But just because students such as Gabriella do not have all their skills down pat or understand all the ramifications of English language arts, we do not serve any useful purpose by keeping those students away from the creative or the inventive in the name of developing skills through worksheets and drills. We hope they will succeed, but keeping them away from creative forms, keeping them from attempting, reaching, stretching, is probably far more searing than possible failure.

Use literature circles

Literature circles allow students to work together in small groups and to talk about a single book, often a book that the students themselves have selected. Although you can give your students real guidance as they work in their circles (you can offer lists of books from which to choose and procedures for discussion), literature circles allow students to be more autonomous than they might be in a whole-class configuration. Think of literature circles as a sort of small-group book club where students, not the teacher, run the show. Guidelines, journal checks, and teacher visits to the group can help students stay organized.

Do remember that literature circles need preparation. Sometimes students are not ready to talk among each other day after day—or even a few times a week—without some specific direction. Assigning students small-group roles (facilitator, recorder, timekeeper), giving them possible lists of things to talk about (yesterday we considered the main character; today let's list possible themes), giving students incremental deadlines (by the end of the week each group member will need to have completed two journal entries) are all part of your job structuring literature circles.

Also, you will need to make sure that the discussion group members are relatively compatible as that is essential to this kind of extensive small-group work. Harvey Daniels' book *Literature Circles* is devoted entirely to the subject, and you might want to check it out (see also the Bonnie Hill and colleagues' text) if literature circles seem appealing to you in your classroom.

Let them act it out—after they have warmed up first

Creative dramatics can make magic in a classroom, and certainly students can base short skits not only on full-length plays but also on poems, short stories, and pieces of nonfiction. Regardless of what you base your creative dramatics on, do not forget the human being in all of this; just because your students are young does not mean they have no inhibitions. Just telling students to "get in front of the class and act it out" is a recipe for disaster. Students need some help; like most people, they need to get ready.

First, students need to be warmed up for such a skit. This can involve breathing exercises, movement exercises, and games (see the following sections about mirror images, farmyard, and statues). Students can then, in groups or pairs, work on brief skits or do impromptus and present them with much less inhibition and fear.

To expect students just to *do it*, to perform on *your* moment's notice, is unfair and something, frankly, you most likely would not want to do either. Let's look at a few ways to warm up students (the following can be done in sequence).

Relaxation   This activity loosens people up and encourages them to stretch and breathe deeply. Have students stand up and move away from each other so that they can extend their arms out and not hit someone else in the face or back. Let students slowly take a number of deep breaths. Have students stretch their arms above their heads, to their sides, and then bend over and "bounce" with their arms hanging loosely to the floor. Let students put their hands on their waists and twist their upper torsos to the left and the right. Have them rotate their heads (*gently*, this can be dangerous) on their necks. Finally, let students shake their arms at their sides, then their legs (one at a time, obviously!).

A variation on this stretching exercise is for students to imagine that they are standing at the foot of a tree and trying to pick an apple just out of reach. Ask students to see the tree, see the apple, then stretch first the left and then the right arm so that they can "pick" the apple. (Standing on tiptoe is allowed.)

Farmyard   This is a silly, childish exercise that usually makes students laugh; it also requires that deep breaths be taken, which has a tendency to relax people and loosen inhibitions. Farmyard makes a lot of noise; be prepared for someone down the hall to call for quiet or to investigate what's going on.

Students should be standing and positioned so they can see one another and you. I tell students to imagine we are in the country in a farmyard. We are now all chickens and we must make chicken noises. So we all cluck a bit for about a minute or so. Then we become a much bigger animal in the farmyard, a pig, and we snort and snuffle for a minute. Watching the chickens and the pigs are the family pets. What does that cat say? We meow a bit. The cat, of course, is chased away by its natural enemy, and we bow wow as a dog for about a half a minute. (Keep these short—students can get tired of all these ridiculous noises.)

Finally, we see the largest animal in the farmyard and the one (I think) that makes the most satisfying noise. We are a cow, and we all moo as a finale. (Make sure everyone makes these noises randomly; there should be no orchestration of the sounds.)

Mirrors   Once students have relaxed with these two exercises, they are ready to pair up for Mirrors. The purpose is to watch the other person and to mimic, without words or extraneous facial expressions, exactly what that person does. One of the pair stands directly in front of the other and starts lifting hands, moving arms, whatever. The other person, for a minute or so, must be that person's mirror image and do the identical actions he or she sees. Then the roles are reversed.

Statues   Statues adds plot to Mirrors and can be done while the class watches a few students or can be done with everyone in the class participating. You need to put students in trios and have them number off 1, 2, and 3. The three will be given roles (reminiscent of a nineteenth-century tableaux), and they must, again wordlessly, indicate their role by body gesture and position. Imagine that all the students have counted off. Here are a few scenarios they can arrange in about thirty seconds and then hold for ten seconds or so:

- 1 and 2 are angry at 3.
- 2 is cheating, and 1 is telling 3 about it.
- 3 is in love with 1, and 2 approves.
- 2 is in love with 3, and 1 thinks it's a bad situation.
- 2 is jealous of 3; 1 intervenes.

Clearly, this exercise asks more of students than the others and can be expanded into impromptus:

- Students can strike a pose and have the class guess the general situation.
- Students can be given a situation and have to show it.
- Students can experiment with a tableau and then write about it.

Before I do creative dramatics of almost any sort, I go through most or all of the four exercises outlined. By the time students are through, they are relaxed, inventive, and ready for experimentation. You may think this is a waste of valuable time, but it is my experience that warming up students for creative dramatics is essential. Regardless of what your purpose is in using creative dramatics, your students need some time, as the song says, to get in the mood.

Art and music

As response through creative dramatics can inspire students, so also can the use of art and music. Letting students who like to draw or paint or put together collages interpret or respond to literature through that medium can unlock a world of connection that might otherwise not exist. One project that I have found students enjoy is making an ABC book based on a novel. Using the letters of the alphabet, students make an ABC book/list using each letter of the alphabet and citing appropriate events/ideas/concepts. For example thinking of *The Great Gatsby*,

> **D** is for **DAISY**, who was Gatsby's love and inspiration.
> **E** is for **ENIGMA**, the mystery that was Gatsby.

Like my student Susan, described in Chapter 4, students can illustrate the alphabet book or use different typefaces to make it visually appealing.

Likewise, our students are often fiercely loyal to certain groups or styles of music, and using the lyrics of their favorite songs or asking them to connect reading with what they listen to can also make literature real or illuminating in a way that would not be otherwise possible. A book on this topic is *Hip-Hop Poetry and the Classics for the Classroom* where poems are paired to hip-hop songs for analysis and comparison. Teacher authors Alan Sitomer and Michael Cirelli link, for instance, Dylan Thomas' "Do Not Go Gentle into That Good Night" with Tupac Shakur's "Me Against the World"; "Harlem" by Langston Hughes with "Juicy" by Notorious B.I.G. The lesson plans are specific, and poem texts and excerpted song lyrics are provided. If your students love hip-hop, check it out.

A key to success in using art and music with literature is allowing students some freedom and yet being specific with expectations. Asking students to respond to literature with art or using music and not giving them any other boundaries can result in poorly focused projects. For example, ask students to select a certain number of songs and discuss how the lyrics relate to the literature; give students dimensions or number of elements to be incorporated into art projects.

Whenever possible, give them a choice

Even the most well-thought-out activity, one that has worked for other teachers and in other classes, can fall flat with a specific group of students. Giving students choice regarding what they will do with literature is often essential to student motivation and success, and there are many sources of activity ideas that can help you provide your students a menu of activities they will find appealing. Diana Mitchell, who is one of the most creative teachers I know, offers a number of inventive suggestions in our book *Both Art and Craft* (2000):

- **Yearbook entries** where students imagine what characters in the literature were like in high school and create, for each, a yearbook entry that includes a picture, a nickname, school activities, clubs, sports they might have participated in, a quotation that the character might have selected, favorite colors or foods, plans after high school.

- **E-mail directory** of people the character in the literature might keep in touch with by e-mail. Students are asked to justify the selections and explain why those names might be in their character's directory. Finally, students are asked to create a number of e-mail messages between the character and those in his or her directory.

- **Word test** for the literature where students create a fifteen-item vocabulary test of words that are essential to the understanding of the particular piece. Students also have to explain how they selected the words and how they would define each word in terms of the literature itself.

- **Creation of a home page** where students create an appropriate electronic site that a character might have. Students must use appropriate background, pictures, information, and at least five links to sites that the character would be interested in. Students need to justify all choices.

- **Creation of a chat room** conversation where a character has found other people to talk with. Students should describe the chat room the character is in and why the character would be drawn to the kind of group that operates the chat room. Students can also construct a conversation the character has with others while in the chat room.

- **Creation of a childhood** for a character where students include the character's earliest memory; memory of being scared, embarrassed, happy; the character's biggest worry; the one thing the character really dislikes; the one thing the character wishes his or her parents had realized about them. (53–58)

If they can't—or won't—read it

Who says that reading aloud to students is just for elementary school? The pleasures of *hearing* literature are manifold and, indeed, can help students who are struggling with material too difficult for them to comprehend easily. Hearing a piece read and seeing it simultaneously on the page can double comprehension; it can also give you the opportunity to gloss or define words that you are relatively sure your students would not readily understand. I read aloud most of the Edgar Allan Poe short stories my students studied; my cadence and my vocabulary synonyms helped them get through a lot of the difficult, vocabulary-rich nineteenth-century prose. I also read other, less challenging pieces to classes that featured reluctant readers or virtual nonreaders.

I love to read aloud and always apologize to students for my hogging the reading. Occasionally, though, I ask students to take turns reading literature whose syntax and vocabulary would not be a torture for a volunteer. Reading aloud adds to the drama of the literature and provides, especially with short works, an impact and power that only a single, sustained reading can provide. If your students can't read or if they really struggle over certain kinds of literature, read it to them or have relatively confident volunteers read all or part of it.

Reading aloud is also very important in drama and poetry. I, for one, cannot imagine reading poetry silently. Reading a poem a number of times is part and parcel of the experience of the genre, and even if students have looked at a piece in preparation for a discussion or for homework, they should hear it again—aloud—before discussing or writing or anything.

Reading aloud can also address another issue: that of students not doing homework or reading outside of class. Certainly for schools that feature high absentee rates, the expectation that students will prepare their reading before class can lead to serious teacher frustration when a small percentage of students—if any—actually come to class having read what was assigned.

In one teaching year, I had about a 40 percent absentee rate for three of my five classes; that meant that I could never count on who would be present for any given class on any given day. The continuity of assignments was destroyed ("No, I didn't read it—I was absent" many of my students would tell me), and in this situation, there was little I could do but adapt. Otherwise, I was forced into the situation of not only failing the students because of school-mandated policies about absences but, when the students did come to class, ensuring that they would not be able to participate. I didn't like that option, and, accordingly, I used poetry, short stories, and very short dramas that could be read in class. I then set up some form of activity that we either started or completed within a fifty-minute period. Students, despite their spotty attendance, could complete work within a class and, for some, it not only meant the difference between passing and failing but also gave them a daily sense of accomplishment and completion.

While this accommodation may strike you as caving in to a bad situation—weak student reading skills and excessive student absences—I would defend it as a realistic compromise. Faced with failing them all virtually from the onset or working with the reality of my students and my school, I chose the latter. And I do believe some of my students learned something along the way as they listened.

If you don't like it either

I've read the sentiment before, and I happen to agree with it: if you really don't like a piece of literature—and this is particularly true of poetry—you probably shouldn't teach it. As self-indulgent as that may seem, I think it is good advice and, within some limits, I follow it myself. The point is that enthusiasm is catching. The reverse is also true. To give one example, if "To the Virgins to Make Much of Time" seems impossibly silly to you, skip it and maybe even Robert Herrick altogether. There is surely some other seventeenth-century British poet whom you can present to your students in an effective and enthusiastic manner. On the other hand, don't assume that what one year you absolutely could not bring yourself to teach will remain on your "yuck list" forever: your tastes will change as you teach, and you need to give literature a second look every year or so. You might surprise yourself.

Remember why you're doing this

When you're faced with objectives and those very official-looking textbooks and five classes of thirty students or so each, it is hard to remember just why you are reading literature. Don't forget the joy of it, the possibility that some of your students, not all certainly, but some, will become lifelong readers due in part to what happens in *your* class. Don't forget the laughter and the joy; it's why you are doing this.

For many beginning teachers the curriculum requirements and what it seems the school or the school system expects can become an overwhelming weight; there is the fear, reasonable or not, that you will be judged by how much material you cover or how efficiently you cover it. For some teachers, the scores their students make on large-scale exams are also a concern.

But at some point, although you cannot wave away or minimize these very real issues, you also have to make some choices about what school expects versus your responsibility to your students. To some people, even some teachers in the classroom, a "free" reading day once a week would seem a waste; time spent becoming mirror images and creating skits would appear frivolous. But what you are about is more than pages in the textbook and passing scores on literature tests. As highbrow as it may seem when you contemplate the down and dirty realities of third period, you are in that class to invite reading and thinking, to give students with minds and hearts and psyches windows onto the world we know is in books. You are a guide to something bigger than the state competency test, the unit exam, the departmental requirements, or even the SATs and admission to college. While it is not always true that there will be conflict between reading and talking and thinking and what school "expects," there may be. And when that occurs, remember why you are a teacher, why you got into this business in the first place.

Long after the multiple-choice test on *Beowulf* has faded, long after the students can no longer identify who wrote about a raisin in the sun or tell with certainty what happened to Willy Loman or Heathcliff at the end, this connection to literature will endure. Thus your guiding North Star is not the curriculum guide; you need, while trying to be responsible to the demands of your job and the expectations of the system, also to hold true to your vision for yourself and your students. It's a lot to ask; it's also very important. Without holding true to that vision you may find yourself relatively lost and feeling, as some do, that you are in the classroom "delivering" a package of instruction at someone else's behest. That's not what you want to spend any part of your life doing; while balancing the expectations may be the tightrope act of your life, the stakes are huge, and the effort is worth it.

············· **FOR YOUR JOURNAL** ················

Pick a favorite piece of literature—a play, a poem, a short story, an essay, a novel—that you think you could teach in middle school or high school. How would you prepare students for this piece of literature? Think about three or four activities you could do during or after the reading; write about them. Can you imagine this piece of literature being challenged or censored? For the sake of argument, imagine it is. What reasons would you advance for using it in the classroom?

A Final Note on Choosing Literature

If we want our students to respond to literature, then it is crucial that we choose literature—or let them participate in the choosing of literature—to which they can have a response. While much of the literature you use in your classroom will be dictated by the textbook anthology, that ubiquitous fixture of the classroom, there are ways you can expand beyond what your text has selected for your students. There is just not time for you to duplicate or scout out a parallel text for everything, but, on the other hand, as well as young adult literature and graphic novels, don't forget these rich and often overlooked sources of reading:

- magazines of all types
- paperback books (from the school bookroom, students' attics or basements, secondhand bookstores, yard sales)
- newspapers and tabloids
- catalogs of all sorts
- advertising newsletters
- pamphlets, booklets, informational brochures

While we have a contractual obligation to adhere to what the school system and our English language arts department encourage or mandate that we "cover," we also need to remember that we have a similar obligation to our students to give them reading to which they can truly respond. It is not completely revolutionary to have a classroom library of materials such as those listed and to let students read and browse through them at specified times. Devoting an entire class period to free reading can encourage students who would not otherwise spend—or find—the time. The reading can be supervised, academic credit can be given, but it can come from the *Guinness World Record*, *Road & Track*, *Sports Illustrated*, *People*, *Sassy*, *Seventeen*; a maintenance manual; horror, sports, and romance novels; and technical brochures and catalogs. Real readers are omnivorous; if we insist that reading means only one thing—that is, "good" literature of which we specifically approve and the "best" literature, which appears on sanctioned lists—we are not only lying to our students, we are in our own way discouraging the young reader.

To open the world of the printed page to our students, we must open the covers of all kinds of reading matter, Harlequin romance to *Hamlet* to *Hemmings Motor News*. Making a reader is a broad and messy business, and we need to become inclusive, not exclusive, in our own tastes and in what we offer to our students and encourage them to read. As one of my students recalls:

> [My English teacher] allowed seniors to pick out their own reading material for the remainder of the school year after spring break. I dare say she would have allowed a college-directed student (aren't they all?) to read *Chitty Chitty Bang Bang* if they had so desired, but she stemmed this with a "water seeks its own level" speech that made one want to read *An American Tragedy* just to show her.
>
> —Heather Talley

A Story: Thurman and *Architectural Digest*

At one point in my teaching life almost all of my students were reluctant readers or virtually nonreaders. I read aloud to them, I brought in carts of library books on selected topics, I took them to the library, I scouted for class materials, and I established a classroom "library" of magazines of all types and a free reading time. For two of the classes, the two I felt could productively use the periods (my other classes were just not psychologically ready for fifty minutes of quiet reading), I established every Friday as a time to read silently, individually. I encouraged students to bring something in, but I also kept my magazine library; most students forgot materials or, frankly, would find access to such materials difficult. But as the months went on, my collection seemed to suffice: the magazines I had scrounged from friends and relatives and back issues of my own subscriptions included a really broad range of newsmagazines, music tabloids, traditional "women's" journals, literary digests, and the occasional technical or car magazine.

It was the reaction of one of my students to this magazine reading that hooked me on its utility and importance—and, indeed, on its unpredictability. It made what I think may have been a permanent difference in the life of one young reader, and I hope that he sees the world a bit differently to this day because of his reading.

Thurman was tall, had long, blond hair that fell below his shoulders, wore sunglasses most of the year (in class as well as out), and sported the chains, boots, and studded jacket that in my school signaled his membership in a group of rather tough, white males who endured school rather than enjoyed it. Thurman lived in a public housing project and hung out with a group who had a reputation for drugs and trouble. With most of his teachers he was silent, almost mild-mannered, but he actually had a strong temper and a violent streak; he had been suspended a number of times from school and, out of school, he was prone to explosions. Too many fights and a final assault conviction led him to a thirty-day jail sentence. But the judge wanted Thurman to stay in school, so the sentence was served on weekends. He checked into the city jail on Friday afternoon and checked out to return to school on Monday morning.

Thurman was in my English class and was struggling with his reading, if not his behavior. He usually wanted to be let out of our afternoon class early; between jail, his job, and his personal life he didn't feel he had much time to waste. It was a request I almost always refused, regardless of the urgency or sensibility of reasons, and Thurman would eventually settle into work. For some reason—one of the mysteries of teacher/student chemistry—we got along very well, and he became one of my absolute, all-time favorite students. After a semester or so of contact, I thought he was wonderful, and he, in his own often elusive way, seemed to like me, too.

Maybe that was why he would be one of the first to wander to the back of the room on Friday and leaf through the magazines. He seemed to have a sense of loyalty to me as his teacher and could, most times, be enticed to try something because I recommended it. After all, I had listened to his favorite rock group of the time and even, on his recommendation, bought one of their albums. We had, of a sort, a deal.

Loyalty aside, Thurman was not a strong reader. He stumbled over words; he refused to complete outside reading. His writing was careful but jerky and unsure. It was, however, on one of the Friday afternoon reads that Thurman intersected with *Architectural Digest*, the pricey journal of multimillion-dollar homes and furnishings I had scrounged from relatives who could not only afford the hefty subscription price but who could occasionally purchase some of the cheaper items featured in it. While I had been really reluctant to add the journal to my class library—its relation to almost anyone's real life was pretty tangential—there were issues and issues of *Architectural Digest*, they were free, and I needed variety.

What possible connection could *Architectural Digest*, this monument to gold-plated faucets of the stars, sunken living rooms of the mega wealthy, marble and terrazzo floors of the famous, have with a hot-tempered white kid from the projects? Photographs and text, it was a bombshell to Thurman; he read intently, steadily; he borrowed copies between Fridays. He didn't want to talk about it at first; he just, ravenously, miraculously, wanted . . . to read. He looked at the pictures, read the captions, and graduated into the text. When he did talk, and it wasn't for some time, he wanted to know about such homes, such designs, such lives. He had, he admitted, no idea that the world in *Architectural Digest* had ever existed. And I could tell, thankfully, that that fact did not depress him a bit; he was filled with understandable wonder, but with a young person's optimism, he was also filled with exhilaration. This was a world of excess, to be sure, but also of beauty and grace where the aesthetic was discussed seriously.

When Thurman wandered out of my life—he did pass my class, graduate from high school, get a job, stay out of jail, and eventually marry—I felt the loss of a favorite student. But also I felt pretty good. Thurman had looked, he had read. I never would have guessed that magazine and that young man would intersect. But they did. And I felt overwhelmingly happy and convinced, once again, that hooking kids into reading is a wide-ranging, broad-moving experience. If *I* had selected reading material for Thurman, it never, in my wildest dreams, would have been *Architectural Digest*. He made the selection himself; all I did was give him a little freedom and some time to read, and then get out of the way.

I wonder if that isn't quite enough.

When I was president of the National Council of Teachers of English, part of my work was traveling around the country to give talks and workshops. One early fall I was the keynote speaker for a two-day session involving all the middle level and senior high school English teachers in a large school district in Maryland. The teachers were a committed and interested group of professionals, and I outlined my deep belief that we must widen the definition of reading and give students more than classics, that we must try to entice them into the world of literature by offering other choices. I talked abut the variety of magazines, the range of nonfiction, and urged those present to encourage those works in their classroom curriculum and, more to the point, to give students credit for work done with this kind of literature. The members of the large audience listened avidly, and at the end there were numbers of questions. One teacher asked about my allowing students to read magazines— I had specifically mentioned car magazines—in English class. I answered his question from the podium but, after the talk, he came up to see me one-on-one. He was incredulous and told me he thought that I was surely not doing my job as a teacher to allow such material in an English classroom and to give students credit for it. I made my point again, but I know I did not convince him that morning, either answering his question from the audience or talking to him individually. Invited to speak to a large professional group, having prepared carefully, I want to be well received, and at times for me resulting conflicts and criticisms can be unsettling. But I left that conference and that one teacher with hardly a backward glance. I kept thinking of Thurman, and I knew, deep and sure, that I was right.

References

Professional sources

American Library Association. *Hit List: Frequently Challenged Books for Young Adults*. Chicago: ALA, 1996.

Appleman, Deborah. *Critical Encounters in High School English: Teaching Literary Theory to Adolescents*. New York: Teachers College Press, 2000.

Burress, Lee, and Edward B. Jenkinson. *The Students' Right to Know*. Urbana, IL: NCTE, 1982.

Carlsen, G. Robert. *Books and the Teenage Reader*. 2d ed. New York: Harper & Row, 1980.

Christenbury, Leila. "Creating Text: Students Connecting with Literature." In *Literature and Life: Making Connections in the Classroom. Classroom Practices in Teaching English*. Edited by Patricia Phelan. Vol. 25. Urbana, IL: NCTE, 1990.

———. " 'The Guy Who Wrote This Poem Seems to Have the Same Feelings as You Have': Reader-Response Methodology." In *Reader Response in Secondary and College Classrooms*, 2d ed. Edited by Nicholas J. Karolides. Mahwah, NJ: Lawrence Erlbaum, 2000.

———. "Problems with *Othello* in the High School Classroom." In *Teaching Shakespeare into the Twenty-first Century*. Edited by Ronald E. Salomone and James E. Davis. Athens, OH: Ohio University Press, 1997.

———. "Rosenblatt the Radical." *Voices from the Middle* 12 (March 2005): 22–24.

———. "What Oft Was Thought But Ne'er So Well Expressed: The Use of Quotations in Teaching Shakespeare." In *Teaching Shakespeare Today: Practical Approaches and Productive Strategies*. Edited by James E. Davis and Ronald E. Salome. Urbana, IL: NCTE, 1993.

Coates, Nathan. "Why We Need Neil Simon's *Lost in Yonkers*." *English Journal* 85 (September 2005): 23–28.

Daniels, Harvey. *Literature Circles: Voice and Choice in the Student-centered Classroom*. 2d ed. York, ME: Stenhouse, 2002.

Freedman, Samuel G. *Small Victories*. New York: HarperCollins, 1990.

Frey, Nancy, and Douglas Fisher. "Using Graphic Novels, Anime, and the Internet in an Urban High School." *English Journal* 93 (January 2004): 19–25.

Gallo, Don. "Bold Books for Innovative Teaching." *English Journal* 94 (November 2004): 114.

Gilbert, Miriam. "Teaching Shakespeare Through Performance." *Shakespeare Quarterly* 35 (5) (1984): 601–608.

Hill, Bonnie, Nancy J. Johnson, and Katherine Noe, eds. *Literature Circles and Response.* Norwood, MA: Christopher-Gordon, 1995.

Johannessen, Larry R. "When History Talk Back: Teaching Nonfiction Literature of the Vietnam War." *English Journal* 91 (March 2002): 39–47.

McCloud, Scott. *Understanding Comics.* New York: Harper, 1994.

Mitchell, Diana, and Leila Christenbury. *Both Art and Craft: Teaching Ideas That Spark Learning.* Urbana, IL: NCTE, 2000.

NCTE. *The Students' Right to Read.* Urbana, IL: NCTE, 1982.

Ransom, John Crowe. *The New Criticism.* Westport, CT: Greenwood Press, 1979.

Rationales for Challenged Books Grades 4–12. Urbana, IL: NCTE and IRA, 1998. (CD-ROM)

Ressler, Paula. *Dramatic Changes: Talking About Sexual Orientation and Gender Identity with High School Students.* Portsmouth, NH: Heinemann, 2002.

Rosenblatt, Louise. *Literature as Exploration.* 3d ed. New York: Noble & Noble, 1976.

Rutsky, Joshua. *Beyond the Bard: Fifty Plays for Use in the English Classroom.* Boston: Allyn & Bacon, 2001.

Schade, Lisa. "Demystifying the Text: Literary Criticism in the High School Classroom." *English Journal* 85 (March 1996): 26–31.

Schjeldahl, Peter. "Words and Pictures: Graphic Novels Come of Age." *The New Yorker* (October 17, 2005): 162–68.

Selden, Raman. *A Reader's Guide to Contemporary Literary Theory.* 2d ed. Lexington, KY: The University Press of Kentucky, 1989.

Sitomer, Alan, and Michael Cirelli. *Hip-Hop Poetry and the Classics for the Classroom: Connecting Our Classic Curriculum to Hip-Hop Poetry Through Standards-Based Language Arts Instruction.* Beverly Hills, CA: Milk Mug Publishing, 2004.

"Teacher to Teacher: What Play by a Playwright Other Than Shakespeare Has Been Especially Effective with Your Students?" *English Journal* 95 (September 2005): 20–22.

Tillyard, E. M. W. *The Elizabethan World Picture.* London: Chatto & Windus, 1943.

Tovani, Cris. *Do I Really Have to Teach Reading? Content, Comprehension, Grades 6–12.* York, ME: Stenhouse, 2004.

Wagner, Betty Jane. *Educational Drama and Language Arts: What Research Shows.* Portsmouth, NH: Heinemann, 1998.

Weiner, Stephen. *Faster Than a Speeding Bullet: The Rise of the Graphic Novel.* n.p.: NBM, 2003.

Zarnowksi, Myra, Richard M. Kerper, and Julie M. Jensen, eds. *The Best in Children's Nonfiction: Reading, Writing & Teaching Orbis Pictus Award Books.* Urbana, IL: NCTE, 2001.

Literature cited

Achebe, Chinua. *Things Fall Apart.* New York: Anchor Books, [1959] 1994.

Agee, James. *Let Us Now Praise Famous Men* (with photographs by Walker Evans). New York: Houghton Mifflin, 2000.

Austen, Jane. *Pride and Prejudice.* New York: Penguin, [1813] 1996.

Barlow, Judith, ed. *Plays by American Women: The Early Years.* New York: Avon, 1981.

Barnes, Kim. *In the Wilderness: Coming of Age in Unknown Country.* New York: Random House, 1996.

Bowers, Neal. "Black Walnuts." *North American Review* 273 (June 1988): 19.

Bradstreet, Anne. "Upon the Burning of Our House, July 10th, 1666." In *The Women Poets in English*. Edited by Ann Stanford, 52–53. New York: McGraw-Hill, 1972.

Brontë, Charlotte. *Jane Eyre*. Edited by Richard J. Dunn. New York: Norton, 1971.

Capote, Truman. *In Cold Blood*. New York: Vintage, 1994.

Chaucer, Geoffrey. *Canterbury Tales*. In *The Works of Geoffrey Chaucer*. 2d ed. Edited by F. N. Robinson. Boston: Houghton Mifflin, 1961.

Chopin, Kate. *The Awakening*. New York: Bantam, 1988.

———. "The Story of an Hour." In *Introduction to Literature*. 2d ed. Edited by Dorothy U. Seyler and Richard A. Wilan. Upper Saddle River, NJ: Prentice Hall, 1990.

Cisneros, Sandra. *The House on Mango Street*. New York: Vintage, 1984.

Clugston, Chynna. *Queen Bee*. New York: Scholastic, 2005.

Coleridge, Samuel Taylor. *Selected Poetry and Prose*. New York: Holt, Rinehart & Winston, 1951.

Connell, Richard. *The Most Dangerous Game and Other Stories of Adventure*. New York: Berkley Highland Books, 1970.

Cormier, Robert. *The Chocolate War*. New York: Dell Laurel-Leaf, 1974.

Cox, Lynne. *Swimming to Antarctica: Tales of a Long-Distance Swimmer*. New York: Harcourt, 2004.

Dickens, Charles. *Great Expectations*. New York: Collier, 1969.

Dickinson, Emily. *The Complete Poems of Emily Dickinson* ("Frigate," #1263; "Hope," #264). Edited by Thomas H. Johnson. Boston: Little, Brown, 1960.

Donne, John. "A Valediction Forbidding Mourning." In *Donne*. Edited by Richard Wilbur. New York: Dell, 1962.

Dreiser, Theodore. *An American Tragedy*. New York: Boni and Liveright, 1925.

Ehrenreich, Barbarba. *Nickel and Dimed: On (Not) Getting by in America*. New York: Henry Holt, 2001.

Faulkner, William. *As I Lay Dying*. New York: Random House, [1930] 1964.

Fitzgerald, F. Scott. *The Great Gatsby*. New York: Scribner, [1925] 1995.

Fleischmann, John. *Phineas Gage: A Gruesome but True Story About Brain Science*. New York: Houghton Mifflin, 2002.

Fox, Paula. *Borrowed Finery*. New York: Henry Holt, 2001.

Frankenstein: The Graphic Novel. Adapted by Gary Reed. Illustrated by Frazer Irving. New York: Puffin Graphics, 2005.

Frost, Robert. "The Road Not Taken." In *Modern Poetry*. 2d ed. Edited by Maynard Mack, Leonard Dean, William Frost. Englewood Cliffs, NJ: Prentice-Hall, 1961.

Gallo, Donald R., ed. *Center Stage*. New York: HarperCollins, 1990.

———. *First Crossing: Stories About Teen Immigrants*. Cambridge, MA: Candlewick, 2004.

———. *No Easy Answers: Short Stories About Teenagers Making Tough Choices*. New York: Laurel-Leaf, 1997.

———. *Short Circuits: Thirteen Shocking Stories by Outstanding Writers for Young Adults*. New York: Doubleday, 1992.

———. *Sixteen*. New York: Dell Laurel-Leaf, 1984.

———. *Ultimate Sports: Short Stories by Outstanding Writers for Young Adults*. New York: Laurel-Leaf, 1995.

Golding, William. *Lord of the Flies*. New York: Coward-McCann, 1962.

Guinness Word Records. n.p.: Guinness World Records, 2006.

Guralnick, Peter. *Last Train to Memphis: The Rise of Elvis Presley*. Boston: Little, Brown, 1994.

———. *Careless Love: The Unmaking of Elvis Presley*. Boston: Little Brown, 1999.

Hansberry, Lorraine. *A Raisin in the Sun*. New York: Random House, [1994] 1987.

Hayden, Robert. "Those Winter Sundays." *Angle of Ascent*, 113. New York: Liveright, 1975.

Hawthorne, Nathaniel. *The House of Seven Gables*. New York: Viking, 1983.

———. *The Scarlet Letter*. Edited by Brian Harding. New York: Oxford University Press, 1990.

Hearst, James. "Cold Snap." *A Single Focus*, 56. Prairie du Chien, WI: The Prairie Press, 1967.

Hentoff, Nat. *The Day They Came to Arrest the Book*. New York: Dell Laurel-Leaf, 1982.

Herbert, George. "Easter-Wings." In *Herbert*. Edited by Richard Wilbur. New York: Dell, 1962.

Herrick, Robert. "To the Virgins to Make Much of Time." In *Seventeenth Century Poetry: The Schools of Donne and Jonson*. Edited by Hugh Kenner. New York: Holt, Rinehart & Winston, 1964.

Hillenbrand, Laura. *Seabiscuit: An American Legend*. New York: Ballantine, 2001.

Hinton, S. E. *The Outsiders*. New York: Viking, 1967.

Hughes, Langston. "Dream Deferred." *The Collected Poems of Langston Hughes*. New York: Random House, 1994.

Hurston, Zora Neale. *Their Eyes Were Watching God*. New York: Harper and Row, [1937] 1990.

Jackson, Shirley. "The Lottery." In *Fiction 100*. Edited by James H. Pickering. New York: Macmillan, 1978.

Juster, Norton. *The Phantom Tollbooth*. New York: Alfred A. Knopf, 1961.

Krakauer, Jon. *Into Thin Air: A Personal Account of the Mt. Everest Disaster*. New York: Anchor Books, 1999.

Larson, Erik. *Isaac's Storm*. New York: Random House, 1999.

Martin, Ann M. The Baby-Sitters Club series. New York: Scholastic, 1986 (and years following).

Marvell, Andrew. *Selections*. Edited by Frank Kermode and Keith Walker. New York: Oxford University Press, 1990.

McCourt, Frank. *Angela's Ashes*. New York: Scribner's, 1996.

McCullough, David. *John Adams*. New York: Simon and Schuster, 2002.

Miller, Arthur. *Death of a Salesman*. New York: Penguin. 1977.

Milton, John. *Areopagitica*. In *Complete Poetry and Selected Prose of John Milton*. New York: Modern Library, 1950.

Moore, Alan, Kevin O'Neill, Ben Dimagmaliw, and Bill Oakley. *The League of Extraordinary Gentleman, Vol. 1*. La Jolla, CA: America's Best Comics, 2000.

Oates, Joyce Carol, and Robert Atwan, eds. *The Best Essays of the Century*. New York: Houghton Mifflin, 2001.

Oliver, Mary. "First Snow." *New and Selected Poems*. Volume 1. Boston: Beacon Press, 2004.

Orwell, George. *1984*. New York: Harcourt Brace Jovanovich, 1949.

Pascal, Francine. Sweet Valley High series. New York: Bantam, 1983 (and years following).

Paul, Jay S. "Central School." *Artemis XVI*. Roanoke, VA: Artemis Artists/Writers, 1993.

Philbrick, Nathaniel. *In the Heart of the Sea: The Tragedy of the Whaleship Essex*. New York: Penguin, 2000.

Poe, Edgar Allan. *Great Tales of Horror*. New York: Bantam, 1964.

Pope, Alexander. *An Essay on Criticism*. In *Alexander Pope: Selected Poetry & Prose*. Edited by William K. Wimsatt Jr. New York: Holt, Rinehart & Winston, 1961.

Riis, Jacob A. *How the Other Half Lives*. New York: Dover, 1971.

Sacco, Joe. *Safe Area Gorazde: The War in Eastern Bosnia 1992–95*. Seattle, WA: Fantagraphics Books, 2001.

Salinger, J. D. *The Catcher in the Rye*. Boston: Little, Brown, 1951.

Shakespeare, William. *The Complete Plays and Poems of William Shakespeare.* Edited by William Allan Neilson and Charles Jarvin Hill. Boston: Riverside Press, 1942.

Schlissel, Lillian, ed. *Women's Diaries of the Westward Journey.* New York: Schocken Books, 2004.

Schlosser, Eric. *Fast Food Nation: The Dark Side of the All-American Meal.* New York: Houghton Mifflin, 2001.

Shelley, Mary. *Frankenstein.* New York: Bantam, [1816] 1984.

Smith, Jeff. *Out of Boneville.* New York: Scholastic, 2005.

Spiegelman, Art. *Maus: A Survivor's Tale. Vol. 1: My Father Bleeds History.* New York: Pantheon Books, 1986.

Steinbeck, John. *Of Mice and Men.* New York: Penguin Great Books, [1937] 1993.

Stine, R. L. Goosebumps series. New York: Scholastic, various years.

Sullivan, George. *Built to Last: Building America's Amazing Bridges, Dams, Tunnels, and Skyscrapers.* New York: Scholastic, 2005.

Swift, Jonathan. "A Modest Proposal." In *Jonathan Swift.* Edited by Angus Ross and David Woolley. New York: Oxford University Press, 1984.

Taylor, Henry. "Breakings." *An Afternoon of Pocket Billiards,* 3. Salt Lake City: University of Utah Press, 1975.

Twain, Mark. *Adventures of Huckleberry Finn.* Berkeley: University of California Press, 1985.

Vaughan, Brian K. *Runaways: Pride & Joy.* Illustrated by Adrian Alphona. New York: Marvel, 2003.

Ware, Chris. *The Adventures of Jimmy Corrigan, the Smartest Kid on Earth.* New York: Pantheon Books, 2000.

White, E. B. *Charlotte's Web.* New York: Harper, 1952.

———. *E. B. White: Writings from* The New Yorker, *1925–1976.* Edited by Rebecca M. Dale. New York: HarperCollins, 1990.

Wright, Richard. *Native Son.* New York: Harper & Row, 1940.

Yeats, W.B. "The Second Coming." In *Modern Poetry.* 2d ed. Edited by Maynard Mack, Leonard Dean, William Frost. Englewood Cliffs, NJ: Prentice-Hall, 1961.

Resources

Recent resources for teaching poetry

Barton, Bob, and David Booth. *Poetry Goes to School: From Mother Goose to Shel Silverstein.* Portland, ME: Stenhouse, 2004.

Though the focus is elementary school, this book is a rich resource of teaching ideas and sample poems.

Brewbaker, James, and Dawn J. Hyland, eds. *Poems by Adolescents and Adults: A Thematic Collection for Middle School and High School.* Urbana, IL: NCTE, 2002.

This anthology mixes poems by accomplished, award-winning poets and poems by young people from grades 5–12. Organized by themes (such as Generations; Love; Body, Mind, and Spirit), this is a great resource for teachers looking for fresh poems and thematic connections.

Focus Issue: Teaching and Writing Poetry. *English Journal.* Volume 91, Number 3, January 2002.

Focus Issue: Poetry: The Best Words in Their Best Order. *Voices from the Middle.* Volume 10, Number 2, December 2002.

Both of these issues of respected professional journals provide numerous strategies, resources, and websites for the teaching of poetry in the middle and secondary school.

Jago, Carol. *Nikki Giovanni in the Classroom*. Urbana, IL: NCTE, 1999.

> A savvy and accomplished high school teacher, Jago outlines teaching strategies for looking at Giovanni's poetic language, writing poems modeled on her work, analyzing the poems, and integrating Giovanni's poetry into other literature study.

O'Connor, John S. *Word Playgrounds: Reading, Writing, & Performing Poetry in the English Classroom*. Urbana, IL: NCTE, 2004.

> Containing twenty-five real-world activities for teaching poetry in middle and high school classrooms, this practical book offers suggestions on how to dramatize poems and enjoy the wordplay of poetry.

Paschen, Elise, and Rebekah Presson Mosby. *Poetry Speaks: Hear Great Poets Read Their Work from Tennyson to Plath*. Naperville, IL: Sourcebooks, 2001.

> Poets Billy Collins, Sharon Olds, Richard Wilbur, Mark Strand, and others contribute critical essays and biographical sketches of dozens of classic poets; the oversized book, with full text poems, also includes three audio CDs.

Powell, Joseph, and Mark Halperin. *Accent on Meter: A Handbook for Readers of Poetry*. Urbana, IL: NCTE, 2004.

> Meaning, rhythm, and meter are all part of poetry, and this very detailed book offers information on scansion and metrical terms, fully illustrated through specific poems.

Recent resources for teaching Shakespeare

Focus Issue: Shakespeare for a New Age. *English Journal*. Volume 92, Number 1, September 2002.

> This issue of *EJ*, entirely devoted to the teaching of Shakespeare's plays and sonnets, offers ideas on teaching *The Tempest*, *Romeo and Juliet*, *Julius Caesar*, and shows how technology and slide shows can be used to bring the Bard to students. An annotated bibliography of helpful websites is also included.

Greenblatt, Stephen. *Will in the World: How Shakespeare Became Shakespeare*. New York: W.W. Norton, 2004.

> If you are interested in an up-to-date interpretation of the life of Shakespeare, Greenblatt's account is readable and riveting. Drawn from recent scholarship and an intensive study of Shakespeare's plays, this book goes far to probe the Bard's motivation, personality, and artistic craft, information, which may be of great interest to students—and their teachers—as they read the plays.

Rocklin, Edward L. *Performance Approaches to Teaching Shakespeare*. Urbana, IL: NCTE, 2005.

> Inspired by an issue of *California English*, Rocklin insists that students explore the genre of drama and see how it is different from prose fiction and that they also engage in performance, not just reading of the plays. Specific plays explored in depth include *Taming of the Shrew*, *Richard III*, and *Hamlet*.

Shakespeare and the Classroom.

> In publication since 1993, this wonderful newsletter/journal appears twice a year. Articles concentrate on performance approaches to Shakespeare, and issues routinely include theatre reviews, film reviews, and many ideas for teaching Shakespeare in the middle, secondary, and college classroom. Packed with information, *Shakespeare and the Classroom* is a great resource.
>
> (For $8 yearly subscriptions, write *Shakespeare and the Classroom*, English Department, Ohio Northern University, Akron, OH 45810.)

Recent books about Young Adult literature

Donelson, Kenneth L., and Alleen Pace Nilsen. *Literature for Today's Young Adults*. 7th ed. Boston: Pearson, 2005.

> The most comprehensive and authoritative text on the history and genre of Young Adult literature, this useful and well-researched book is in a deserved seventh printing.

Herz, Sarah K., and Donald R. Gallo. *From Hinton to Hamlet: Building Bridges Between Young Adult Literature and the Classics*. 2d ed. Westport, CT: Greenwood Press, 2005.

> This is a great book to learn about Young Adult literature and how to approach it by linking to the classics and contemporary issues. Teaching through themes, archetypes, and author biography are also included as well as a wealth of reference material.

Kaywell, Joan F., ed. *Adolescent Literature as a Complement to the Classics*. Norwood, MA: Christopher-Gordon, Volume 1, 1993; Volume 2, 1995; Volume 3, 1997; Volume 4, 2000.

> The four volumes in this series provide numbers of Young Adult titles paired with classics and show how teachers can link the two to improve student understanding and interest. Practical lessons and ideas are provided.

Recommended and recent Young Adult literature

There are dozens of "best" lists from which to choose great Young Adult literature. The following is a short, personal list of recent YA books that I recommend for middle and high school reading. The designation adult themes *indicates that the book is most likely better for senior high school students.*

Blizzard. Jim Murphy. New York: Scholastic, 2002. (nonfiction/natural disaster)

> A retelling of the Great Blizzard of 1888, a March snowstorm that paralyzed the East Coast and is considered one of the United States' most devastating natural disasters. This Newbery Honor book is generously illustrated with maps, photographs, and newspaper articles from the time.

A Corner of the Universe. Ann M. Martin. New York: Scholastic, 2002. (fiction/friendship)

> This Newbery Honor book details one summer in twelve-year-old Harriet's life where she makes friends with a girl who travels with a carnival and uncovers the mystery of her Uncle Adam. Beautifully written, this portrait of small town life and a summer of discovery also touches on mental illness and prejudice. Adult themes.

Feed. M. T. Anderson. Cambridge, MA: Candlewick Press, 2002. (science fiction/dystopia)

> Far in the future, everyone has attached to their brain a "feed" that transmits individually tailored commercials and gives constant commentary on the world. Titus is satisfied with this life until he meets Violet, a young woman who not only has no feed but also thinks that there is a different way to live life.

Godless. Pete Hautman. New York: Simon and Schuster, 2004. (realistic fiction)

> Jason is tired of his parents' religion so, on a whim, he creates a new one and influences his friends to join him in worship. The new god is the town water tower, however, and what happens as Jason and his friends begin their rites is unexpected. A provocative book and National Book Award winner, *Godless* will inspire discussion and debate.

Harry Potter Series. (*Harry Potter and the Sorcerer's Stone*, 1997; *HP and the Chamber of Secrets*, 1999; *HP and the Prisoner of Azkaban*, 1999; *HP and the Goblet of Fire*, 2000; *HP and the Order of the Phoenix*, 2003; *HP and the Half-Blood Prince*, 2005). J. K. Rowling. New York: Scholastic. (fantasy)

> Despite the fears of some, the books in this well-written, well-plotted, and engrossing series do not advocate witchcraft and do not celebrate evil. The books have, however, caused an epidemic of renewed interest in reading and in the genre of fantasy. Harry Potter, who ages from middle school to senior high school in the titles that have appeared so far, is the archetypal epic hero, the hero/orphan who is rescued from obscurity and who must fight evil and win. Harry is a battler who is under threat of death from the feared Lord Voldemort, but he is also fallible, a real young man who must study at the Hogwarts School of Wizards, make friends, endure heart throbs, and occasionally fail to live up to his potential. The books have caused an understandable sensation, breaking all rules regarding young adult literature length and also readership, attracting fans from early elementary years to adults. Even their plot complexity and increasing length (*Order of the Phoenix* weighed in at 870 pages) have not daunted readers' appetites for Harry Potter, and, like them, I await the next book eagerly.

Holes. Louis Sachar. New York: Farrar, Straus, and Giroux, 1998. (fiction/fantasy)

> Through an accident rather than wrongdoing, Stanley Yelnats finds himself sentenced to a juvenile detention facility, the idyllically named Camp Green Lake. Camp Green Lake is a grim place, however, and actually located on a dried-up lake bed. Stanley, like the other detainees, must dig a huge hole every day—an odd punishment in which the warden takes a keen interest. By the end of the novel, Stanley has solved the mystery of Camp Green Lake and made fast friends with his fellow inmates. Written with humor and using absurd coincidence, this Newbery Medal book exerts a charm all its own.

The Last Book in the Universe. Rodman Philbrick. New York: Blue Sky Press, 2000. (science fiction/dystopia)

> The world has been destroyed by the Big Shake, and violent gangs rule what civilization is left. While most people don't worry much as mind probe needles provide all that anyone wants, some individuals, such as Spaz, wonder if life could be better. When Spaz meets Ryter, a holdover from the "backtimes" who, it is rumored, knows about long forgotten things called books and writing, his life is unalterably changed. This is epic science fiction and a compelling read.

Monster. Walter Dean Myers. New York: Scholastic, 1999. (realistic fiction)

> Written in the form of a screenplay, this intriguing book charts the felony trial of Steve Harmon, a young man who may or may not be guilty of murder. Nuanced and complex, *Monster* is a unique young adult book. Adult themes.

Shipwreck at the Bottom of the World: The Extraordinary True Story of Shackleton and the Endurance. Jennifer Armstrong. New York: Crown, 1998. (nonfiction/adventure and survival)

> In 1914 Ernest Shackleton and a crew of twenty-seven men sailed from England to Antarctica in an attempt to be the first explorers to cross from one side of the continent to another. The expedition was not successful, but the story of survival and the nineteen months the group was trapped on Antarctica is charted in riveting detail in this generously illustrated Orbis Pictus winner.

Speak. Laurie Halse Anderson. New York: Puffin Books, 1999. (realistic fiction)

> A Prinz Honor Book and National Book Award finalist, this is the story of Melinda, a freshman who enters high school so traumatized by the events of the previous summer that she refuses to speak. First-person narrative makes this a riveting read. Adult themes.

When the Emperor Was Divine. Julie Otsuka. New York: Random House, 2002. (fiction/Japanese American Internment)

> Written in a plain and spare prose style, this is an affecting tale of a Japanese American family that is ordered from their home in Berkeley, California, and removed to a desert internment camp for the duration of World War II. The experience of the parents and the two children are different and yet the same, and the novel's final chapter offers a ringing condemnation of the injustice of the Japanese American internment. Adult themes.

Witness. Karen Hesse. New York: Scholastic, 2001. (poetry/historical fiction)

> Told in verse, this is the story of a 1924 Vermont town and the citizens' varying reactions when the Ku Klux Klan moves in and begins recruiting. An array of characters presents their reactions, and issues of prejudice and justice are explored. Winner of the Christopher Award.

Anthology of Young Adult classics

Frey, Charles H., and Lucy Rollin, eds. *Classics of Young Adult Literature*. Upper Saddle River, NJ: Pearson, 2004.

> The complete text of eleven young adult novels, moving from the early works by Horatio Alger and L. M. Montgomery to the more contemporary novels of Robert Cormier, Judy Blume, Gary Paulsen, Victor Martinez, and others.

Recent graphic novels you can use

With many thanks to my student Jake Tucker and to Velocity Comics, Richmond, Virginia.

(Note: Because in the world of graphic novels publishing houses can go in and out of business with startling swiftness, ISBN numbers are also included in this list.)

Clowes, Daniel. *Ghost World.* 4th ed. Seattle, WA: Fantagraphics Books, 2001. ISBN: 1560974273.

A fine portrait of teen angst, the *Catcher in the Rye* of graphic novels.

———. *Ice Haven.* New York: Pantheon Books (Random House), 2005. ISBN: 037542332X.

A funny and poignant look at the misfit inhabitants of a small American town.

Eisner, Will. *A Contract with God: And Other Tenement Stories.* New York: DC Comics, 2000. ISBN: 1563896745.

The first true graphic novel by comics pioneer Will Eisner. At times overly dramatic, this book is a collection of stories centering on the occupants of a 1920s tenement and has devoted fans.

Gaiman, Neil, et al. *The Sandman. Vol. 1: Preludes and Nocturnes.* New York: DC Comics, 1993. ISBN: 1563890119.

The literary fantasy that made one of today's most popular children's and young adult fantasy writers famous.

Johns, Goeff, Mike McKone, and Tom Grummett. *Teen Titans: A Kid's Game.* New York: DC Comics, 2004. ISBN: 1401203086.

An extremely entertaining and character-driven action story starring teenage superheroes. For older teens only.

Kesel, Barbara, Steve McNiven, and Joshua Middleton. *Meridian. Vol. 1: Flying Solo.* Denver, CO: Cross Generation Comics, 2002. ISBN: 1931484031.

A beautifully drawn, entrancing fantasy that will appeal to younger female readers.

Millar, Mark, Bryan Hitch, and Andrew Currie. *The Ultimates. Vol. 1: Super-Human.* New York: Marvel Comics, 2002. ISBN: 0785109609.

Well-known superheroes, including Captain America, the Hulk, and Thor, are updated for the twenty-first century.

Moore, Alan, and Dave Gibbons. *Watchmen.* New York: DC Comics, 1995. ISBN: 0930289234.

The book that brought emotional realism to superheroes; considered by many to be one of the finest works of science fiction of the past twenty years.

Morrison, Grant. *We3.* New York: DC Comics, 2005. ISBN: 1401204953.

A touching and twisted take on the classic *Incredible Journey* story. A dog, a cat, and a rabbit— all turned into cybernetic killing machines by the government—try to find their way home.

Morrison, Grant, and Howard Porter. *JLA. Vol. 1: New World Order.* New York: DC Comics, 1997. ISBN: 156389369X.

Intelligent and well-written superhero action.

Naifeh, Ted. *Courtney Crumrin. Vol. 1: Courtney Crumrin and the Night Things.* 2d ed. Portland, OR: Oni Press, 2005. ISBN: 1929998600.

For those who like Harry Potter, this spooky little series should appeal.

Robinson, James, and Paul Smith. *Leave It to Chance. Vol. 1: Shaman's Rain.* Berkeley, CA: Image Comics, 2002. ISBN: 1582402531.

Fantasy and adventure with a young female protagonist.

Tezuka, Osamu. *Astro Boy.* Milwaukie, OR: Dark Horse, 2002. ISBN: 1569716765.

These charming, exquisitely drawn comics are considered possibly the most important and influential Manga.

For further suggestions on using graphic novels, see

Frey, Nancy, and Douglas Fisher. "Using Graphic Novels, Anime, and the Internet in an Urban High School." *English Journal* 93 (January 2004): 19–25.

6

Words, Words, Words

Language, be it remember'd, is not an abstract construction of the learn'd, or of dictionary-makers, but is something arising out of the work, needs, ties, joys, affections, tastes, of long generations of humanity, and has its bases broad and low, close to the ground.

—Walt Whitman, *Slang in America*

It Ain't Necessarily So: The English Language Arts Teacher as Language Expert

It may not be right, but it is true: very few of us in English teaching have the sense of language that Walt Whitman celebrates; most of us don't see the linguistic nature of language as central to life or vital to our professional preparation. If on the other hand you have had courses in the history of the English language or in applied linguistics or in comparative grammar, you are in the lucky minority. Most people who are prepared to teach English language arts do not have a strong language background although, clearly, language—words, words, words—is at the heart of our business.

Jane Dowrick describes a teacher who was definitely the exception:

My teacher began the year by explaining the importance of knowing what words meant and why they came to mean what they did. *Etymology*, he explained, might be difficult to distinguish from *entomology*, since words, like insects, could wriggle away from close examination. He introduced the idea that all words had roots, many of which were Latin. In all of my public school years, I had never before realized that there was a history to our language, stretching back to the beginning of the spoken word. As I recall his approach, I realize that he was actually teaching us the language of English, almost as if he had been teaching a foreign language. . . . Using etymology as a focal point, the lessons covered a wide range of literature and grammar topics. His delight in teaching us was obvious. My enduring interest in the English language, and my own desire to teach was surely influenced by him.

Very few of us entering teaching are like the teacher Jane Dowrick describes. As readers and appreciators of literature, however, it is most often *assumed* that we know something about language, when actually for most of us, our knowledge is spotty at best. As George

Gershwin's song from *Porgy and Bess* proclaims, "It ain't necessarily so." Most of us know little about language or about the science of language; for most people, linguistics is unfamiliar territory.

Prescriptive Versus Descriptive: The World of Linguistics

Linguistics, the study of and the science of language, is a very complex field with a dizzying array of areas. There is, in one branch, **psycholinguistics** (language in relation to mental processes). Psycholinguistics includes **morphology** (the shape of language), **phonology** (the sound of language), **semantics** (the meaning of language), and **syntax** (the structure of language in word and sentence patterns). Another branch of linguistics is **sociolinguistics** (language in relation to culture or behavior) and **stylistics** (the study of literary language). **Historical linguistics** considers the history of language through time, and **anthropological linguistics** looks at language as a social phenomenon, a form of behavior. Linguistics looks at all aspects of language, from how very young children acquire speech to how remote Indian tribes in South America transcribe their language to the history of a verb form. Linguists work as much in laboratories (with actual tapes of people's speech) as in classrooms (with students) and libraries (with research studies); theirs is virtually a universe of study.

In a well-known and widely quoted article, "Never Mind the Trees," linguist Suzette Elgin writes that an English teacher needs to know a few basic linguistic principles. Among other concepts, Elgin urges all of us to know about **grammar**, **dialect**, **register**, and a little bit of the **history of our language**. She also notes that we as teachers should have a basic grasp of **"normal" human language development**, **what languages do**, and, crucially, **how to find answers to questions** about language and linguistics.

For the purposes of this chapter, we are going to look at a very small (more restricted even than Elgin cites) and practical portion of language, **applied linguistics**. Please look at the references at the end of this chapter for further resources; this section on language is a quick excursion, not a full tour, and you may want to know much more about a number of other areas of language. We know that many people, especially those who equate others' pronunciation or vocabulary or usage with their innate human worth, are highly frustrated by the field of linguistics. These individuals are often looking for authoritative, definitive rules of right and wrong when it comes to language use and language choice. They want, essentially, **prescriptive** information from linguistics, rules and regulations, dos and don'ts, shoulds and oughts and musts.

Linguistics, however, is anything but prescriptive. In fact, maddening to many, it does little or nothing about decreeing right and wrong; it assumes no right or wrong except in context. Linguistics tells and defines what *is* and is thus not *prescriptive* but *descriptive*. It looks at *ain't* and *he don't* and *I should of done my homework* as legitimate, recognizable, definable (if variant) forms of language. When you study historical linguistics, in fact, you find that *ain't*, a scorned and generally unacceptable usage, was standard in Dickens' time in England. Indeed, it is considered appropriate today for many upper-class English speakers—Queen Elizabeth and Prince Charles among them—in the United Kingdom. Linguistics would also tell you that the scorn for *ain't* is almost wholly disproportionate: it communicates and has only lately, historically, become the despised form it is in some contexts today. Similarly, *he don't* is nothing more than the mismatch of a singular pronoun and a plural form of the verb *to do*; linguistics would note that there is no diminution of meaning in *he don't*, while it certainly is what is called a class marker of a negative sort. (Some would assume the utterer of *he don't* is not particularly well educated.) Finally, *I should of done my homework* could be described, if we took purely a descriptive approach, as a transcription of *have* to *of*, an understandable equivalency based on what most people actually hear when they rapidly say *should have*, *could have*, and so on: the *have* sounds, to many speakers, sound like *of*, and they therefore write *of* for *have*.

In all cases in the study of linguistics, English language arts teachers seeking immutable standards of correctness will not find the ammunition they may be looking for. And linguistics will remind us again and again that what is considered acceptable and what is considered unacceptable shifts over time. It is the very nature of language to change. Linguistics also reminds us that

- **There are no languages or forms of language that are inherently "superior" to others.**
- **There are no languages or forms of language that are inherently easier or harder to learn or even "prettier" to the ear.**
- **The association of certain usage forms with class markers—certain people from certain economic strata will use certain linguistic forms—is not only arbitrary in almost all cases but will also shift over time.**

Two principles: Language changes/there is no "bad" language

The poet Pablo Neruda once wrote, "Is a dictionary a sepulcher or a sealed honeycomb?" It is a powerful question and powerful metaphor and pinpoints the tension regarding words and language. To that end, James Stalker, former chair of the NCTE Commission on Language, reminds us what English teachers should remember about language. Stalker tells us

- that all languages, including our own, are in a constant state of flux;
- that all languages are comprised of variants, which are used for different purposes and enjoy different levels of acceptability;
- that all languages and varieties of languages serve a multitude of functions;
- that all languages and their varieties are orderly and, therefore, can be described and explained through complex structures, including syntax (sentence structure) as well phonology (the system of sounds), morphology (word structure), semantics (meaning), discourse (structures larger than the sentence), and pragmatics (language use in context). (4)

This is a fairly extensive list, but it is unified by two important principles: first, that language never stays the same—it changes—and, second, that variations in language do not make that language *wrong*, *bad*, or even *inappropriate*.

These two principles may be odd if we believe that our language is stable and that changes in it—new words, imported from other languages such as *glasnost*, *jihad*, *manga*, and *tattoo*; new meanings for old words, such as *the Web*, *mouse*, and *gay*; new combinations, such as *24/7*; nouns that are now used as verbs, such as *impact* and *interface*; and other variations, such as *lite* for *light*—are to be resisted. As Simon Winchester writes in *The Meaning of Everything*, his history of the making of the Oxford English Dictionary, the language is ever expanding:

> Since Shakespeare—and since William Hazlitt and Jane Austen, since Wordsworth and Thackeray, the Naipauls and the Amises, and the fantasy worlds of the hobbits and Harry Potter . . . the language that we call Modern English has just grown and grown, almost exponentially. Words from every corner of the globalized world cascade in ceaselessly, daily topping up a language that is self-evidently living, breathing, changing, evolving as no other language ever has, nor is ever likely to. (17)

Winchester reminds us:

> For English is not to be regarded in the same way as, say, French or Italian, and in one crucially important way. It is not a fixed language, the meaning of its words established, approved, and firmly set by some official committee charged with preserving its dignity and integrity. The French have had their Académie Française, a body made up of the much-feared Forty Immortals which has done precisely this (and with an extreme punctiliousness and absolute want of humor) since 1634. The Italians have also had their Accademia della Crusca in Florence since 1582 . . . the task of both [French and Italian] bodies was to preserve linguistic purity, to prevent the languages' ruin . . . to prescribe the use of the language. No such body has ever been set up in England, nor in any English-speaking country . . . English is a language that simply cannot be fixed, nor can its use ever be absolutely laid down. It changes constantly; it grows with an almost exponential joy. It evolves eternally; its words alter their sense and their meanings subtly, slowly, or speedily according to fashion and need. (27, 29)

This growth with "exponential joy" is a far different vision than what many hold about our language. The misperception by many is that rules fix a language—and, of course, that English teachers enforce those rules. As Winchester and others know, such is not true.

Think for a minute about your knowledge of literature: from Old English to Middle English to modern English, from *Beowulf* to *Hamlet* to James Joyce's *Ulysses*, from Edmund Spenser to Gerard Manley Hopkins to Sylvia Plath, from Addison and Steele's *The Tatler* to the *Washington Post* or the *Los Angeles Times*. Language changes, and the evidence is all around us. For instance, consider for example the humble word *fun*. Is it a noun or an adjective? Is it both? We say, "I had fun at that party," and it is a noun; we go to a "fun house" at a carnival or a Halloween celebration, and *fun* in that construction functions as a compound noun. But what do we say about the commonly heard comment, informal though it may be, "It was a fun time"? Clearly *fun* in that circumstance is an adjective modifying *time*; while a speaker in a formal situation would not be likely to use such a construction, is it wrong? Is it not the use of *fun* as an adjective? What we are seeing is a developing acceptance of *fun* as both noun *and* adjective, which will mean that in years hence "It was a fun time" or "I had fun" will be widely acceptable usage.

In addition to the concept that language never changes—as it does—is a second misperception that language can be *wrong* or *bad*. The latter ignores the fact that certain language forms provide what linguists call **class markers**. Thus, when a student of yours says "He don't know" rather than "He doesn't know," there is an immediate assumption about that student's educational—and social and economic—background. Truth be told, there is little real difference between the two sentences; they both convey that *he does not know*. The subject/verb disagreement of the first, however, is a form that is associated with the uneducated or economically disadvantaged and, regardless of its ability to convey information, is considered unacceptable to many speakers. It is, in fact, so marked, that we would call that usage **stigmatized**. You can think, I'm sure, of similar constructions that in your community and your context are equally powerful class markers, which, for some hearers, reveal the speaker's lower status.

The arguments can get terribly petty, zeroing in on acceptable variations rather than on the big issues of standard and nonstandard practice. I once encountered a woman who was most interested in my work as an English teacher, and inquired intently how I pronounced the word *mauve*. My pronunciation, she said, would tell her a great deal about my education and erudition because, according to her standards, there was only one right way to pronounce the word. Of course, I failed her test: my pronunciation is from my regional heritage, *mawve*. Hers was the other variant, *mowve,* and she instructed me to change the way I pronounced the word. While most dictionaries cite both pronunciations, this speaker found her choice the only right choice. We were both talking about the light purple color, but, for this person, it became much more than color and intelligibility; the pronunciation of *mauve* became a crucial issue.

Clearly, I don't like conversations such as these. I find them unhelpful and unpleasant. One speaker corrects another; someone gets to feel superior; someone gets to feel wrong. It is, of course, one thing to encounter such a dispute with a peer. It is another to encounter it in class. We need to remember that language variants are not just of the egregious sort (*he don't know, teacher*); they can wander into more rarefied territory.

When we discuss "good" English, most of us rely on the language used by the most reputable of speakers. And yet, as Robert C. Pooley in *The Teaching of English Usage* reminds us, the issue is complicated:

> "[G]ood usage is the usage of the best writers and speakers" . . . is probably the expressed or implied standard of good English in almost every American schoolroom today . . . [yet] the chief difficulty lies in the interpretation of the terms "reputable" and "the best writers and speakers." For example, at the same time that these definitions of "correct" English were current, nearly all grammar books listed as undesirable English the use of the split infinitive, the dangling participle or gerund, the use of the possessive case of the noun when naming inanimate objects, the objective case of the noun with the gerund, and the use of *whose* as a neuter relative pronoun, among many others; yet all of these uses may be found in the authors who form the very backbone of English literature and who are "reputable" and "the best writers" in every sense of the words. If the standard makers defy the standards, to whom shall we turn for authority? Moreover, the use of literary models tends to ignore the canon of *present* usage, for by the time an author has come to be generally recognized as standard his usage is no longer "present." And among present speakers, who are best? Any careful listener who has heard a large number of the most prominent platform speakers of the day has still to hear one who does not in some manner violate the rules of the books. Are all great writers and speakers at fault, or is it possible that the rules are inaccurate?
>
> The way out of this perplexity is to shift the search for standards away from "authorities" and traditional rules to the language itself as it is spoken and written today. (11–12)

Thus we turn to what is actually around us in language and from that source make determinations about "correct" and "incorrect."

Spelling and Vocabulary

In *The Mother Tongue: English and How It Got That Way*, writer Bill Bryson notes that over
300 million people in the world speak English. He calls the language "one of the world's
great growth industries" (13) and cites the existence of over 600,000 English words,
expanding every year. This is a very large number of words both to define and to spell correctly, and one aspect of "correct" language is spelling and vocabulary and its importance.
In fact, many people outside of schools equate most of what we do as English language arts
teachers not only with correct grammar but also with correct spelling and appropriate use
of vocabulary. Let's start with spelling.

I know of no study that shows a correlation between intelligence and correct spelling.
And yet many people equate misspelled words with stupidity and certainly ignorance. Certainly as a teacher you are expected to be almost perfect in your spelling—an expectation that,
frankly, is often hard to fulfill. Yet, as the teacher, you have a responsibility to spell consistently and correctly. On the other hand, spelling is really only a small part of English language
arts and should not take a disproportionate amount of class time.

It will help you, however, if in their language study, your students learn a little bit about
the history of English spelling. Bryson reminds us that we have forty sounds in English but
more than 200 ways of spelling those sounds (120). Linguist Mario Pei terms the English
spelling system "the world's most awesome mess" (310), and for many of our students, that
description is pretty accurate. Students need to know that correct spelling was only very
recently perceived as an important issue. In fact, only in the last few hundred years has the
spelling of English words been at all standardized and have dictionaries, as repositories of
the "correct" way to spell a word, entered wide use. Samuel Johnson published his *Dictionary* in 1755; spelling instruction in this country entered the classroom around that same
time. We have only to look at our own nation's original documents—and the correspondence
of our not-so-distant forebears—to see that literate people used a dizzying array of forms
to spell the very same words.

The history is, of course, helpful. On the other hand, the practical reality is that we
want our students to spell correctly. Even with the use of spell check, students can do some
individualized work to enhance their own list of "demon" words. Having students

- **keep a spelling log with their own frequently misspelled words,**
- **explore the "spell check" feature of most word processors, and**
- **research a few words and their variant spellings over the years**

are three avenues by which students can improve their spelling and appreciate its diversity. While not in every assignment—such as spontaneous writing in class or journal entries—but in final draft writing, we can expect that students check their spelling and conform to a standard. Of course, many students with learning disabilities and English language learners have more than ordinary difficulty with correct spelling; for those students more patience and more time is necessary.

With vocabulary, many English teachers trust they are expanding their students' language by giving them a number of vocabulary words to learn, both spelling and definition, every week or so. In many schools across the country, the words are chosen by the teacher (or the text), given to the students, and tested regularly. This is a staple of the English language arts classroom, but it may surprise you to know that, as it is often practiced, it is virtually useless. As educators Don and Alleen Nilsen remark wryly in a recent and excellent book on vocabulary instruction, "Except for saying, 'You might be tested on this word,' . . . most teachers [are] unable to answer . . . questions about why students should be memorizing the meaning of words they had never heard spoken, never seen in writing, and never anticipated using" (vi).

As Nilsen and Nilsen are saying, the lasting effect of this practice is negligible; most students forget the words and their definitions almost immediately after the test. A student of mine, Laurie Messer, recalls:

> The vocabulary tests [in English class] were standard tests taken from the teacher's manual, and some last minute cramming was all that was required to learning the spelling and definitions of the words for the multiple choice tests. Some teachers did try to individualize the vocabulary exercises to make them more interesting and to show us how to use the vocabulary words in "real life" . . . But generally no one really ever learned the vocabulary words, and I think the teachers hated the exercises just as much as the students.

The point is that people will expand their store of words, their language, their vocabulary, when they use the words *in context* or when they have a *need* for the words. As language lovers and as teachers we must create vocabulary/spelling lists that have some relevance for our students, lists that come from

- **Reading (words they recently read that they did not know the meaning of).**
- **Life (words that are used frequently by their family or in their neighborhood or on their after-school job that they do not think are as frequently used by those outside those contexts).**
- **Classwork (words that they have encountered in English or other classes that are new to them or that they consistently misspell or stumble over).**

It is not impossible to have students working on individual lists within a class setting; a teacher can keep track of such lists by collecting them on a regular basis, and students, with some prior direction and organization, can demonstrate their mastery of their *individual* spelling lists by choosing a selected number of words and using them or defining them on a quiz. I did this with my students in English 11 when I returned to teach high school, and I found it one of the more successful activities of the semester.

At any rate, to present students isolated lists will not help them score higher on the state-mandated test or any other vocabulary or language-based measure. It will, however, encourage them to see language as nothing more complicated than the memorization of disconnected lists of words. Letting students participate in their own spelling/vocabulary lists and encouraging them to expand those lists can not only give students more control over this aspect of English language arts but also show them that they, too, live in a world of language. It is not confined to the vocabulary presented in a textbook; it is in their world and all around them.

····················· **FOR YOUR JOURNAL** ·····················

Make a list of words that you have difficulty spelling; write a brief statement of why you think you stumble on those words (actually, most spelling mistakes are logical!). Then go to the library or online and look up the *etymology* (origin and development) of your spelling demons in a resource such as the *Oxford English Dictionary*. What are the origins of the words? What different spellings do they have? What are their different meanings?

The Five Grammars

Most people associate English language arts—and language in particular—with the idea of grammar. "I'd better watch my grammar," they tell you when they find out you are or are planning to be an English teacher; "I liked English, but I hated grammar," they might recall; "What's the grammar rule?" they might ask you. Actually, what people are referring to is not grammar at all but **usage**. You probably already know that, but you might wonder about these different manifestations of what most people call **grammar**. They are not all the same animal, and that is why researchers discuss at least three or sometimes more grammars. What are they?

The five grammars described by Patrick Hartwell are summarized by Mark Lester in *Grammar in the Classroom*:

Grammar 1: Our internal, unconscious rule system. The grammar that we have in our heads.

Grammar 2: The scientific analysis of grammar. The linguist's model of Grammar 1.

Grammar 3: Usage. What people mean when they say that someone doesn't use very good grammar.

Grammar 4: The schoolroom version of traditional grammar. The grammar that is found in secondary textbooks.

Grammar 5: Stylistic grammar. The use of grammar for the purpose of teaching style. Among the approaches included here would be sentence combining. (335)

Grammar 3 and Grammar 4 are what most of us are familiar with; note, however, that they are only part of the picture of grammar. Lester notes:

The best-known grammar of English is traditional grammar, or more accurately, the conventional schoolroom version of traditional grammar. The latter has been the mainstay of English education in America since the time of the Revolutionary War, and every educated person in the English-speaking world has at least a passing familiarity with its terms and concepts. (187)

Thus, as teachers, our major emphasis is on Grammar 3, which is essentially usage. In order to teach Grammar 3, we may use a handbook or textbook, Grammar 4. When we analyze literature or with sentence combining (see later in this chapter), we are using Grammar 5.

Don't be confused, then, when people talk about grammar and its importance in your classroom; they are probably referring to usage rules and to the usage texts themselves.

So What Do We Do About Teaching Grammar?

What do we do with grammar? Many teachers and members of the public assert that the teaching of grammar is important because they believe it improves our students' writing and speaking. Unfortunately, however, especially when done through books and worksheets and rule memorization, the teaching of grammar does not result in better—or even different— speaking and writing. Many assume that when students do not improve after years of grammar study it is either the students' fault (they just didn't get it) or the quality of instruction (the teacher did not teach it enough; the teacher did not teach it clearly enough; the teacher didn't teach it at all). It is, however, the opinion of many researchers who have looked for decades at the results of formal grammar instruction on student language and composition that that is just not the case. The difficulty seems to lie in two areas: how grammar texts are set up and how teachers are encouraged to teach grammar.

Let's consider the issues. We acquire language messily, aurally, by mimicking patterns. The verb *acquire* is deliberate here: we don't really *learn* our native language as we learn most other things. We do, however, *acquire* it by a rather indirect process. The small child does not consciously choose verbs or adverbs or clauses or phrases; he or she produces what he or she hears and by trial and error becomes an accomplished language user. By the time that small child is ready for school, he or she actually has most of the syntax needed to produce relatively complex conversation or discourse.

We often seem to ignore this competence, though. In secondary and middle school, we ask students in traditional "grammar" classes to go back and label with abstract terms and possibly with conceptual representations (such as diagramming) what they are naturally producing. The hope is that understanding the abstract framework of what they are doing will make their language "better." And that transfer just does not readily occur.

Think about the abstract pattern that students study: in most classes, it proceeds from rule memorization to worksheet/example practice to actual writing. The problems lie directly in that pattern: the rules are not sufficiently inclusive or clear; the examples for practice are deliberately restricted so that they will fully conform to the rule; and unfortunately the rule and the example often do not bear a relationship to real student speaking or writing. And we expect our students to move from rule and restricted practice to the universe of their own sentences. The transition is most times just not made.

For example, consider the last time you needed to verify a grammatical construction you used in a research paper or an essay. If you went to a standard usage "handbook" (or "grammar"), you probably had a very hard time finding a direct answer to your question. The fact is, however complex they might sound, the rules in most "grammars" are presented in very simplified versions, and the illustrations of those rules are rarely comparable to the highly complex constructions even elementary school-age children are capable of producing.

So what do we do? In some cases, regardless, we are expected to teach grammar in our classrooms. While no research buttresses the transfer, school authorities can insist that knowledge of the rules will indeed improve our students' speech and their final drafts. Accordingly, some feel that "grammar" instruction, a familiar and traditional part of language arts, should remain part of the twenty-first-century English class and enforce that in curricular decisions. Jim Meyer summarizes the issue:

> Public school teachers who have a strong background in linguistics and in language study find themselves in a bind. Their commitment to serious research and study, to the discipline of linguistics, and to intellectual honesty is in conflict with their responsibility to their employer and to the legally constituted education authorities. Even to obtain a license to teach [at least in some states] they must be willing either to parrot definitions that they know to be misleading or to accept no credit for their answers. To continue as teachers they must engage in continual gymnastics, balancing contrary expectations of what is to be taught in their classrooms. (39)

But enough of the hand wringing.

In an issue of *English Journal* that I edited some years ago, twenty teachers wrote about how grammar should and should not be taught. Although all twenty had very different approaches, the conclusions were clear. Grammar and usage, they maintained, should be:

- taught in connected units of study;
- taught in small and targeted doses;
- taught in relation to student writing;
- taught when there is a real need for it and when teachers can persuade students there is a need. (Christenbury, 12)

For instance, teachers need to provide students with grammar and usage instruction in some sort of logical sequence (when students are writing their short story dialogue they need information on quotation marks and capitalization, not necessarily on semicolons). Teachers need to spend limited amounts of time on such instruction (two solid weeks spent on clauses and phrases will not be helpful to most students). Teachers also need to look at what specific students are having difficulty with—and at what they have clearly mastered—before they drag the entire class through, as one example, subject/verb agreement. It just may be that in a class of twenty-five only five students have this as a problem area. Finally, teachers also need to provide students with outside audiences for their work, audiences that may give the students more of a feeling that, somehow, their writing, their correct final draft writing, matters. If the teacher is the only one who reads the students' work and cares about correct usage, many students will remain indifferent to making their writing careful with regard to surface errors.

If nothing else, if no single other strategy, we need always to remember context. If we teach grammar, we need to teach it not as a separate unit but as it relates to specific issues in our students' writing and in their speech. We need to make sure that the students who study an aspect of grammar have a need for it and can, in fact, use that aspect in their class work. To do otherwise is to teach a skill or a piece of knowledge that has no application at all or has application to only a very few students in our classes. Lester suggests teaching grammar in four general areas:

- grammar terminology to provide a shared vocabulary for talking about grammar and writing;
- key grammatical concepts (the sentence, inflection, tense, agreement) that underlie most written error;
- practical techniques for monitoring error in their own writing; and
- sentence combining (more on this later in the chapter) as a unique bridge between grammar and writing. (366)

Doesn't this seem logical? Why, then, do many teachers continue to use unrelated content from handbooks and employ worksheets and tests to teach grammar? If you think about it, that kind of teaching is easier as it becomes a one-size-fits-all instruction. When a teacher chooses to pay attention to what an individual student needs as opposed to delivering blanket instruction for all in a single class, then life is a bit more complicated. Yet the effort is worth it: students will respond to instruction to grammar and usage if, indeed, they need the instruction and if it bears some relation to their own writing.

As far as the time spent on these subjects, linguist Constance Weaver, like Nancie Atwell in *In the Middle*, advocates using minilessons for such grammar instruction, devoting no more than ten minutes or so at the beginning of class to go over what a number of students—if not all—need to know or review. Confining instruction in grammar, in usage (the choices speakers make when they talk or write), and in mechanics (surface conventions of spelling, punctuation, capitalization, and so on) can be very helpful to students. Asking students to generate their own rules from their reading—and their own writing—can also be very beneficial.

All of this discussion about grammar may make you relatively uneasy, especially if you feel that you do not know much about grammar and usage yourself. Even though you may have taken a course in the history of the English language and possibly in comparative grammars, you might still wonder if you can identify a comma splice in a student's essay or explain a nonrestrictive clause to your class. You may not be able to: many traditional English majors do not delve deeply into this subject and certainly not in the way that it is taught in most secondary and middle schools. On the other hand, if you are going to do something in your own teaching about grammar and usage—beyond having students do the exercises at the end of the grammar handbook chapter or fill out a worksheet another teacher has shared with you—if indeed you are going to try to teach grammar in context of your students' writing, it is important that you know the subject yourself.

There are, fortunately, many sources to which you can turn, and you should not despair if, at this point, you feel your knowledge is inadequate. You can learn and it may be, like many teachers, that the concepts are easier to handle now than they were when you were younger. Popular books such as the best-seller Lynne Truss' *Eats, Shoots, and Leaves* may be helpful. More germane to us professionally, however, are books by teachers such as Brock Haussaman and colleagues' *Grammar Alive!*, Jeff Anderson's *Mechanically Inclined*, Harry R. Noden's *Image Grammar*, Martha Kolln's *Understanding English Grammar* and *Rhetorical Grammar*, and Weaver's *Teaching Grammar in Context*, all enormously helpful. The January 2003 *English Journal* focus issue on grammar is packed with teaching ideas,

and you may find the NCTE Assembly on the Teaching of English Grammar (ATEG) a
source of information as well as ATEG's practical newsletter, *Syntax in the Schools*.

······················ **FOR YOUR JOURNAL** ···················

Find a grammar-and-usage or grammar-and-composition text. You
might borrow one from a teaching friend or a high school or middle school student. Leaf through the text and pick one rule of usage
or "grammar" and look at the exercises in the book that relate to
that rule. Now rewrite the rule in your own words and make up
your own examples to help students practice that rule. Put both the
rule and your examples on a sheet of paper and then exchange the
paper with a friend. Have your friend do your examples. How successful is your grammar sheet? Finally, browse through some of
your own recent writing: can you find a sentence you have written
that illustrates the rule you have selected? If so, how helpful is
your rewritten rule in telling you why what you wrote is correct?

English Language Learners

Depending on where you teach, you will have either some or many students for whom English is a second language. Few communities in America today are populated entirely by
native speakers, and when the children of non-English speaking parents come to school,
many of them will need a great deal of support to succeed. Some of these students will know
virtually no English at all and, depending on your school district, they may not be given
many resources to learn English quickly and effectively. You, probably a traditionally prepared teacher with little background in English as a second language, may be very concerned abut these students mainstreamed into your classroom and about what you can do on
a daily basis to help them with their vocabulary (academic vocabulary in particular), their pronunciation, and their reading comprehension. The scope of this book is not wide enough to
give you even part of what you might need to effectively serve these students, but I can
sketch out for you some principles and also point you to some resources to help your English language learners make progress, stay in school, and graduate.

Let's start with some principles for teaching second language learners. The following
is taken from a favorite book of mine, *When They Don't All Speak English*. If you read these
principles carefully, you will see, much perhaps to your relief, that what is good for first language students is also good for second language ones. Pat Rigg and Virginia Allen articulate
the following guidelines:

- People who are learning another language are, first of all, people. "Children's developmental stages are more important than levels of English proficiency."
- Learning a language means learning to do the things you want to do with people
  who speak that language. Learning a language "doesn't mean learning forms of

language to use someday in some possible situation: it means using the language (however badly) today, now, to do things."

- A person's second language, like the first, develops globally, not linearly. "Talk is the 'warm bath of language' . . . the second-language learner hears and participates in conversation that is usually meaningful because the context makes the meaning clear."

- Language develops best in a variety of rich contexts. "Ideal situations are those in which the student understands what's happening and is also learning something new."

- Literacy is part of language, so writing and reading develop alongside speaking and listening. "Even students just beginning to learn English can write, as long as the writing is authentic; that is, it is the student's own composition for the student's own purposes, not a product for the teacher's evaluation." (vii–xv)

What do these principles imply? They mean that you can create a positive environment for all your students, including your English language learners, by extending to them the kind of rich context you would create in your classroom anyway. But remember, also, that this is a long-term process and one where you may not see the kind of quick progress you would like. While most English language learners will have a basic oral competence after about two years in school and, as I've implied, quickly acquire what is needed to actually function in school and life, academic language (and this is what they will need in your class and other content classes), takes five to seven years to master. So just because an English language learner is competent orally, he or she may, as Kimberly Gomez and Christina Madda tell us, "continue to need vocabulary and conceptual support in reading and writing in content-area study" (46). Modification of instruction is key, and if you don't have background in this area, do know that the kinds of individualization you would provide for any of your struggling students is also appropriate for English language learners. You will also want to keep in close contact with the ESL/ELL teachers in your school; their expertise is wonderful, and many of them are familiar with numbers of helpful programs and strategies such as the Center for Applied Linguistics' SIOP Program, Sheltered Instruction Observation Protocol. (For more information on SIOP, see the Short, Hudec, and Echevarria book in References.)

Let's turn to some specific activities you can do to help your students become more proficient in English.

Activities for ELLs

Danling Fu, who taught for some years in New York in Chinatown, suggests that, first and foremost, teachers "forget the grade level curriculum" (8) and literally **teach students where they are**. This means that if students don't have basic English skills, you need to adjust what they do and what are your expectations. It may mean that these students need something as basic as a review of the English alphabet; it may mean that they need to read different texts (such as children's books, picture books, magazines) than what other students are using in your classroom.

In addition, giving English language learners regular **opportunities to speak** in class is very important. English pronunciation and cadence of word clusters in sentences may be quite foreign to your English language learners; if they don't have an opportunity to read aloud—prose or poetry—or to dialogue with others, they will not progress in language mastery.

But what about writing? Certainly if a student is struggling with the alphabet and the vocabulary and the syntax of English, shouldn't we just back away? Fu says no, and advocates that teachers help students **work into writing** by, first, giving them a topic of interest, such as describing themselves and their lives, and letting students address that subject by:

> using drawings or photos;
>
> writing captions for the pictures;
>
> reading the caption aloud. (13)

Small-group and pair work, a staple of the English classroom, can also be especially effective with second language learners. Working with another student who is more proficient in English, Fu notes, can help the English language learner make an easier transition; get to know other students; and, mostly importantly, use English more effectively by talking with peers.

Finally, remember that your English language learner may not have mastered English vocabulary or pronunciation, but that does not mean that he or she does not come to your classroom without intelligence, background, and skills. While it may be difficult to individualize, try to study your English language learners and make real adaptations for them. Many English language learners are highly motivated, and with encouragement from you and a positive classroom atmosphere, they can make remarkable progress.

For the past five years I have taught Applied English Linguistics to teachers who work with English language learners, and I have learned a great deal from these people and their extensive experience. In class we often share stories to illustrate or reinforce theories and best teaching practice, and one session a teacher told a story that reminded all of us about assumptions and misperceptions and how we need to be open to the varieties of experiences and background that our English language learners bring. In this case, one of the teacher's students, new to this country from Central America and with little English background, was given a basic school-screening test and subsequently labeled mildly retarded, a diagnosis that did not seem consistent with what the teacher had briefly observed in class. When, however, the teacher talked with the tester about the student's results, she understood the incorrect diagnosis immediately. One of the major parts of the test had been to ask the student, using pictures, to put in order the steps for baking a traditional layer cake. The student had hopelessly confused the order of the task, and the sad conclusion was that she was deficient cognitively. The teacher, though, knew enough about the student's rural background and country to understand what had happened: this student had never seen a layer cake, must less baked one. In her country, though, she knew cooking sequences of a different sort, and if she has been presented pictures regarding the steps to kill, pluck, and bake a chicken, she would have scored 100. When this fact was presented to the school, the student's diagnosis was changed.

Indeed, we need to be open to our English language learners and ready to adapt, modify, and, of course, enjoy what they bring to enrich our classes.

Language Play/Language Games

We also need to remember the wonderful world of language play and language games. As children, all of us had some exposure to—and delight in—games with words, rhymes, riddles, puns, jokes, and stories. How sad it is that in middle and high school we seem to leave all of this richness behind in the name of being more serious and academic. We need to recapture the broad and fine idea of play—experimentation—with language.

There are many resources available that can lead you and your students to working with a number of areas of language study. **Etymology** (the origin and history of words), **semantics** (the meanings of words), **doublespeak** (deliberate deception in language, often used in politics and brilliantly described by George Orwell in a famous essay, "Politics and the English Language"), and **dialect** (the wonderful variations of both pronunciation and word choice) are just a few of the fascinating topics you can pursue.

You need to remember that language is literally all around us and that although it may not be immediately apparent to you, your students are adept at language play. What they play with and toy with may be wholly outside the classroom—in the cafeteria or in the parking lot or at the mall—but you can, with some encouragement, have them bring what they know and use into the classroom—and this includes your English language learners, for whom language play is also very important. The following is a sampler of activities.

Puns and plays on words

Puns and plays on words are used in menus, billboards, bumper stickers, advertisements, and other aspects of daily life. A local church billboard reads, for example: "Seven days without God makes one week [weak]." Such puns and slogans are creative uses of language and can be tools not only to encourage students to explore homonyms but to look at how such homonyms are effective. (*Week*, a noun, is the direct object; *weak*, a modifier, is the predicate adjective; *one* is, in the first sense of the sentence, an adjective but a pronoun in the second sense of the sentence.) Another such pun or slogan is the insult terming a person "a legend in his own mind," a play on the more familiar phrase, "a legend in his own time." Both words, *mind* and *time*, are nouns used in parallel constructions that not only have a near rhyme, but also convey widely different meanings.

Bumper stickers have become wonderful examples of wordplay. A few of my favorites include:

- I USED TO BE INDECISIVE; NOW I'M NOT SURE
- ESCHEW OBFUSCATION
- TEACHERS DO IT WITH CLASS
- ANYTHING FREE IS WORTH WHAT YOU PAY FOR IT
- EDITING IS A REWORDING ACTIVITY
- WHAT IF THERE WERE NO HYPOTHETICAL QUESTIONS?

Advertising offers many such puns and plays on words. Some of my students collected a few recently, taken from billboards, signs, and print advertisements:

- YULE LAUGH; YULE CRY (billboard advertisement for a Christmas movie)
- COFFEE BRAKE (sign on outside of convenience store)

- TIPPING IS NOT A CITY IN CHINA (sign on wall of restaurant)
- SOME OF OUR GUESTS LIKE THE IDEA OF A MOUSE IN THE ROOM (advertisement for a motel chain featuring in-room computers)
- FASTER THAN THE SPEED OF FRIGHT (billboard advertisement for a roller coaster at a local amusement park)
- HO³ (T-shirt slogan for Christmas: Ho Ho Ho)

My friend and book editor, Jim Strickland, is tickled by:

- AND LEAVE THE REST TO US (from a mattress company)

and, finally, from Alleen and Don Nilsen's work:

- JUST A SHADE BETTER (advertisement for a lamp shop)
- AFTER 35 YEARS, WE'VE GOT THE HANG OF IT (advertisement for a drapery company) (20)

Puns can also be the basis for jokes, as in the following *Snakey Riddles*:

Question: What does a polite snake say after he bites you?
Answer: Fangs a lot! (Hall and Eisenberg, 18)

Question: What did the snake say when it stopped biting the giraffe's neck?
Answer: It's been nice gnawing you! (Hall and Eisenberg, 26)

There are also countless "punny" anecdotes that are familiar to many and that depend on not a single word but on an aphorism or a well-known phrase, as in this case below, "the lesser of two evils":

Two boll weevils grew up in South Carolina. One went to Hollywood and became a famous actor. The other stayed behind in the cotton fields and never amounted to much. The second one, naturally, became known as the lesser of two weevils.

Students can also create Hink-Pinks where the answer to the question is a one-syllable rhyming word, such as:

What do you call an obese feline?
   Fat cat.

To complicate the matter, students can also create Hinky-Pinkys, where the answer is a two-syllable rhyming words, such as:

What do you call pasta for pooches?
   Poodle noodles.

(Ohanian, 94)

Oxymorons, contradictions in terms, are also fun and can be, within limits, wonderfully insulting. A few popular ones include: *found missing; jumbo shrimp; alone together; taped live; new classic; military intelligence; small crowd; plastic glasses; diet ice cream; exact estimate.*

Have students recall puns, plays on words, oxymorons, or even jokes they have seen or create new ones that make a statement, promote a product, advance an idea, or provide humor. Then have them:

1. List the possible homonyms or similar sounds for the crucial word or words.
2. Label the part of speech and the sentence function of the word or words.
3. Explain, in prose, how the sentence can be read two—or more—ways.

Do know that some of these activities will be very challenging for English language learners and, in fact, may not be appropriate unless adapted extensively. As Yu Ren Dong writes, "the complexity of understanding multiple layers of meaning" is not quickly mastered, and many second language speakers "acquire one meaning of a word, often . . . associated with concrete, sensory referents, without knowledge of other meanings or abstract and metaphorical referents" (30). When using these kinds of games in your classroom, consider if all of them are appropriate for all students.

Relative meanings/semantics

Certainly the women's movement has sensitized all of us to the varying uses of language, especially when describing people's behavior. "He's assertive, she's pushy" shows how language can be used to stereotype genders. Our language also provides an array of degrees of intensity, of approval or disapproval, all of which can be conveyed by words. Look at *minimal*, *average*, and *maximum* as degree distinctions for color (pink, red, scarlet) or weight (slim, thin, emaciated) or any other characteristic you might want to describe. Your students can come up with a number of "families," and this kind of language play can be especially effective for vocabulary expansion for your English language learners. Use the following headings, and have students make a chart such as the one that follows:

MINIMAL	AVERAGE	MAXIMUM
creek	stream	river
pebble	rock	boulder
big	huge	gargantuan
unhappy	depressed	miserable
dislike	hate	detest

First names

Names are important in any culture and often reveal a great deal about the thing named and its importance. Ask your students to consider the following as they list first (not last) names:

1. List as many names for each category as you can.
2. The names should come from your own experience or that of someone in the group.
3. After you have listed the names for each category, try to write a brief statement about what the names seem to have in common or what observations could be made about this group of names. (Look in particular for the number of syllables, incidence of consonants, and incidence of vowel clusters.)

Categories: Names with definite English meaning (Pearl); names with definite meaning in a foreign language (Marguerite is *daisy* in French); names that are considered in this culture "clearly masculine" (Robert) or "clearly feminine" (Angeline); names that are androgynous (Courtney); blended names (Jonalee); foreign equivalents (John, Juan, Jean, Johannes); nicknames (Spike, Cool); names for pets (Spot, Red) (Born, 83).

Where words come from

The origin of words is fascinating; some words are derivations of other words (*present/presentation*), some are abbreviated forms (*flu/influenza, ad/advertisement*), some blend two or more familiar words (*smoke-and-fog/smog*), some are acronyms made from the first letters of each word in a phrase (*AIDS, ASAP, CD*), some come from proper names (*bourbon*). Look at the following list: can you find out where the words come from? Can you add any words to the list?

fan	Camcorder	Dacron
NASA	bra	hamburger
Kodak	orient	fax

(Parker and Riley, 99–100)

Euphemism

Newspapers and magazines, like most forms of the popular press, often use phrases and words that mean something relatively different from their surface meaning. Politics, too, uses euphemism all the time; think of the widely used phrase for overtopping an extant government, "regime change." This country's recent experiences with war have also yielded numbers of euphemisms for bombing ("surgical strike"), dead combatants ("casualties"), and tactical mistakes where troops inadvertently attack their own ("friendly fire"). A candidate promises to investigate "revenue enhancement," for example, while an ad in a local newspaper touts "friendly service," and a letter to the editor discusses the "human spirit of America." What do these phrases really mean? What is gained by using such phrases? What is lost?

Look at an issue of a magazine or newspaper and find as many "doublespeak" or euphemistic words and phrases as you can. For each:

1. List the phrase or word.
2. Define what you assume, from context, it *really* means.
3. Suggest a more accurate replacement or defend the word or phrase as it stands.

NCTE's *Quarterly Review of Doublespeak* is a great resource, and you may want to look at it.

Minidictionaries

Dictionaries can be great fun and can provide not only information but also a look at what is popular, what is in, and what is out. Within a group, have students compile a minidictionary of words or phrases that seem indigenous to their school and its students. Have students:

1. List the words or phrases.
2. Define the words or phrases.
3. Use the words or phrases in a single sentence.

Games and activities such as these can open the world of language for our students; students can also design and enjoy their own language play.

Daffy definitions

In the spirit of puns, students can also make their own lists of unusual definitions of words, using a first and second definition. While this activity might be a little advanced for many English language learners, my students came up with the following double and very daffy definitions, complete with grammatical explanations:

dilate: 1. To grow in size 2. To die late, live too long (*die*, verb, cease to exist + *late*, adverb, after the usual time)

fast days: 1. Days of abstinence from food 2. Days you live and eat in a hurry (*fast*, adverb + *days*, noun)

nitrate: 1. A salt of nitric acid 2. Night rate as opposed to day rate (*night*, adjective + *rate*, noun)

shamrock: 1. A four-leaf clover 2. A fake stone having the appearance of something valuable (*sham*, adjective + *rock*, noun)

Students can compile similar definitions for a specialized dictionary of "punny" words.

Sentence Combining

Sentence combining is an activity where students put together very short sentences into one longer sentence. For example, a student, given the following short sentences:

1.1   My friend is furry.
1.2   My friend is fuzzy.
1.3   My friend is named Dog.

could combine the three into one:

My friend is furry, fuzzy, and named Dog.

Equally correct would be the following minor variations:

My friend, Dog, is furry and fuzzy.
My friend is furry, is fuzzy, and is named Dog.
My furry, fuzzy friend is named Dog.

As William Strong, a major proponent of sentence combining, writes, the origin of sentence combining comes from linguistic research:

The transformational model proposed that language is governed by a finite set of rules for sounds, word formation, and syntax, all operating harmoniously. It is these rules, linguists hypothesized, that all neurologically normal children figure out and internalize, without being taught them in the conventional sense. . . . [Transformational grammar asserted] that typical sentences are actually comprised of many constituent kernels, each contributing in a patterned way to overall meaning. (3)

The practical application of sentence combining stems from the observation that older writers have a tendency to produce sentences that are longer, denser, and more **syntactically mature** (Strong, 4, 6, 12). Such writers would never string very short sentences together ("My friend is furry. My friend is fuzzy. My friend is named Dog."). Younger or beginning writers do, however, use such short sentences. Getting beginning writers to "make" more complicated sentences could be speeded up, researchers hypothesized, by practice in combining sentences. Researchers also hoped that practice would enable student writers to generate those more complex structures with ease and **fluency**.

Previous research studies questioned how long-lived the "gains" were: in other words, if students continue to combine sentences over a period of time, will they, after the exercises are over, maintain those more syntactically mature sentences and write more complex structures? An influential article by Robert J. Connors (2000), however, reviewed the history of sentence combining, and concluded that it is an effective and beneficial strategy. Consistent work with sentence combining can help students' writing become more syntactically complex and, in addition, can be an important way to teach grammar and usage. Sentence combining is a relatively no-risk, no-threat technique to allow students to play with language and along the way to increase their native abilities to make new sentence structures. **Fluency**, the characteristic of writing with relative ease, is also a reason to use sentence combining; the exercises often help students become more comfortable with writing and to spin out sentences with less hesitation. While some of the almost extravagant claims for the benefits of sentence combining have faded, the gains cited are strong enough to make sentence combining a useful activity in the English language arts classroom.

Let's take a look at some typical sentence combining exercises. They come in two varieties, **open** and **signaled**. With open exercises, students combine the sentences in any order to make a single, longer sentence. The following is an example taken from William Strong's excellent sourcebook, *Sentence Combining: A Composing Book*. Students make eight sentences from the pairs listed below.

1.1   Carol was working hard on her test.
1.2   Sue slipped her a note.

2.1   Carol unfolded the paper carefully.
2.2   She didn't want her teacher to see.

3.1   The note asked for help on a question.
3.2   The question was important.

4.1   Carol looked down at her paper.
4.2   She thought about the class's honor system.

5.1   Everyone had made a pledge.
5.2   The pledge was not to cheat.

6.1   Carol didn't want to go back on her word.
6.2   Sue was her best friend.

7.1   Time was running out.
7.2   She had to make up her mind.

8.1   Her mouth felt dry.
8.2   Her mouth felt tight. (Strong, 19–20)

There are truly dozens of ways each pair could be combined, and each combining is, unless it strays significantly from the original sentences, equally correct. While you and your students could come up with eight sentences rather different from the following, here is one version of the combined sentences:

1.   Carol was working hard on her test when Sue slipped her a note.
2.   Carol unfolded the paper carefully; she didn't want her teacher to see.
3.   The note asked for help on an important question.
4.   Carol looked down at her paper, and she thought about the class's honor system.
5.   Everyone had made a pledge not to cheat.
6.   Carol didn't want to go back on her word, but Sue was her best friend.
7.   Time was running out, and she had to make up her mind.
8.   Her mouth felt dry and tight.

These sentences about a real school issue can also be used by students as the beginning of a writing exercise—what should Carol do?

Signaled exercises, unlike the open exercises, ask students to do specific things with sentences and to combine the sentences in a directed way. The directional signals are, in this instance, noted at the end of the sentence and are set in all caps. Try to combine using the signals:

1.1   Ten months of sales indicate SOMETHING.
1.2   The market for new houses has changed. (THAT)
1.3   The change is abrupt. (-LY)
1.4   The change is permanent. (-LY)

While the combinations of the first, "open" exercise cited can be very varied, the final sentence generated by these four sentences should, according to the signals, read:

> Ten months of sales indicate that the market for new houses has changed abruptly and permanently.

Using these kinds of exercises, either signaled or open, once or twice a week for brief periods can help students "play" with structures. Using the blackboard or an overhead projector, you may want to start by showing students how to do this in a class demonstration. Students can do these exercises at their desks, with a friend, or in a small group. Sharing the different variations is always helpful, and taking a limited amount of time is important. Spending repeated class periods on sentence combining exercises, however, can wear everyone out; in this case, as with much in instruction, less is more.

Once students are comfortable combining sentences in either both open and signaled mode or just the open mode, they can move to what I consider one of the more useful aspects of sentence combining. I have students take open exercises and look at the semantic effects they have created. For example, consider the following short sentences. The two sentences were made (*decombined*) from one original sentence in Richard Wright's *Black Boy* (Memering and O'Hare, 265):

1.1   I went upstairs.
1.2   I felt like a criminal.

We could, without much effort, generate a number of combinations:

I went upstairs, and I felt like a criminal.
I went upstairs, feeling like a criminal.
I went upstairs and felt like a criminal.
Upstairs I went and felt like a criminal.
Upstairs, feeling like a criminal, I went.
Upstairs I went, and I felt like a criminal.
Feeling like a criminal, upstairs I went.
Feeling like a criminal, I went upstairs.

If this were a class, I would record these possible combinations on the board or the overhead and ask a number of questions. I would want students to look at the sentences and then to discuss, in turn: which seem to be the most effective sentences? powerful? personal? What are the differences? similarities? Why? Without going into a great deal of explanation, we as readers know that every combination conveys a slightly different meaning, done through language and placement of that language. Simply put, the meaning—and effect—conveyed by "I went upstairs, and I felt like a criminal" is a bit different from "Upstairs I went, and I felt like a criminal" or "I went upstairs, feeling like a criminal." And, in order to talk about that semantic difference, students have to deal with issues of language; in the sentences cited, students will, sooner or later, have to mention the place of *upstairs* and why that inverted location makes a difference (as it certainly does). In fact, to talk about *upstairs*, students will have to deal with the concept of its relation to the verb *went* and, possibly, name *upstairs* and its function (adverb) in the sentence. Also, how does the participial phrase *feeling like a criminal* make a different impression than the complete sentence *I felt like a criminal*? Why? What does it convey? Why would we want to use a complete sentence instead of a participial phrase? Voilá! We have not only considered semantics, but we have done some grammar teaching.

This is not, as with other issues in sentence combining, a question of what Richard Wright actually wrote in *Black Boy* (as mentioned the two sentences are formed or decombined from one original sentence) or what, indeed, is the "best" answer. We are looking at choices and options and shades of meaning, and while some combinations may not reflect the intent of the two sentences or make much sense (for example, "I went criminally upstairs" or "Criminally, I went upstairs"), making sense is not the point of this exercise. You need not feel that you, by the way, should know precisely the difference between the many variations

I've cited. It is enough, rest assured, that you and your students consider those choices and semantic differences. Whether or not you agree or can always precisely define why one sentence is doing something a bit different than another, looking at them and talking about them gives you a forum and an occasion to consider and discuss subtleties and nuances in word order and phrasing. This exercise gives all of us as readers an invitation to talk.

On the other hand, if you are starting this exercise with little or no knowledge of traditional grammar, you will be handicapped in your teaching and discussion. In order to talk with your students and deal with what they combine, you need to know, on sight, the basic terms and structures. These include the parts of speech, phrases, clauses, subjects, and objects. If you are not ready for that now, you will have to stick to more confined exercises and wait to introduce such discussions until your own knowledge of terminology and function is up to speed. You can, of course, start with a few sentences and, on your own, study what your students might come up with. However, you'll need to know your grammar before you launch into using sentence combining to discuss semantics and usage. But you knew that anyway, didn't you?

Students' Right to Their Own Language

One of the most controversial—and difficult—issues for English teachers is their responsibility to students who speak what is considered "nonstandard" English, English that violates the usage rules we often mistakenly call "grammar." For traditionalists, the role of the English teacher is that of corrector and keeper of the standards; in this scenario, English teachers need to stop their students from speaking or writing in a nonstandard way. The question involves the definition of dialect and also whether it is prestigious or nonprestigious. Linguistics tells us that meaning or intelligibility is rarely the issue; social attitude and cultural norms determine the value and prestige of a dialect. We know that nonstandard English does not affect the ability to read or think or write and rarely interferes with meaning. It is therefore hard to defend logically the traditional English-teacher-as-corrector role. When we advocate the eradication of nonstandard English in our classroom, we are more in the business of linguistic etiquette than in the business of better communication.

And, for some, the eradication of nonstandard English also means that we are more in the business of racial discrimination than language learning. When some years ago the Oakland, California School Board made public statements regarding Black English Vernacular (BEV), or Ebonics, a firestorm erupted across the United States. Spurred by weak test scores and concerned about Oakland students' ability to perform on such measures, in late 1996 the Oakland School Board sought extra funding for their schools. Specifically, the Oakland School Board argued that BEV constituted a separate language and, therefore, the Oakland public schools, populated primarily by Ebonics speakers, were eligible for federal funds.

One of the surprising results of the ensuing debate was the revelation that many educators were unfamiliar with much of the research and extensive literature regarding BEV. Some educators, with only a sketchy knowledge of the field, concluded that the Oakland School Board and its defenders were, essentially, bringing a new issue to the table—possibly for political and financial reasons. Linguists and knowledgeable language arts teachers know that BEV has been studied, documented, and discussed in the education world for some sixty years or more and, as the noted linguist William Labov convincingly demonstrated, BEV is, like any dialect, entirely rule-governed.

The controversy subsided, however, when it was made clear that the motivation of the Oakland School Board was students' acquiring Standard English. On the other hand, the political volatility of this issue cannot be overemphasized. When Anglo/Caucasian teachers are the prime transmitters of Standard English to Latino and African American students, there is often a real concern about equity and racism. You as a beginning English teacher need to be aware that, for many parents and members of the school community, how we talk and how we teach that talk in the classroom are sensitive and controversial matters.

What, though, should a teacher do? People outside and inside the school really expect us, as English language arts teachers, to address the issue of standard and nonstandard language in our classes. After debate and discussion and even some soul searching, the National Council of Teachers of English issued *Students' Right to Their Own Language*, a position statement, which, among other things, maintains:

> The history of language indicates that change is one of its constant conditions and, furthermore, that attempts at regulation and the slowing of change have been unsuccessful. . . . Dialect is merely a symptom of change. . . . Diversity of dialects will not degrade language nor hasten deleterious changes. Common sense tells us that if people want to understand one another, they will do so. Experience tells us that we can understand any dialect of English after a reasonably brief exposure to it. And humanity tells us that we should allow . . . [all] the dignity of . . . [their] own way of talking. (18)

What does this mean? It means, practically, that when students perceive a need to adopt a different dialect, they will do so—as they do when they leave your class and enter the lunchroom or their cars or their homes. As discussed earlier in this chapter, telling or teaching students that their language is *wrong* or *bad* is not only damaging but also *false*. Reminding students, however, that different choices of language are appropriate for different contexts—for example, that their language may influence whether they get a job or a loan, that their language could be a barrier to some people—may be more accurate. If students perceive the need to change, they will do so.

Thus teachers need to offer students a choice of expanding their language rather than wholly rejecting their "home" language. Teachers need to offer students instruction but also to be sensitive to the fact that students who do not consistently or firmly conform to standard English or what they perceive as "school talk" may be doing this deliberately. And, I firmly believe, *they have that right*.

Teacher Mark Larson addresses this very issue. Invited to a luncheon honoring a writer, he found that he was dressed too informally and was, to confound his feelings of being out of place, confronted at the meal with "a table spread with, among other things, three forks, two spoons, a stack of plates in graded sizes, and several glasses, one of which contained a napkin folded like a swan" (92). This is simple etiquette stuff, and, Larson, an adult and a professional, was attending the luncheon voluntarily. He found, however, that the event not only made him feel uneasy and resentful—which rule was he going to break next?—but he also connected the event to his students. He writes:

> Not knowing the rules of so complex a meal, I knew I ran the risk of making my next ignorant blunder at any moment . . . I felt conspicuous, as if every move I made revealed my status as an outsider. As my uncertainty increased, so did my resentment . . . I wanted to grab the wrong damn fork, use it as conspicuously as possible and holler, *I don't want to be one of you anyway!*

How often have we heard variations of *I don't want to be one of you anyway!* in our classrooms? When we listen, we can hear it in our students' anger, in their withdrawal, in their refusal to do "our" work, in their defiant rejection of the prescribed rules of "proper" grammar. Every year, students will proclaim what they think is a fail-safe rule of thumb for taking grammar tests: "If it sounds weird, it's right." I believe they are saying, What you are teaching feels wrong. It isn't me. It's you. I'll play along, but I won't incorporate it into my real life. (92)

While Larson is not, in this anecdote, offering us a way to teach grammar and usage more effectively, we would be wise to listen to what he is saying about our students who often will resist the teaching of standard usage. For many, and it is not a small issue, *I don't want to be one of you* may be at the heart of their resistance to incorporating "correct grammar" in their writing and their speech. While I am not sure that any of us can do a great deal about this by ourselves, it puts some student behavior in context. Teaching is, as you know, also a political act, and there is little that is more political than correcting and trying to change another's language.

That said, certainly we need to be in a position to offer students language choices and options. African American educator Lisa Delpit writes in "The Silenced Dialogue":

> To imply to children or adults . . . that it doesn't matter how you talk or how you write is to ensure their ultimate failure. I prefer to be honest with my students. Tell them that their language and cultural style is unique and wonderful but that there is a political power game that is also being played, and if they want to be in on that game there are certain games that they too must play. . . . [S]tudents must be *taught* the codes needed to participate fully in the mainstream of American life. (96, 100)

We would hope, as Geneva Smitherman has advanced, that every student will know three languages: first, the "standard" dialect of English or what she terms "the language of wider communication" (170); second, a street or home dialect of English; and third, one foreign language. With this "tripartite language policy" (Smitherman-Donaldson, 170), students might be more equipped to thrive in the world. It is not outlandish to give students exercises in which they speak or write in first one and then a second dialect. Certainly the Shakespeare-summary exercise in Chapter 5 asks students to write using different forms of language, and its language-play aspect is a large part of the exercise's appeal to students.

Students who want to be taken seriously will choose different language from that chosen by people who are trying to make their audience laugh; their **purpose** will guide their language. All students know—and instinctively adjust to—the different demands of **context**, shifting language choices depending on where they are—school, home, work. Students also know that language choices are often made in response to the listener; for example, there are certain phrases and words they would not use with grandparents that would pass unnoticed by their peers. Knowing when to adjust and how to use language successfully to communicate is a more powerful skill than is any monolithic list of (to steal from a title of a language book) *dos*, *don'ts*, and *maybes* of usage.

The Language of Hate

While this chapter has discussed language change and that there is actually no "bad" language, what about the language of hate, language used to demean, exclude, shock, or hurt? All of us, some perhaps more frequently than others, have been the target (possibly the originator?) of language that was designed to wound. And schools and classrooms are places where such language can crop up and be an issue both for teachers and their students.

We must acknowledge that language is a two-edged sword and while, in this book, we concentrate on the positive power of words, we would be naive if we did not recognize that language can also be used as a potent weapon. As teachers, one way we can blunt such language is to demystify it and to examine it rationally. It is not inconceivable—or even that shocking or daring—to place the insult of the week or even the obscenity of the month on the board and to bring it directly into our lesson plan. We can briefly discuss origin and meaning and use and, yes, examine with our students why the word or words are so powerful and so repugnant. There may be some snickers and some inappropriate comments at first, but looking directly at the language of hate can defuse it.

Talking about such language and bringing it into our classroom is one way to deal with it. While we can forbid its use within our classroom walls, forbid it being used against us as teachers or against students by students, we cannot, realistically, wipe the halls or the cafeteria or our communities or even the printed lyrics of today's popular songs of certain words or phrases or language used to demean. Taking the power of language—its negative power—into account may be one of the more potent aspects of language we can bring into our classroom.

The Glory of Language

In all cases it is good to remember that while we may want students to know and be able to use "correct" or "standard" English—the language of those who approve loans, give diplomas, and hire employees—we need to remember two things.

First, we need to understand that "standard" language is arbitrary, and second, that "correct" language has changed and will continue to change. We have an obligation to make our students' options broad, to help them—and invite them—to learn "standard" and "correct" English, but we need to place the issue in perspective and to acknowledge that those two terms get placed within quotation marks for a reason. And that reason is that there is just no immutable, definable, *standard* English and no immutable *correct* English.

The English teacher as Language Cop is a sad picture, but you know very well that most people associate your role in the classroom with the primary task of correcting and reshaping speech. Even for many of your students for whom such school experiences were painful—or futile—there is the expectation that you, new English language arts teacher, will do it right, do it effectively, and do it a whole lot.

Knowledge is your armor. Language shifts. Differences in language are not to be condemned or squelched. Mechanics and usage have a place in final draft writing. Without them we would have a difficult time understanding meaning; our students need to be able to present finished prose that is clear. On the other hand, we are about larger things than teaching students to memorize the functions of the semicolon and to fear the split infinitive and, regardless of the circumstances, rarely to use slang or colloquialisms. As difficult as it may be, we need to balance our obligation to teach correctness with an ethical mandate to respect our students and the language they bring to us, and to honor meaning before form.

When students walk into our classroom self-conscious about their speech, worried about how they talk, afraid to express what they know—or don't know—we are in a territory of pain and difficulty. Many of our students don't have an academic vocabulary; some have variations of speech that are unfamiliar even to some of their peers; some use, almost exclusively, a lot of slang and street talk. Your students may seem confident, brash, even display a certain linguistic bravado. But underneath that may be a fair amount of insecurity. It is your job to create a lively, positive, language room: there is a place for all kinds of talk in our classes, just as there is a place for all of our students. To do any less is to silence them; and that is the one thing we simply cannot, in all conscience, do.

·············· FOR YOUR JOURNAL ··············

Choose *one* of the following activities; both of them can be very illuminating about *your* own language background and, of course, they are also appropriate for your students.

Your language acquisition

Elizabeth A. Poe writes that students can answer the questions in Part I; they will need to interview parents for Part II to find out the answers about themselves and their own language acquisition. The following are excerpts from her suggestions.

Part I

1. List the children in your family according to their birth order, age differences (number of months older or younger than you), and sex.
2. What language or languages are spoken in your home?
3. Do you remember anything about learning to talk?

Part II (for parents)

1. What are your first recollections of my speech development?
2. What were my first words?
3. How old was I when I spoke them?
4. Did I have any problems with my ears? If so, what?
5. Did I play with children who were older than I was? Who?
6. What sort of things were done that helped my language development?
7. Who did these with me?
8. Did I talk much once I learned to talk?
9. Do you remember anything I said that you thought was funny? (Poe, 113–14)

Writing a linguistic autobiography

Mark A. Christiansen writes that students need, in order to write linguistic autobiographies, some data about themselves. The following are excerpts of some of the questions he suggests that students consider for their final paper.

Family Background

1. What is your racial or ethnic background?

2. To what extent have members of your immediate family affected your language? (Remember that your mother was probably your first English teacher.)

3. Have any elderly relatives influenced your language growth? How?

4. Does anyone among your relatives speak a foreign language? As a result, have you looked upon the English language differently?

5. What are your father's and/or mother's occupations? Are there specific words associated with their jobs?

Leisure Time Activities

1. What is your favorite hobby/sport? Are there words associated with it that you have learned?

2. How much recreational reading do you do? Has your vocabulary been expanded because of this reading?

3. Have you traveled much? When you have been away from home, have any people ever called attention to certain expressions you use? Have people ever made fun of your dialect? If so, how did their cajoling make you feel?

4. Have your peers had any effect on your pronunciation or vocabulary? Do you use much slang? Are there certain idioms that you use with your friends or in a social group that you do not use with your parents?

5. Do you work after school or during the summer? Has your vocabulary been affected as a result of this employment?

Formal Education

1. What is (are) your favorite subject(s) in school? Have you encountered any new words from studying this subject?

2. Have you studied a foreign language? Do you use any terms from that language?

3. Have you made any attempt to change your grammatical constructions or usage? If so, what specifically have you altered?

4. When you speak, are you conscious of using certain gestures, facial grimaces, and vocal inflections? If so, how do they support what you say?

5. Do you have more difficulty expressing yourself in writing than in speaking? If so, why?

Residence

1. To what extent has the urban, suburban, or rural area in which you live affected your speech?

2. Do you watch much television? Have you adopted certain expressions used by your favorite TV performers?

3. Have you moved from one residence to another? If so, how have the neighborhoods been different? Has the neighborhood in which you now live affected your speech? (Christiansen, 119–21)

References

Anderson, Jeff. *Mechanically Inclined: Building Grammar, Usage, and Style into Writer's Workshop*. Portland, ME: Stenhouse, 2005.

Association for the Teaching of English Grammar (contact NCTE, 1111 W. Kenyon Road, Urbana, IL 61801-1096, for more information and how to subscribe to *Syntax in the Schools*).

Atwell, Nancie. *In the Middle: New Understandings About Writing, Reading, and Learning*. 2d ed. Portsmouth, NH: Boynton/Cook, 1998.

Beowulf. Edited by Rowland L. Collins. Bloomington: Indiana University Press, 1965.

Born, Bernice. "Studying Personal Names." *Virginia English Bulletin* 37 (Spring 1987): 81–88.

Bryson, Bill. *The Mother Tongue: English and How It Got That Way*. New York: Perennial, 2001.

Christenbury, Leila. "From the Editor." *English Journal* 85 (November 1996): 11–12.

Christiansen, Mark A. "Writing a Linguistic Autobiography." *Virginia English Bulletin* 37 (Spring 1987): 119–21.

Connors, Robert J. "The Erasure of the Sentence." *College Composition and Communication* 52 (September 2000): 96–128.

Delpit, Lisa. "The Silenced Dialogue: Power and Pedagogy in Educating Other People's Children." *Harvard Educational Review* 58 (August 1988): 280–98.

Dong, Yu Ren. "Don't Keep Them in the Dark! Teaching Metaphors to English Language Learners." *English Journal* 93 (March 2004): 29–35.

Elgin, Suzette Haden. Never Mind the Trees: What an English Teacher Really Needs to Know About Linguistics. National Writing Project: Occasional Paper No. 2, 1–15. n.d.

Fu, Danling. "Teaching ELL Students in Regular Classrooms at the Secondary Level." *Voices from the Middle* 11 (May 2004): 8–15.

Gershwin, George. "Porgy and Bess." New York: Gershwin Publishing, 1935.

Gomez, Kimberley, and Christina Madda. "Vocabulary Instruction for ELL Latino Students in the Middle School Science Classroom." *Voices from the Middle* 13 (September 2005): 42–47.

Hall, Katy, and Lisa Eisenberg. *Snakey Riddles*. New York: Dial, 1990.

Hartwell, Patrick. "Grammar, Grammars, and the Teaching of Grammar." *College English* 47 (February 1985): 105–27.

Haussaman, Brock, with Amy Benjamin, Martha Kolln, Rebecca S. Wheeler, and members of NCTE's Association for the Teaching of English Grammar. *Grammar Alive!* Urbana, IL: NCTE, 2003.

Hopkins, Gerard Manley. *The Poetical Works of Gerard Manley Hopkins*. Edited by Norman H. Mackenzie. New York: Oxford University Press, 1990.

Johnson, Samuel. *Dictionary*. Philadelphia: J. Maxwell, 1819.

Joyce, James. *Ulysses*. Paris: Shakespeare and Company, 1924.

Kolln, Martha. *Rhetorical Grammar: Grammatical Choices, Rhetorical Effects*. 5th ed. New York: Pearson, 2007.

———. *Understanding English Grammar*. 5th ed. Boston: Allyn & Bacon, 1998.

Labov, William P. *A Study of the Non-Standard English of Negro and Puerto-Rican Speakers in New York City*. Final Report, U.S. Office of Education. Cooperative Research Project no. 3288, 1968.

Larson, Mark. "Watch Your Language: Teaching Standard Usage to Resistant and Reluctant Learners." *English Journal* 85 (November 1996): 91–95.

Lester, Mark. *Grammar in the Classroom*. New York: Macmillan, 1990.

Memering, Dean, and Frank O'Hare. *The Writer's Work*. Englewood Cliffs, NJ: Prentice Hall, 1980.

Meyer, Jim. "Living with Competing Goals: State Frameworks vs. Understanding of Linguistics." *English Journal* 92 (January 2003): 38–42.

NCTE. *Quarterly Review of Doublespeak*. Edited by Harry Brent. Urbana, IL: NCTE (various years).

———. *Students' Right to Their Own Language*. Urbana, IL: NCTE, 1974.

Neruda, Pablo. "# LXVII." *The Book of Questions*. Translated by William O'Daly. Port Townsend, WA: Copper Canyon Press, 1991.

Nilsen, Alleen Pace, and Don F. Nilsen. *Vocabulary Plus High School and Up: A Source-Based Approach*. Boston: Pearson, 2004.

Noden, Harry R. *Image Grammar: Using Grammatical Structures to Teach Writing*. Portsmouth, NH: Boynton/Cook, 1999.

Ohanian, Susan. *The Great Word Catalogue: FUNdamental Activities for Building Vocabulary*. Portsmouth, NH: Heinemann, 2002.

Orwell, George. "Politics and the English Language." In *Shooting an Elephant and Other Essays*. New York: Harcourt, Brace, 1950.

Oxford English Dictionary. New York: Oxford University Press, 1971.

Parker, Frank, and Kathryn Riley. *Linguistics for Non-Linguists: A Primer with Exercises*. 4th ed. Boston: Little, Brown, 2005.

Pei, Mario. *The Story of English*. Philadelphia: J. B. Lippincott, 1952.

Plath, Sylvia. *Collected Poems*. Edited by Ted Hughes. Boston: Faber & Faber, 1981.

Poe, Elizabeth Ann. "Teaching High School Students About Language Acquisition." *Virginia English Bulletin* 37 (Spring 1987): 113–18.

Pooley, Robert C. *The Teaching of English Usage*. Urbana, IL: NCTE, 1974.

Rigg, Pat, and Virginia G. Allen, eds. *When They Don't All Speak English: Integrating the ESL Student into the Regular Classroom*. Urbana, IL: NCTE, 1989.

Shakespeare, William. *Complete Plays and Poems of William Shakespeare*. Edited by William Allan Neilson and Charles Jarvis Hill. Boston: Houghton Mifflin, 1942.

Short, Deborah, J. Hudec, and J. Echevarria. *Using the SIOP Model: Professional Development Manual of Sheltered Instruction*. Washington, DC: Center for Applied Linguistics, 2002.

Smitherman-Donaldson, Geneva. "Discriminatory Discourse on African-American Speech." In *Discourse and Discrimination*. Edited by Geneva Smitherman-Donaldson and Tuen A. van Dijk. Detroit, MI: Wayne State University Press, 1988.

Smitherman, Geneva. "'Students' Right to Their Own Language': A Retrospective." *English Journal* 84 (January 1995): 21–27.

Spenser, Edmund. *The Complete Poetical Works of Edmund Spenser*. Boston: Houghton Mifflin, 1908.

Stalker, James C. "What Should English Teachers Know About Language?" *Virginia English Bulletin* 37 (Spring 1987): 323.

Steele, Sir Richard. *The Tatler*. Edited by Donald F. Bond. Oxford: Clarendon, 1985.

Strong, William. *Creative Approaches to Sentence Combining*. Urbana, IL: NCTE, 1986.

———. *Sentence Combining: A Composing Book*. 3d ed. New York: McGraw-Hill, 1994.

Truss, Lynne. *Eats, Shoots, and Leaves: The Zero Tolerance Approach to Punctuation*. New York: Gotham, 2004.

Weaver, Constance. *Teaching Grammar in Context*. Portsmouth, NH: Boynton/Cook, 1996.

Whitman, Walt. "Slang in America." *Walt Whitman Prose Works 1892*. Vol. 2, 573. Edited by Floyd Stovall. New York: New York University Press, 1964.

Winchester, Simon. *The Meaning of Everything*. Oxford: Oxford University Press, 2004.

Wright, Richard. *Black Boy*. New York: Harper & Row, 1945.

7

Writing and Rewriting

Experience has shown me that here are no miracles in writing. The only thing that produces good writing is hard work.

—Isaac Bashevis Singer

Fifth Period, Wednesday Afternoon

It is fifth period, Wednesday afternoon. The English teacher of this tenth-grade class has placed the writing topic of the day on the board: "What Democracy Means to Me." The students walk into class and see the large letters on the board; they groan a bit as they get into their seats. The bell rings. After taking attendance, the teacher begins the class briskly and tells the students, "Class, I would like you to write your response to the topic I've put on the board. It's something that I am sure all of you have an opinion on. You have the entire period. You might start by outlining your thoughts and then writing from that outline. All papers are due at the end of class and will be graded on both content and form. Do try to be careful with your work—remember, neatness counts."

While there are grumblings from the students and some pained looks exchanged between the rows, the class gets down to work. The teacher stands at the podium, grading some quizzes from the earlier periods, and keeps an eye on the students. While occasionally she walks to a desk to answer a question from an individual, the group is generally quiet. Some fidget at first, some make a few notes, and some start to write, stop, and then ball up their paper and start fresh. Most destroyed papers result in a trip to the trash basket; too many of those trips, and our teacher begins to frown at the offenders.

Quiet reigns for almost fifteen minutes, but after that time, about two-thirds of the class are clearly through. The students shift in their seats, talk a bit; some put their heads down on their desks and retreat. The teacher calls for silence, reminding the class of the importance of the assignment and of not disturbing their neighbors. The students settle down, and those who are still working on their essays work until the final bell. Standing at the door, the teacher collects the finished papers as students file out of the room. Everyone has turned in something, and the students leave, looking largely relieved to be through with this particular fifth-period English class.

That night, our English teacher looks over the essays. She first frowns, then groans. These final drafts, the product of fifty minutes of writing and recopying are, first of all, terribly short: they average a little over a handwritten page in length. Worse, they are largely lifeless, filled with clichés, and seem to repeat endlessly the same stale points about the necessity of democracy punctuated with the same old platitudes about how wonderful it is to live in America. There are precious few original thoughts, not to mention much evidence of care in writing. Nevertheless, our teacher gamely attempts to respond to the pieces and give the students a grade, as promised, on form and content. About three hours later, she dispiritedly calls it a night and goes to bed. Just why can't those students in fifth period write? There are no miracles in these student papers and no real evidence of hard work.

What went so wrong for this teacher and her students? Why is this scene so familiar in schools and why, further, is the outcome so predictable—and so unsatisfactory?

A Traditional Model of Teaching Writing

This scenario reflects what we might call a traditional model of teaching writing. It is not the model you will find reflected in many of today's composition texts, but it is how most people have been taught—if not how they have actually learned—to write. What are its elements?

In the traditional model, **topics** are wholly teacher determined and are relatively divorced from student experience and knowledge. "What Democracy Means to Me" is an extreme example but not that unbelievable. Many school writing topics tend to be fairly abstract and, for most middle and high schoolers, of little burning or immediate interest.

There is in this model limited attention to helping students "get in" to a draft of writing. There is little attention to invention strategies or **prewriting**. Students are expected to come up with ideas on their own, and they may be asked to submit an outline of those ideas—which it is assumed is constructed before the writing—with their final paper. As we all know (many of us from experience as students), most students write the outline *after* they have completed their final draft.

Another feature of the traditional model is limited **time** to write; most students are given a class period or a very few days to complete a final draft. Many times this writing is done wholly outside class, which means that **collaboration** among students or sharing of drafts is rare and **help** from teachers is infrequent. In the traditional model, students write in isolation, by themselves, and figure out, by themselves, if what they have written can be revised or how it can be revised.

A further characteristic of the traditional model is the type of **response**. First, this response comes only from the teacher, and second, it is a response that is almost wholly **summative**, in that it results in a final grade with limited comments on content and extensive comments on organization and form. The opportunity to **revise** and resubmit the paper for a second look is usually not possible in the traditional model.

The **audience** in the traditional model is always the teacher. Because no students see drafts and the teacher alone reads and grades, the paper is written for him or her; sharing or even publication of work in an outside source or even within the classroom is rare.

Finally, the **structure** of a writing assignment is often given to students in the form of a formula that they are to follow and from which they are not encouraged either to vary or move beyond. The five-paragraph theme and similar structures are part of this formula approach.

Jenni Gallo, looking back on her high school career, describes writing in the traditional model:

> We were . . . alone when we wrote; one set of eyes saw our papers. Our rhetorical situation was narrowly defined; we never would have thought of writing a paper for anyone but our teacher. Our parents might have seen our writing, but their advice was usually editorial; peer input would have been seen as violating the honor code. We essentially wrote in a vacuum; we were not even writing for ourselves. . . . When we wrote, we were supposed to know our ideas already; we found out about organizing note cards and creating an outline, but we never discussed how papers actually got written or about the lack of a "correct" process. We never had the option to revise our mistakes so I viewed my papers and their ideas as immutable.

What is limited about the traditional model?

There is one central flaw in the traditional model of writing; it ignores much of what we know about how real writers write and thus inadvertently makes the practice and learning of writing pretty difficult. Real writers are folks who work at the newspaper as well as those who create novels and poetry. Real writers are also in offices of varying types; they write letters, contracts, ads, informational brochures, manuals, and procedures. Real writers make their living writing all sorts of things and, sadly, what they experienced in most middle school and high school classes bears little relation to what they actually practice in their jobs.

I have not been a teacher all my life. In the middle of my career I left teaching; for four years, I wrote and edited full-time, working on press releases, memos, letters, ads, brochures, newsletters, and a magazine. I wrote in an office every day for a variety of audiences and with an end product, publication, in mind. Those four years were not easy ones—I found I missed students and the classroom and did not particularly like the isolation of an office. On the other hand, what I learned a lot about real writing during those four years has helped me put the teaching of writing into clearer perspective.

I found in my four years of writing and editing that I wrote about things I knew about—or wanted to know about—and that in my job, I could take some time coming up with ideas. I rarely had to produce a finished product in fifty minutes or less although at times I did write to a tight deadline.

I also did not write alone; I asked the advice of other writers and readers, read aloud to them, shoved drafts under their noses, and made extensive revisions: changing, adding, deleting, sometimes rewriting entirely. At times what I wrote was not anywhere near what the powers that be wanted; in those cases, I went back to my office and tried again. In short, in the real world I was never "failed" for writing that missed the mark. I was not demoted or fired, and my salary was not cut when whatever immediate piece of writing was not up to standard. I was expected, simply, to go back and do it again.

The traditional model does not take much of my experience into account and, further, restricts the writing to one audience—the teacher—a grade-giving, credit-determining audience at that. The traditional model also posits that writing can be done in a limited period of time, by formula (a number of formulas are routinely taught, including the five-paragraph theme), and that that formula will be relatively all-purpose for a writer's needs. Finally, the traditional model does not allow for rewriting or even starting all over again, as I often did in my job. Again, this is not the experience of real writers.

Listen to a few student voices as they recall their school experiences trying to write:

> We learned how to formulate thesis statements. And to back them up with examples. Of course there is a negative involved here too. There was only one way to write a paper. You had to

include your thesis in the first several sentences of the paper, and it had to contain three topics that were to be the subjects of the next three paragraphs, and then you had a conclusion. No variations allowed.

—Mitra Palmer

I also found among my memories graded papers that were bleeding red ink with corrections on grammar, but no comment on structure, style, content, or tone. Although I was taught the correct format for a composition paper, I had no recollection of lessons on writing. We were expected to follow the basic format including an introduction, body, and conclusion, which was a great place to start, but after that, we were lost. Our revisions consisted of correcting all grammatical errors and resubmitting the paper to the teacher.

—Melissa Chai

I was not a student who possessed "a gift for writing" and was told that I lacked depth and breadth to my writing. . . . It is difficult to forget those endless "themes" assigned and "cringing with fear" when asked to develop my own paper topic. My inadequacy resulted from the lack of writing skills, and from the inability of teachers to guide students to think for themselves.

—Brenda Gates

[My teacher] taught us to write. That is, she taught the five-paragraph theme, that crumbling pillar of the high school curriculum. [She] espoused what she termed the Keyhole Approach to organization, illustrated here.

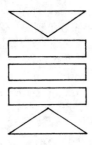

The inverted triangle represented the introduction, which began broadly but which culminated in the specific thesis statement listing the three points. It was always placed at the end of the first paragraph. The three blocks represented the three paragraphs that made up the body of the paper—one paragraph for each point. The first sentence of each paragraph identified the point to discuss, and the last sentence provided some kind of transition into the next point. The final triangle illustrated the conclusion, as it began with a restatement of the thesis and then grew more general.

As you can imagine, such a strict form can be confining, and this form spawned such thrillers as "Three Benefits of Reading" (an actual student paper—mine). It produced lifeless, predictable prose, and a safe outline to follow forevermore. But this outline did make me see the need for a clear sense of organization in writing, and made me aware of the moves I was making as a writer. . . . However, for the longest time I didn't realize that the Keyhole Approach *wasn't* the best idea *all* the time. I had decided that, since it always worked for me (those hideously boring essays earned me "A"s), it would work all the time. So, for a while at least, I wrote uninspired papers limited to three main points and one-paragraph introductions and conclusions.

—Connie Chantelau

Many students do learn to write despite experiences similar to the ones just mentioned, but for others the whole learning-to-write process is an ordeal, especially when it follows closely the characteristics of the traditional model. Some students never learn and have, for their pains, uncommonly uncomfortable memories of what, in English language arts class, it meant to "write." And for teachers, upon whom the determination of what is good writing solely rests, the traditional model can be exhausting and difficult. The teacher in the traditional model controls, determines, and judges all: he or she makes the assignment, sets up the relatively unvarying structure, and is the sole responder to and evaluator of the writer.

When the traditional model demands that writing follow a formula, students can adhere to a cookbook approach only too well, as Debbie Martin, in her student teaching, observed in a writing assignment on satire:

> The general pattern for the seniors was to copy *verbatim* the definition of satire for their opening paragraph. Then they added a sentence that stated the three satirical characters they were going to discuss. They wrote a paragraph on each of the three characters which was a listing of the characteristics copied off the study sheet. . . . they then added one original sentence to each of the three paragraphs that explained why these characteristics were other than expected. They closed with an original one-sentence concluding paragraph.

What Debbie Martin describes is not what most writing teachers want. But what can we offer in the traditional model's place?

·············· **FOR YOUR JOURNAL** ··············

Think about your own writing history in school—how you "learned" to write. How did you get your ideas? What kind of computer or writing instrument did you use? Did you have a special place or time of day to write? Did you share your writing with a parent? a friend? Did you make notes before you wrote? talk to yourself? draw? How was your writing received in school? What help did you get to improve? What happened when you went to college and wrote? Was it different? Why? Why not?

A New Model of Teaching Writing

The traditional model of teaching writing has not been a comfortable way for many students to learn to write—although, admittedly, many have taken the structure and used it and modified it to their advantage. Today, most English language arts teachers use what is termed a "new" or "process" model for teaching writing, a model that is not so much based on an ideal of how writing *should* proceed but on how studies of the behaviors of real writers show that it actually proceeds. This model of teaching writing is more closely based on what we know real writers do. While this movement probably has its origins in the 1950s, the work of composition teacher Janet Emig in the 1970s triggered a reconsideration of the traditional way of teaching writing when she focused her research on the actual behavior of student writers as they wrote rather than an idealized conceptual schema of writing.

What was Emig's research? Emig observed students as they drafted and revised and asked them questions, to which they responded, during their actual writing. What she found—again, based not on theory but on observation of behavior—was far removed from the "ideal" writing procedure that had governed writing instruction. Students did not appear to get their ideas, outline them, write, and then revise—but seemed to jump among activities, writing not in a linear step-by-step manner but in more of a recursive pattern. Students Emig studied got their ideas as they wrote, and they revised their writing not at the end but throughout the entire writing. As composition researcher Frank Smith describes it, "Writing is not a matter of taking dictation from yourself; it is more like a conversation with a highly responsive and reflective other person" (27). This insight into writing behavior, accompanied with an understanding of the importance of invention—that writers needed to use techniques more like artists in their creative processes to find ideas—became the centerpiece of writing best practice and the "new" model of teaching writing. In essence, how students *got there* was far more important than what they produced at the end. More important to teachers, however, Emig's research also showed that how students got there was not consonant with much of the direction they were then receiving from their writing teachers.

The picture that has emerged is far different from what went on in the fifth-period class described at the beginning of this chapter. Much composition teaching today concentrates on the act of writing and rewriting and less on the finished draft; it is oriented more toward process, not product.

In this model, the **topic** of writing is one which students help determine and which is related to their interests and knowledge. Students are given an opportunity for and help with **prewriting** to give them ideas and a starting place. The **time** to write is extensive and takes place in *and* outside class. Students show their drafts to each other and to the teacher in a **collaboration**, which gives them response at the draft-writing stage. Peer groups are a major source of feedback to writers during their drafting.

A final draft receives a **response**, and if it needs work in areas, students can **revise** and resubmit the paper. This response is **formative**, in that it helps students change and refocus and possibly improve. The audience for this writing is not just the teacher but also other students. Widening the audience is achieved through collaboration in **peer groups** and also through the publication of student writing through anthologies, class display, and school-wide posting and distribution. Finally, the **structure** of the writing emerges from the topic; it is not predetermined by the teacher.

The following chart summarizes the two models:

	TRADITIONAL MODEL	NEW MODEL
Topic	teacher determined	teacher-and-student or student determined
Prewriting	limited or none	extensive
Time	limited	extensive
Help/Collaboration	none	extensive
Response	from teacher only summative	from teacher and peers formative and summative
Revision	limited	extensive

	TRADITIONAL MODEL	NEW MODEL
Audience	teacher only	teacher and others
Structure	provided by teacher	provided by student and nature of topic

A student preparing to enter teaching recalls an especially successful writing assignment; while it does not contain every element of the new model previously cited, it worked powerfully because of two factors, topic and prewriting:

> One year our teacher led a class discussion on busing at the time just before it became a reality. Our class was all-white and the discussion did not get very lively, but I still remember coming away from the discussion with very definite opinions—just what I needed to get started on the assigned paper. Though it was a very simple topic, we just had to argue for or against busing, we really had to think to come up with why we felt the way we did and why we took the positions we did.
>
> What made this an effective activity, and one that should have been part of most writing activities in high school English was the fact that it was a current issue, one that was in the news and very controversial. Students knew busing could affect them; it was close to their lives instead of being some vague and unreal topic that would have been hard to get a handle on . . . [it was a] real issue to grapple with.

—Lori Shacreaw

A new-model writing class

The traditional model for teaching writing emphasized the end result, the final product. As we have pointed out before, the new model, by contrast, puts a great deal of attention on the specifics of getting to the product—on the process. Thus the new model for teaching writing is often called a process model.

What does this mean? Process writing asks us to pay attention to the ways real writers write. Real writers do not write in a straightforward or linear fashion, as below:

> **STEP ONE: Get an idea.**
>
> **STEP TWO: Outline that idea (Do not go back to Step One).**
>
> **STEP THREE: Write (Do not go back to Step Two).**
>
> **STEP FOUR: Revise what is written (Do not go back to Step Three).**
>
> **STEP FIVE: Recopy (Do not go back to Step Four).**

Looking at how real writers write, we see that very few writers follow this pattern. And yet this is often what we expect within English language arts classes and how we "organize" our students.

What happens with real writers? Watching such writers write and asking them to talk about their writing, we find that the various "steps" in the process very often occur with amazing simultaneity. A writer might get an idea and start to put something down, which gives her another idea; while adding that idea, perhaps she realizes that something is not right with what she first wrote, and she crosses it out. She has, essentially, gotten an idea, written, gotten another idea, written, revised, even edited, all in a fairly unorderly way and sometimes virtually simultaneously. We call this pattern *recursive*, and it is far from being the step-to-step or *linear* pattern of Step One to Step Two to Step Three to Step Four to Step Five.

We think real writing looks something more like this, with the "steps" going forward and backward and forward:

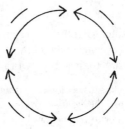

The implications for us as teachers are serious: we cannot spend Monday getting ideas, Tuesday writing, Wednesday revising, and Thursday editing. If we put students on such a schedule, even in the name of process writing, we are not truly letting students explore or use their recursive process.

We need to help students get started and then give them time to use and develop their own patterns for working through drafting to a final (or somewhat final) version. They may be getting ideas on Wednesday and Thursday, writing on Friday and Sunday, and getting more ideas on Monday. If we believe writing is truly recursive, we create a schedule that allows for that recursiveness. This does not mean we abandon our students and give them three days to figure it out for themselves; we need to help them during this time and by using a workshop format. In a process model, however, you cannot completely confine writing behaviors to certain blocks of time—because it doesn't work that way. Teachers who try to schedule the process are actually abusing the term—and not really helping their students. Giving students time over a period of days to write and prewrite and revise is more helpful than predetermining which writing "step" a group will be involved in on any given day.

When Students Have a Choice: Getting Writing Ideas

While students often resent teachers who consistently tell them what they are to write about, when, and how, it is also, paradoxically, no solution to tell students to "write about anything you want." In fact, few students will take that freedom and do much with it other than become frustrated and anxious. As teachers we can help strike a balance: we can present our students with a general direction in which they can go and yet allow them to be creative and inventive on their own. How can we do this? By adhering to three principles of successful writing assignments. These assignments

- must be interesting to the student
- must be both specific and general
- outside of research projects, must be within the student's area of expertise

Let's look at each of these in turn.

The first principle for any successful writing assignment is that it must be **interesting** to the student; it must, in essence, be perceived by the student as worth doing. Many times, then, ideas that really appeal to us as adults—such as municipal regulations in apartment buildings or legal requirements for day care centers or what will happen to social security, issues which may be affecting *us* right now—are often of little concern to our students. We need to think of topics with which they, not just we, can have some intellectual and emotional engagement. Linking the granting of a driver's license to school grades, for instance, may be of far more import to your students than the issue of the price of prescription drugs. Try to present students with topics that appeal to them.

The second principle for a successful writing assignment is that it must be **both specific and general**: while this seems like a contradiction, it really isn't. Building choice for students is vital so that while we can satisfy, for instance, the need (or the curricular mandate) to have students write an "argument" paper (taking a stand on an issue and presenting a case), we let students determine what issue in specific they will pursue. As another example, we could ask students to write a memoir, but, obviously, the memoir will be based on their own experience and life history details, not on someone else's.

One example of this kind of assignment is "Scars," a personal narrative and exposition with which I have with some success. In Scars students write about a physical scar they have: where it came from, when they acquired it, who was involved, why it happened, and what (if anything) the scar means to them now. Students have boundaries regarding this assignment—it is a narrative and exposition with a structure—but they and they alone determine the specifics.

The third principle for a successful writing assignment is that it must, somehow, be **within the area of the student's expertise**. While research papers are legitimate places for students to learn about new topics, essay writing assignments are rarely successful if they require students to take stands on comparatively unfamiliar issues. Thus, if students have no specific background regarding college admissions policies or water control, why ask them to research and write about the topic? Letting students select an area about which they have knowledge—and you may be surprised at what they know—can yield a far more successful essay.

There are countless sources of "ideas" for writing and, naturally, asking students about what they are interested in can result in excellent suggestions. Think also of the following:

- **Quotations:** have students bring in a quotation (with attribution and source) and write about why they chose that quotation, what it appears to mean, and how the quotation might relate to their lives. Students can write about their own quotations or even each other's; students can make a "bank" of quotations for the use of other students and other classes.

- **Childhood memories:** ask students to select a childhood experience (that occurred from age 12 or younger) and write about it. Topics can include finding something valuable; doing something forbidden; trying not to cry; getting an unexpected present; mastering a task; being somewhere you weren't supposed to, and getting caught; making an important friend; being laughed at and not knowing why (Tanner).

- **The daily news:** have students pick a single news article from the day's paper or the local television station and write about what it *doesn't* say: what facts appear to be left out? Why? What more would a reader want to know? What can you speculate will be the implications of this event on individuals? The community? To what extent do you think this is news important enough to include in a paper or as a segment on CNN? Why or why not?

- **A holiday memory:** students can recall the holidays that their family celebrates and select one and write about its activity, memory, and/or tradition. (Burkhardt, 269)

- **Letter to self:** as the first writing assignment of the New Year, students write a letter to themselves with five parts (me, now; my world; what I do; people in my life; my future). The letter deals "with the things that are important and real" in the students' lives and can be returned to students at the end of the school year. Students can include with this letter a supplementary packet including photographs, maps, videotapes, montages, or other information that they feel will illumine who they are. (Burkhardt, 270, 273)

- **Observing nature:** in Fran Claggett and colleagues' *Learning the Landscape,* the authors set up a wonderful writing assignment where students pick an animal, plant, or natural object and observe it over a period of days, taking focused field notes and writing. The assignment requires multiple, defined journal entries, a drawing, and, more important, a conclusion, and it culminates in a finished piece of writing. Even for urban kids, who might end up observing a rock or a star or a house plant, this assignment is accessible.

Another interesting avenue is the **multigenre paper** where students combine letters, news articles, cartoons, prose, poetry, and other media (including art and type using different type styles and sizes) in one paper. James Agee's *Let Us Now Praise Famous Men* used this format seventy years ago; Agee, writing about the Depression-era South, made lists and used dialogue, prose, and Walker Evans' photography to paint his portrait. Similarly, students can break the boundaries of traditional papers by using a multigenre format and, through that perspective, present more than one perspective of an event or topic. While W. David LeNoir issues teachers a "multigenre warning label" (99) regarding unity—the papers need not just be multigenre but must be coherent in what they say—this is an interesting and promising format. For more information, check out Tom Romano's *Blending Genre, Altering Style.*

When Students Have No Choice: Writing on Demand

Timed writing tests are part of the current educational landscape, and as much as we want to think about student writing that is expressive and individual, based on student interest and expertise, workshopped in writing groups, and open to revision, such is not always the case. Both many state and national tests—in particular the SAT, ACT, and AP tests—use writing on demand, giving students predetermined topics or prompts and a narrow window of time in which to respond. It would seem, at first blush, that such writing is completely antithetical to everything outlined in this chapter. As I and my coauthors argue, however, in *Writing on Demand: Best Practices and Strategies for Success*, this kind of writing is a genre in itself, and the good work that we do in our writing classrooms need not be abandoned when we prepare our students for timed writing tests. When students are comfortable getting writing ideas, drafting, and revising, when they read perceptively and can understand what a prompt is asking them to do, they can indeed perform well in a timed writing situation. While the scope of this book does not allow for a long discussion regarding the genre of writing on demand, it may be helpful to consider two issues of importance in this kind of specialized writing, negotiating a predetermined topic or prompt and dealing with time.

Negotiating a prompt

Let's imagine your students are in a timed writing situation and are confronted with the following prompt:

> Sophocles wrote, "The greatest griefs are those we cause ourselves." What do you think of the view that the worst sorrows are those for which we are responsible?

There are, in essence, a number of things that students need to consider regarding the prompt and their roles as a writer. The following Prompt Analysis Questions (or PAQs) can help students approach any prompt, including the previous one:

1. What is the *central claim/topic* called for?

   Do I have choices to make with regard to this claim/topic? Will I need to focus the claim/topic in order to write a good essay? What arguments can I make for this claim? What do I know about this topic?

2. Who is the intended *audience*?

   If named specifically, what do I know about this particular audience? If the audience is implied or not identified, what can I infer about it or them? In either event, how might the expectations of this audience affect my choices as a writer?

3. What is the *purpose/mode* for the writing task?

   Is the purpose stated or must it be inferred? What is this writing supposed to accomplish (besides fulfilling the demands of the prompt/assignment)? What does the goal of this writing suggest about the mode (narration, exposition, description, argument) or combination of modes that I should consider in responding?

4. What *strategies* will be most effective?

   What does the purpose/mode suggest about possible strategies? Of the strategies I am comfortable using—strategies like examples, definitions, analysis, classification, cause/effect, compare/contrast—which will be most effective here? Are there any strategies—such as number of examples or type of support—that are specified as required?

5. What is my *role* as a writer in achieving the purpose?

   Have I been assigned a specific role like *applicant* or *representative*? If I have not been assigned a specific role, what does the prompt or assignment tell me about the level of expertise I should demonstrate, the stance I should assume, or the approach I should take? (67)

With this prompt, the *claim* is Sophocles' comment about grief, and it appears open to debate or discussion; there is nothing in the prompt that seems to suggest what kind of attitude the writer is to take. The *audience* is not specified—the writer is not asked to make an argument to a specific figure, so we can assume the audience is the reader/scorer of this wring. The *purpose or mode* is the presentation of a point of view (*what do you think* is how the prompt reads). *Strategies* are open and not specified in the prompt. Writers could tell a story, give hypothetical examples, or just express an opinion, but it is good to look at the pronoun *we*, which implies a personal approach to this prompt, not a distanced one. As for *role*, the writer is to tell what he or she thinks—to express a point of view—regarding Sophocles' comment.

Students can use the PAQs with a number of prompts; the time they take to assess the prompt itself is well worth it and can help them produce a solid piece of writing in a brief period.

Dealing with time

Using time in a writing test is something that is far different from writing in a regular classroom environment. Students need to understand that they will, once they get their writing ideas in place, have to produce very quickly. As a first step, students need to know how long they have to write and then, as we suggest in *Writing on Demand*, they need to practice the following procedure:

- Look at the clock and write the following on a piece of paper:
  - time writing test begins
  - time that marks one quarter of the available minutes
  - five minutes before test must be completed
- Use the first quarter of available time to plan your writing. This includes reading the prompt and instructions, prewriting, and developing a thesis or main point.
- When the clock indicates that a quarter of the time has elapsed, consider where you are in the planning process. If necessary, you can take a few more minutes to finalize your thoughts.
- Start writing your response after no more than half of the available time has elapsed.

- As you write, glance at the clock occasionally and keep looking at your thesis and prewriting to keep them in the forefront of your mind.
- Five minutes before the end of the test, draw your writing to a close.
- In the last few minutes, reread and proofread your writing, making corrections, inserting missing words, or deleting unnecessary ones. Changes that are inserted or deleted neatly are acceptable—in most cases you will not have a lot of extra time, so do not try to recopy the entire selection. (143)

Giving students practice with prompts and timed situations can help them feel more comfortable with the specific requirements of writing on demand. It's only part of the writing picture, but it is one that we cannot ignore—and working with students before the test can help them feel more confident.

Writing Groups: Questions, Answers, and Reasons

Whether in a timed situation or in our classroom, helping students with their writing is part of our task as teachers. One way to do that is by using writing groups that both capitalize on the collaborative aspect of writing and help students see their work as broader than just between themselves and the teacher. Sure, the very idea of writing groups scares some teachers. There is of course the fear that students will get out of control in the groups, but an even greater fear is that students not only don't know what to do but will do nothing in their groups but share their own ignorance about writing. It is, after all, the teacher's job, isn't it, to be the determiner of what is good writing?

These fears need not be realities. When students are told what a writing group is for, when the tasks and procedures are outlined and consistently reinforced, there is little real chance that a writing or response group will either get out of control or get lost. Students need to be introduced to writing groups; they need to model the behavior in a "fishbowl" kind of exercise (discussed later in this chapter); and they need an accountability structure for what they do in their groups. Some groups will be able to talk about drafts and take notes on their copies productively; other groups will need checklists and worksheets that they turn in with their drafts to encourage them to stay on task. Regardless, writing groups can work very effectively in the middle school and the high school.

Don't writing groups "do" the teacher's job?

But what about the concern that response to writing is the teacher's job and that students in a writing group are doing nothing more but sharing their ignorance?

The utility of the writing group is that it exposes students to the writing of others. Gone is the isolation of one person writing his or her draft and never hearing or seeing what other students are doing. The writing of other students teaches; a draft presented in a writing group may be significantly better or significantly worse than the work of the other members of the group. Nevertheless, in a writing group students get to read and consider a range of writing—one another's drafts. Often I wonder what effect it has on students to read only and see only the polished, analyzed, credentialed work of the great, whom we know can write: Annie Dillard, Lewis Thomas, Henry David Thoreau, Martin Luther King Jr. Letting students see and work with the writing of those like themselves who are learning to write can be a heartening experience.

Writing groups also tap into the collaborative, *each one teach one*, aspect of learning. If a student gets lost reading another student's draft, if the point just seems to disappear, that student—the reader, not the writer—will need to figure out why and articulate it. By trying to help a peer, the person will have to put a name on the problem area, give some sort of advice about what to do. It makes all students in the group consider and grapple with issues of writing in an immediate way, which is far more active than responding in a large group to whatever the teacher asks students to look for and discuss. Students can become more independent, and there is a double learning that can take place. In order for Ellen to help Mark with his writing, Ellen has to figure out what the issue is; by helping Mark, Ellen is helping herself.

The numbers game: Help with the paper load

In addition, we need to think about the sheer impossibility of the teacher's task in the area of writing. It is an overwhelming job: the numbers, ladies and gentlemen, are just not in our favor and will not be in the near future, unless there is a major overhaul of the educational system.

In a famous article in the very first issue of *English Journal* (Vol. 1, No. 1, 1912), Edwin M. Hopkins asked, "Can Good Composition Teaching Be Done Under Present Conditions?" The article lamented the number of students in the average English teacher's class and noted that with the time it took to teach and respond to writing, it seemed an impossible situation. Little has changed between 1912 and today. Most English language arts teachers see a large number of students every day; I have a student teacher who recently, in a burgeoning suburban school, saw 167 students a day. What, practically, does this mean?

Let's look at the numbers. Let's imagine that you give *one class a week* a writing assignment. They are taking their writing seriously, and you want to give them a response to their drafts before they do a final version. You are not using writing groups; you want to make all the comments and suggestions yourself.

Let's say you spend a moderate amount of time—*ten minutes per draft*—for this one class of twenty-five to thirty students. That's anywhere from 250 to 300 minutes—between four and five hours—just to give students an intermediate response to a draft. When you receive final versions, of course, you will spend another ten minutes or so per paper—and that's another four to five hours. This is for *ONE CLASS* to do a single piece of writing to which you respond and then evaluate and grade; it has worked out to about eight to ten hours of your time outside of teaching and preparation.

This eight to ten hours is, by the way, in addition to work for your other three or four classes and outside whatever else you are having this same writing class do. Is it any wonder English language arts teachers avoid giving writing assignments and, if they do, only work with final drafts?

The writing group can help a teacher handle some of the paper load. He or she can circulate among the groups and feel confident that with proper preparation, students can share what they are working on and get feedback from other readers, not just the teacher. It's a practical solution that not only has a sound pedagogical basis, but that also may help to save a committed writing teacher's sanity.

Procedures for implementing a writing group

The composition of a writing group can be heterogeneous or homogenous; in other words, you can either mix writing ability or keep writers of the same ability in a single group. I have had most success with a heterogeneous group of three or four members; I also always mix males and females and members of majority and minority racial or ethnic groups. I think diversity works well and prefer to use it in my classes.

I always ask my students for an ungraded writing sample a few days before we get into writing groups. We do some prewriting together, and I have students write about a personality characteristic of theirs or something that they are good at outside of school. It's an assignment that allows students to talk about something they know about and are interested in—themselves. I read these writing samples, looking at them with an overall general eye; it is holistic grading. While I respond to what students have written, I do not give the papers a letter grade. Students get credit, of course, for having done the writing, and for my own purposes, I place the papers in stacks; one stack for the strong writers (1s); one stack for the middling writers (2s); and one stack for the writers who, at this point at least and within the context of this group, look like they will need work and help (3s). Whereas one writing sample is no sure indicator of writing ability, and this sort of 1 to 3 holistic scoring has limitations, the procedure gives me a handle on where the student might be at that moment in my class. Using this quick diagnosis, I then construct the writing groups, mixing the 1s, 2s, and 3s as well as the males, females, and ethnic groups. So, for example, a single writing group of four might have, in ability, one 1, one 3, two 2s; in gender, two females, two males; in an ethnic mix, three Caucasians, one Latino. I do not, by the way, share the numerical designations of their writing sample with students until the end of the course.

It is initial diagnosis, based on a single piece of writing, and its function is only to allow me to create intermediate groupings.

I talk with my students about why writing groups are important, giving them much the same argument I have outlined here. I assure them I will be circulating among the groups as they work. I then give them the following handout, and we go over it:

WRITING/REVISION GROUPS

In groups of three or four, you will have about an hour to share one another's papers, suggest changes, and reinforce what you feel are the strongest parts of the shared papers. Every member of the group must participate in the revision and should, while being respectful of the others' writing, make a conscientious effort to help the others improve their drafts.

TIME

Group of three, 15 minutes apiece
Group of four, 10–12 minutes apiece

PROCEDURE

1. One person should give copies of his or her rough draft to the members of the group.

2. The person should then read the draft aloud to the group—there should also be no preliminary apologies or explanations, just the reading.

3. The person should then pause for a few minutes to allow the group to consider, look over the draft, make marks, make notes.

4. The discussion of the draft should then start and include both negative and positive remarks. In all instances, the group should try to be specific about the paper. Comments such as "I don't like this paragraph" are not helpful; comments such as "In this sentence, this word seems too strong" or "This section seems out of place—could you move it more to the beginning of the paper?" are more useful and will help an author in changing and revising a draft.

5. While the writer of the draft would do well to listen to suggestions and comments, the paper belongs to the writer, not the group. It is conceivable that the writer will listen to suggestions and hints and decide to accept only some of them in revision.

QUESTIONS TO CONSIDER*

- Ideas and Content: To what extent is the draft clear? interesting? convincing? Are details used well? Are main and secondary ideas balanced?
- Organization: Can a reader follow where the draft is going? Are there helpful transitions? Where can points be made clearer?
- Voice: Does this draft read as if it were written by a real person? Can you "hear" the voice of the writer? Is there flavor, honesty, humor here?
- Word Choice: Are the words used fresh? striking? appropriate for the content?
- Sentence Fluency: To what extent does the writing move the reader along? Are the sentences varied or do they all sound the same?
- Conventions: Are there areas where the writer needs to check spelling? punctuation? paragraphing? capitalization? Do any of these errors interfere with the meaning of the draft?

Then, using a duplicated copy of an anonymous student draft, I ask students to enact a "fishbowl" writing group and role play.

Four student volunteers sit at the front or in the center of the room and pretend they are the group discussing this draft; one student volunteers to be the author, and the others are members of the writing group. The group follows the procedures outlined in the handout. The "author" begins by reading the draft aloud. The discussion then proceeds. The rest of us watch in silence, noting not so much what is said about the draft but what kinds of remarks are made and by whom: who talks, who doesn't, how it goes. After about ten minutes of observation, we stop the role play, and we talk about what we saw.

Then I have four different student volunteers do the fishbowl again. Not surprisingly, the second group is always different from the first; they have the benefit of having watched the first fishbowl, and they usually have different ideas of their own and different ways of interacting. Again, we discuss how the group went.

It is only after taking a writing sample, grouping students, explaining the purpose and intent of a writing group, giving students some written instructions, and doing a number of fishbowl exercises that my students are comfortable beginning work in a writing group. Even then checklists can be necessary to keep students on task—checklists that I discuss and briefly review—as well as teacher circulation among the groups. Groups can take a bit of time to bond, and they may have questions that need to be answered. To have students just "get in groups and talk about one another's drafts" is not possible for most; if we care about the process, we need to:

1. Model the process, step by step.
2. Reinforce the process.
3. Monitor the process.

When students are asked to take on roles they do not understand and for which they are not prepared, chaos and anxiety can ensue.

---

* These questions are adapted from *Creating Writers* by Vicki Spandel and Richard J. Stiggins.

How often groups are reformed is a context issue; I prefer groups that last for a semester at least, but you may want to change your groups more frequently. Personality conflicts between students, discipline issues, students whose writing skill changes so drastically that they would benefit from other peers, groups that for whatever reason are not productive or harmonious, are additional reasons to reconfigure writing groups. As you circulate among groups you will be able to sense who is working well and who is not; use your judgment to determine when and if a writing group needs change.

The work of a writing group: Revision, editing, and proofreading

As the title of this chapter indicates, writing is also rewriting—revision—and the most important work of a writing group can be to help with that vital function. A note, however: most students confuse revision with editing and proofreading. The three are not interchangeable. Revision, editing, and proofreading are different and represent very different levels of activity during the final draft of writing. Many students, in fact, believe that the alteration of a single word or the correction of capitalization and punctuation is revision, but such is not the case. Students must look at the whole writing, not just at the word or sentence level. Revision is the major work of changing writing; editing and proofreading are last-stage polishing activities.

To briefly recap: *revision* is best thought of as re-vision, relooking, reworking of a piece of writing. It can occur at all stages of the composing process to clarify and improve a draft or to completely rework a draft and start over. Revision activities may include: changing significant portions of the writing, such as rearranging and rewriting sentences, rearranging sections, deleting sections, adding sections, rewriting openings and closings, or even refocusing the entire piece. Revision can transform a piece of writing, and the advice of writing groups can be invaluable.

Editing, on the other hand, is a look at a revised piece of writing. It is ongoing and also used during the later composing stages. During editing—and writing groups are helpful here—a writer reviews and changes word order, sentence structure, and checks usage issues (such as pronoun references, subject/verb agreement). At this stage the major changes in the writing have been established; the changes made in editing are less intrusive and far less significant to the meaning of a final piece of writing.

Proofreading is a last look at a revised, edited piece, and occurs at the very end of the writing and just before submission or publication. Activities during proofreading include verification that all minor details of usage are addressed (such as capitalization, indentation of paragraphs, sufficient spaces between title and body, etc.). It is a final polishing and can be done outside a writing group setting.

Most students who find writing difficult from the onset resist revision and hope that proofreading and some minor editing will be all that is needed to improve their hard-won first draft. For most students, however, revision is the vital activity to learn and practice—and one of the most powerful ways to encourage students to revise their work is to use writing groups.

Conferencing with Students

Besides groups, another activity that is helpful to students is the brief conference. It may seem impossible to talk about a draft individually with each student in a class of thirty, but you can do it if the conferences are kept brief and are conducted while other writing/reading activities are going on. Let's imagine that students are working on their writing and you are available, at your desk, for five-minute conferences with people who want to talk. You could, conceivably, confer with seven or eight students and still have some time to circulate among the class or do some large-group instruction. Many students want the privacy—and the reassurance—of a conference.

In *Learning by Teaching*, Donald M. Murray, discussing writing conferences, notes they should be short and frequent and limited to one concern at a time. He also offers conference guidelines for teachers:

- **The student responds to the text or to the experience of producing it.**
- **The teacher listens to the student's response to the text and watches how it is presented.**
- **The teacher reads or listens to the text from the student's perspective.**
- **The teacher responds to the student's response.** (163–64)

Practically, what does this mean? It might mean that a conference would start with questions that ask the writer how he or she views the draft. Questions I use include:

- **What do you think of what you have written?**
- **How difficult was it to get this far?**
- **How easy was it to write about this subject?**
- **What do you want to work on?**
- **Where are the draft's strengths? weaknesses?**
- **What can I help you with?**

Notice that all of these questions, and the whole tenor of the conference itself, are focused not on the teacher's making the draft better—or correcting it or improving it or criticizing it—but on making the writer look at his or her own work and selecting what he or she sees—or doesn't see—as an issue. This kind of indirection may make you worry that you are not doing your teacherly job; after all, aren't we supposed to mark up and evaluate and determine what is good writing and not good writing? Not really. A conference that allows students to focus on selected aspects of their writing will ultimately produce more *learning* than a list of "corrections" we might hand a student in a conference setting.

The Place of Correctness and Grammar in Its Place

Correctness is important. The key, though, is where and when. Correctness is important in a final draft. We need to school ourselves as teachers not to expect students—and not to ask students—to be concerned about spelling or grammar or surface issues while they are "getting it down," as Dan Kirby and his coauthors write in *Inside Out* (39 ff.). Getting it down is first. Getting it right is second. If we ask students to do both simultaneously we can cripple them and their writing. They need to draft and cross out and struggle first, then they need to go back and consider correctness. Asking students to do it all at the same time is asking for something that real writers don't practice at all; correctness has a place, but that place is firmly at the end of the writing process.

When I work with student drafts, if it is near the end of the process I will note that students should edit and proofread, look up certain words or check for punctuation or rework certain constructions that are either not standard or not conveying clearly what the writer means. Sometimes I will place a mark by every line of a draft where something needs to be reconsidered; students can ask one another, their group members, or they can consult their usage handbooks or dictionaries. They can, of course, also ask me, but I try to get them to pursue other sources—and thus learn to be more independent of me—as much as possible.

The point, of course, is not that correctness should be valued in and of itself but that our students need to see that correctness serves meaning. When surface errors interfere with reading, they are serious impediments. As preservice teacher Julie Morrison writes in her journal:

> If teachers can make their students actually see how grammatical mistakes rob their papers of the meaning intended, then they will see the importance of "correctness," not for a good grade or just to appease the teacher, but because they deserve to be taken seriously. Their ideas warrant the reader's attention, not the grammatical errors. So if students realize that their misspelled words, or subject-verb disagreement trips the reader and distracts his attention, then maybe they will see worth in writing correctly.

Correctness is important, but *what* students say is paramount. Too many people associate writing only with spelling, English language arts class only with using "correct" grammar. We read that the public worries about declining standards in language, but most of those worries seem to refer only to the most surface of surface errors! Would that the public criticize recent graduates of high school because they are writing lifeless stuff, not because that lifeless stuff is misspelled. We need, as with literature, to remember why we are in the classroom: it is not to point out errors; it is to get students, in their writing, to grapple with ideas and then, only then, to present those ideas in a correct form.

And this is where grammar comes in.

As argued in the previous chapter, you can teach a definition of a part of speech and test it. You can have students label participles in sentences and mark if the choices are right or wrong. You can put a fault-ridden sentence on the overhead or board and have students pick out the errors. It's testable, gradable, and can be put in fill-in-the-blank or multiple-choice format. It's harder, on the other hand, to gauge whether an opening to an essay is "effective" or not; it gets difficult putting into words why one description says more, is more evocative, than another.

What we need to do is integrate the terms, the description of the language, with the actual production of language in writing. Grammar study *before* writing will not improve writing; no studies confirm that cause-and-effect relationship, although most people assume it has just got to exist. Grammar study *with* writing or with revision is useful.

Imagine you have a student who keeps writing the same sentence patterns, subject/verb, subject/verb, subject/verb: "He drove down the lane. He saw it. He had been looking for it." You want the student to break out, vary what he is writing. Now would be the time to look at sentence patterns, at inverted verbs, introductory participial phrases, adverb clauses, periodic sentences. Maybe the student does not need to look at all of these; maybe the student doesn't need all of the nomenclature or terminology to know that you can start a sentence off with something describing something, and then complete the sentence as usual ("Driving down the lane, he saw what he was looking for"; "What he was looking for was down the lane"; and so on). Work with sentence combining could also certainly help such a student (see Chapter 6).

Imagine you have a student who cannot get straight where to use commas as opposed to semicolons to separate parts of sentences. The student writes, "Natural disasters such as Hurricane Katrina bring out the best and worst in people, this is obvious from news reports." Now is the time to learn how to identify complete sentences and to learn the term *conjunction*. If the student understands that she has written two complete sentences (*disasters bring/this is*) and not used a conjunction, she can use a semicolon and not a comma (*Disasters bring; this is*). If the student adds a conjunction (*and* would be logical here; *Disasters bring, and this is*), she can keep her comma. At this point, this student needs not only to be able to identify complete sentences but she also needs to know how conjunctions work with commas and semicolons.

Memorizing the usage handbook's definitions, making lists of pronouns or adverbs for example, identifying items on tests, rewriting or identifying someone else's usage mistakes are contextless acts that rarely relate to real students' problems and questions in their own writing. These kinds of activities, although still frequent in many English language arts classrooms, are not, I think, worth our time. They may give us marks for our grade book and they may lull us into thinking that we are being conscientious teachers, but the fact is these kinds of isolated activities just do not do what we want—which is to improve student writing.

Now They've Written It—What Do You Do with It?

There are a number of activities you can perform with the final versions of student writing. In general, the major activities are **response**, **evaluation**, and **grading**, and each one of these can have a clear relationship to the assignment rubric that you will create (more on that later).

The three activities are not necessarily mutually exclusive, but each differs somewhat from the others. When we **respond** to students, we make an effort to talk to them, writer to writer, reader to writer; the issues of quality, good/better/best, are not of primary importance. When I respond to a student paper, I try to do three things:

1. **I link something the student has written to me personally.** Yes: I had a similar experience; that would anger me, too. That happened to a friend of mine.

2. **I tell the student what I like about what he or she has written.** I pick one or two things the student does well and I ask the student to think about it. Your introduction really grabs me—do you have any idea why that opening image is so powerful? You are using parallel construction effectively here—do you see how?

3. **I ask the student questions about the draft.** Look at your title—is that what this paper is really about? If not, what is it about? Can you find where you could break this long section into two paragraphs? What effect do you think this word has on what you are trying to say in this paragraph?

When I **evaluate** a paper, I put more emphasis on how well I think the paper is doing what it does, on how close the paper seems to come to what it is trying to do. That may mean more emphasis on number 2 and more direction on number 3. (You might say, I am lost in this section; what is it about? Your paragraphs are so long you are combining a number of points; can you break the section on page 2 into two—or three—paragraphs?)

To **grade** a paper requires a letter or numerical designation *and* some sort of final evaluative comment. I use single letter grades and have never found the "split" grade of one letter for content and one for form to be successful. While many teachers like the split grade, as it seems to make a distinction between content and mechanics (surface errors), I have a hard time accepting that distinction anymore. If surface errors diminish meaning—and they can—then content is really intertwined with form. How can we separate them? Is it really possible, if form is so related to content, that a paper receives a B in content but a D in form? For me, one grade seems more logical.

And this leads us to constructing rubrics.

Creating and Using Rubrics

Whether it is for a timed writing test or for an assignment you have created, rubrics are invaluable instruments to assess students fairly and, when shared with students beforehand, help them understand what they should emphasize or concentrate on in their writing. Traditionally, rubrics involve five or six standard items or traits—*ideas, organization, word choice, voice, sentence fluency,* and *conventions* are typical—although the "weight" or emphasis on each one of these can appropriately vary. This is important; while it may seem tempting to use the same rubric for all your writing assignments and make all of the traits of equal importance, it's not a good idea. You need to adapt your rubrics so that they reward what the assignment itself emphasizes. There is, accordingly, no "perfect" or template rubric that is appropriate for all assignments.

For example, a traditional paper that emphasizes a logical argument would probably want to reward ideas and organization and perhaps make each of those items worth more points. A narrative that tells a personal story might want to give emphasis and significant point credit for organization and voice. If the assignment involved description, word choice might be truly important and thus rewarded in the rubric more than other aspects. At any rate, the assignment itself and the rubric should be clearly related: if you ask students, for instance, to cite three examples to buttress their point, the rubric should pay attention to the presence—or absence—of three examples. Let's take a look at two documents, an abbreviated assignment sheet for a writing that my students and I often enjoy, the epiphany paper, and the rubric I used to grade it. Students had both of these before they wrote. Can you see how the two are related?

EPIPHANY PAPER

Purpose:	To describe convincingly a significant incident in your life
Audience:	A fellow writer
Function:	Narrative description
Length Suggestion:	Three to four pages, typed, double spaced
Discussion:	An epiphany is a manifestation or, literally, a showing. Christian theology designates the visit of the Magi, the three wise men, as the epiphany of Christ to the world, and many other religions and also mythological tales feature epiphanies. In our own lives, all of us have experienced incidents that operate as moment or revelation or insight, some of which last for many years, if not a lifetime. These incidents—and there can be many depending on the individual—serve as emotional, psychological, even spiritual touchstones in our lives.

Think, in your life, of such an incident or epiphany. Questions to consider:

- What was the nature of the epiphany?
- Who, if anyone, was involved in the event?
- How did anyone inside or outside the event help you assess its significance?
- What did you think you learned at the time? now?
- What happened in what sequence?

If moments of epiphany in your own life are far too personal to write about, consider such an event in the life of a close friend or relative. Do understand that being highly revelatory is NOT expected as part of this assignment, and it is not anticipated that you will share in this essay—which your writing group will see and which is for credit and a grade—something that for you is intensely private and sensitive. If you can select an incident that is not supercharged, do. Otherwise, focus on another person's epiphany.

What kind of rubric would be useful for this assignment? While, in this case, I followed the traditional ideas/organization/word choice, and so on, notice how I made a 30-point rubric that reflected, at least in some sections, the specific assignment requirements itself. As constructed, the rubric also rewards what was most important about this memoir, ideas and organization, and, because of the personal nature of the assignment, voice.

EPIPHANY PAPER RUBRIC

Ideas   7   6   5   4   3   2   1
What was the nature of the epiphany?
Who, if anyone, was involved in the event?
How did anyone inside or outside the event help you assess its significance?

Organization   7   6   5   4   3   2   1
Who, if anyone, was involved in the event?
How did anyone inside or outside the event help you assess its significance?
What did you think you learned at the time? now?
What happened in what sequence?

Voice   7   6   5   4   3   2   1
What did you think you learned at the time? now?

Word Choice   3   2   1

Sentence Fluency   3   2   1

Conventions   3   2   1
Three to four pages
Typed, double spaced

TOTAL SCORE   _____

Key:
30–25   A
24–19   B
18–13   C
12 or below D

Rubrics keep our writing evaluation and grading on target and also tell students what is expected in a writing assignment. This is a win/win situation for both teacher and students and a real incentive to use rubrics with all graded writing assignments. In our comments we can respond and evaluate students, but the use of a rubric with headings such as those shown are also helpful when we consider student writing.

Finally, we need to be aware that however we react to student writing—response, evaluation, grading, or any combination of the three—we wield a certain power and influence. Julie Morrison, a student who now teaches English, writes how my feelings about her writing even affected her choice of which piece would be printed in our class anthology. I try not to let all of my prejudices show, but I didn't fool Julie one bit:

> To be perfectly honest, I chose the paper that I thought you liked better, the childhood myth. I trust your opinion, much more than my own, and I rely on your experience as a writer to show me what's strong, what works . . . etc. This makes me think about my own responsibility as a responder, when I teach. It's a lot of pressure, I guess, because the teacher's response really affects the students' own appraisal of the writing. I know we've discussed this many times in class, and it's really a scary issue for us since we don't have a whole lot of experience with something that [matters] *so much.*

Without letting this influence overwhelm us, we need to remember that we carry a weight—and thus a responsibility—when we look at student writing.

·············· **FOR YOUR JOURNAL** ················

Ask a friend who teaches in a secondary or middle school to lend you a copy of a student's draft (with the student's permission and with his or her name removed) or get a draft from a peer. Imagine you are the teacher and need to *respond* to the draft. Write a paragraph that you feel gives the student feedback and that offers formative comments. Then write a paragraph that *evaluates* the paper with summative remarks. Finally, place a *grade* on the paper as if it were a final draft. Look over what you have done: how helpful do you think your response and evaluation is? Write a paragraph about how you felt doing this exercise.

Using a Writing Portfolio

Using student portfolios is also very helpful in grading and evaluating. Such portfolios can showcase not only students' work but can also show their growth and their ability to assess themselves. In a portfolio, students select from a group of papers what they feel is their best or most representative writing. No writer shines on every effort, and with a portfolio, students not only have some control over what is evaluated, but also they can select the pieces they feel are indicative of their talents. In addition, most portfolios also include self-evaluation, an aspect that can be indispensable as students put perspective on their own work and their growth.

Much like artists have done for years, students present their portfolios, which can demonstrate their range of writing and also their changes in a given space of time. In writing portfolios, usually presented at the end of a semester or marking period, students can include:

- **daily writing** (such as journal entries, reading logs, and so on)
- **project writing** (such as a research paper)
- **creative writing** (such as poems, song lyrics, short stories)
- **a writer's memo**, which describes not only the pieces included in the portfolio but details what those pieces show (such as change, focus, improvement, personal investment) and how the writer judges those pieces (most successful, most difficult, most memorable)

Properly applied, portfolios can give students a sense of satisfaction and also can help them take appropriate responsibility for their writing growth.

The Wonderful and Varied Journal

If we believe that people learn to write by writing, that practice helps with fluency—we are right. How, nevertheless, does even a highly conscientious teacher deal with a lot of writing in a number of classes? The answer for me is the journal, a great tool that can be used in a variety of ways.

I like to start classes with ten minutes of writing; in a **class** or **learning log journal**, the topic relates to the class discussion, the readings we have done for homework, the activity we just finished. Typical topics might be: in last night's reading, what two things did you notice? What surprised you? List three questions you have.

Another journal is the **personal journal**, which allows students to keep more private and introspective thoughts. It gives students an outlet for their ideas and emotions, and it capitalizes on a powerful subject, themselves. While there are always issues of confidentiality (students may want to write in this journal but not share with you or with others every page), this type of writing can be very effective. Typical topics might be: what is the best thing that happened to you this week? Imagine you are going on a long trip and can take only one personal item with you—what would it be?

A **writer's journal** can be a place where a student keeps notes, records dreams, writes out phrases and story fragments, preserves other prose or poetry he or she has read, all with the idea of using the journal as a basis for future or current writing. Many artists, inventors, and scientists keep notebooks of this sort—writers need them, too. Typical topics might include lists of interesting words, opening lines, snatches of dialogue that could be used in any piece of writing.

Dialogue journals are written on one side of the page with space for someone else—another writer, the teacher, other students—to write back and respond; the subject of a dialogue journal can be quite varied, but its strength lies in the fact that one writer writes to another, and there is an immediacy that this format captures. Typical topics might be: what two things does this class really need? What did you think of the last assembly? What is one question you've always wanted to ask an adult?

Whatever their type, journals need to be written consistently, taken up on a regular schedule, and responded to in a nonthreatening manner. Surface correctness and even neatness are nonissues in journals—although the writing should be legible so that it can be read. Letter grades that absolutely judge quality are more than likely inappropriate for journals; some teachers assess journals on completion or on number of pages written. I usually put a check at the top of each page read or skimmed and write a comment at the end responding to what the student has written.

Journals are a direct answer to the paper-load issue. If students write regularly in their journal, they are working on their writing, and their sheer writing fluency can be very positively affected. It is hard to stay afraid of writing—to have what is known as **writing apprehension**—when you have to write regularly. Students also learn a few other things through using a journal: they can "work out" intellectual and personal issues through their own writing; not all writing needs to be perfect; not all writing needs to be graded. The wonderful and varied journal can be a powerful part of your classroom.

The Research Paper

It is, as student Beth Hagy notes, "the research paper, commonly known as going to the [web] and expanding" that strikes fear in the hearts of both teachers and students. Most students hate this assignment; most teachers dread not just the difficulty of getting students through the process but the lifeless results of what seem to be hours of preparation. Further, in the age of the Internet, plagiarism is *the* serious issue in the research paper.

What advice do I have about combating plagiarism? It's actually pretty simple: give students an opportunity to write about something in which they are interested. Years ago teacher Ken Macrorie wrote about the "I-Search" paper, a paper that encouraged students to pursue in their research something they want to search out. Certainly we need to remember that primary and secondary research can be done on an amazing range of subjects. It is not just the Romantic Movement in England in the early 1800s or the use of fire imagery in a novel that should be the sole subject of student investigation. Certainly there are students in your English language arts class who may want to research Edgar Allan Poe's short stories or Toni Morrison's metaphors. But there are those who can also do excellent jobs researching the history of their neighborhood, the latest innovations in SUV technology, the newest theories on the global warming and the high incidence of hurricanes, or the influence of the Internet on just about everything.

I know this is *English* class. But I also know that when we talk about research, we need to broaden what that definition is and not insist that our students mimic what we necessarily did in our college Victorian Poetry class or American Novel course. Getting students to read and write and ferret out information is the purpose, I think, of a research paper. And, as noted in other chapters, if you insist that students write only on classic pieces of literature, you are opening the door to your students' going to a website to cut and paste (Jeffrey Klausman calls this "patchwork plagiarism"), download and present others' writing as original work. When you allow students to choose unusual topics you can minimize plagiarism.

Using his experience with the research paper, teacher Henry Kiernan offers teachers eight points about research papers and students. His advice is worth reproducing:

1. Spend instructional time teaching students to develop and frame questions, using notebooks, journals, and logs to help them define what they are pursuing.

2. Use interdisciplinary ideas that reach across a number of subject areas and that can "transcend" the English classroom and also connect it to other disciplines

(in his English class, Kiernan uses the environment as the general topic area for research papers).

3. Think about organizing research in small teams, not just individually. (Kiernan suggests local history projects and community and state issues as two areas that lend themselves well to research in project teams.)

4. Have students construct and use interviews, surveys, questionnaires. Traditional databases and literature searches do not always yield what students need in their research.

5. If students do research on literature, have them pick a novel that may lead them to other interdisciplinary questions (for instance, *The Great Gatsby* could inspire a research project on aspects of the 1920s).

6. Get students to write letters to a number of institutions and people (government offices, businesses, individual professionals) so that they learn how to request information and also how to evaluate responses.

7. Have students share and discuss the final papers in a forum atmosphere.

8. Publish the best papers for student models in the future. (7)

If teachers follow these kinds of guidelines listed, students can broaden the idea of what research actually means, concluding that research sources can come from many areas. It is not just journal articles, books, and even information from Internet searches that can constitute quotable and useable research sources. Also, when we give students a platform to display their findings—such as in a discussion forum and through publication—we reinforce the fact that research is more about finding answers and pursuing ideas than fulfilling some kind of disembodied English teacher assignment.

Jim Strickland, writing in *English Journal*, offers a creative research paper alternative based on the widespread use of FAQs, Frequently Asked Questions, on websites. Strickland has his students select a topic of interest, research it, and then use the FAQs format to convey the information. The format has "real-word relevance and can be created after someone has researched a topic of interest, using library skills and information literacy" (25). Strickland notes:

> The FAQs format accomplishes the goals of a traditional research paper assignment but capitalizes on the advantages of computer technology. Students start with their research questions; employ the technology to satisfy their inquiry; collect, synthesize, summarize, and organize the information; and present what they've found to variety of audiences in a format with which they are familiar from surfing the Internet. (28)

It also discourages plagiarism as students must transform all original documents into FAQs format.

One assignment with which I have also had a great deal of success is asking students to research the day of their birth. Students have to read the newspapers—one national, one from the community in which they were born—for the events of the day. They have to interview family members, in particular their parents, about recollections of the momentous date and use personal material such as their own baby book. Students can then concentrate on any aspect of the day: the international scene, the movies playing, the cost of any goods or items, the weather, the sports scores, the car ads. How they weave this together is an individual choice, and I give them guidance on writing this personal yet scholarly account of a day in history.

This assignment gives students a sense of history; it gives them a sense of themselves within and as a part of history. It makes them turn to primary not just secondary sources; it gives them an opportunity not only to interview but to use and interpret those interviews; it asks students to choose what is most important to them; it capitalizes, again, upon that undeniable interest all of us have in that ever-fascinating subject, ourselves. I have never had, I might add, a student plagiarize this assignment or fail to turn it in. There are few activities I can say this about, but "The Day I Was Born" is a relatively surefire assignment.

One caveat I would add to these ideas about research projects is that it is a teacher's responsibility, if there are multiple parts to a research paper assignment, to set up an incremental system so that students can not only keep track of what they are doing but also garner points along the way. Thus, you might give students an assignment sheet with deadlines and progressive credit. Both of these, the deadlines and the point credit, will help keep students on target and give them a sense of progress in their project and in their final grade. What kind of steps will students need to take as they do their research? The deadlines and the points for each step will be ones that you want to establish, but the following topics should probably be included:

Preliminary Topic (discussion and tentative outline)

Final Topic (submission and teacher approval)

Research Source List (submitted and approved)

Research Source Notes (submitted and approved)

Optional Conference with Teacher

Draft 1 (submitted to Revision Group and revised)

Draft 2 (submitted to Revision Group and/or teacher and revised)

Final Draft

As a parting note, a survey reported by NCTE's *Council Chronicle* revealed that when teachers talked to their students about copying work from the Internet, it actually seemed to make a difference. The survey involved almost 170,000 students, K–12, and students whose teachers did *not* discuss plagiarism and copying work from the Internet were less likely to feel that it was wrong. Conversely, students whose teachers did discuss copying from the Internet understood it was cheating. We need to take a proactive approach with students and discuss citation and paraphrase; prevention, not detection, is the issue. If we rely on Google to detect plagiarism (by entering phrases from the suspicious paper) or for-fee websites such as Turnitin.com and MyDropBox.com to scan an entire paper, we have taught students little. Michael Freedman's recipe is "avoiding generic assignments and topics that rely on recounting information, developing writing [assignments] . . . that make plagiarism difficult, and teaching our students how and when to document their sources of information" (548). It couldn't be clearer.

What We Are About as Teachers of Writing

Every summer for eight years I worked with classroom teachers in my local site of the National Writing Project, one of many sites across the country. The National Writing Project insists that teachers of writing need to write themselves. This principle is the major point of the almost thirty-year-old program, and it has done a great deal to change what is practiced in the classroom. Every summer teachers of all subject matters and all grade levels meet to consider issues of writing. The core of the program is an opportunity to research and share ideas about writing, but it is also about giving teachers an opportunity to write themselves.

Teachers of writing should write. Yes, that is you, too. Whether you keep a journal at home, prewrite with your students in class, contribute an article to your local education or language arts newsletter, dash off a poem or so every month, you need to write. I suspect that one reason English language arts teachers often do such silly stuff in class with writing is that they are not writing themselves and have forgotten what it took, what they needed as writers.

And, yes, I write with my students. It's not that I do every assignment with them from beginning to end; I take a low-level approach, and it is workable for me. I've done this for years, and when I went back to teach high school a few years ago, my students and I wrote in our journals together for ten minutes at the beginning of every class. They shared theirs aloud, and I shared mine, too. I also, though less frequently, freewrote drafts on the board or the overhead while students wrote at their desks; and over the years, in the classes I have taught, I occasionally show students the revision agonies I go through to produce my own final draft writing for publication.

All of it seems to cheer them up immensely: my journal entries are not always profound; they often ramble, and sometimes I can't read my own handwriting. Students whisper and chuckle a bit over the drafting I do in front of them, and once they get to know me, they do ask, looking at my revisions, why I don't get it right the first time when it's clear (hey, it's right here in this section) that the whole point was in that fifth paragraph of the second draft. After all, I'm the teacher. But then, again, maybe all writers are like that, huh?

Yes. And that's the point, and I think you can do that, too. The power of writing with your students makes you a writer with them, not a gamemaster giving them another assignment from which you are completely removed. As Isaac Bashevis Singer tells us in the opening of this chapter, there are few miracles in writing; it is consistent and hard work, it is writing and rewriting, and it is work that we, as teachers, can do with our students. While not completely devastating, the picture Connie Chantelau sketches does not, I think, describe how we can help our students become confident writers:

> I don't remember ever using peer groups or having individual conferences about my writing; I recall no encouragement to experiment with writing beyond the standard forms; I recall no personal engagement with literature encouraged in writing. I learned how to edit, not revise. I learned to view writing as a product to be written in fifty minutes and graded based on content and grammar. I had no notion of audience other than the teacher and some faceless college examination board. I was trained, however inadvertently, to stay well within the confines of certain forms and language when I wrote, and I never learned how to handle criticism constructively. In high school I wrote safe, well-organized and entirely correct essays with so spunk, no pizzazz, no chutzpa. I was afraid to expand, to try anything different, and none of my English teachers encouraged me to. I never saw my English teachers write; I never heard them read anything they had written. While we wrote, they sat behind their desks, watching, reading, and grading.

What do we want in our classes when we teach writing, when we have our students write? It may be the vision that Julie Morrison describes:

Students need to write for the sake of writing and not to show that they've read a book or mastered the basic punctuation skills. I want my students to be challenged with their writing and value it as much as they do their own speaking voice. This will take time and lots of practice. We'll need to work together, and learn together. And when my students learn to value what they can say on paper, they will value how they say it, and mechanics will find its place and finally be of some use.

I can't say it any better.

················· **FOR YOUR JOURNAL** ·················

Think about the more successful writing experiences you have had in school. What one paper or papers was the most satisfying to you? Why? Was it the grade? the topic? the process of getting the words down? the feeling after you had turned it in? Try to analyze *why* that writing assignment stands as one of your favorite. Finally, what about that experience can you bring into your English language arts classroom? Are there elements you can use with your students? How? Be specific.

References

Agee, James. *Let Us Now Praise Famous Men* (with photographs by Walker Evans). New York: Houghton Mifflin, 2000.

Burkhardt, Ross M. *Writing for Real: Strategies for Engaging Adolescent Writers*. Portland, ME: Stenhouse, 2003.

Claggett, Fran, Louann Reid, and Ruth Vinz. *Learning the Landscape: Inquiry-Based Activities for Comprehending and Composing*. Portsmouth, NH: Boynton/Cook, 1996.

Emig, Janet. "The Composing Process of Twelfth Graders." *NCTE Research Report No. 13*. Urbana, IL: NCTE, 1971.

Freedman, Michael. "A Tale of Plagiarism and a New Paradigm." *Phi Delta Kappan* 85 (March 2004): 545–48.

Gere, Anne Ruggles, Leila Christenbury, and Kelly Sassi. *Writing on Demand: Best Practices and Strategies for Success*. Portsmouth, NH: Heinemann, 2004.

Hopkins, Edwin M. "Can Good Composition Teaching Be Done Under Present Conditions?" *English Journal* 1 (January 1912): 1–8.

Kiernan, Henry. "The Research Paper Redux." *CSSEDC Quarterly* 12 (May 1990): 7.

Kirby, Dan, and Tom Liner, with Ruth Vinz. *Inside Out: Developmental Strategies for Teaching Writing*. 2d ed. Portsmouth, NH: Boynton/Cook, 1988.

Klausman, Jeffrey. "Teaching About Plagiarism in the Age of the Internet." *Teaching English in the Two Year College* 27 (December 1999): 209–12.

LeNoir, W. David. "The Multigenre Warning Label." *English Journal* 92 (November 2002): 99–101.

Macrorie, Ken. *The I-Search Paper*. 2d ed. Portsmouth, NH: Boynton/Cook, 1988.

Murray, Donald M. *Learning by Teaching: Selected Articles on Writing and Teaching*. Portsmouth, NH: Boynton/Cook, 1982.

Romano, Tom. *Blending Genre, Altering Style*. Portsmouth, NH: Boynton/Cook, 2000.

Smith, Frank. "Myths of Writing." In *Rhetoric and Composition: A Sourcebook for Teachers and Writers*. 3d ed. Edited by Richard L. Graves. Portsmouth, NH: Heinemann, 1990.

Spandel, Vicki, and Richard J. Stiggins. *Creating Writers: Linking Assessment and Writing Instruction*. 2d ed. New York: Longman, 1997.

Strickland, James. "Just the FAQs: An Alternative to Teaching the Research Paper." *English Journal* 94 (September 2004): 23–28.

Tanner, Marcia. "Writing and Richard Wright." NCTE Talk. October 9, 1997. Available email: NCTE-Talk@listproc.org\.

"Teachers Shape Student Attitudes Toward Online Cheating." *The Council Chronicle* 15 (September 2005): 1.

8

The Craft of Questioning

*How do I know what I think until I hear what I say?**

The Power of Talk

The power of talk is one of the English teacher's great resources. Our classrooms can be arenas of conversation where students argue, question, challenge, comment, and observe. And in frequent instances, we and our students can find out what we think or believe through our own conversation—discovering, as the chapter epigraph describes, "what we know" when we have the opportunity to talk and "hear what we say." Certainly, even though some of us would like for students to practice that art of discussion a bit more courteously or calmly or maturely, what we do in class is largely talk.

You as the teacher will mostly initiate and, yes, somewhat control that talk, and one of the most frequent activities in the English language arts classroom is the asking and answering of questions. It can be a highly adaptable, malleable activity when it comes to the consideration of language, literature, and our students' writing. In fact, most teachers are not aware of just how much they do use questions in their classrooms: numerous research studies of actual teaching confirm that teachers who think they are asking only a moderate number of questions—around twenty—in any given class were actually asking as many as four to eight times that amount—up to 150 questions a class.

Talking and answering and asking questions can help clarify our own ideas, not only to others but also to ourselves. In its proper context, the craft of asking and answering questions can be the heart of a lively and learning class.

When I think about the many discussions I have had with classes and students, I remember how awkward it was for me in the beginning of my teaching career to initiate and maintain a discussion. But I did have some successes, and I recall one class in particular, a class with which I never felt I had much rapport, and I remember the day that that class, more than any other, showed me what a discussion could actually achieve.

---

* This quotation is variously attributed and variously written; while some give the twentieth-century British novelist E. M. Forster credit, others do not. But it's a great quotation whoever said it.

We had been talking about a poem and the speaker's choices and how—or if—those choices could relate to our own lives.

Learning to question, to talk with these students, I had had a hard time creating an environment where anyone *wanted* to talk. I had taken some advice and tried to slow down, tried to open up spaces in the conversation, tried not to follow my "list" of questions so precisely. My new mode, and I had instituted it for only a week or so, was a bit more comfortable to me. There was for the first time some silence in the classroom, silence that I thought was positive in that it gave students some space to think and to consider. I had, I felt, finally allowed for breathing room.

It only happened once quite this way with this class, but in the space of forty minutes we moved from the poem and its relation to any real person's choices into an area of great interest to my students: drugs. In that conversation, we moved beyond the platitudes about buying and selling and doing drugs and into the realities of the issue. Cassandra, as I recall, got teary in this class talking about how difficult it was for her to curb her own interest in drugs when her stepfather used *and* dealt. James insisted she should be stronger, said he would be in a similar situation; Maurice chimed in with a companion story and a happier ending. Towanda snorted her disapproval of the entire issue and told everyone they were fools. That made Michael laugh, but then he gave his opinion, too.

This was not in my lesson plan and, frankly, some of the details of some of this class conversation alarmed me. In a way, we were all learning names and specifics and incidents and there were, of course, ethical ramifications to what was being revealed, however tentatively, in this class. But the students wanted to talk about this, wanted actually to talk to *one another* about this, and the poem and my classroom structure had seemed to provide the space to do so.

When the bell rang and the students left (and we had, by the way, agreed not to share this conversation with others outside the class), I was both unsettled by what had happened and profoundly satisfied. The class' environment had changed; the students had talked, for the first time in my presence, about something that was truly important to them, about something that was not purely *school*. The students had, further, connected that real thing to what we were reading. What had happened was spontaneous and appropriate; while I would not expect or demand students to reveal so much about their personal lives, to talk, as in this case, of their own experiences with drugs, in this class the sharing was student initiated and treated confidentially. It was, despite the disturbing nature of the subject, a glimpse of teacher heaven.

I think most of us want such solid and worthwhile experiences when we ask and answer questions in our classrooms. Indeed, we ask questions not only to prompt personal sharing from our students about their relationship to literature but for a number of other reasons. Asking questions can:

- **Provide students with an opportunity to find out what they think by hearing what they say.** In responding to questions about literature or ideas, students often discover their opinions or reactions. In responding to questions about writing, students discover their ideas in prewriting or clarify their ideas in revision.
- **Allow students to explore topics and argue points of view.** Through questioning, students can pursue an aspect of a topic that appeals to them or can logically defend a theory or belief that they hold, sharpening not only oral but also thinking skills.

- **Let students function as experts.** Through questioning, students as well as teachers can probe, explore, and move a discussion into a number of areas.
- **Present students with the opportunity to interact among themselves.** Given the proper setting and environment, students can—and will—argue and debate with one another. Student talk is very important, and it can not only be a stimulus for learning but also lead students to explore topics further or to pursue new topics.
- **Give the teacher immediate information about student comprehension and learning.** Through questioning, particularly through paying attention to answers, teachers can check for comprehension and mastery. Questioning can serve as a diagnostic tool.

What follows may help you with your use of questioning in your classroom. It is, actually, an overlooked and at times misunderstood resource. Researcher Larry Cuban found this in his observation of thirty-two classes and sixteen teachers in two California high schools. While the classes he observed were on task and productive, the questioning was unimaginative and more of a control mechanism than a learning tool:

> Of the 26 teachers who engaged students in question-and-answer for a portion of the period, all but 6 (74%) depended largely upon factual recall questions from the text, worksheet, homework, or previous lecture. Seldom did a student in these classes (whether college-bound or non-college-bound) recite answers more than a few words in length. The 6 teachers who probed student answers by asking for explanations, elaboration, or evidence to support statements did so [only occasionally] with the whole class. (207)

So how can your class be different?

Questions That Teachers Ask

The issue of questioning hierarchies

Confronted with something—anything—to talk about in a classroom, most beginning teachers make an effort to write out the questions they think might be useful and put them in a lesson plan. Certainly for the class previously described, I had questions prepared on the poem we were going to discuss. Many times, especially with literature, teachers will use questioning hierarchies, scales of importance or categories of schemata that classify question types. Within these schemata or hierarchies, the assumption is that certain kinds of knowledge—and the answers to certain kinds of questions—are considered superior to, more sophisticated than, or requiring higher cognitive skills than certain others.

Following this belief, most creators of questioning hierarchies suggest that teachers ask questions at the lowest level of the scale and then move up, spending the majority of questioning time in the upper reaches of the questioning hierarchy. The logical assumption is that spending all questioning time on "lower-level" or purely factual questions (What was the main character's name? Who wrote this and when? Who is the protagonist's enemy?) is not as productive as spending time on "higher-level" or more sophisticated questions (To what extent is this novel realistic? How does this incident relate to the opening of the short story? What do you think you would do if a similar incident happened to you?). Further, we know that students in so-called remedial or lower-tracked classes are often asked *nothing* but factual or recall questions and are never or rarely asked to consider *why*, *how*, or *what if*.

A number of sequential (ordered and hierarchical) and nonsequential (nonordered and nonhierarchical) questioning schemata are depicted at the bottom of this page.

Each of the schemata represents a type of question or conceptual activity. The sequential schemata imply that certain questions require higher thinking skills than others and probably should be attempted in a set order. Look, for instance, at the Sanders: memory is lower on the scale, literally and figuratively, than analysis, and memory should, according to the schema, precede analysis. Some of the schemata, however, simply name different activities without giving them a value or order. Look at the Hyman schema where there is no valuative difference between definitional and evaluative and no assumption that one should precede or follow the other.

If the workings of the human mind were as orderly as some of the questioning schemata suggest, there would be no problem using such hierarchies when we plan for questioning in our classroom. We know, however, that the studies of real classrooms do not

Sequential Questioning Schemata*

Benjamin Bloom
To evaluate
To synthesize
To analyze
To apply
To comprehend
To know

Norris M. Sanders
Evaluation
Synthesis
Analysis
Application
Interpretation
Translation
Memory

Hilda Taba
Apply concept
Interpret concept
Form concept

Harold L. Herber
Applied comprehension
Interpretive comprehension
Literal comprehension

Nonsequential Questioning Schemata*

Arthur Kaiser: Open ——— Closed ——— Suggestive ——— Rhetorical
Richard Smith: Convergent ————————————— Divergent
Ronald T. Hyman: Empirical ——— Definitional ——— Evaluative ——— Metaphysical

---

* Adapted from Christenbury and Kelly, 4.

confirm such clean divisions regarding what actually happens when people talk and when they ask and answer questions. While questioning hierarchies can be a useful starting point, they are not true descriptions of human conversation—and that includes conversation in school. Researchers recording classrooms and classroom talk confirm that schemata are not that accurate a picture and that their use does not always yield what we think it might. For instance, we know:

- Few people—students and teachers—actually approach knowledge in an orderly, paced way, moving smoothly, as the sequential hierarchies would imply, up from one level to another.
- The categories of most questioning hierarchies are not only arbitrary but often overlap, leading to difficulty in actually constructing questions (for example, a question in the Bloom schema that features **analysis** as opposed to **evaluation**).
- The categories of most questioning hierarchies also imply that more superior cognitive sophistication is required for certain operations than for **others** (for example, the act of **synthesis**, in the Sanders schema, is superior to **application**).

In addition, the absolute, consistent benefit of asking "higher-order" questions is also debatable. We know, for instance, that:

- Most research studies are unsuccessful in classifying higher-level questioning in actual classroom discussions.
- Research studies are similarly mixed regarding higher-level questions resulting in greater student achievement.
- Not all students prefer or are comfortable with answering higher-level questions, especially if those questions are not matched by corresponding higher-level questions on tests.

While some order of questioning is necessary and while a mixture of question types, however defined, is essential, it seems that discussion and questioning in the language arts classroom need not be so rigidly organized as some theorists and practitioners would imply. And while many of the creators of questioning schemata would be the first to caution against using them inflexibly, many lists similar to those I have included have been abused. They have become prescriptions rather than suggestions or guidelines, and further, they have given an unrealistic picture of human discussion.

A story

I learned about that unrealistic picture in my first year of teaching. My eighth graders, spurred on by one of my more memorable students, Walter O'Brien, taught me.

I had assigned a short story from the literature anthology and, for my afternoon eighth-grade class, had to the best of my fledgling abilities prepared a lesson plan for a large-group discussion. I had questions written out and notes in the margin of my copy of the story; I was ready to start; my materials were arranged on my desk, and on the board behind me were written the date, the title of the story, and the notation "Discussion." I was organized and ready. But I really hadn't counted on my students, specifically on Walter: what I was organized for was not what happened.

The bell rang, and I moved into the hall to await my lively eighth graders. They had some three minutes to change books and classes, and they came toward me, as was customary, laughing, shoving, talking, arguing, bringing all that energy and craziness and bright-eyedness into the classroom. They were energetic and even silly and boisterous at times (the class was right after lunch), but I was coming to like this group caught somewhere between the hilarity of late childhood and the seriousness of teenhood.

Depending on their mood and personality, they entered the class, threw their books on the desk, catcalled across the room, made faces at each other, flirted, hurled insults, yawned, told jokes, smiled shyly, twirled around, stretched, pushed each other, checked hair or makeup in mirrors, and, after their fashion, got ready for the beginning of class.

The second or late bell was ready to ring, and I moved to the center of the class to begin. And then, in the midst of the din and the hubbub, Walter, who with his glasses and careful clothes looked even at thirteen like a young physician or lawyer in training, called out, "Mrs. C., Mrs. C, just tell me, *why did he do that to her?*"

Why did he do that to her? We all knew that Walter's question was about the reading, and I knew that his question was, essentially, the heart of the short story. But I was disconcerted: I had not called roll and started the class; I was not ready to begin the discussion I had planned; further, the issue of *why he had done that*, that question and the answer to it, was way down on my lesson plan for this class discussion.

But it was, I found, what the class was going to start with. People started talking to Walter, started talking to me, started answering and arguing and looking around to see others' reaction to their answers. In the space of my confusion and Walter's loud voice, the late bell rang, the students got into their seats and, virtually without me, continued arguing with one another as to just *why he had done that*. And we were off.

I think, to this day, my students thought I had somehow planned all this. They were a generous group of people and seemed to always give me the benefit of the doubt, believing implicitly that most good things that happened in the classroom were somehow my doing. But I hadn't planned this at all. I did, however, have the good sense to follow their lead, to seize the moment, to start calling on people and refereeing the discussion, to allow the chemistry to work.

Sure enough, by the end of the class, we had "covered" all the introductory questions I had in my lesson plan. We had also come to some consensus on the overall meaning of the story. We had not started where I had planned; we had not begun as I had envisioned; we had, however, started not only where the students wanted to start but with the most important question. In the middle of the discussion some students had asked about factual details—we dealt with those facts then returned to *why he had done that*. It was wholly out of "order": it also was very effective.

I chewed over that particular class again and again in my mind. While I don't recall that that exact level of excitement ever occurred again—or even in a similar pattern—I knew then that Walter O'Brien and his classmates had taught me something about questioning. In hindsight, I think they taught me to:

- Follow your students' lead—if they want to talk about something that is not in your order or on your list, let them.
- Be flexible with your questions: let a discussion have its own evolution. You don't necessarily have to start with the basic, the recall, questions.

- Don't always play it safe: students can lead a class into exciting territory, and giving them that opportunity can be one of the more valuable instructional decisions you make.

Your classes, like most classes, will be filled with such opportunities. Your job is to get your teacher antenna tuned and when it is appropriate, seize the moment.

The Questioning Circle

Years ago my friend and colleague Pat Kelly and I wrote a book on questioning. We had a good time writing and talking together, but the most exciting part of our joint writing venture was our talk about questioning hierarchies and how we felt they did not serve us or our students well. On the other hand, we knew beginning teachers needed a place to start when they constructed questions to ask in the classroom: what could we offer them?

We cooked up an alternative questioning schema, which we called "the questioning circle." We felt that this schema, nonsequential and nonhierarchical, offered a logical yet flexible format for questioning and could guide teachers in constructing questions. In the years since we wrote *Questioning: A Path to Critical Thinking*, we have heard from teachers all over the country who have used the schema in English language arts, in social studies, and in elementary classrooms.

The schema is made of three areas or circles: the **matter**, **personal reality**, and **external reality**. The first area, the matter, represents the subject of discussion or of the questioning. The second area, personal reality, represents the individual's experiences, values, and ideas. The third circle, external reality, is actually "the world": the experience, history, and concepts of other peoples and cultures.

These areas overlap—as does knowledge—and are not ordered (see the shaded areas in the diagram). In addition, there is one place where *all* the circles or areas intersect—the union of the subject, the personal experience of the individual, and the experience of others. This dense area (the black area in the diagram) contains the most significant questions, those that others might term "higher ordered," but it is absolutely open as to how and when anyone arrives at the answers that reflect the intersection of the matter, personal reality, and external reality.

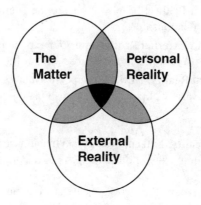

How would a teacher use the questioning circle?

I think that any discussion should contain questions not only from the three separate circles (the matter, personal reality, external reality) but also from the areas any two circles intersect (the three shaded areas) and from the area where the three circles intersect (the black area).

Let's look at the questioning circle as applied to a piece of literature. "Cold Snap" by American poet James Hearst is a brief, image-filled piece about love and loss. My students have little problem picking up on the cold and winter imagery, and they use the outline of the poem as a springboard for discussion: who of us, by thirteen or so, has not experienced a difficult personal relationship, romantic or otherwise?

Cold Snap

The winter night in your face
darkened, and sparkling stars of frost
enameled your eyes. My words
caught on a splinter of ice
and bled to death. As their last heartbeat
sang to the music of the band
my ears felt empty and now
I can't dance with anyone else
with my blood frozen by your white hands.

James Hearst
A Single Focus

Preparing to teach the poem using the questioning circle, and considering a relationship of imagery to reality, a teacher could generate the following:

White questions

Matter: What central image reveals how the speaker's words are received?

Personal Reality: How would *you* define a difficult personal relationship?

External Reality: What part does lack of communication play in relationships?

Shaded questions

Matter and Personal Reality: In what ways are the poem's images appropriate for describing a broken relationship?

Personal Reality and External Reality: Are your experiences with difficult personal relationships similar to or different from those of your friends? How?

Matter and External Reality: How are the poem's images describing a specific incident applicable to a variety of personal relationships?

Dense question

Matter, Personal Reality, External Reality: Which image in this poem do you think best expresses the complexity of difficult personal relationships?

Developing questions for other works of literature is not difficult. While you may choose to write questions for each area—white, shaded, and dense—and thus draw ideas together, the dense question, the intersection of all three, is the focal point of the discussion. In fact, asking the dense question early in the discussion allows students to respond from a variety of perspectives: the text, their personal experience as a reader, and the external reality of the world and other literature. Even if it is entirely personal, students have a basis for responding, and the discussion can build on a variety of perspectives.

Using a dense question early in a discussion can also circumvent the usual, lower-order-to-higher-order movement of a hierarchical questioning schema. The central point, the focal or dense question, need not come toward the end of a conversation at all; you can enter it early and return as the conversation extends and moves and shifts.

············· FOR YOUR JOURNAL ················

Select a piece of literature with which you are familiar and choose one part of it—a scene or chapter or similarly defined section. Think of what is *important* to you about that section and write a dense question from the questioning circle that might reflect the three components: the matter, personal reality, and external reality. Using that dense question as a touchstone, work back into the shaded and white questions. Review what you have. How broad a discussion do you think such a "set" of questions might generate? If you can get an opportunity to try out your questions with a group of students, write about how the class went.

Beyond Hierarchies: Questions You Don't Want to Ask

Whether you use the questioning circle or another questioning schema, there are a few general principles to keep in mind when you construct questions. You need to be aware of some questions that because of the way they are phrased will not encourage students to answer fully or even clearly.

Questions you *do not* want to ask include:

- **Yes/no questions:** Questions that can be answered by one word are often not interesting to answer. Further, if the answer is that "easily" delivered, maybe the question itself is rather one-dimensional. Yes/no questions also require follow-up questions that can, possibly, make your classroom seem like an interrogation, not a discussion. Consider changing a question such as:

    Is this characterization effective?

  to something more subtle, more complex, and, actually, more worth answering:

    To what extent is this characterization effective?

  Use phrases that enrich and expand the question (why, how, to what extent) and keep out of the territory of yes or no.

- **Fill-in-the-blank questions:** I have heard myself ask these, and I always wince. In the heat of a discussion, trying to get students to see one thing or one idea, you can find yourself saying,

The way to describe this passage is _____?

and pausing at the end of the question while you wait for students to come up with the answer. I have also been known to generate this lovely version:

The way to describe this passage is what?

Regardless, both versions are really asking for a single word, as if students were to literally fill in the blank of your question. What you are asking students to do is to come up with one word (your word, by the way) to fill in that blank. Not only are questions such as these difficult to understand, they also require that the students find that one exact word or phrase. That is not what we are about with questioning and discussing, and you want to change such a question to a more straightforward interrogative:

What do you think is a way to describe this passage?

You have a better chance of getting a multiplicity of answers—and, yes, perhaps not the answer you were looking for. The latter possibility, by the way, can be very exciting in a classroom.

- **Double questions:** It is hard enough to answer one question, much less two in the same sentence. It's confusing, there is too much to consider at one time, and students often don't know—or, confronted with such a question, don't care—how to answer two questions at one time. Don't let yourself ask a question such as:

What are the reasons Anna did not wish Julio to speak,
and why did Julio fail to take her advice?

Separating those two good and useful questions will be helpful to you and your students and less confusing. You would ask:

What are the reasons why Anna did not wish Julio to speak?

and then you would proceed to ask:

Why did Julio fail to take her advice?

Further, it may well be that the answer your students come up with to Anna's motivation do not lead into the question about Julio. By not "stacking and storing" your questions, you will, perhaps, be more open to adjusting to what you and your students discuss.

- **Vague questions:** We all ask them, and in your first years of teaching, regardless of your care and planning, you will ask some truly unfocused questions. It happens, but it is also something to work on. Don't let yourself ask your class:

What did Hester Prynne do?

The context is just not clear, and you need to give students guidance about what the question is addressing. Give enough pointers to lead your students into the possibility of answering and discussing. Ask when, where, at this juncture, anything that will open the specifics. Change the question to:

At this point in the novel, what did Hester Prynne do?

With such a specific, students have a better chance of answering your question.

- **Loaded questions:** English language arts teachers are famous for these, and I would surmise that you, like me, hated them as a student. They are questions that tell students that their answers, their discussion, is really not necessary because there is a set path to follow. Loaded questions include gems such as:

Why is suspense necessary in fiction?

Why do you think Arthur Miller is such a famous playwright?

Is this book average or a classic?

While you may really believe all of what I've listed—that suspense is necessary in all fiction, that Miller is indeed famous and justly so, that the book you are discussing deserves to be a classic—those are your assumptions, not your students'. By asking questions like this, you rob your classes of the opportunity to argue, to dispute, to explore. You have set what they are to discuss, and in a way you have also set how they are to discuss it. In addition, be aware that either/or questions, such as *Is this book average or a classic?* are biased toward the last choice. It would be a rare student who would choose average when the question is phrased in that manner.

Surprise can rarely operate in a classroom conversation that features questions like these. Change such questions to:

What do you think is the function of suspense in fiction?

Arthur Miller is a famous playwright; to what extent you think he deserves that fame?

What is your—or others'—definition of a classic? By that definition, how closely does this book fit that category?

·········· FOR YOUR JOURNAL ··········

For fun, let's take a Bad Questions Quiz. Look at the following awful questions and match them with the characteristics they exemplify:

BAD QUESTIONS QUIZ

Directions: Read the following awful questions and decide what is wrong with them. Place the letter of the characteristic you choose in the blank to the left of the question.

a. yes/no question   c. double question   e. loaded question
b. fill-in-the-blank question   d. vague question

_____ 1. Does the short story we have just read have a climax?

_____ 2. How is foreshadowing used effectively in *Oedipus Rex*?

_____ 3. Why is the study of dialect important?

_____ 4. The purpose of figurative language is _____.

_____ 5. How does this image work?

_____ 6. Can you tell me his name?

_____ 7. What is happening in this paragraph and why do you think it is occurring *now*?

_____ 8. Is the main character murderous?

_____ 9. What are the central issues and how do they relate to the piece as a whole?

_____ 10. The best word to describe this section is what?

Answer Key

1. a.	6. a.
2. e.	7. c.
3. e.	8. a.
4. b.	9. c.
5. d or e.	10. b.

Scoring:

If you scored 80 to 100 percent, you are ready to question effectively. Go to the head of the class!

If you scored 50 to 70 percent, you need to get back to work. Study and try again!

If you scored below 50 percent, review this section before you talk with your students!!

Questioning Behaviors

While control is an important issue in the classroom, it is often the death of questioning. When the asking and answering of questions becomes an inquisition, a challenge, a discipline measure, or just a terrifying event where one is asked to speak aloud, it is virtually impossible to move into real, productive conversation. If you have students who, for whatever reasons, cannot or do not wish to participate in a discussion, don't plan for one until they are ready. You would be setting up both yourself and them for failure. Try intermediate steps, such as having students work in pairs or in small groups until you think they would be comfortable in an all-class discussion.

If, however, you do think your students could benefit from discussion, there are some behaviors and some classroom structures of which you need to be aware.

Arrange your class so that students can see each other   If your students sit in rows so that they cannot see other students' faces, it will be difficult to maintain a large-group discussion. Rearrange your room so that the discussion, the conversation, allows the speakers to see one another's faces, not just the teacher's face. If the desks are moveable, you can place them in a square, rectangle, or circle or even in facing rows.

Learn about wait time and practice it   Wait time refers to the length of time between the asking of a question and an answer or the time between the asking of a first and then a second question. What most of you as beginning teachers fear—what you probably have in the back of your mind when you think of the difficulties of questioning—is the silence after you ask a question. Because even experienced teachers can fear that silence, the tendency is to ask, ask, ask. Remember the statistic cited in the beginning of this chapter about the number of questions teachers *thought* they asked compared with what they *actually* asked? Teachers in that study, who assumed they asked as few as twelve questions in a class, asked as many as 150. Imagine, if you can, a fifty-minute period and 150 questions: it works out to about three questions a minute, a question every twenty seconds. It is a pattern that might not be unbearable for part of a period but that could certainly be tiring if continued for almost an hour. In an article from decades ago, questioning researcher J. T. Dillon articulated it well:

> Certain studies report undesirable effects [to teacher questioning]. For example, high rates of questioning may yield negative affective outcomes, encourage student passivity and dependence and make the class appear as if it were an inquisition rather than a reasonable conversation. (217)

Give students time with their own answers   Rushing students with their answers (Yes? And then what?), either by adding too many encouraging comments or by conveying that the class and the discussion need to move on, can inhibit a conversation. Conveying calmness and establishing an unpressured environment gives students an opportunity to think and answer and encourages successful questioning. While some students come from backgrounds in which rapidity of speech and response is a sure sign of a successful conversation, not all students share that experience, and too much overlapping talk too quickly can silence them.

Give students your attention when they answer   Maintaining a certain level of eye contact with students lets them know that they have the attention of their listener. (Extensive, unbroken eye contact can be seen by some students as hostile and challenging, so you will need to adjust the degree of eye contact according to the cultural dictates of your school community.) Head nods and smiles encourage response, while head shakes and frowns generally do not. Turning away from students—even to write their response on the board or overhead—can break the flow of words. Turning toward students and keeping the upper body free of crossed arms (which can be seen as a defensive or negative gesture) can encourage a student to keep talking.

Have students talk to each other, not just to you   One way to let students know that their answers are not solely directed to the teacher is to remind students they are telling the entire class, not just you. That reminder, which should be made in a friendly manner, can be reinforced by alternating eye contact from the student speaker to the class as a whole. The speaker will usually begin, especially if he or she can see other students' faces, to talk to the whole group, not just you, the teacher. In addition, you can move to the side or back of the classroom, taking the visual focus off you and putting it on the students. You are still the teacher, but you are not in front of the classroom. If the class is discussing something— such as a list or a chart—that is on the chalkboard or an overhead, it is *doubly* sensible for you to move to the side of the room. Students can then consider the material and talk without your being between them and the material.

Exhibit a pleasant facial expression and attentive body posture   As I've mentioned, frowns, crossed arms, virtually no eye contact, and a turned back will usually make even the most determined student abbreviate his or her answer or perhaps not answer at all. Be pleasant and encouraging with your face and posture.

Be aware of the consequences of praise   Praise that is too strong can, oddly enough, be inhibiting. Most students, when told their observations are brilliant, will rarely attempt a second one; they stop while they are ahead. In addition, as odd as it may seem, continued praise from you the teacher can make a conversation a game to get teacher points. You can respond positively to comments without resorting to effusive praise.

Use student answers to extend or focus the discussion   As a section in this chapter will reinforce, using student answers in a conversation is the most powerful demonstration of the value you place on student answers. Asking a student how he or she responds to or relates to a peer's observation tells the students that their comments are valued, are important, and can focus a discussion. When students disagree, encouraging them to explore their alternative views and inviting other students to comment on each other's observations can be helpful and interesting.

Let students repeat their own answers   Related to the previous point is the issue of repeating comments that get lost in the occasional noise of a discussion. When a teacher repeats those comments, he or she takes them over. If a student wants a comment repeated, let the maker of the comment do the repetition. The more student voices—and the fewer teacher comments—are heard in a classroom discussion, the more student thinking and engagement is present. While many beginning teachers think they are actually doing students a favor by repeating their comments, it's just not so: letting students "own" their comments gives strong reinforcement to the importance of students in classroom conversation.

Watch student body language and behavior   Some of the keys to getting students to respond to one another is tuning in to their reaction during a discussion. Body language is an important key, and head nods, shakes, smiles, frowns, and shifts of position can all indicate agreement or disagreement. Using that body language to invite students to respond can be nonthreatening and also very accurate: asking Marjorie if that frown meant she had something to say, observing to Ricardo that he just nodded, did he want to comment, can work wonders in a discussion.

Make it a goal to call on *every* student in the class   It is only too easy to let the verbally aggressive students respond to most or all of the questions asked in a classroom. Either use your class roll or keep it in your head, but, in a large-group discussion, make it a general goal to have asked *every* student to respond in some way. Inadvertently, many teachers call predominantly on a handful of students, sometimes based on eagerness, sometimes based on gender. You need to make sure that you open up your discussion and issue regular invitations to talk to *all*. You may be surprised by what you get back; even if students decline to respond or talk, they know that you are interested in their participation and are not willing to let them coast through or hide in a discussion.

················· **FOR YOUR JOURNAL** ·················

Sit in the back of a class where a large-group discussion is going on and watch for behaviors I just mentioned. How many students (keep track and count them) in the class participate? How many comments (count them) are in response to teacher questions? in response to other students' comments? How long (use the class clock or count slowly in your head to measure the seconds) are student answers? How consistent (note this after each question asked) is the teacher's wait time? In general, how would you characterize the teacher's body language and facial expression? Finally, looking at your data and assessing the discussion more generally, write about whether this is a class you would have liked to participate in; why or why not?

When Questions Don't Work

Do remember that questioning is not always the best tool to use in a classroom. Some groups of students may need practice and help before they can function in a relatively orderly manner asking and answering questions. In addition, questions are not appropriate when students:

- Do not have sufficient background or information to respond or to respond well.
- Are not comfortable talking out loud in a large group or even arguing a point in a group.
- Are not at ease in your class or with each other.

Questioning can actually be threatening to students, and you need to remember your classroom context as an important determiner of the appropriateness of asking questions.

If, however, you judge that questioning is appropriate with a specific class and that your questioning behavior is also appropriate, there are some strategies you might use.

When students can't/don't/won't answer questions

When students *cannot* answer a question, it may be because what you asked is just not clear or because what you asked is too advanced. First, do think about making your questions as answerable as you can for your students. Second, be sensitive to students' preparation for the level of your question. Third, remember that not all students are comfortable with the interchange of questioning and answering; these are your quiet students who may be very on task otherwise but not active in discussion (for more information on quiet students and class discussion, see the two Townsend articles and the Greenwood article in the References section; all three are excellent).

Besides the three caveats, however, unless there is a negative chemistry working in a classroom or individual problems with a class, students' general inability to answer a question usually lies in the question or the level of the question.

When students *do not* answer questions, it is possible they did not hear the question. It is also possible they did not understand it. Using your wait time, you may want to rephrase a question as well as make sure you are audible. If you are not allowing appropriate wait time, students may not be answering questions because they are not given time to do so. Pay particular attention to the rhythm of your questioning if students are not answering.

When students *will not* answer questions, it may be that their silence is directed toward the subject or, again, toward the act of answering questions. When questioning is not an opportunity to explore but an occasion of tension and anxiety for your students, you should change your approach and avoid direct questioning. When students are more comfortable talking in the class, they will answer questions.

When students give short answers or wrong answers to questions

Short answers are relatively easy to deal with. First of all, make sure you are not asking questions that call for one-word answers; if you are asking for a single piece of information, you are likely to get just that information. On the other hand, questions that ask for extensive information usually get extensive answers. If you are asking questions that should elicit more than one word but students are still giving short answers, address follow-up questions (to the same student) such as:

- Why do you think that?
- How is that true?
- Could you give us an example that illustrates that?
- How would you compare your answer with John's (or Felicia's or any other student's)?

And, again, make sure that your questioning behavior encourages extensive answers. You may unconsciously be hurrying students along or even cutting them off by your own behavior.

Wrong answers are, frankly, tough to deal with. When students try to discuss and attempt an answer, we as teachers are often very distressed to tell students that their answer is incorrect. An obvious solution is not to ask questions that have right or wrong answers. That solution, however, is not foolproof, since even opinion and judgment involve fact and detail. We can, however, make a more concerted effort to ask students to explore options and weigh opinions rather than to determine right and wrong.

When students are incorrect in their answers, honesty is the best policy. If you give the outward impression that every student answer is right in varying degrees, you are not being fair. "No, I don't think so" or "I'm not sure" are gentle ways of telling students they are in error. Also, when a student response is misguided or mistaken, there is often alternative evidence available. If, for example, a student feels that a minor character is actually the hero of the play, it is better to point out a specific passage challenging the contention and ask the student how the passage relates to his or her point than to tell the student, "No, you're wrong." And allowing students off the hook because they retreat behind "well, it's my opinion," may be tempting, but often it is not appropriate. When students are just out and out wrong, a teacher, like Lauren Dean, has to indicate such:

> There are times . . . when opinions have high value [but I also] enforce the idea that students need to anchor their arguments in facts, quotes, statistics, etc. [Some of my students, though] do not understand the idea that they may simply be wrong. When comparing the Globe to the Dionysian Theater, I had one student say that the Globe had a small stage, was indoors and only attended by poor people—despite the extensive reading on the Globe and my personal testimony about studying there! When I [refuted this] . . . the student claimed that that was his opinion! Another student questioned a definition I [indicated was wrong]. She said, "Well that is what I studied." I responded that I am sorry she studied only part of the definition, but that *satire* did not mean "human weakness," but it is writing that ridicules human weakness, vice or folly to bring about social reform. She looked at me as if I had insulted her.

Finally, moving without comment from a student's wrong answer to another student who you think will supply a correct answer can create problems. Such an abrupt shift may make the first student feel ignored and may in essence place the student providing the "correct" answer in an awkward position. You may want to ask someone else the same question a student has answered incorrectly, but you owe the first student a response and an acknowledgment.

Questions That Students Ask

If the teacher is the only one to ask questions, the process of questioning can be seen as a measure of teacher dominance, inhibiting any student-centered learning environment and encouraging student passivity. The teacher as the only questioner then becomes the arbiter of all answers and classroom concerns, a role that is not only tiring but that does not foster student learning.

Many teachers would like students to generate questions, but teachers need to help the process along. Consider the following techniques:

- **Asking students to write questions for discussion and then using those questions can help students take charge of their learning.**
- **Asking students to write questions for study, for quizzes, or for tests and then using those questions can also help students take charge of their learning.**
- **Turning student comments into questions for other students can be a powerful indicator that you, the teacher, consider student questions important. It also makes the student question the focus.**
- **Encouraging students to question by making an absurd or contradictory statement can also stimulate student questions.**
- **Using questioning games such as *Solve the Situation, What's the Question?, Picture Perfect, or Twenty Questions* can help stimulate student questions (see Christenbury and Kelly, 28–33).**

When students start asking questions in your classroom, it is powerful and useful; breaking their silence and encouraging them to ask questions is one of the more valuable things we can do in the classroom.

Virginia Woolf's novel *To the Lighthouse* contains an image I think of when talking with a class. It is the dining room scene (125 ff.) in which the intelligent and sensitive Mrs. Ramsey, unobtrusively presiding over the table, watches and orchestrates and brings out all the disparate members gathered in her house, some of whom are her children and relatives, some of whom are her guests. There is some tension and conflict in the room; the group is not a homogeneous or even harmonious one. Mrs. Ramsey knows, as the dinner begins, that some individuals feel ignored or patronized or unimportant. But with a glance here, a question there, an encouraging smile when appropriate, Mrs. Ramsey watches over the group, gradually getting them to talk with one another and respond to one another, allowing each his or her turn. Using voice and eyes and words, somewhat as we do as teachers, she creates the ground for conversation, "the whole of the effort of merging and flowing and creating rested on her" (126). And as we do as teachers, Mrs. Ramsey asks the questions, gets others to answer, notices, encourages, bides her time. We are, both male and female, Mrs. Ramsey;

we watch over the dining room table of our classrooms. And the talk that we encourage there can be the stuff of life.

················· **FOR YOUR JOURNAL** ·················

Think about your school history and the asking and answering of questions. Can you describe any questions you wanted to ask in class but didn't? couldn't? Why did you hesitate? Can you describe times when you asked a question that surprised even you? In your classroom as an English language arts teacher, what will your policy be on the asking and answering of questions? How orderly do you want the process to be? how unorderly? Why? What are the kinds of behaviors or remarks that would tend to make you want to terminate a large-group discussion? Why? What behaviors or remarks would tend to make you think the large-group discussion is successful? Why?

References

Christenbury, Leila, and Patricia P. Kelly. *Questioning: A Path to Critical Thinking*. Urbana, IL: NCTE, 1983.

Cuban, Larry. *How Teachers Taught: Constancy and Change in American Classrooms 1880–1900*. 2d ed. New York: Teachers College Press, 1993.

Dillon, J. T. "Alternatives to Questioning." *High School Journal* 62 (February 1979): 217–22.

Hearst, James. "Cold Snap." *A Single Focus*, 56. Prairie du Chien, WI: The Prairie Press, 1967.

Greenwood, Cathleen S. "The Quiet Girls." *English Journal* 86 (October 1997): 82–86.

Townsend, Jane S. "Silent Voices: What Happens to Quiet Students During Classroom Discussions?" *English Journal* 87 (February 1998): 72–80.

Townsend, Jane S., and Danling Fu. "Quiet Students Across Cultures and Contexts." *English Education* 31 (October 1998): 4–19.

Woolf, Virginia. *To the Lighthouse*. New York: Harcourt, Brace & World, 1927.

9

Media Literacy

Equal education [in media] must be about more than the number of DSL lines in a building or computers in a classroom; it must extend to the experiences teachers offer students.

—**Kylene Beers,** *Voices from the Middle*

In school and society we swim in a sea of media, and it saturates almost all aspects of our lives. Through the radios and CD players in our cars, the televisions in our houses, the films we either travel to see or rent from a video store or through the mail, and in particular through the PCs we have in our homes, we are inundated by media and the popular culture it brings to us. And inside school is often just as media-heavy as outside. Though the funding and access may be uneven across states and school districts, the increasing use of laptops both by teachers and students in the classroom, electronic catalogs and databases in the media center, the presence of camcorders and VCRs, the use of television to transmit school and other news is a daily reality in many high schools and middle schools. Extensive electronic educational networks and a variety of databases for computers and satellite dishes for television reception link even the most remote schools to a much wider world.

Through these many outlets we learn, with a startling degree of ease, the latest details of world crises, the newest testimony in corporate scandal trials, the day's international currency rates, the developments in recent political scandals, and even the current Hollywood gossip. And while some members of the public assume that many English teachers ignore media in their personal lives—too busy rereading our Shakespeare to go to the latest movie, log on the Internet, or watch reruns of our favorite shows through TIVO—such is not true of most of us. We as a group are often as avid consumers of media and popular culture as any other, and many of us use and enjoy media extensively.

And this is lucky, for here and now we are teaching young people, most of whom are cutting-edge consumers of media. Consider the following statistics, gathered in late 2005 by the Pew Internet and American Life Project and the Kaiser Foundation and reported by the *New York Times*:

- More than half of teenage Internet users go online daily, an increase of almost 10 percent since 2000;

- The total daily amount of teen exposure to media content is now 8.5 hours a day, up from 7.5 hours a day in 2004;
- The average multitasking teenager spends three hours a day watching television; two hours listening to music; one hour on the computer outside of homework; just under an hour playing video games. (Navarro 2005)

And, from other recent studies:

- 25 percent of all online teens use Instant Messaging as their main communication tool. (Zucco 2003 as cited in Lewis and Fabos)
- Instant Messaging use among young people has surpassed that of other forms of communication, including chat rooms (Herring 2004 as cited in Lewis and Fabos).

While the number of hours may be impressive, as is the range of young people's interest in media, *consuming*, however, does not always mean carefully *selecting*, and many of our students need opportunities to become savvy about what they see, what they are invited to believe, and on what they choose to spend their time and money. In short, our students need to become *media literate*. And this is where we come in.

Issues in Media Literacy

When we consider media literacy, our students, and the classroom, there are a number of issues of importance. Among them are: **access**, **integration**, **issues regarding the Internet**, and **teacher competence**. Of all of these issues, access and integration are the most pressing challenges to today's English teacher.

Access

While almost all school districts and states have technology standards that detail how and when students are expected to be able to perform certain skills—such as using resources from the Internet for a research paper, creating a PowerPoint presentation, sending and receiving e-mails, or analyzing an ad campaign on television—it is not a given that every school has sufficient media to support such activities. A computer lab that is open only on a limited basis, a media center that has only a handful of camcorders or digital cameras with which to complete projects, a single available classroom that is "wired" to showcase a PowerPoint presentation can set up frustration for English teachers—and their students.

In addition, while it might appear from the popular press that most schools have up-to-date, if not completely sufficient media, you may find yourself in a school or school district where working and current computers and other media are the exception, not the rule. In particular with computers, many schools still struggle with obsolete hardware and software, restricted Internet availability, and few working printers. While some schools are now issuing laptops to all their students, it has not become the norm, and you may teach in a school where computers are not readily available.

Another crucial area regarding media is that of technological support. For numbers of less generously supported schools, there is often only one or two people who "do" media-based teaching, only one person who has the experience and the expertise to help teachers adapt and change their lessons and incorporate media. Even the most eager of teachers can become quickly discouraged when there is, frankly, no one readily available to whom to turn for advice and direction.

Accordingly, one thing you need to consider before you require media components as part of your projects and assignments is access: will students be able to complete the project using the available media from the school? Will certain adjustments—in deadlines or in assignment details—need to be made? What support will you need to craft the assignment? Being realistic about what is available in your school setting will help both you and your students avoid unnecessary failure.

And access is important not just for planning issues and avoiding frustration: it is also an ethical issue. Students from wealthier homes are more likely to have and bring computer knowledge and skills to school. For students whose families can afford personal computers and Internet access at home, there is a familiarity with media that carries over well into school assignments. That familiarity, however, is not equally distributed among our students.

The implications are clear: not only do we need, as teachers, to make sure that the technology is available in our schools when we assign the use of media, we also need to remember that the use of technology and the ease of that use will also be influenced by what is at home.

We, as teachers, can work to ameliorate these circumstances. In fact, one of the real worries of educators regarding technology standards is the difficulty regarding access: holding students to standards regarding media is next to useless if they do not have an opportunity to use that media on a regular basis. And as the opening quotation to this chapter suggests, it is we, the teachers, who will provide that experience, not just the presence of DSL lines or computers.

Integration

As tempting as it is to use media in almost all assignments, you need also to keep in mind what media itself can best accomplish. While certain media skills are not negotiable in today's world—all students should be able to download information from the Internet, for instance, and use a word processor—it may be that having every student create a spreadsheet or make their own homepage is just not necessary within the context of our classes. For instance, it could be that the research project needs only half of its sources from the Internet, not every source. It might be that all final presentations do not require PowerPoint. When, on the other hand, media helps illumine a point or provide information and presentation that is otherwise not possible, it can be invaluable—and integral—to your students' work. Look at your media requirements and resources and ask yourself to what extent the use of technology supports the concept or the skills that are your goals in the classroom. While using media may be the right choice, in some instances, the use of electronic media may not be truly appropriate.

Further, in many low socioeconomic school settings, computers are used extensively for remediation and skill reinforcement whereas in more well-funded schools with wealthier students, computers are used to gather an analyze information, reports *Voices from the Middle*. Its editor, Kylene Beers, frets:

> In other words, poorer students are being shown the least powerful ways to use technology. I worry that this digital divide reflects a belief that poorer students—most often our students of color—cannot "handle" or grasp higher-level thinking but must be drilled in basic skills. (5)

Thus the use of media in our classes is not an answer in itself. We as teachers need to help students understand how to select, evaluate, and judiciously integrate media into their work. Otherwise, media becomes merely a glitzy toy. Consider this story from my student Valerie Schwartz, who observed the following in a local school and wrote about it in her journal. It illumines not only the difficulties that can routinely happen with the use of technology—and, in this case, a very low-level form of technology—but, more to the point, a questionable use of technology in the first place. The teacher is determined and resourceful, but we have to ask to what end. Valerie writes:

> Did someone say technical difficulties? Today, my cooperating teacher attempted to listen to "The Pardoner's Tale" on CD and was met with some debilitating technical difficulties. One of the companion resources that comes with the literature textbook is a package of CDs with selected readings; however, most of the selected readings are incomplete and only provide excerpts. Thus, the reading for "The Pardoner's Tale" was incomplete. Regardless, my cooperating teacher decided to use this piece of technology.
>
> In the middle of the reading of the tale, the CD started skipping. As the teacher took the CD out to look at it, she realized that the whole CD was cracked and of no use. My teacher remembered that she had lent out the CD to another teacher last year and figured that he must have broken it. She then sent a student to another teacher in search for the CD (all of the English teachers have this CD, apparently), and the student brought back a burned copy of the CD. Of course, this copy wouldn't play in the CD player.
>
> At this point, the teacher told the students to pull out their independent reading books and read while she fixed the problem. While she sent a student to the library to get a CD player that would play a copy of a CD, I suggested that she try the CD in the computer. She tried this, but come to find out the media software on the computer was not working properly. Finally, the student came back with the CD player, which the teacher tested and got to work properly. She had to fast forward to where the students left off, but did so with the volume turned way down so as to not disturb the students' reading. After about twenty minutes of this, the class continued listening to the tale until it abruptly ended. Flustered, the teacher decided to finish the tale by reading it aloud.

What is the point of this story? Valerie goes on to speculate:

> While I am a huge advocate for the use of technology, it must be used with purpose. At the beginning of the class, I found myself wondering why the teacher would even use the CD recording because I knew that the reading was incomplete. The class rarely listens to selected readings on CDs, and they seem to understand the readings just fine, so what purpose was listening to the selected reading of "The Pardoner's Tale" serving? Was this use of technology really going to help clarify the reading in a way that it couldn't be clarified otherwise? Furthermore, why wasn't there a backup plan for technical difficulties? Okay—the students reading independently, but what did that have to do with "The Pardoner's Tale"? Wouldn't reading a totally different selection for twenty minutes in the middle of a lesson on "The Pardoner's Tale" break any momentum and interest that was building prior to the difficulties? And why wasn't the crack in the CD noticed prior to the execution of the lesson? Shouldn't it have been tested to make sure it worked?

Valerie may be asking many more questions than are realistic, but her major point, the judicious use of media, is important. Technology expert and English teacher Sara B. Kajder insists: "If using a technology doesn't take student readers and writers beyond what they can do without it, don't use it!" ("Plugging In," 7). There is, certainly, a built-in appeal to much of technology—as an example, using PowerPoint can be more fun than using an overhead transparency; listening to a professional recording on a CD may be seen as superior to reading in class by teachers and students—but neither is magic and often convey no more information of and by itself; it just conveys it in a different format.

And format will not solve essential teaching and learning issues: students can soon weary of sitting in front of computer screens if they are not given instruction, reasons, and help. Even the best software does not automatically help someone find ideas for writing or know when or how to revise. Spell check and grammar checks are not foolproof solutions to correctness. Access to numerous databases or the Internet does not frame a research question. A library of videos will not automatically solve a problem interpreting a text.

Thus technology is a tool, not a solution. To make technology integral, not just ancillary, we need to think about what can be accomplished through technology that is not otherwise achievable. And, when we use technology, we need to guide and help students understand what the limits might be.

Issues regarding the Internet

The ever-expanding, increasingly influential Internet can be wild and woolly territory. The information highway has some dangerous detours where individuals post salacious, false, illegal, and pornographic information. While almost all schools have blocks on inappropriate websites—most of which involve explicit sexual content or other questionable information—there is no foolproof filter for the myriad of information on the Net, and it is tempting for students to read and internalize much of what they see on an attractive or official-looking website. Much partial information and misinformation is conveyed electronically, and students need to be skeptical and thoughtful regarding what they might encounter. While certainly no one wants to censor totally students' access to websites, the issue takes on increasing importance as the Internet expands and is accessible in school.

Students, accordingly, need to be aware of hoaxes and other questionable content, which, despite their presence on the World Wide Web, have little else to recommend them. Even Wikipedia, the free online encyclopedia that is one of the world's busiest websites, has become the victim of a hoax in which the father of a popular newscaster was implicated in a Wikipedia entry as being involved in the Kennedy assassination (Seigenthaler 2005). It took some months, but the journalist tracked down the author of the libelous—and false—entry and had it removed.

Teacher Marguerite M. McGlinn wrote this warning over ten years ago, but it still rings true:

> There is no librarian for the Internet. A government-established mega network, the Internet provides a matrix for commercial, corporate, government, and educational networks . . . [millions of] computers currently access the Net, and, unlike a library, the users are adding as well as reading information. A user must judge the validity of the information and be able to distinguish among data, opinions, and interpretations. (46)

To combat the problem of students accessing inappropriate websites, most school systems have crafted official documents termed Acceptable Use Policies. These detail, both for the protection of students and teachers, what types of websites are deemed inappropriate by the school system. A successful Acceptable Use Policy provides guidance, direction, and details regarding consequences for inappropriate use of the Internet—ask about your school's policy before you require students to go on the Web. It may save you and your students some trouble. In addition, as teacher Jeff Wilhelm insists (2004), students can evaluate websites in a more formal manner where they assess design, content, technological elements, and, in particular, credibility (a contact person is noted; the links are current; the host school or institution is cited). See the end of this chapter for some resources for websites that will help students with this evaluation.

As another topic (and addressed in Chapter 7 in the Research Paper section), students can be lulled, particularly regarding projects, into thinking that finding and downloading information, cutting and pasting it, and adding some graphics are viable substitutes for the time-consuming—and often tedious—process of research. As with print matter, students need to reword and remake information, not just cobble it together and call it original research. Otherwise, as with books and articles, such unattributed copying is plagiarism: the issues are the same with electronic sources as with print ones. And sometimes it is not deliberate plagiarism but just a misplaced confidence that if it is on the Internet, it is official and sufficient. For instance, when I returned to teach high school, my students did a research paper, and one of their first steps was to provide a sketch of their topic. One student, who wanted to write on fast food in America, submitted as her outline the first two screens of the McDonald's corporation website. It looked great—bullets, pictures, graphics—but it was nowhere near adequate as a topic outline. When I had my conference with the student, she was more than a little surprised that the website pages were not acceptable, but we talked about the limits of the information and what she, on her own, needed to provide.

Teacher competence

And if much of the discussion of media is a bit disheartening to you, if you feel you are not up to speed in this area, do remember that this is the one place where your students will know as much or more than you do. While you might have been playing video games and surfing the Net during high school and college, you also may be one of those for whom the world of media is relatively uncharted territory. In fact, your familiarity with the electronic world will most likely be directly related to your chronological age. Regardless, many of our students are highly adept regarding electronic and visual media, and asking them to serve as tutors, consult with lesson planning, and provide targeted help to peers during class time can not only make your life easier—it can reinforce, once again, that students can be experts, too. In this area, that is not just wishful thinking; it is a reality.

Computers

Compared to five years ago, my office phone rarely rings, and I receive probably less than a dozen letters a week—most all of my professional communication is electronic. Every day I write in response to messages from the listservs to which I belong, and I correspond with numbers of people, both personal and professional, through e-mail and Instant Messaging. And almost every day I go on the Internet to browse and to check out favorite, bookmarked sites. Through databases on CD-ROMs I look up rationales for challenged books and information on authors. And using my computer to acquire information this way is not just self-indulgent: at this point most of the teaching organizations to which I belong (both state and national) put all of their information in electronic format. If I want to know the names and addresses of officers, the upcoming publications, a preview of conferences, I use my computer. It is no longer optional.

In my teaching life, on my computer I create tests, handouts, charts, and material for overhead transparencies and PowerPoint. Each course I teach has its own site, and there I post documents, make announcements, and hold discussions on our electronic discussion board. Similarly, when I went back to teach high school, I posted my lesson plans and announcements on a personal school-sponsored website and corresponded both with parents and students by school e-mail. Under a recent, tight deadline, I need to write a report with a colleague who teaches in another state. We arranged a time and chatted on speakerphone, and as we talked I keyboarded our ideas. While talking I e-mailed to her our first draft; we revised and changed that draft as we continued to talk. After a few hours and three document drafts e-mailed back and forth to each other, we finished our report together and met the deadline handily.

This is the world now, and it is a far cry from even a few years ago. As an English language arts teacher, this is also your world and that of your students, and while you may not use every aspect of the electronic resources available to you, you will need, in your planning and your teaching, to work with computers.

Word processing

This is the most frequent and most visible use of computers in the schools, and the ability of most word processing programs to help students get their ideas on record quickly, cleanly, and efficiently has transformed student writing. With word processing, the thorny issues of handwriting and manuscript presentation become far less important; also programs that spell check and suggest usage changes help students make improvement to their text. Moving, deleting, and adding material is simple with word processing and, for some students, inspires more revision. While in your classroom you may still have students writing by hand for some assignments (and it is maddening that almost all standardized timed writing tests must be handwritten), for final draft papers, word processing is at this point an essential life skill.

There are many aspects of word processing that are of interest to you and your students. Among them are:

- **Spell check:** this feature can catch misspellings that even the most eagle of eyes miss. Spell check, though, is not at all foolproof. Having students investigate spell check can be most illuminative. Spell check explorations can help students see how homonyms are often not caught by spell check (*to/too/two*, *their* and *there*), and how, if they are not careful, through spell check they can inadvertently substitute words that, while correctly spelled, don't make much sense in context. I do not agree with those who feel that spell check—and even usage checkers—makes students lazy and inattentive. They are modern tools of word processing and, used intelligently, produce cleaner final draft copy.

- **Word count:** many word processing programs will tell students the total number of words in a document (or even part of a document), and, if your assignment requires specific word minimums or maximums, this feature is a great tool. It is also an accuracy checker: certainly with word processing students can enlarge typeface and increase leading (the space between lines) and, as a result, one student's four-page essay may actually have far fewer words than another student's two-page essay. If the number of words in an assignment is important to you or your students, this feature can be very useful.

- **Readability** is a bit thornier of an issue as readability measures that are incorporated into word processing programs are based on number of syllables per word and number of words per sentence. In the case of syllable count as a measure of text difficulty, it is assumed that multisyllabic words are more difficult; this principle may be well confirmed by the comparison of the four-syllable *nefarious* as compared to the one-syllable *bad*; clearly, the latter is the more common word and one that is understandable by even younger readers. But what, however, about the two-syllable word *arcane* and the four-syllable word *information*? In this case, few readers would know the meaning of the deceptively simple *arcane* while even the youngest reader understands the sense of *information*. The other readability measure, length of sentence, is a similarly flawed determiner. Simple sentences linked by conjunctions can be very long—but are not necessarily complex (*I got up and went into the kitchen and fixed my breakfast*). Compare that twelve-word sentence to a two-word example, the paradox *Life kills*. In this case, comprehension is easier with the longer sentence.

    Thus, neither number of syllables or number of words per sentence provides a foolproof indication of text difficulty, and therefore a readability rating may be deceptive. Students need to know the bases for readability measures and use the information the software program provides with some skepticism.

- **Format:** desktop publishing has made available to all of us new typefaces, new type sizes, text markers such as bullets and stars, **bolding**, *italics*, <u>underlining</u>, and other kinds of graphic bells and whistles. Some of these wonderful devices make text more readable and clear; some interfere. Your students should experiment but also should know that some kinds of graphics, not to mention typefaces and type sizes, are distractions, not aids:

    Like this passage, which is both too small and is printed in a virtually unreadable typeface.

    (translation: Like this passage, which is both too small and is printed in a virtually unreadable typeface.)

With those cautions aside, however, your students may enjoy desktop publishing immensely: the software programs PageMaker and Quark can help with page layout, Illustrator and Freehand can help with drawing, and PhotoShop can help students illustrate multigenre papers with photographs they load on to the computer. There is, in fact, no end to the many enhancements students can incorporate into their manuscripts. Actually, the use of restraint and good taste is probably more of a challenge.

E-mail

Almost all schools today have e-mail connections within and without the school community, and students can use these connections to correspond with class members, other students in school, and even those outside the school. While the Pew Internet and American Life Project found that 75 percent of teenagers instant message online, making it "the digital communication backbone of teens' daily lives" (Navarro 2005), e-mail is a bit more formal, and students need to know that they must expand beyond instant messaging and even text messaging on their cell phones. Teaching students the basics—addresses, content, brevity, courtesy (known as Netiquette)—is important, and some of these basics are a bit different from what students may be familiar with when they instant message their friends. Being able to write courteously, coherently, and well in an e-mail, addressed perhaps to someone who is not an acquaintance or a friend, is a life skill that most students need—

experiencing it in your class will help students adjust to the use of e-mail in their lives after graduation.

Electronic books (e-books)

Numbers of classic and contemporary books are now available electronically, mostly through CD-ROMs. For instance, the poetry of Robert Frost, the novels of Mark Twain, and Shakespeare's plays are all available on CD-ROMs. The advantage of using electronic books is that they come with graphics, music, and even hypertext (links within the text itself that can "carry" a reader into another, related area such as the author's life, time, and literary influences). As another feature, students can search for important recurring words and phrases in a text, a process that is very tedious to do by hand but is far simpler when a text is in an electronic format.

In addition, Project Gutenberg (www.gutenberg.org) has also transformed thousands of paper books into electronic ones, which are available on the Web. For some students, not otherwise interested in a classic work, an electronic format might be appealing and interesting, and an electronic book can thus be more accessible than a printed one.

The Internet

The origins of the Internet extend back forty-five years as a military communication system. The Internet has evolved, over time, into a system for different computers to communicate with each other; it is, as technology expert Sara B. Kajder calls it in *The Tech-Savvy English Classroom*, "a worldwide network of networks" (49). Twenty-five years ago, the Internet took the shape that now is a bit more familiar, the largest electronic network in the world and home to hypertext documents that, through links, provide a huge, interconnected "web" of research, communication, entertainment, and shopping.

In school, too, the Internet is the key to the World Wide Web (also known as the Web and the origin of the www you see in website addresses). Using graphic Web browsers, such as Netscape and Microsoft's Internet Explorer, can help students view websites. Further, Web investigation is made easier by search engines (such as Google and Yahoo!) that can yield thousands of sites related to the topic of interest. Through websites, students can find many great sources of information: there are sites for literary figures, historical eras, scientific, athletic, and cultural topics, almost anything one could imagine.

While sites on the World Wide Web can be used very successfully to complete research projects on common topics, along with traditional subjects, it is also possible to help students become more comfortable with the Web by asking them to find answers to relatively unknown subjects. Teachers Stephen Tchudi and Diana Mitchell suggest a scavenger hunt where students "choose four or five relatively obscure or difficult questions . . . [such as] where will the national bowling championships be held next year? How much does it cost to send airmail *from* England? What's today's newspaper headline in Moscow or Johannesburg?" (351). Finding the answers to these kinds of questions, not just information about Byron or the Jazz Age, can help students expand their expertise on the Web.

Again, however, one serious issue about using the Web for research is its undeniable ease; students can plagiarize quickly. Deciding how you will approach these issues is important when you ask your students to use the Web as part of their research. Asking students to provide copies of their sources, giving students guidelines regarding reputable websites, and even requiring students to mix both traditional print and electronic sources can all address some of these issues.

WebQuests

The WebQuest incorporates research and furthers student learning; it is one of the richest activities that we can do electronically. Students can read websites, create hyperlinks, scan and download photos, and otherwise enrich the standard research project with all the many resources the Web can provide. One drawback of WebQuests, however, is that, if you create your own WebQuest rather than use one already posted online, it is tough on teacher time. Constructing an original WebQuest means that you have to do significant legwork before you set up an assignment and investigate sites to which you will direct your students. And, unlike research you might normally do for a literature or language unit, you will need to check and recheck sites every time you revisit this WebQuest as sites will rapidly morph, change, or even disappear from the Web. But that's the bad news. There is, actually, plenty of good news.

Let's take a look at topics and procedures for WebQuests.

Topics that your students might want to pursue should be topics where the kind of up-to-the-minute information found on the Web is important. For instance, my student who wanted to research the fast food industry (and this was part of an American culture unit) would find a WebQuest really helpful. Someone who was interested in the origin of haiku, however, would probably find the information in print sources just as readily. The topic needs to have a connection to the kind of information found on the Internet; otherwise, an encyclopedia online or in print would be just as helpful.

General procedures for WebQuests involve keeping students on task and in bounds. For that reason, in particular, it is important that students who pursue a topic be given a menu of sites to which they need to refer. Otherwise they not only may get lost in the research—think of the number of sites which usually can refer in some way to any topic—but they may also be sorely tempted to check out the latest NASCAR statistics or celebrity gossip on the Web. Also, because you do not necessarily want to manage over twenty-five or more individual quests, it is helpful to have students work in groups; for a WebQuest whose task is the development of an educational, interactive website on a specific issue, teacher Sara B. Kajder designated team manager, archive manager, content specialist, and Web designer as four roles students could take (*Tech-Savvy*, 83 ff.).

Specific procedures, beyond the general ones above, involve an **Introduction**; a **Task** (which could be a PowerPoint or a website, a writing activity); a **Process** (how the students should approach this task, what roles they might take); **Resources** (these should be preselected by you and can also include other print and film materials); **Evaluation** so that students know how they will be judged; and a **concluding presentation** so that students can share their WebQuests within the class or beyond.

Listservs and chat rooms

Listservs are electronic communities where everyone on the list receives messages that any individual posts or sends; a chat room is a stable site that anyone can enter and post messages. Regarding both, there is a continuing discussion that can include the mundane and the very weighty. Asking students to join one of the many school-related listservs and chat rooms for a period of time and to keep track of what happens on that listserv can be a useful and profitable project.

New Jersey teachers Elaine Insinnia and Eileen Clary Skarecki use teacher-sponsored chat rooms and discussions with their students and list the advantages:

- Absent students participate in class discussions from home (or read the saved chat).
- Reticent students answer without fear.

- Thoughtful students express opinions without the discussion boomeranging to a new topic.
- Teachers "listen" to all students, not just the most vociferous one.
- All students "hear" the question—no repetition necessary.
- Students stay engaged and focused for longer amounts of time.
- Teachers and students have a record of discussions.
- Students' recall of facts improves due to the visual repetition. (16)

One serious caution: there are less than reputable communities that use listservs and chat rooms to discuss topics that are not appropriate for young people or to lure the unsuspecting into sexual encounters. If you ask your student to work on listservs or enter chat rooms, be sure you review the sites beforehand so that you do not, unwittingly, send your student into some of the darker, less savory areas of the Internet.

Blogs

Blogs (or web logs) are online journals and have become increasing popular, especially through www.blogger.com/start where anyone can learn how to publish a blog that is not only free but also easy to use without knowing sophisticated coding. Today, almost 17 million blog sites are active. Currently blogs are used by a wide range of writers, and your students may not only be involved in blogging but may, with some encouragement from you, want to do more. Teacher Will Richardson uses web logs and notes:

> Web logs are as diverse as their creators. In their most common forms, Web logs act like diaries that are updated once a day or like notebooks that store information. Some serve as collectors and filters of Web content on a particular topic with potentially many entries in a single day. Most Web logs are filled with hyperlinks to other Internet sites, and they allow commentary from readers . . . joining people from diverse geographic, political, and socioeconomic groups in one place. (39)

Interactive and dynamic, blogs can entice students to write more and to feel the pride of publication and interaction. While the same strictures apply regarding care in access (Richardson suggests the Web log software Manila to facilitate site security), blogs are another of the almost infinite variations that the Internet offers the English classroom and students.

·············· **FOR YOUR JOURNAL** ··············

Pick a topic in which you are interested and research and find a related WebQuest using a search engine (such as Google). You can start by entering the term *WebQuest* or by entering the topic and *WebQuest* (for example, *WebQuest and Scarlet Letter*). How do you assess this WebQuest? How difficult do you think it would be for students to do? How specific are the directions and steps? To what extent do you think this WebQuest really addresses the topic of your interest?

Television

It is not fashionable for English teachers to admit that they watch TV, but it is, for most of us, a reality. Like my students, I *do* watch TV, and it has been a part of my education. One of my first remembered literacy moments was due to TV: I recall standing on tiptoe in front of the TV screen, reaching up to trace with my finger the letters that appeared there. I was four, and while I had many books in my room and was read to constantly by my parents, TV also was also, for me, an effective vehicle for letters and words. The screen was, in its own way, magical and held, like my books, something I wanted to know.

Later, as a young child living in an area with limited cultural offerings, it was TV that brought me my first Shakespeare (I saw, on a Saturday afternoon "oldies" show, Laurence Olivier in *Richard III*), my first Arthur Miller (*All My Sons*), my first opera (I can't remember which one, but I know I liked the forceful singing, the elaborate costumes, and the drama). Television also brought to me many other less uplifting shows that delighted and intrigued me. Today, I watch news avidly and browse the ever-increasing number of channels at my disposal. TV continues to teach me.

Whether you share my views regarding TV, it is a powerful arm of media. Our students watch hours every day of talk shows, court trials, dramatic programs, reality shows, sports events, MTV, and, of course, advertisements. Rather than bewail the amount of time students invest in front of the TV set, we need to think of how we can use television in our English classroom.

For teacher Barbra S. Morris, television helps create a research community, and she suggests that students pursue specific aspects of television and then present them both orally and in a formal paper. Here is one of her scenarios:

> As a model research project, let's imagine Keith, who wants to research . . . how many close-ups occur in one quarter of a football game and what functions they serve. . . . Keith designs a coding chart so he can discriminate among persons in each close-up on screen as game play progresses. He creates columns or categories for players and coaches and fans and officials. (39)

When Keith presents his findings, he concludes that close-ups are used to shape viewers' perception of the importance of players' contributions, regardless of the actual facts of the game.

In another television project, one of Morris' students researches "how many women appear in a half hour newscast as anchors, reporters, experts, victims witnesses, and perpetrators" (41) and, using a chart, she concludes that women are just not seen regularly as experts. In a third project, Morris reports a student who creates a questionnaire that, after the viewing of a sitcom, she administers to the viewers and follows up with a discussion. All of these projects are legitimate research studies using TV and may inspire students to view critically the powerful medium of television.

Advertising also is a large part of television, and our students, by the time they graduate, will have viewed almost half a million TV commercials. Teacher Marnie Curry-Tash suggests that students consider TV ads and, as possibilities, analyze TV commercials, considering, as large questions, the role of consumerism in American society, the presence of minorities in advertisements, the use of gender stereotypes, and the connection between advertising and literature (48).

·········· **FOR YOUR JOURNAL** ··············

- TV: Pick a television series (sitcom, reality show, drama) that you particularly like and watch it over a series of three to five weeks. For each viewing, chronicle, in writing, the plot of the show (including what occurs during each segment or section), the characters, the dialogue, the set(s), and the theme or "point." Then, using your notes, analyze this show:

  Why it is a good or very good television show?

  To whom do you think this show appeals? (Be specific.)

  If you were asked, what changes would you suggest in the cast, characters, plots, sets, or themes? (Be specific.)

- MTV: MTV is a staple on the video scene. When it first appeared on television, people who enjoyed certain artists and groups were upset because they felt that any visual interpretation of a favorite song would destroy the song for them. While that feeling has faded, still, for many, the video version of a song can be wildly different from what one expects.

  Choose an artist you like a great deal and pick two or three of his or her songs or raps. Reproduce the lyrics and also write a page on each detailing what the piece is about, why you like the arrangement or instrumentation, why you think it may be some of the best of this artist's performances. Then, if you can catch the video on MTV or another music channel, view the version of the song and discuss how the visual version enhances or detracts, what you found surprising or not surprising at all about the video version, and what you would have added or taken away from the video version (camera angles, dance steps, sets, supporting characters, and so on). Because music videos are routinely rotated so that the most popular songs are the ones whose video versions are shown, be prepared to start with an artist's video and then work backward to the song and the lyrics. Videotaping the version will help you as you do your analysis and research.

Film

I confess: I adore film almost as much as books. The visual has a huge power for me, and a number of significant films have shaped my ideas and values. Many of our students, too, love film, whether they go to the local multiplex or watch DVDs for home viewing. Film is, it must be remembered, as varied as literature: some of it is truly art; some of it is geared largely for entertainment. Though most teachers are severely restricted regarding the showing of film in school—"R" ratings usually doom a class viewing in most school districts—you can still use film in your teaching.

Remember that film and literature share characteristics: theme, plot, character development, setting, climax, symbol, point of view. Further, film techniques do the same things, though in different ways, that prose description and dialogue accomplish in literature. The connections between movies and books are strong and, for some students, using the examples of film helps them appreciate and understand basic literary techniques as well as, of course, providing them with a more nuanced appreciation of film itself. Framing, focus, camera movement, lighting, sound, editing, and a director's choices are all part of the craft of film and all legitimate topics to explore when your bring a film into your classroom.

Certainly there are many films based on famous and not so famous literary works: in recent years current best-sellers as well as the novels of Jane Austen, the short stories of Annie Proulx, and many of the plays of Shakespeare have been brought to the screen. Linking these visual interpretations of literature can be excellent. But don't also forget the importance of film itself. On its own, film can provide theme, idea, and often thought-provoking pieces of work for classroom discussions. Film does not have to be linked to an established piece of literature to be worth your and your students' time.

In addition, documentaries are a rich source of film study. The entire issue of truth versus fiction is never so clearly delineated as in the documentary, and teacher John Golden in particular notes the three components of documentaries. He cites the **visual track** (self-explanatory), the **audio track** (dialogue, narration, music, and the normal background recorded during dialogue as well as sounds added to emphasize the text), and the **text track** (such as subtitles identifying speakers) of nonfiction films ("Reel," 2005). Documentaries range across topic areas: sports, music, politics, crime, history, science are all topics of documentaries that can be studied in class.

Two superior sources for film study for English teachers are William V. Costanza's *Great Films and How to Teach Them* (which also has a CD-ROM study guide for twelve films) and John Golden's *Reading in the Dark: Using Film as a Tool in the English Classroom*. The latter is one of the very best books I have ever seen on teaching film with step-by-step procedures for teaching students about film and discussing film excerpts and entire films, and I strongly recommend it.

················· **FOR YOUR JOURNAL** ·················

You can do this with your students but, first, try it yourself. Go to a movie that is popular and watch it carefully, looking for character development (and how that may relate to the actors cast in the roles), camera angles, plot development, background music, theme. After you've seen the movie, write a review (you might want to look at a newspaper for an example) detailing two things you think were very successful and two things you would have changed if you had been the director. Justify all four observations. Finally, write a paragraph telling why you think this movie has been/is so popular with your peers: what about it appeals to them? What does or does not appeal to you? If you had the power to recast the movie, who, do you think, would be more successful in the roles?

The Popular Culture and Media Literacy

In many ways, this discussion of media and the need for media literacy involves the popular culture, a force that is incredibly strong in today's society. When you think back on your own years in middle school and high school, you may remember that you were acutely aware of what was in and what was out in a variety of fields: music, video games, film, television shows. While you may have been less involved in these areas than some of your classmates, you were probably as aware then as you have ever been of what is termed popular culture.

Your students, too, are also involved in popular culture and are more likely to share common media experiences than a common novel or short story or poem. Thus media literacy is a vital part of education in and of itself. To do nothing with the Internet but use it for traditional classroom research, to only pair film with literature, to study TV largely to condemn its overuse or mindlessness are all shortsighted. To condemn the shorthand abbreviations of text and instant messaging is to ignore the utility of such communication in its own context. Media, which conveys to all of us the popular culture, is a legitimate area of study. Although it may not appeal to everyone, we need to remember that there is an entire world that is powerful and influential—and is largely unrelated to books and libraries and historical sources of English language arts.

As responsible teachers, we must use the popular culture. We must teach media literacy and bring it into the classroom rather than constantly pushing it out as if it were something beneath us and our students. Our classroom is, in many ways, the world, and media literacy is a skill that we can give our students as surely as any skill in traditional English language arts. It may be an aspect of the journey you did not anticipate, but it is, here and now, a significant part of your teaching responsibility.

················· **FOR YOUR JOURNAL** ·················

The NCTE/IRA Standards discuss media literacy in Standard 8, which urges that "Students use a variety of technological and informational resources (e.g., libraries, databases, computer networks, video) to gather and synthesize information and to create and communicate knowledge." Thinking of your own teaching, sketch out a student project that can be relatively easily accomplished for each of the categories of library, database, computer network, video. To what extent do the projects require information gathering and synthesizing that cannot be truly accomplished without that form of media? What will students learn using that form of media that would otherwise be lost?

References

Beers, Kylene. "Equality and the Digital Divide." *Voices from the Middle* 11 (March 2004): 4–5.

Costanzo, William V. *Great Films and How to Teach Them*. Urbana, IL: NCTE, 2004.

Curry-Tash, Marnie W. "The Politics of Teleliteracy and Adbusting in the Classroom." *English Journal* 87 (January 1998): 43–48.

Golden, John. *Reading in the Dark: Using Film as Tool in the English Classroom*. Urbana, IL: NCTE, 2001.

———. "Reading in the Reel World: Teaching Documentaries and Other Non-fiction Texts." Presentation at 2005 NCTE Annual Convention, Pittsburgh, PA, November 2005.

Insinnia, Elaine, and Eileen Cleary Skarecki. "Power Chatting: Lessons for Success." *Voices from the Middle* 11 (March 2004): 10–16.

Kajder, Sara B. "Plugging In: What Technology Brings to the English/Language Arts Classroom." *Voices from the Middle* 11 (March 2004): 6–9.

———. *The Tech-Savvy English Classroom*. Portland, ME: Stenhouse, 2003.

Lewis, Cynthia, and Bettina Fabos. "Instant Messaging, Literacies, and Social Identities." *Reading Research Quarterly* 40 (October/November/December 2005): 470–500.

McGlinn, Marguerite M. "Moving and Grooving on the Information Highway: One Teacher's Experience with the Internet." *English Journal* 84 (October 1995): 45–47.

Morris, Barbra S. "Toward Creating a TV Research Community in Your Classroom." *English Journal* 87 (January 1998): 38–42.

Navarro, Mireya. "Parents Fret That Dialing Up Interferes with Growing Up." *New York Times* (October 23, 2005): Section 9; 1, 10.

Richardson, Will. "Web Logs in the English Classroom: More Than Just Chat." *English Journal* 93 (September 2003): 39–43.

Seigenthaler, John. "A False Wikipedia 'Biography.'" 2005. *USA Today* (November 30): 11A.

Tchudi, Stephen, and Diana Mitchell. *Exploring and Teaching the English Language Arts*. 4th ed. New York: Longman, 1999.

Wilhelm, Jeffrey D. "Inquiring Minds Use Technology!" *Voices from the Middle* 11 (March 2004): 45–46.

Resources

Organizations for media literacy

Assembly on Media Arts, National Council of Teachers of English (publishes the newsletter *Media Matters* and sponsors workshops and sessions at NCTE conferences: contact NCTE, 1111 W. Kenyon Road, Urbana, IL 61801 or www.ncte.org).

National Telemedia Council (publishes a quarterly newsletter *Telemedium* and provides information on media literacy: contact 120 E. Wilson Street, Madison, WI 53703 or www.nationaltelemediacouncil.org).

Center for Media Literacy (publishes newsletter *Connect* and sponsors a wide range of resources for teachers: contact 3101 Ocean Boulevard, #200, Santa Monica, CA 90405 or www.medialit.org).

Association for Media Literacy is a professional organization for media literacy in Canada (contact 95 Bannatyne Drive, Toronto, Ontario M2L 2P4 or wwww.aml.ca).

The **International Society for Technology in Education** (www.iste.org) is a great site for conferences, publications, and teacher resources. The organization's journal, *Learning and Leading with Technology*, known as *L&L*, is also helpful.

The **International Visual Literacy Association** (which can be found at www.ivla.org) is also an excellent site. Their periodical, *Journal of Visual Literacy*, will give you ideas for your teaching.

Other useful websites

NCTE, the International Reading Association (IRA) and the Marco Polo Project have collaborated on a great website for lesson plans, www.readwritethink.org, where you will find superior lessons and resources.

To help students evaluate websites, check out:

Web Evaluation for Intermediate Grades (www.siec.k12.in.us/~west/edu/rubric2.htm)

Web Page Evaluation Worksheet (www.hu.mtu.edu/teachtech/search2.htm)

Evaluating Web Sites (www.ehhs.cmich.edu/~pstohrer/eval.html)

Other sites of interest (thanks to Nancy Patterson, editor, "Tech Connect," *Voices from the Middle* 11 [March 2004]: 62–63.)

Web English Teacher (www.webenglishteacher.com)

Visual Literacy (www.pomona.edu/Academics/courserelated/classprojects/Visual-lit /intro/intro.html)

10

A Question of Ethics

What makes teaching a moral endeavor is that it is, quite centrally, human action undertaken in regard to other human beings. Thus, matters of what is fair, right, just, and virtuous are always present.

—Gary Fenstermacher, *Moral Dimensions of Teaching*

The consideration of questions of morality and ethics, of right and wrong is not confined to churches and mosques and synagogues; it exists outside religious frameworks, too, notably in the schools and in teaching. "The implications for education have had to do with . . . the resolution of moral dilemmas" (119) writes educational theorist Maxine Greene, and those issues of ethics and morals relate to us as teachers. Historian Joel Spring notes:

> Whose moral and social values will permeate the American school? [Nineteenth-century American educator] Horace Mann argued that there were certain moral values that all religious groups could agree upon and that these shared values would become the backbone of the moral teachings of the school. A variety of religious groups have disagreed with this idea from the time of Mann up to the present. (13)

Yet, despite the ongoing tensions in the American public school about whose ethics, whose morals, will be directly taught or even discussed, the issue remains. Certainly not only the question of ethics in our content, as characters confront dilemmas and make choices is one issue, but so also is the act of teaching itself. Gary D. Fenstermacher observes in a book on teaching and ethics:

> Whenever a teacher asks a student to share something with another student, decides between combatants in a . . . dispute, sets procedures for who will go first, second, third, and so on, or discusses the welfare of a student with another teacher, moral considerations are present. The teacher's conduct, at all times and in all ways, is a moral matter. For that reason alone, teaching is a profoundly moral activity. (133)

We must, as teachers, be fair in our dealings with students and have classrooms where, literally, justice prevails. Further, much of what we consider in language and literature and writing also touches on issues of morality and ethics, and our classrooms should be places not only where individuals demonstrate fair behavior but also where issues of right and wrong can be discussed.

English Class as Ethics Arena?

So is English class an ethics arena? Beyond issues of the ethics of teachers and teaching itself, is there something about the subject matter that we need to also address? It seems impossible in a pluralistic society where, first, not everyone agrees on what is right and what is wrong, and where, second, the schools are secular and public in nature. Disagreement among our students and the nonreligious nature of the public school are not, however, reasons for us to avoid moral and ethical questions. While we need to be aware of prevailing community standards, we would be shortsighted as English teachers to sidestep the important issues that permeate language arts.

Thus, Brutus' choices, the actions of Huck, the decisions of Celie are all issues of ethics and morals. In *Julius Caesar*, *Huckleberry Finn*, *The Color Purple*, what were the options, the considerations, what do you think was right, was wrong, and why? For sure, you and your students will not always agree, but it seems a waste of all of our time and of the literature itself not to consider, discuss, and weigh. Our classrooms are not just for the consideration of the art of literature or the craft of language—the way dialogue reveals, imagery enhances, sentences balance—but also of content, characters who confront life and make decisions which affect themselves and those around them. How, then, do you approach literature or language using an ethical lens? While not automatic, it seems to me that such questions fall well within our discussion of content. For instance, Jonathan Swift's "A Modest Proposal" makes little sense unless the reader understands than absolute indifference of English absentee landlords toward their starving Irish tenants. Only then does Swift's savage satire, where he advocates the eating of children, have the weight it surely deserves. George Orwell's essay "Politics and the English Language" is not about word origins and sentence structure but about the power of language to distort and even corrupt the perception of reality; its critique of totalitarian regimes and language is pertinent today. The civil disobedience both Thoreau and King advocate in their writings are worth serious discussion; to what extent are their arguments pertinent to the defense of those today who break the nation's laws in the name of morality? We may feel great sympathy for the tormented Othello, manipulated and deceived by his evil lieutenant Iago, but does that excuse his murder of his innocent wife Desdemona? It is unfair that Rochester is duped into marrying a woman who had insanity in her family and who actually is now insane (and who he cannot divorce), but is his response in *Jane Eyre*, confining her indefinitely to a locked attic room, justifiable? All these questions are worth asking and while we most likely cannot—should not—enforce one group or class answer, they are important to explore and important to discuss.

To ignore or avoid what literature often addresses—the world of ethics moral choices—is to eviscerate the English class and make what we read and what we discuss divorced from reality.

Ethical Issues for the Classroom Teacher

Beyond our content, though, as the opening quotation for this chapter implies, are also ethical issues for us as professionals and teachers. The following discussions may seem preachy to you, and if so, I apologize. I want, however, to call your attention to some topics, rarely discussed in books about teaching, that will affect—and possibly tempt—you as a teacher. We have great power to do good in the classroom. We can also do great harm. Student privacy, fairness to all students, protection of students who are vulnerable, being friends with your students, and sexual ethics are five issues we need to consider.

Finally, the next-to-last section of this chapter, Breaking the Rules, addresses the scary but inevitable time when you find you must make a decision that is outside the official regulations. While it might surprise you to think that such decisions may be part of your beginning life in the classroom, they most likely will. If your career parallels that of most conscientious teachers, it is likely that very soon in your teaching career you will confront such a time when you must break the rules.

Student privacy/student rights

Along with our teaching, what we do and discuss and direct in class, is the way we deal with our students and deal with what they choose to share with us and with their peers. As English teachers we are often in a position to hear revelations of sorts from our students, stories, embellished and true, of choices, decisions, triumphs, disasters. In journals, in narratives, in classroom discussions, and in role plays, students often reveal large chunks of their lives. Some of those stories involve fairly intimate details and the public revelation of such would be a personal invasion of privacy. Some of those stories further involve legal issues that have bearing outside the classroom.

Because laws differ from state to state as do school practices, you need to inform yourself about your obligations regarding certain student revelations. Issues involving threats of suicide, drug use or sale, physical or sexual abuse, may come to your attention in your students' writing or conversation. When and how to inform the guidance staff, a building administrator, the school nurse, or school social worker of behavior that may be life threatening or illegal is something you need to investigate. Ignorance of the law is not an excuse; ask what your school policies are and act accordingly.

For example, when I returned to high school teaching, I had one young woman who was experiencing academic difficulties; I had called home a number of times to talk about Keisha's work and her inability to meet most deadlines. While Keisha's mother seemed supportive and positive on the phone, one day after my class I found on the floor a folded, handwritten note that Keisha had evidently passed to her friend Erin and which had inadvertently been dropped. I picked up the note to throw it away and also read it. In the note, Keisha complained about her mother restricting her and said that Erin just ought to see "the bruises." In my state, that is grounds for charges of child abuse, and I took the note immediately to a counselor. The counselor called Keisha in that next day to talk and arranged for an interview with Keisha's mother. Charges were not filed, but to my knowledge, at least for that semester, the abuse stopped.

As teachers, we also need to remember that students have a right not only to our respect but also to privacy. Beyond the very serious situation inadvertently shared, students may reveal other details of their lives and those of their family and friends. Tempting as it may be, we should not carry their revelations outside the school sessions for our friends' or relatives' edification or amusement. What we may consider atypical or informative or even entertaining stuff is our students' lives, and we need to honor the fact that often—and often with implicit confidence in our discretion—they share those lives with us.

Being fair to all students

None of us finds all of our students equally likeable, and we are kidding ourselves if we think we will be completely compatible with every one who comes to class. We have an obligation, however, not only to teach but to evaluate fairly everyone with whom we come into contact. We should not use assignments or grades—it is *wrong* to use assignments or grades—to punish or keep in line whomever we do not like or with whom we have a personality clash. That sort of punitive power is one of students' deepest fears—being failed or downgraded because of the teacher's personal tastes—and we should do nothing to further that fear. While we often cannot change our feelings about students, we are *not allowed* to act on them. It may not be comfortable for us as teachers, but it is part of our obligation to our students to treat all fairly and to rise above petty behavior.

For this reason, you once again need to be aware that you come from a culture and a background that espouses certain values. Further, you have a definite personality that expresses itself in certain traits. To ignore that background and your own personality, to assume that either you have no particular values or tastes or that those values and tastes are generally universal, is misleading. You will teach students with whom you have little in common, and ignorance of that fact is naive.

You cannot, of course, adopt all of the values and background and personality traits of all of your students, nor should you jettison your own values. You do need, though, to acknowledge that you will at times react both negatively and positively to students on the basis of their class and race and sex, sexual orientation, and other individual characteristics. You will also have students with whom you share unresolvable tensions, and some of those tensions may be related to personality issues. Fair or unfair, your job as a teacher is to be just, to be professional, and to look at the student as student untinged by personal antipathy.

Frankly, when I returned to teaching high school, I was surprised by my own strong reaction to some of my students. Even with all of my experience and background, I found certain individuals could inspire in me anger and irritation. Keisha, for instance, almost made me crazy, and her consistent inability—unwillingness?—to follow instructions and deadlines tempted me to be sarcastic with her when she presented yet another excuse for her work. I do think I resisted, although it was an effort. But then there was Justin, so bright in many aspects of English study, who decided research paper deadlines were meant for others, certainly not him. I did not react well to his refusal to participate, and it took me many months into the semester before I was able to overcome my early dislike of him and his dismissive attitude. I think he returned the favor. Later in the semester, when Justin's father had a near fatal accident and I had to talk to his mother on a regular basis, I became closer to Justin. His parents were divorced, he had been living with his now incapacitated father, and now he had to move back in with his mother. Justin was in a personal crisis, and it led to our talking about our mutual perceptions and responses. I felt it was important that I take responsibility for my attitude, and I told Justin so. After that discussion, we both agreed to a truce. I found that *my* perception of Justin improved, and his work actually evened out.

Like me, you are human, and you are certainly allowed to have negative feelings. You are, on the other hand, not only human but a human teacher, and the problem, the ethical dilemma, emerges when your feelings actively influence your evaluation and your interactions with students. Do not indulge yourself in making favorites or making enemies. You are in the classroom to teach all and to teach all fairly. It may be hard—you will have your own

Keisha and Justin and heaven knows who else. It may take some conscious consideration on your part, but you must, as an ethical responsibility, deal evenhandedly with all those who share the classroom.

Protecting the vulnerable

Middle school and high school can be a time when apparent difference is especially unacceptable, and students can participate in a number of negative and ultimately damaging activities that target others who appear vulnerable. While you cannot police the entire school—and sometimes you cannot police even much of the hallway outside your classroom—you can enforce, in your own space, a code of respectful and kind behavior and language. This involves your active vigilance, and while you may be reluctant to intervene, it is your obligation to assert yourself in your classroom.

Any form of bullying and hazing, either physical or verbal, should be outlawed in your class. Whether a member of the majority or minority, *no student* has the right to harass those who are of a different race, religion, gender, sexual orientation, or appearance. Mocking someone's speech or accent is unacceptable; making fun of a student's clothes or hygiene practices is not to be allowed. Cliques and groups and gangs are inescapable in most school settings, and today "Internet-enabled bullying" (Conn) is also a reality. Realistically, in school or out, there is little we can do to ensure all of our students are socially comfortable and successful. But within our own classrooms, we can indeed rule and outlaw, immediately and precisely, the kind of harassment that some students will more than willingly inflict on others and that some students, in fear, will watch silently if not approvingly. Protecting the vulnerable is part of your ethical responsibility as a teacher, and while it may not always be comfortable or make you feel wonderful, creating an environment of respect and tolerance is part of your work in the English language arts classroom.

When I returned to teaching high school, I so wanted everything to go smoothly, especially at that crucial beginning of the semester. My very first week, though, during a large-group discussion I was making a list on the board of comments students were calling out as I recorded them. It was going well, but after one student's contribution someone objected, "Oh, that's just so gay." The remark was not delivered lightly and even writing on the board with my back to the room I knew that whoever said it meant it to silence, if not to wound. Turning around to face the class, I wished with all my heart that that comment had not been made because I knew that I had, right then and there, to call the language out of bounds and to say that I never wanted, in this class, to hear it again. And so I did. Many of the students' faces registered honest surprise, and the large-group discussion quickly sputtered. I sensed some students were shocked by the rebuke and resentful. For my part, the only good news—the only important news—was that I never heard the slur again.

Being friends with your students

One of the hardest things for beginning teachers to do is to draw a line between their roles as professionals, teachers, and their understandable desire to be friendly, even friends, to students. If you are close in age to those you teach, if you come to know about their lives and care about them, it can be an even more difficult balance. For their part, students are often curious about teachers, especially young teachers, and if you are younger, your students may want to know a great deal about you and your personal life. While it is understandable, certainly in the beginning of your career, that you may feel more of a peer to your students than a teacher, you need to remember that you are now fulfilling a professional role and one that requires a necessary gulf between you and them. This is the nature of the business: friends do not give friends grades or credit for work; friends do not reprimand friends or impose sanctions for disciplinary infractions. Teachers, though, do all of these with and for their students, and it is part of your new professional life.

While being kind and supportive in class is important, you are there to teach, not to join your students' social circle. It is essential that you maintain a professional distance; students are not entitled to sensitive information about your private life, and you do not necessarily need to get involved in their private lives. You are not their mother or their father, an older sister or brother, but their teacher, and you must maintain a professional role. The balance is not always easy, but it can be done. Brian Durrett, writing at the end of his student teaching experience, notes:

> I feel that I have made a difference in the lives of some of my students. There is one in particular that has been a really tough relationship to sustain. This gentleman has had expectations of me that I could not meet because I was his teacher and not his buddy. I did not compromise my job and responsibilities to foster our friendship. I think it lasted. There was time that I think it was stronger than it has been as of late because I feel that I have had to be tough with him. In the long run, I think he will value my presence in my life, and I know that I have valued his presence in mine.

Similarly, during her semester as a student teacher, Kara Elder needed to set the record straight for one persistent student:

> One student went to far as to ask me to the prom. I first responded he must be silly. He persisted. I told him that I was his teacher, and such would not be appropriate. He didn't think it would be a big deal. I told him I was also too old and married, not to mention uncomfortable with such. He said he didn't know why. I finally got the student to drop the subject by saying if I was still around come prom time (which I probably will not be), I would try to go as a chaperone, but definitely not as his date or a peer he could hang out with once there.

And this leads us to a more serious ethical issue, that of sex and our students.

Sexual ethics and your students

When you walk down the halls of your middle school or high school as a beginning teacher and you see relatively immature, even awkward young people, some clearly with one foot still in childhood, you may wonder if I have lost my mind to even suggest that you, a teacher, could ever think of having an intimate relationship with one of your students. Even when you consider the more socially sophisticated, physically mature students you deal with, it may, early in your career, seem a sheer impossibility that you would ever think of any of them in a romantic or sexual fashion.

You may never fall in love with one of your students, but experience teaches that many of the ingredients for strong mutual attraction exist in the school. Working closely with students over a period of time, getting to know and like and trust them—and they you—your feelings about their availability and their attractiveness may undergo a marked shift.

In a culture that deifies—and sexualizes—the young, it may become hard to remember that the attractive and often appealing students you teach are not your peers and are not available for socializing and/or romance. When you spend the bulk of your time interacting with young people, you may well find yourself in a position, mutual or not, of being strongly attracted to one of your students. This happens to male and female teachers of almost all ages, to those married and unmarried, and it is a serious ethical issue in our field.

The heart has a mind of its own, and at some point in your career you may convince yourself that a relationship with one of your students is eminently justifiable. You may find yourself in a vulnerable time of your own life; the student in question may be troubled or confused or lonely or just really infatuated with you. As the daily news tells us, there are numerous cases of students and teachers falling in love, having sexual relations, even having children with each other and marrying. Some of these cases result in scandal and ruined careers and criminal charges; some of them go on to happier and even permanently happy endings. I doubt there is a school system in this country where intimate teacher/student relationships have not occurred.

The entire issue, nevertheless, is poisoned by the sheer inequality of the players. A student is never in an equal power relationship with a teacher, the latter of whom holds authority, standing, and the weight of the grade. Further, in high school and middle school, students are almost always younger than their teachers, even their young teachers, and regardless of the number of years between the two groups, teachers are generally viewed as parental or older sibling figures.

Using your power as a teacher, consciously or not, to further a sexual or romantic relationship with a student is wrong. It preys on students' vulnerability and trust; it makes school just another place where a young person can be used or exploited. Further—and very practically—states have laws prohibiting sexual relations with minors, and almost all your students will fall into that legal category. In most states, the legal penalties can be severe; in most states, teaching contracts and even certification can be terminated for such behavior, generally lumped under the rubric "moral turpitude."

In specific, touching and physical proximity are areas of concern. Often our students, male and female, will attempt close physical contact. Sometimes this is done from a sense of affection and care; sometimes it is done from a sense of curiosity and adventure. Certainly, also, some student-initiated physical contact is nothing more than an expression of veiled aggression. Regardless, you as a teacher must insist on maintaining appropriate physical space between yourself and any student. In addition, while any and all individual conferences with our students can be conducted out of earshot of others, they should never be conducted out of eyesight. Thus, meeting with a student in quiet corner of a public space— such as the media center, the school courtyard, or the cafeteria—is acceptable as is, of course, meeting with a student in a classroom with an open door. If you are alone, conferencing with a student—either of the same or different gender—behind a closed door is asking for misinterpretation.

If this talk of professional distance seems abstract, there are a few specific behaviors you can practice in the classroom that may help to ensure a healthy distance between yourself and your students:

- minimize touching students and, when in conference, meet with them in public spaces and in view of others;
- decline to share with students details of your own past or present personal life, including dating, sexual practices, or romantic involvement;
- avoid extensive personal conversations in the classroom;
- avoid in class what could be seen as flirtatious behavior and do not participate in sexually provocative conversations or jokes;
- adopt a dress that is more like the teaching staff than like the students;
- exhibit characteristics that are professional and adult.

Despite all of the cautionary nature of this discussion, however, this is not a plea for a return to some sort of puritanical past. All of us as human beings are endowed with a sexual identity. It is unrealistic to insist that you not appreciate the attractiveness of your students, that you be immune, as another human being, to their appealing natures. Our students are working on their sexual identities and practicing their personal charm, often in our classrooms and with us and their peers. We would be less than human if we did not respond, if we failed to appreciate in a very real sense their emergence as accomplished young men and women. But beyond that appreciation we must not go. Young people need to find romantic and sexual partners outside the school teaching staff, and you as a teacher need to draw a line over which no one crosses. You are in a trusted position as a teacher, and violating that trust while the student is in your charge is serious and regrettable. Admiration from a certain distance is the more honorable path. Taking care not to give students the wrong signals about your relationship with them is essential.

················· **FOR YOUR JOURNAL** ·················

Ethics is a broad field, and the topics listed in this section probably touch on only some of the issues. Identify an ethical issue that you think affects the English classroom and that is not discussed here. What is the issue? Why, in your opinion, is it important to teachers and students? What do you feel are possible guidelines for teacher/student behavior with regard to this issue?

Breaking the Rules

The idea of going against the established order of school is a tough topic, but it's one, early in your career, that I think is important for you to think about. If that institution called school always operated in our students' best interest, we as teachers would not have to ever consider breaking—or bending—school rules. Those rules can be in the areas of curriculum or discipline or just procedure, and it is part of your ethical code that you may, at some time for some good reasons or cause, have to move outside the regulations. To what extent and when and how you do this is no mild issue: breaking too many rules too blatantly will get you fired. And, of course, there are some rules, especially those regarding ethical teacher conduct, that should never be breached. Yet, you will face times in your teaching career when breaking the rules is just about the only thing to do. There are clearly risks to this, but it an area that you will need to contemplate.

I had just finished writing the first edition of this book when I was named editor of *English Journal*. I knew that my first *EJ* issue would be a crucial one, and as I planned that issue I kept coming back to a student whose story I had not included in *Making the Journey*. For some time I thought about what Ray meant to me as a teacher and why I couldn't get him out of my mind. One day it came to me that Ray's story was central to an idea I wanted to discuss, breaking the rules in school, and that idea became the theme of my first issue as editor of *EJ*.

When I asked other teachers to submit manuscripts for this issue of *EJ* and to write about a time when they had, for good reasons, broken the rules of school, they responded generously. The overall tone was struck by Carmela M. Cotter, an Ohio teacher who wrote: "Be courageous; no one ever said that teaching was 'safe'" (45). Many other articles in that issue of *EJ* stand out in my mind. One, "Culture Wars and the Rules of the English Classroom," was written by teacher F. Todd Goodson who allowed his students freedom to pursue the research topic of their choice. In Goodson's class, a student wrote a paper on WICCA, the oldest American church of witchcraft. Goodson was fully aware of how controversial the topic might be—as part of her research the student even interviewed a member of a local witches' coven—but Goodson noted that the incident with his student had broader implications:

> If this were an isolated incident, it would not be that big of a deal. In fact, however, I felt a constant tension throughout my tenure as a high school teacher—tension that was the result of the process of negotiating social boundaries of taste for students' reading and writing activities—to the point that I always felt that I was doing my most effective job as a high school English instructor when I was on the verge of getting in trouble. (21)

In fact, the idea of trouble—getting in it and staying out of it—was a theme of many of the articles. A number of teachers wrote of using censored books in class and one, Roberta C. Young, dryly remarked:

> My department chair . . . advised me not to teach [*The Outsiders*] and refused to purchase [a] class set. . . . What to do? Simple. I had one copy of the book and a door to my room that closed. (45)

Another teacher, Iona Whishaw, discussed how she bent the prevailing "English Only" rule in her school and allowed her Chinese students to use their first language in English class and to translate poetry. Teacher Melissa Whiting skirted school regulations and let her students present their original play in the school auditorium—although all assemblies had been forbidden. In another instance, teacher Sylvia Garland explained why she filled out the required interim report on her student Pete—and then threw it away. The idea of breaking the rules seemed to be a thread, too, in subsequent *EJ* issues: in an article on veteran teachers and staying in the classroom, Richard Argys wrote that it was, at least for him, difficult "to imagine an educator lasting until retirement without developing a talent for breaking rules" (63). All of these teachers are thoughtful, dedicated people, and, just as I had so many years ago with Ray, they made decisions for the best of their students, not for the best of a rule or a regulation that did not, in their professional opinion, serve their students' teaching and learning.

Breaking the rules and my student Ray

In my high school teaching, I bent many rules to reward students and to keep them encouraged *about* school, a place to some of them that was more than occasionally inhospitable. Much of this rule bending was minor stuff and was not terribly remarkable. In the case of Ray, though, I put my teaching career on the line. While I am not sure I would have the courage to do it again, it made a significant difference for one young man, and I am glad I did it.

To this day I can see Ray vividly: he was a very small, sharp-featured, blue-eyed fifteen-year-old with pale skin and hair and eyebrows so blond they were almost white. He came from a single-parent home and lived with his mother and a four-year-old sister. Ray's mother was struggling to keep the little family together and was not, frankly, doing well at it. She was prone to deep depressions and had a hard time maintaining her life, her hourly wage job, and her two children. As with many such situations, Ray, at fifteen, operated more as a peer to his mother than as a child and took increasing responsibility in the home.

How did I know any of this? I knew this because Ray was in my class and because, particularly in response to home pressures and his mother's periodic breakdowns, he would cyclically drop out of school only, when things got calmer at home, to return, hopeful that he could salvage the year and salvage his grades. He knew that his academic career was imperiled by his family issues but, like many kids in similar situations, when the issue arose about sacrificing himself or turning his back on the family, there was no question as to what he should do.

I wish I could tell you that those of us who knew why Ray came late to school, didn't come to school, dropped out of school only to return again and again were sympathetic and knowledgeable and helpful. But such is not the case at all. Ray was a ghostlike boy, pale and unassuming; he did not share much with anyone, and many of his teachers and his counselors were unaware.

Accordingly, the administration, particularly the vice principal responsible for Ray's numerous changes of status, became increasingly impatient with his pattern of attendance and dropping out. Because Ray was reticent, silent about this issue, his dropping out seemed as much about indecision as anything else. Few even suspected home responsibilities.

One memorable day, there was a climax of sorts. Ray, having dropped out twice that year, was reentering school once again. As Ray was exiting the vice principal's office after completing the latest set of forms, the vice principal followed him out into the hall. It was obvious that the vice principal had had it with Ray's most recent return to school and took the opportunity to vent his frustration. It was during a change of class, and the vice principal raised his voice at Ray's departing back and shouted at him over the noise of students *You aren't even worth the trouble you're causing.*

I was on hall duty at that change of class and saw the incident and heard it. I watched as Ray stood frozen outside the vice principal's office, both furious and humiliated. I knew Ray, watched his reaction, watched him whirl and move toward the vice principal. I immediately intervened: as small as he was physically and as calm as he usually was, it seemed clear to me that Ray was ready to assault the administrator at that very moment. I stood in front of Ray and moved him out of the hall. In the relative quiet of my classroom, Ray and I briefly discussed the incident. I, who had often silently observed that the vice principal was neither one of the most tactful nor even one of the kindest of human beings, told Ray in forceful terms that the administrator was *wrong.* It was a risky thing to tell a kid, but, at the same time, what I said was true, and both Ray and I knew it.

That was when Ray and I connected. Ray, thankfully, never quoted me. So Ray and I had a relationship and when, some months later, things got bad at home again, I was called to do something more serious than intervene in a potential assault and criticize a vice principal behind his back.

Ray's mother had collapsed again, and it seemed that the only solution was, one more time, for Ray to drop out of school and to be there, in the apartment, to take care of her and his sister. It would have, once again, put him behind, and as he was getting near the end of his junior year, it seemed hopeless that he would ever complete high school.

I talked to Ray after school; he saw no compromise. I was concerned. But what would happen, I asked him, if he went to school only part of the day and left early? Then, he would have the afternoon and night with his family. We released students after sixth period, at 2:20 P.M., but not all students had all six periods of classes. Ray had my English class fifth period. If he left right at lunch, fourth period, he could have the whole afternoon to take care of things at home and still keep his morning classes. Ray thought that those hours might be enough—but what to do with my class? We had a strict, mandated attendance policy, and if Ray missed more days, there was an automatic F with no chance of appeal. Ray needed to be marked present.

Looking back, I think I was at a crossroads in my life as a teacher. I knew that I would have to be the person to break the rules for Ray: the system, in my judgment, would just not accommodate Ray any more.

So every day for a matter of months I marked Ray present in my class although he was at home with his mother and his baby sister. The deal was that Ray would do independent written work for the class and turn it in. I would accept it and grade it as if he were present and working along with the other students. Only he and I would know that he was not *in* class at all; the other students, preoccupied with their own lives and hardly interested in the colorless Ray, were not likely to notice and not likely to turn either of us in.

And so we went for almost two months. If, indeed, the scheme had been discovered, I would have been in very serious trouble as I was deliberately lying, marking Ray present, day after day. It was not lost on me that attendance records are, in my state, virtually legal documents. I just lived on the promise and hope that Ray was a trustworthy kid who needed a break that not the school but I could provide. I also trusted that Ray would indeed turn in his written work and get grade and credit from me.

Would I ever risk this again? Most likely not; it could have ruined my career as I was clearly lying. Also, if Ray had been in an accident or discovered off school premises at a time when his teacher vowed that he was present in her class, the school—and I, his teacher— would have been liable. In my case, I think it would have been just cause for dismissal. But I did it then because I knew the school would not bend, and because, I hoped and prayed, I knew Ray. I certainly knew that he was worth the risk of breaking the rules.

And, in the end, I did know Ray. He was not a stellar student, and I cannot tell you that he went on to be a brain surgeon or that his time at home cured his mother and that everyone lived happily ever after. But Ray did return to my class, did his work, turned it in. I recall the afternoon when he handed me an inch-high sheaf of paper, done in careful handwriting and painstakingly correct and thorough. Where he had found the time to do this writing and reading, I'll never know. But Ray had fulfilled his part of the bargain, and I could tell from the expression on his face when he gave me his work folder, he felt a certain sense of accomplishment. For my part, I was incredibly relieved.

Ray passed my class, and my consistent subterfuge was never discovered. He finished the year, and he finished English 11.

Why am I sharing this story? Am I encouraging you to lie and to tell falsehoods? To make deals with kids and mark them present in your class when they are not even on school property? No, I'm not encouraging you to do that at all, but this is a teacher's story and a teacher's story about a kid and a compromise that a teacher could make and no one else could, a compromise that the school would not allow. I broke the rules, took a risk, and in my case, it worked. In larger ways and in small ways, you, too, will find yourself bending the rules and moving the regulations because you, a teacher, have a kid like Ray and a need to make a bureaucratic system of rules more flexible, more responsive, more humane.

············· **FOR YOUR JOURNAL** ·················

Despite my story of Ray, the very idea of a teacher breaking rules may strike you as unnecessary or even unethical. What is your feeling about teachers and school and curricular regulations? To what extent can you imagine a time when a teacher would be tempted to break a rule? From your perspective, what kinds of guidelines would dictate when or when not to break the rules?

Being and Becoming an Ethical Teacher

When I first began teaching, I thought I was smarter than most and, as a rule, I did not have much patience with people or, even, despite my education, much tolerance for opposing viewpoints. Some of these personal characteristics were part of being young and simultaneously both insecure and arrogant. Some of these characteristics were the product of years of being encouraged and even rewarded to be concerned about myself, my grades, my life, my career, my needs, and the endlessly fascinating *me*.

As I have tried to describe in this book, going into the classroom changed many of those characteristics. For the first time in my life and on a sustained basis I had to engage with, respond to, and meet the needs of countless others. The fact that they were shorter and younger than me didn't change the nature of their needs, and the fact that I was being paid didn't blunt the compelling aspect of the work. The people with whom I shared the classroom became, in essence, a real part of my world and my life, and I began to work as hard as I ever had to live up to their expectations and to treat them fairly and well. In direct and indirect ways my students eroded my well-developed egocentricity and asked me to open my mind, be kind, be funny, be smart, be attentive, and be patient.

And so the bulk of my life has been, in essence, in the service of my students and, along the way, I think I have had a chance to become a better person. In Cormac McCarthy's *No Country for Old Men*, he writes, "It's a life's work to see yourself for what you really are and even then you might be wrong" (295). It's a haunting statement, but for me the work of seeing myself as I am has been a bit easier because I am a teacher. These people, these students, have shaped my life and led me, through the years, to consider how and what I teach and to invite me to make ethical choices. Because of them, I continue to work on my teaching and work on myself. Through books such as this one, through the work of other teachers and your own experiences in the classroom, I wish for you a similar experience.

Our time in the classroom can be transformative in profound ways. For some, this issue becomes more than dealing with content and students in an ethical way but expands into a broader realm, that of social justice. Sonia Nieto observes:

> Teachers enter the profession for any number of reasons, but neither fame nor money nor the promise of lavish working conditions is at the top of that list. Instead . . . for many of them, social justice figures prominently among the motivating factors underlying their choice to

teach. The urge to live a life of service that entails a commitment to the ideals of democracy, fair play, and equality is strong among many of those who begin teaching. (91)

Nieto continues, though, to remind us that "teachers are not miracle workers. Nor are they social workers or missionaries." Instead, they must balance:

> Teachers need to understand their roles as involving more than simply attending to the minds of students; it also entails nurturing their hearts and souls . . . to do this without taking on the world of injustice is tricky business . . . an equilibrium that is difficult at best. (105)

Finding this equilibrium is one of the many challenges you face on the journey, and one of the most important. And remembering this aspect of our teaching, being true to it in a way, can be hard at times. While policy makers and politicians often want us to educate only for test scores and efficiency, we are—inescapably—about bigger things. Educator Marilyn Cochran-Smith makes the point:

> From a social justice perspective, the purpose of education needs to be understood not simply as constructing a system where pupils' test scores and wise monetary investments are the bottom lines. Rather, the purpose of education must also be understood as preparing students to engage in satisfying work, function as lifelong learners who can cope with the challenges of a rapidly changing global society, recognize inequities in their everyday contexts, and join with others to challenge them. (416)

This is our challenge on the journey. It is personal, it is social. It has profound consequences for ourselves and for our students.

References

Argys, Richard. "Surviving a Career in Public Education." *English Journal* 85 (September 1996): 63.

Bronte, Charlotte. *Jane Eyre*. Oxford: Oxford University Press, 1994.

Christenbury, Leila, ed. Breaking the Rules Focus Issue. *English Journal* 83 (September 1994).

Cochran-Smith, Marilyn. "Teacher Education and the Outcomes Trap." *Journal of Teacher Education* 56 (November/December 2005): 411–17.

Conn, Kathleen. *Bullying and Harassment: A Legal Guide for Educators*. Alexandria, VA: ASCD, 2005.

Cotter, Carmela M. "Respecting Your Right to Parent, Respecting My Right to Teach." *English Journal* 83 (September 1994): 44–45.

Fenstermacher, Gary D. "Some Moral Considerations on Teaching as a Profession." In *The Moral Dimensions of Teaching*. Edited by John I. Goodlad, Roger Soder, and Kenneth A. Sirontnik. San Francisco: Jossey-Bass, 1990.

Garland, Sylvia. "The Form in the Wastebasket." *English Journal* 83 (September 1994): 37–38.

Goodson, F. Todd. "Culture Wars and the Rules of the English Classroom." *English Journal* 83 (September 1994): 21–24.

Greene, Maxine. *The Dialectic of Freedom*. New York: Teachers College Press, 1988.

McCarthy, Cormac. *No Country for Old Men*. New York: Knopf, 2005.

Nieto, Sonia. *What Keeps Teachers Going?* New York: Teachers College Press, 2003.

Orwell, George. "Politics and the English Language." In *Eight Modern Essayists*, 3d ed. Edited by William Smart. New York: St. Martin's Press, 1980.

Shakespeare, William. *Complete Plays and Poems of William Shakespeare*. Edited by William Allan Neilson and Charles Jarvis Hill. Boston: Houghton Mifflin, 1942.

Spring, Joel. *American Education: An Introduction to Social and Political Aspects*. 3d ed. New York: Longman, 1985.

Swift, Jonathan. "A Modest Proposal." In *Jonathan Swift*. Edited by Angus Ross and David Woolley. New York: Oxford University Press, 1984.

Twain, Mark. *Adventures of Huckleberry Finn*. Berkeley: University of California Press, 1985.

Walker, Alice. *The Color Purple*. New York: Harcourt Brace Jovanovich, 1982.

Whishaw, Iona. "Translation Project: Breaking the 'English Only' Rule." *English Journal* 83 (September 1994): 28–30.

Whiting, Melissa E. "The Play's the Thing." *English Journal* 83 (September 1994): 32–35.

Young, Roberta C. "A Novel Rule." *English Journal* 83 (September 1994): 45.

Note: The magazine *Teaching Tolerance*, published by the Southern Poverty Law Center, is a great resource for teachers who want to ensure just and equitable classrooms. For more information, write: 400 Washington Avenue, Montgomery, AL 36104 or call 334.956.8200 for subscriptions.

Teaching Today

Plus ça change, plus c'est la même chose.
(The more things change, the more things stay the same.)

—French Proverb

Things Have Changed/
Things Have Stayed the Same

It is a truism of the age that times have "changed," that little of what we experience as adults today would be familiar to previous generations because our twenty-first-century society has been utterly transformed by modern life. Changes are undeniable, advances in science and technology are startling, and what most of us take for granted in communication, medical care, transportation, and standard of life was hardly imaginable fifty years ago.

In education, however, change is not quite so clear-cut: we can turn to the French proverb with which this chapter begins and agree that things have changed but things have also stayed the same. In our schools, while the specifics vary, the broad outline of teaching today is not vastly different from what it was decades ago. For some, this fact is comforting, giving school a familiarity and dependability that is occasionally lacking in other parts of our society. For others, however, the fact that school has not changed so very much is an indictment, a demonstration of the institution's inability to respond effectively to societal change.

The future and predictions of change in the future are not, as one wag noted, what they used to be. It seems that many of the predictions for sweeping revolution in school have just not come to pass. As an institution, school appears to be remarkably resilient to being reformed and transformed, however frequent the calls for restructure, however detailed the state standards, and however dire the reports of student test scores on high-stakes test. Certainly, when I returned to high school teaching almost thirty years after I began my career, I was not overwhelmed by the changes in my students or in school. While some aspects were different, I found my semester in Trailer 11 remarkably like the very first classes I taught in the beginning of my teaching career. And in some ways that is not very good news for you.

What *does* this mean to you? It means that while in your career you may see aspects of school change, you need to know that that change will probably not be overnight or even all that obvious to the outside observer. And if you are coming into teaching with the sure belief that schools as we know them will be transformed in the next few years and really reflect these calls for reform, you will need to adjust your expectations.

School has changed. School has stayed the same.

In high schools and middle schools all over the country, as in years before, classes meet, bells ring, lockers slam, buses arrive and leave. Sounds of band practice float through the halls; announcements are made over the loudspeakers for club meetings and sports and dances. There are cheerleaders, football players, brains, geeks, jocks, Goths, freaks, heads, and all the other attendant groups. Some students study; some never take home a book.

But there have been changes: the library is now called the media center, and the labs hold not just beakers and microscopes but rows of computers linked to the Internet. Many students bring school-issued laptops to class, and often the Internet connections are wireless. The school nurse tends to many more serious complaints than headaches, and the guidance counselors deal with problems far beyond deciding which college to attend. Metal detectors guard most school entrances, but deadly violence periodically erupts on school groups or in the community, and students by the score use—and occasionally sell—drugs and alcohol. In many American middle and high schools a myriad of languages other than English can be heard in cafeterias, and the student body is a mix of races and ethnic backgrounds.

There are still proms and field trips and romances and schoolwide testing days and pep rallies and bake sales; there also are security guards in the halls, classes for new mothers, police sweeps of student lockers, and information on teen obesity, AIDS, binge drinking, and date rape.

It's school; it's stayed the same in outline, but it has also changed as our society has changed. And it may be frustrating or it may be heartening, but there are virtually no arguments or issues or controversies in education that have not surfaced in some form in previous years and been discussed and debated in previous years. While the issues are of course never identical, perennial concerns abound in education. Let's look at four such issues that today and in the future will shape—and challenge—your professional life.

Four Contemporary Challenges

The influence of standards

Remember in Chapter 1 where we talked about the "sea of mediocrity" and the standards and testing movements? If not, recall that in 1983 the United States Department of Education issued *A Nation at Risk*, a report that contended that education was currently drowning in "a sea of mediocrity." Widely read and widely quoted, this report jump-started a movement to establish standards and tests related to those standards in every state in the country. The crafting of curricular benchmarks and skills standards became far more important than ever before, and, not surprising, the professional organizations, not just the individual states, also were involved.

So, in the early to mid 1990s, The International Reading Association (IRA) and the National Council of Teachers of English (NCTE) joined forces to craft standards for English language arts. The process was a long and laborious one that involved countless drafts and meetings and conversations at the local, state, regional, and national levels. As to be expected when you bring together large numbers of independent-minded professionals, there was consistent drafting and revision and, along the way, a certain amount of controversy. At one point, federal monies, which had helped fund the standards-writing process, were withdrawn. But both NCTE and IRA believed that the establishment of standards by those in the profession would be far superior to those written by people outside the classroom, and the meetings and drafts continued on. It is no exaggeration to observe that thousands of English language arts teachers participated in the writing, discussing, revising, and editing of the NCTE/IRA Standards. The story does not, however, have a neat and predictable ending.

Once published in 1996, the NCTE/IRA Standards came under intense criticism and scrutiny and, even these many years later, not all constituents—including many English teachers—are satisfied with them. While those who like the NCTE/IRA Standards felt that their broad and inclusive language would be helpful, others wanted much more specificity, including lists of recommended works of literature and classroom activities. Sometime in the future, it may be that you will see a new set of English language arts standards drafted and promulgated. Currently, however, many find the twelve NCTE/IRA Standards for the English Language Arts helpful:

1.   Students read a wide range of print and nonprint texts to build an understanding of texts, of themselves, and of the cultures of the United States and the world; to acquire new information; to respond to the needs and demands of society and the workplace; and for personal fulfillment. Among these texts are fiction and nonfiction, classic and contemporary works.

2.   Students read a wide range of literature from many periods in many genres to build an understanding of the many dimensions (e.g., philosophical, ethical, aesthetic) of human experience.

3.   Students apply a wide range of strategies to comprehend, interpret, evaluate, and appreciate texts. They draw on their prior experiences, their interactions with other readers and writers, their knowledge of word meaning and of other texts, their word identification strategies, and their understanding of textual features (e.g., sound-letter correspondence, sentence structure, context, graphics).

4.   Students adjust their use of spoken, written, and visual language (e.g., convention, style, vocabulary) to communicate effectively with a variety of audiences and for different purposes.

5.   Students employ a wide range of strategies as they write and use different writing process elements appropriately to communicate with different audiences for a variety of purposes.

6.   Students apply knowledge of language structure, language conventions (e.g., spelling and punctuation), media techniques, figurative language, and genre to create, critique, and discuss print and nonprint texts.

7.   Students conduct research on issues and interests by generating ideas and questions, and by posing problems. They gather, evaluate, and synthesize data from a variety of sources (e.g., print and nonprint texts, artifacts, people) to communicate their discoveries in ways that suit their purposes and audience.

8. Students use a variety of technological and informational resources (e.g., libraries, databases, computer networks, video) to gather and synthesize information and to create and communicate knowledge.

9. Students develop an understanding of and respect for diversity in language use, patterns, and dialects across cultures, ethnic groups, geographic regions, and social roles.

10. Students whose first language is not English make use of their first language to develop competency in the English language arts and to develop understanding of content across the curriculum.

11. Students participate as knowledgeable, reflective, creative, and critical members of a variety of literacy communities.

12. Students use spoken, written, and visual language to accomplish their own purposes (e.g., for learning, enjoyment, persuasion, and the exchange of information).

Again, along with these standards from our professional organization, almost all fifty states have crafted agreed-upon standards. One important difference between the NCTE/IRA standards and state standards is that the latter is tied to regularly administered, standardized testing. And while the NCTE/IRA Standards are linked to no test or testing program, many find them useful as a benchmark against which to judge curriculum and planning. Certainly the NCTE/IRA standards may not be wholly reflective of all aspects of English language arts—or even phrased as many would like them—but they are, for all of us, a comprehensive list of what can and should be accomplished in the English language arts classroom. Encouragingly enough, most state standards are compatible with those of NCTE/IRA.

Thus, for the foreseeable future, state standards, as well as those created by professional organizations such as NCTE and IRA, will continue to guide not only the curriculum but also testing. You need to be familiar with these standards and knowledgeable about how to implement them in your planning and classroom activities.

High-stakes testing and reporting

Since the widespread administration of the Standardized Aptitude Test (SAT), American high schools have been rated largely in terms of how students perform on that measure. While the SAT (and also the ACT) was at one point used to predict success in college, most people outside—and many inside—schools use SAT scores to judge the effectiveness of the high school and the achievement of students. Although the controversy continues unabated as to what the SAT and other similar tests measure and how they measure it, not to mention the value of measuring at all, standardized testing appears to be here to stay. It is, further, often directly linked to the teaching and learning of established standards, and many feel that standardized test scores offer the only true "accountability" of the public schools to the public.

And now the federal government has entered the arena with the No Child Left Behind (NCLB) legislation, a comprehensive and far-reaching program that further ties student test results to school funding and the rating of schools. Schools whose students' test scores are not either meeting set levels or showing improvement (Adequate Yearly Progress or AYP) are targeted for remediation and, further, the student scores of their schools and their school districts are published in the community.

And this is the world you now enter as a teacher. Surely you can recall many tests in your school life, and it has been suggested that the current generation is the most tested group of students ever. What will ultimately happen to this huge emphasis on testing may not be completely clear, but it does seem that, for the foreseeable future, the influence of standardized tests will do little but expand. Unless school systems agree to adopt a more comprehensive—and more time-consuming and expensive—method of testing, paper-and-pencil standardized tests, at the district and state level, will continue to dominate testing modes.

But do know that this kind of testing is not the only way to assess students. For example, noted educator Theodore R. Sizer recommended some years ago in *Horace's Compromise* a year-end "exhibition of mastery" (215) by each student. Such a demonstration would be individual, specific, and fair and based on more than the ability to determine the one correct answer to a multiple-choice question. Practically, such exhibitions are also unlikely to be widely adopted in public schools, since they require a heavy investment in teacher and student time and would have to be evaluated by methods other than electronic scan sheets. But the idea is solid. Sizer notes:

> The requirement for *exhibitions of mastery* forces both students and teachers to focus on the substance of schooling. It gives the state, the parents, prospective employers, and the adolescents themselves a real reading of what a student can do. It is the only sensible basis for accountability.
>
> [But] effective exhibitions will be complicated to construct and time-consuming to administer. To be fair, they need to be flexible: not all students show themselves off well in the same way. They cannot, then, merely be standardized, machine-graded, paper-and-pencil tests. (215)

The issue for you the English language arts teacher is that much of what you do in class will not always relate to the standardized test, which traditionally relies on multiple-choice questions with single right answers. In addition, the standardized test is largely based on knowledge retention, not judgment or speculation or argument. Finally, because many states feel the pressure to have all students score consistently well on these tests (after all, most states publish these scores by district and even by school), you may find yourself pressured to teach only what is noted in your state standards and which, therefore, appears on your state standardized test. You might even, as has happened in my area schools, be told to test only in multiple-choice format so students are completely familiar with that kind of test question. If either of these is the case, influencing content or test format, it could well change your sense of freedom and individualization.

For the present and near future, issues of high-stakes testing and reporting will continue, at least for the thinking teacher, to be a source of tension and contradiction. The balance between authentic teaching of English language arts and the test will continue to be uneasy.

English language learners and multiculturalism

As emphasized throughout this book, the public schools are for the public, and that public comes in different colors and from different ethnic and religious and cultural backgrounds. The presence of *multi*cultural in school is surely not new. But what is new, what you will face more squarely in your career than many of your predecessors in the classroom, is the proportion of students from many cultures and backgrounds and for whom English is a second language. As of this writing, the Latino population in the United States is rapidly increasing and has, in some school districts, outstripped the Anglo population. Immigrants from the Pacific Rim and Asian countries are also growing in influence and number, as are those from Africa and Europe.

The result is an increased awareness in the schools, and somewhat in the nation, of differing populations that require, appropriately, representation in the curriculum and in school staff and school culture. Like every one of the issues cited in this section, this is not a passing fad but an issue that is here to stay and that you will face in the classroom.

As the English language arts teacher, your responsibility is to be aware of the variety of your students and, if the material from which you teach is not representative of that variety, to amend or supplement it. As Latino writer Rudolfo Anaya demanded in a speech at an NCTE conference, later reprinted in the *English Journal*:

> Our community stretches from California to Texas, and into the Northwest and the Midwest. But not one iota of our social reality, much less our aesthetic reality, is represented in the literature read in the schools. . . . If you are teaching in a Mexican American community, it is your social responsibility to refuse to use the textbook which doesn't contain stories by Mexican American authors. If you teach Asian American children, refuse the textbook which doesn't portray their history and social reality. . . . But you don't have to be teaching in a Mexican American barrio to insist that the stories and social reality of that group be represented in your textbook. You shortchange your students and you misrepresent the true nature of their country if you don't introduce them to all the communities who have composed the history of this country. To deny your students a view into these different worlds is to deny them tools for the future. (19–20)

Multiculturalism has serious implications for our classroom, our materials, and our interactions with our students. It is our obligation to provide English language learners with support and appropriate instruction.

Today the literal complexion of school is being transformed, and you, as a new teacher, need to be aware of, receptive to, and prepared for students from varying walks of life and for whom English is not their first language. You will also need to ensure that your classroom materials are balanced and inclusive.

Teachers as activist professionals

Most of us who enter English language arts teaching are not fully prepared for its intimate connection to politics. Whether we like it or not, though, our classrooms and our content are often queried and even controlled by outside forces. While we need to be responsive to a community, I also think we need to assert ourselves as the professionals we are. We need to be activist, to reclaim our classroom in the face of Democrats and Republicans, in the face of liberals and conservatives, in the face of religious right and nonreligious alike, in the face of anyone who would dictate to us, use legislation and funding, loss of accreditation and other punitive measures or threats, how to shape our classrooms and our discourse with our students.

While these people are often well meaning, sometimes they are not. And most times they are so distant from our schools and our students that their policies have far more to do with partisan ideology than with the reality of teaching and learning. Accordingly, it is often hard to determine who is our friend and who is not in this business; we must look critically at what others outside the classroom advocate for the good for our students and our schools. Then we must make our professional choices, choices that are based on our earned authority, our teaching experience, and choices that are based on sound research and what we know of best practice. And we have that right.

I have always believed in the primacy of the teacher, in the fact that the teacher, who logs more time in the classroom than any local or national politician, than any administrator or school superintendent, is the expert and the professional. He or she knows English language arts, knows students, and knows the institution in which he or she works. I don't accept stories about the widespread presence in our schools of lazy and incompetent and uncaring teachers: the teachers I know are thoughtful, conscientious, hardworking people. They are the members of my community, and I am proud to be one of them. As teachers, then, I think we must reclaim our authority in the classroom: the classroom is ours, our province, our field of endeavor, and I know for us that that work, that reclaiming, is wholly in service not of our egos or of our professional advancement but in the service of our common treasure, our students.

And this is something I think we need to make a concerted effort to tell our parents and the public. While it is simply not possible for many of us to directly refuse school district or state mandates, to resign from our teaching positions, to put, as it were, our lives and careers and finances at stake, if what we are told to do in our classrooms contradicts what we know is best for students, we must take action. I think all of us need to remember that we have a civic, yes, a moral responsibility, to inquire, to question, and, at times, to challenge what is going on around us in the name of education and educational reform. This means asserting yourself in department, school, and PTA meetings and becoming active with your professional organization. There is strength in numbers, but no one will listen to you if you don't first speak.

Remember: what is essential is not the national directive, the local curriculum guide, the standards, state or national; it is not the expertise of the administration, the funding of the school district, or even parental support. The foundation, the bedrock, the basis of any change or improvement in education in this country is the individual teacher in the individual classroom, working in service of our students' learning. As teacher Todd DeStigter expresses it in *Reflections of a Citizen Teacher: Literacy, Democracy, and the Forgotten Students of Addison High*:

> In my view, this sense of urgency, this keenly felt desire to do some good in this world, may serve as a prompt for citizen teachers to adopt an expanded notion of their work, especially when that work takes place in contexts where students represent a diversity of cultures and languages. That is, teachers must cultivate an identity not just as instructors of academic content or even as activists dedicated to promoting democracy. Rather, citizen teachers must also think of themselves as social scientists striving to be more attuned to how their students view the world and how their culturally situated values shape the ways they think and live . . . For I have come to believe that in order to change the world for the better, our actions should begin and end face-to-face, *cara-a-cara*, with others. In communities such as these, people could no longer be forgotten. (301–302, 324)

As you begin your life in the classroom, remember that you are a professional, and asserting your authority is not just an option, it is an obligation. As an activist professional, you will ensure that your students and those in your teaching community are not forgotten.

FOR YOUR JOURNAL

The four issues cited may be very different from the ones you assume will be the unresolved tensions/perennial problems you will face in your first years as a teacher. If so, what other issues do you think you will have to confront and solve? How will you deal with them? If, on the other hand, the four issues discussed approximately cover what you expect to confront in the classroom, choose *one* and discuss what you feel is an approach to that dilemma, if not a total solution to it. What can a classroom teacher do with this issue?

Staying in the Classroom

The strain of teaching is acknowledged, if not understood, by the popular and educational press. *Burnout*, the accumulation of stress to a critical breaking point, is frequently cited as a reason experienced teachers leave the classroom temporarily or even permanently. And, according to the National Commission on Teaching, the number of beginning teachers (those in their first three years) who do not return to their classrooms hovers anywhere between 40 and 30 percent. As exciting as teaching can be, as rewarding as students are, teaching is a high-intensity profession. It is marked by consistent, almost unyielding expectations from a large number of people, students, parents, and administrators alike. In addition, life in a classroom always entails a certain amount of isolation from other professionals; teachers can spend most of their day without any sustained contact with other adults. The pressure, the isolation, and the frequent feeling of being overwhelmed by the demands of the classroom can seem insurmountable after even a few years teaching in school. One of my students, Lauren Dean, wrote in the middle of her student teaching:

> I have realized something that I do not like about my new life as a teacher. I am completely oppressed by my workload. What I mean is that I feel as if I am always playing catch-up. The very minutes I finally finish grading sixth period's essays, I then have another set of quizzes to grade, or journals to read, or journals to write, or lessons to write . . . right now I do not have a single moment's peace where there is not some type of schoolwork that I could be doing.

Kara Elder, also writing during her student teaching, echoes this, but she has come to what she sees as a partial solution:

> I have spent at least three nights a week at home working, one day a week at school late and every weekend working on school matters. The pace has stressed me to the point of affecting my health . . . One thing has become clear to me, after my first year as a teacher, the only work I will do for school (except for the occasional task) will be done at the school. My home has to be my sanctuary, and I am even beginning to take that to heart and lessen my loads home as I student teach.

As mentioned elsewhere in this book, an excellent work that addresses burnout and workload is *What Keeps Teachers Going?* by Sonia Nieto, where Nieto interviewed dozens of teachers on what kept them in the classroom. Their stories are equally different and heartening. Nieto captures the many different reasons teachers stay teaching—love of students, intellectual engagement, the chance to make a difference in society, the chance to shape futures. It's a positive and interesting book, and you might think of reading *What Keeps Teachers Going?*

In *Supporting Beginning English Teachers: Research and Implications of Teacher Induction*, authors McCann, Johannessen, and Ricca note the kind of comments beginning teachers make and what those comments might imply. According to *Supporting Beginning English Teachers*, teacher talk is different for those who are likely to leave the classroom after a short period of time. Such teachers will:

- Talk about how the workload is unreasonable and hopeless.
- Talk about the futility of any efforts to correct the problems they see as inherent to teaching.
- Talk more about their needs than the needs of the students.
- Talk about their plans to "escape" from teaching.
- Talk about their limited career choices and their view of teaching as a career compromise.

To the contrary, teachers who are likely to stay in teaching talk about the issues in very different ways. They:

- Talk about a sense of duty to help the young people who can benefit from the teacher's instruction.
- Talk about an interest in developing their teaching skills.
- Talk about their growth as teachers and can account for factors that have influenced their growth.
- Talk about strategic plans to make bad situations better.
- Talk about bad experiences in the school as evidence of the need for good teachers.
- Talk about disturbing episodes in the school year as shared experiences between students and faculty and not as personal obstacles, aggravations, or attacks. (McCann, Johannessen, and Ricca, 35)

As another aspect of this topic, a favorite article of mine published in the *Kappan* urges beginning teachers to remember the importance of "maintaining a life." Author Margaret Metzger reminds teachers to take care of themselves as human beings, not just as professionals. Among other things, Metzger urges teachers to:

1. Sign up for season tickets to cultural events; otherwise you'll think you are too tired to attend anything. Schedule regular social events with friends.
2. Hunt for a place to work. . . . Beg for some space in the school for yourself, even it's an old closet. Try to get your own classroom. Moving all your belongings every fifty minutes will make you crazy.
3. Try to stay out of petty politics. There is more squabbling in schools than you can imagine.

4. Find a friend with a sense of humor. Schools are full of chaos and drama, and . . . you need at least one friend who can laugh with you about the absurdity of schools. (351)

It is also good to remember that teaching is something we need to continue to work at; it is not alchemy but an ongoing journey. In *Who's In Charge?*, teacher Susan Ohanian also tells us:

> Those who hope to be effective teachers must recognize that teaching is a craft of careful artifice; the profession requires more than a spontaneous overflow of good intentions or the simple cataloguing and distribution of information. It is possible, I suppose, to have an inborn talent for teaching, but I am sure that those teachers who endure and triumph are *made*—rigorously trained—and not born. (210)

Staying in the classroom will, actually, require continuing work on your part. Donald Graves, a teacher for many years, urges teachers to consider the classroom as a source not of stress but of energy and to energize from a number of areas: what we do well ourselves, what our colleagues and students offer and even from the curriculum itself. My student, Lauren Dean, finally concluded that she would need to accept that "teaching is a way of life" and that she could "find some way to celebrate minor accomplishments and minor freedoms" so that she did not continue to feel overwhelmed. And that is where professional organizations may offer you real help and encouragement.

The personal nature of professional organizations

Some years ago, on the occasion of the seventy-fifth anniversary of my state English-teaching organization, I wrote about how that association helped save my fledgling and troubled teaching career. In "Growing Up in VATE," I named names and told stories; without the organization and its members, other teachers, I doubt I would be here today, still in the classroom. For me, VATE (the Virginia Association of Teachers of English) and NCTE have been professional homes, providing me conferences and workshops, books and journals, and more important, teacher friends who continue to stimulate, challenge, and inspire me.

Starting as a member of my local affiliate and then moving through different levels of the organization, I have spent over thirty years in VATE. I have spent as much time in NCTE. Through those two organizations, I have had opportunities to read and talk and learn; I also have met other teachers who have strongly influenced what goes on in my classroom.

I recommend that if you plan to stay in teaching, you join your local *and* national English-teaching organization. This is, in my opinion, not a luxury but a necessity: those organizations will give you access to thoughtful and tested teaching ideas and provide conferences and workshops where you can share with other teachers. Those people are your colleagues and may, in time, even become your friends—there is, in fact, a highly personal aspect to professional organizations. Regardless, they will influence your own teaching and also give you important companionship in this journey.

Your own reading

Under the pressure of writing papers and reports and preparing for class, it may be very tempting to begin—and to continue—to dispense with time for your own reading. Certainly many conscientious teachers take that route, taking time only to glance quickly at the daily newspaper or to skim professional magazines and articles. With their long hours and very time-consuming work, gone are any and all afternoons engrossed in a novel or Sunday evenings with the latest best-seller.

If you wish to stay in the classroom, I strongly recommend that you not neglect your own personal reading—whatever that reading may be. Whether it be poetry or science fiction, history or romance, gardening or sailing, accounts of Inuit tribes or Italian countesses or hunting in the African veldt, fine literature or popular schlock, I encourage you to keep reading. It's one of the reasons that you got into this business; it feeds you mentally and emotionally. Without time for your own reading interests, your life can become devoid of the special joy that reading gives us.

Unfortunately, there are many English language arts teachers who have stopped reading; most all of them regret it, and most all of them, citing time pressures, can justify it. If you suspend your own reading, however, I think it will show in your teaching, and it may contribute to some professional unhappiness. On the other hand, if you continue to read you will find that your tastes change and grow, deepening unexpectedly in an area or perhaps shifting into new areas. You will be able to share with your students what *you* are reading; you will be doing something for *you*; and your own reading will reinforce, once again, the power and magic of this business of reading and learning.

Becoming a teacher researcher

You do not have to be taking a graduate course to do research in your own classroom. As a teacher you may have questions about how or why something did not or did "work" in your classroom. You may want to try out a new technique of instruction or evaluation or organization. Doing your own research with your own students can keep you interested in what is before your eyes and can revitalize your teaching. While it may seem intimidating or terribly complicated, setting up research in your classroom is not impossible and actually not that difficult; the books cited at the end of this chapter can be a real help to your work and are written by classroom teachers for classroom teachers. Being a student of your own teaching can be illuminating and rewarding.

There are a number of good books on teacher research, but two names you will want to remember are Ruth Shagoury Hubbard and Brenda Miller Power: in *Living the Questions* they offer solid, practical advice about looking at your own teaching and coming to useful conclusions.

The End of the Lifetime Teacher?

It may seem odd that at the end of this section about *staying* in the classroom, I raise the issue of the end of the lifetime teacher. I'm not sure all would agree with me, but it is my feeling, given both the pressures of the classroom and the fairly recent phenomenon of multiple careers within a lifetime, that the person who stays in the classroom teaching for twenty or thirty years will be an increasing rarity. Certainly those who do will have survival skills of the highest order, but some will opt for a second—or even a third—career. Some will leave teaching, of course, only to return, as I did after my four years of writing and editing.

On the other hand, I am not sure that going into the classroom and doing a good or even fantastic job for five or ten years is all that harmful both to the individual teacher and to his or her students. Years and years of experience are valuable, no doubt, but I am not sure that either the students or the system completely benefit from a teaching staff that has unbroken decades in the classroom. Perhaps what I am suggesting is that while you may want to adopt some of the strategies previously listed to make sure you stay in teaching and stay there happily, you might reconsider just how long any person can—or should—remain in the classroom.

As I wrote in an editorial for an *English Journal* issue focused on veteran teachers:

> As a beginning teacher, like most novices, I was bothered tremendously by the very newness of everything. In my first years in the classroom, I was creating new lesson plans, new tests, new approaches. . . . Like so many beginners, I was more than occasionally exhausted by the newness, the strangeness, and I longed for the time when the plans and the material and the routine would be familiar, even routine.
>
> Now, some 20 years later in my teaching career, I know that the challenge of the veteran is how to make it new *again*, how to recapture that freshness, that excitement, even that edgy fear, that is part of a beginner's life. At times I recall those days with real nostalgia and wish, once again, that I was doing some school-related task for the very first time. (11–12)

While this feeling may be a bit in the future for you, it is the challenge of making it new, every day, that confronts the veteran teacher. As you will soon see in your own professional life, it is a challenge to which some rise and to which some, for many reasons, decline to pursue. Regardless, you will want to make all of your time in the classroom useful, rewarding, and, to a very real extent, new. And when it fails to be that and when that change appears permanent, it is time to think of leaving the classroom, both for your students and for yourself.

················ **FOR YOUR JOURNAL** ···············

For a minute, imagine that you do plan to be a lifetime teacher and stay in the classroom until you are ready to retire. Imagine further that you are entering your fifth year of teaching with many more years ahead of you and with a mild case of burnout. What, for you, do you think are *two* problems you are confronting, two sources of burnout? How do you think you will handle those two problems and renew yourself? Be practical; be specific.

Making the Journey

Most teachers know that of all the figurative language we "explain" to our students, metaphor actually comes easiest. Almost all of us use metaphor regularly in everyday language and, possibly, many of us think in terms of metaphors. In literature, in fairy stories, legends, myths, epics, folktales, not to mention poetry, novels, and plays, metaphor is a central element. The metaphors that seem to linger in our minds, the ones that appear and reappear in varying sources, are more likely than not the more central, the more elemental, the more archetypal. And for me, there is a metaphor in life and literature that at least partially represents what I feel this business of teaching is all about.

The metaphor is that of making the journey, a concept so prevalent in literature, in religion, in philosophy, in music, in everyday speech and aphorism that it requires virtually no elaboration. Some describe human existence as a journey from birth to death, and certainly our literature, from across the world and the centuries, is replete with heroes, both male and female, who journey out to discover, rediscover, and confirm. First steps, length, destination, and merit are all part of the lore of the journey metaphor.

The epic heroes Ulysses, Theseus, Psyche, Oedipus, Beowulf, Gawaine, Arjuna, to name just a few, go on long and arduous journeys; the more humble travel not so far but with as great an effect. From classic literature to the more contemporary, the metaphor of the journey is widely used.

From Christian, John Bunyan's central character in *The Pilgrim's Progress*, to Gulliver in Johnathan Swift's *Gulliver's Travels*, from Milkman in Toni Morrison's *Song of Solomon* and Inman in Charles Frazier's *Cold Mountain* to the rabbits in Richard Adams' *Watership Down*, from the questing Miyax in Jean Craighead George's *Julie of the Wolves* to Russel in Gary Paulsen's *Dogsong*, characters in classic, contemporary, and young adult literature make the journey. The American poet Robert Frost wrote of a journey and a road not taken, and, in an even more famous poem, of a journey and the need to go miles and miles before rest. In Virginia Woolf's first novel, Rachel makes a portentous journey in *The Voyage Out*; the journey from Appalachia to Detroit changes Gertie forever in Harriette Arnow's *The Dollmaker*. The beat writer Jack Kerouac went *On the Road* literally, as did William Least Heat Moon in *Blue Highways*; they were making their own internal journeys as well.

Who we are when we begin the journey is not, of course, who we are when we end. The journey, of and by itself, shapes and forms us, and often we arrive at a destination a bit differently from the way we had anticipated. And that is the stuff of literature and, of course, of life. The Native Americans who started the Trail of Tears, the African Americans who endured the Middle Passage, the surviving pioneers in the Donner party, the hopeful immigrants who came to Ellis Island, were all different at the end of their journey. Across the Atlantic and Pacific oceans, the borders of Mexico and Canada, immigrants have made the journey into this country, and that journey has shaped them.

As a teacher, you too make a journey, and you too will change. Your reading, your life in the classroom, and inevitably, the lives of those people with whom you will have such extensive and consistent contact, your students, will alter if not transform you.

What I hope for you as you make your journey is what I hope for myself: that we remain open as teachers not only to the wonder of the literature and the language but also to our students' minds and hearts. On my journey, which continues as my teaching life continues, the twists and turns of the path challenge and provoke and inform me and, I hope, help make me a better teacher and a better human being. I hope the same for you.

I have written in this book of the tough times of teaching, and I do not think I have exaggerated. But there is also magic and passion and joy in the classroom; I hope I have written convincingly of that, too. You, also, will see many sides of the teaching life as you make your journey and continue to be and become a teacher of English language arts.

For me—and that is a large part of the authority I claim in this business, my own experience—what is contained in English language arts has shaped my life. The characters in books, the lines from poems, the language I use, the conversations I have, the writing I do, have all formed me as a person. Teaching is, for me, utterly central: I am never more myself than when I am in the classroom, and I often think that within the four walls of my classroom is a universe in itself.

Tomorrow I will teach again. I will bring into the classroom all of me, all of what I know, what I feel, and I will, once again, learn something from the experience and from the students. My journey continues. While I don't make anyone's blood run quicker in every class, every day, I try, and what I teach, the great and glorious English language arts, makes it easier. And the students, for their part, are all the reason to keep trying, are all the reason to make the journey.

·············· FOR YOUR JOURNAL ················

The metaphor of the journey is just one possible description for teaching. I have changed my own personal metaphor for teaching numerous times—and expect to change it again and again. If at this point in your career you were to pick a metaphor for what you think your teaching life will be or currently is, what would it be? Draw the metaphor or describe it (or both); choose a central image that means something to you and that illustrates your current thinking about the profession of teaching.

References

Adams, Richard. *Watership Down*. New York: Macmillan, 1972.

Anaya, Rudolfo. "The Censorship of Neglect." *English Journal* 81 (September 1992): 18–20.

Arnow, Harriette. *The Dollmaker*. New York: Avon, 1954.

Bunyan, John. *The Pilgrim's Progress*. 2d ed. Edited by James Blanton Wharey. Oxford, UK: Clarendon Press, 1967.

Christenbury, Leila. "From the Editor." *English Journal* 85 (September 1996): 11–12.

———. "Growing Up in VATE." *Virginia English Bulletin* 32 (Fall 1989): 77–80.

DeStigter, Todd. *Reflections of a Citizen Teacher: Literacy, Democracy, and the Forgotten Students of Addison High*. Urbana, IL: NCTE, 2001.

Frazier, Charles. *Cold Mountain*. New York: Atlantic Monthly Press, 1997.

Frost, Robert. *Collected Poems*. Garden City, NY: Halycon House, 1942.

George, Jean Craighead. *Julie of the Wolves*. New York: Harper & Row, 1972.

Graves, Donald H. *The Energy to Teach*. Portsmouth, NH: Heinemann, 2001.

Heat Moon, William Least. *Blue Highways: A Journey into America*. New York: Fawcett Crest, 1984.

Hubbard, Ruth Shagoury, and Brenda Miller Power. *Living the Questions: A Guide for Teacher-Researchers*. York, ME: Stenhouse, 1999.

Kerouac, Jack. *On the Road*. New York: Bucaneer Books, 1957.

McCann, Tom, Larry R. Johannessen, and Bernard P. Ricca. *Supporting Beginning English Teachers: Research and Implications for Teacher Induction*. Urbana, IL: NCTE, 2005.

Metzger, Margaret. "Maintaining a Life." *Phi Delta Kappan* 77 (January 1996): 346–51.

Morrison, Toni. *Song of Solomon*. New York: Alfred A. Knopf, 1977.

National Commission on Teaching and America's Future. *No Dream Denied: A Pledge to America's Children*. Washington, DC: National Commission on Teaching and America's Future, 2003.

NCTE and IRA. *Standards for the English Language Arts*. Urbana, IL: NCTE/IRA, 1996.

Nieto, Sonia. *What Keeps Teachers Going?* New York: Teachers College Press, 2003.

Ohanian, Susan. *Who's In Charge? A Teacher Speaks Her Mind*. Portsmouth, NH: Boynton/Cook, 1994.

Paulsen, Gary. *Dogsong*. New York: Bradbury, 1985.

Sizer, Theodore R. *Horace's Compromise: The Dilemma of the American High School*. Boston: Houghton Mifflin, 1984.

Swift, Johnathan. *Gulliver's Travels*. Edited by Paul Turner. New York: Oxford University Press, 1986.

United States Department of Education. *A Nation at Risk*. Washington, DC: GPO, 1983.

Woolf, Virginia. *The Voyage Out*. New York: Harcourt Brace & World, 1920.

Index